Competition and Regulation in the Data Economy

ELGAR STUDIES IN LAW AND REGULATION

Series Editor: Roger Brownsword, *Professor of Law, King's College London, UK*

Regulation is a ubiquitous concept in today's world. The proliferation of new technologies necessitates continual re-appraisal of the rules that govern them, whilst globalization increases the complexity of interaction between governance systems on a national, regional and international level. As a field of study, regulation continues to grow and evolve, both in consideration of specific sectors, and at a conceptual level, as the rationale and motivation for regulation are scrutinized.

This new and exciting series is an important forum for original works of scholarship that explore regulation and its interaction with the law. It favours work that has a critical, innovative or analytical perspective and, whilst having a primary focus on legal writing, welcomes approaches that draw on other disciplines. The scope of the series encompasses a wide range of regulatory fields, from biotechnology and ICT to machine learning and AI, from security, food, and environment to health, leisure, and employment. At the same time the series plays host to broader discussions on the nature of risk, governance models, the role of democracy, regulatory theory and many others.

The primary mission of the series is to stimulate the development of original thinking across law and regulation and to foster the best theoretical and empirical scholarship in the field.

Titles in the series include:

From Chasing Violations to Managing Risks
Origins, Challenges and Evolutions in Regulatory Inspections
Florentin Blanc

The Scales of Weighing Regulatory Costs
Technology, Geography, and Time
Jamison E. Colburn

Generic Top-Level Domains
A Study of Transnational Private Regulation
Tobias Mahler

Regulatory Stewardship of Health Research
Navigating Participant Protection and Research Promotion
Edward S. Dove

Competition and Regulation in the Data Economy
Does Artificial Intelligence Demand a New Balance?
Gintarė Surblytė-Namavičienė

Competition and Regulation in the Data Economy

Does Artificial Intelligence Demand a New Balance?

Gintarė Surblytė-Namavičienė

Lecturer, Faculty of Law, Vilnius University, Lithuania

ELGAR STUDIES IN LAW AND REGULATION

Edward Elgar
PUBLISHING

Cheltenham, UK • Northampton, MA, USA

Published by
Edward Elgar Publishing Limited
The Lypiatts
15 Lansdown Road
Cheltenham
Glos GL50 2JA
UK

Edward Elgar Publishing, Inc.
William Pratt House
9 Dewey Court
Northampton
Massachusetts 01060
USA

A catalogue record for this book
is available from the British Library

Library of Congress Control Number: 2020944280

This book is available electronically in the **Elgar**online
Law subject collection
http://dx.doi.org/10.4337/9781788116657

ISBN 978 1 78811 664 0 (cased)
ISBN 978 1 78811 665 7 (eBook)

Printed and bound by CPI Group (UK) Ltd, Croydon, CR0 4YY

Contents

1. Introduction

It is often claimed that the Fourth Industrial Revolution is taking place.[1] This revolution has been said to be "building on the Third" and "characterized by a fusion of technologies that is blurring the lines between the physical, digital, and biological spheres".[2]

Yet the question is, first of all, what exactly the "Fourth Industrial Revolution" is supposed to be and whether it can, indeed, be claimed that it is already taking place. It could be asked whether the claimed effects of such a revolution are, in fact, comparable with those brought by inventions such as the steam engine, electricity and computer technology. On the one hand, it is true that the developments of artificial intelligence (AI) have been significant. On the other hand, however, intelligent machines on a par with human beings in terms of their intelligence and sovereignty in dealing with a wide range of tasks, thereby making decisions on their own and maybe even capable of autonomously (re)writing their algorithms, do not seem to have arrived yet. Thus, it might be that the Fourth Industrial Revolution is rather the *Hannibal ante portas*, and – for a good reason (?)[3] – has not yet arrived.

---

[1]   See, for example, Bundesministerium für Wirtschaft und Energie, Memorandum der Plattform Industrie 4.0, 2015 (https://www.bmwi.de/Redaktion/DE/Publikationen/ Industrie/memorandum-plattform-industrie-4-0.pdf?__blob=publicationFile&v=13); Eine europäische Studie von Roland Berger Strategy Consultants im Auftrag von BDI (Bundesverband der Deutschen Industrie e.V.), Die digitale Transformation der Industrie, 2015 (https://bdi.eu/media/user_upload/Digitale_Transformation.pdf).

[2]   *Schwab, K.*, The Fourth Industrial Revolution: what it means, how to respond, 14 January 2016, World Economic Forum (https://www.weforum.org/agenda/2016/ 01/the-fourth-industrial-revolution-what-it-means-and-how-to-respond/): "The First Industrial revolution used water and steam power to mechanize production. The Second used electric power to create mass production. The Third used electronics and informa- tion technology to automate production. Now a Fourth Industrial Revolution is building on the Third, the digital revolution that has been occurring since the middle of the last century. It is characterized by a fusion of technologies that is blurring the lines between the physical, digital, and biological spheres."

[3]   The risks associated with the developments of AI were highlighted and thus a word of caution towards such developments was expressed, for example, by Stephen Hawking: *Hawking, S.*, Stephen Hawking says A.I. could be "worst event in the history of our civilization", 6 November 2017 (https://www.cnbc.com/2017/11/06/ stephen-hawking-ai-could-be-worst-event-in-civilization.html); *Hawking, S.*, Stephen Hawking warns artificial intelligence "may replace humans altogether", 2 November

However, AI and related developments have already caught the attention of the regulators and academia. For example, a debate was launched by the European Parliament on the "European civil law rules" applicable to robotics and artificial intelligence. On 16 February 2017 a European Parliament resolution was adopted with the recommendations of the Commission on Civil Law Rules on Robotics.[4] In academia, fears have been expressed with regard to the danger of intelligent machines autonomously colluding on the basis of their algorithms (the so-called "algorithmic collusion") and thus posing risks to competition.[5] Studies have been made on whether there is a need to reconsider some of the concepts of EU competition law owing to the novel features of the "digital era".[6]

Yet it is not a given that economic changes have actually been as revolutionary as they are sometimes claimed to be. On the one hand, it is true that doing business in an economy that has been coined the data-driven[7] or the algorithm-driven[8] economy (in the following, the data economy[9]) may be different. On the other hand, however, it can be questioned whether the

---

2017 (https://www.independent.co.uk/life-style/gadgets-and-tech/news/stephen-haw king-artificial-intelligence-fears-ai-will-replace-humans-virus-life-a8034341.html); *Hawking, S.*, Stephen Hawking warns artificial intelligence could end mankind, 2 December 2014 (http://www.bbc.com/news/technology-30290540).

[4] European Parliament resolution of 16 February 2017 with recommendations to the Commission on Civil Law Rules on Robotics (2015/2103(INL)) (https://www .europarl.europa.eu/doceo/document/TA-8-2017-0051_EN.html?redirect). See also, European Parliament, Press Release "Robots and Artificial Intelligence: MEPs Call for EU-Wide Liability Rules", 16 February 2017 (http://www.europarl.europa.eu/news/ en/press-room/20170210IPR61808/robots-and-artificial-intelligence-meps-call-for-eu -wide-liability-rules).

[5] See, in particular, *Ezrachi, A./Stucke, M.E.*, Artificial Intelligence & Collusion: When Computers Inhibit Competition, (2017) University of Illinois Law Review 1775 (Oxford Legal Studies Research Paper No. 18/2015; University of Tennessee Legal Studies Research Paper No. 267, available at SSRN: https://papers.ssrn.com/sol3/ papers.cfm?abstract_id=2591874); *Ezrachi, A./Stucke, M.E.*, Virtual Competition: The Promise and Perils of the Algorithm-Driven Economy, Cambridge: Harvard University Press 2016.

[6] See the report for the European Commission by Jacques Crémer, Yves-Alexandre de Montjoye, Heike Schweitzer, "Competition Policy for the Digital Era", 2019 (http:// ec.europa.eu/competition/publications/reports/kd0419345enn.pdf).

[7] OECD (2015), Data-Driven Innovation: Big Data for Growth and Well-Being, OECD Publishing, Paris.

[8] *Ezrachi, A./Stucke, M.E.*, Virtual Competition: The Promise and Perils of the Algorithm-Driven Economy, Cambridge: Harvard University Press 2016.

[9] In the following, it is the term "data economy" that is used throughout this book. It is meant in terms of the economy, where companies do business on the basis of employing algorithms and using data as an input for such algorithms. Thus, the term covers both the data-driven and the algorithm-driven economy, since data and algo-

fundamental economic principles have changed in a way that would raise entirely new legal questions, which may, in turn, beg for legal changes. The clarification of the latter question is of utmost importance, not the least when it comes to an assessment of any necessary regulatory changes. Therefore, this book starts with an analysis of the notion of AI and the question whether the impact of the data economy, from a legal point of view, has indeed been so revolutionary that the existing legal rules have to be thought over from scratch (Chapter 2).

For the purposes of this analysis, it may be helpful to revisit to the roots of the classic economic theories, such as the theory of Adam Smith. Smith's book *The Wealth of Nations* was published at the dawn of the First Industrial Revolution.[10] However, this is not the reason why it should be delved into for analysis of his economic, and to some extent moral, theory.[11] The purpose of such an analysis is, first and foremost, to clarify whether the economic principles on which the data economy functions are in any way different from the classic economic theory, so that the question can be answered as to whether there is a need for drastic legal changes. The theory of Adam Smith may help to explain some of the concepts of the data economy, such as the "privacy paradox", and may provide answers to widely debated questions such as the implications of considering data as a commodity. Importantly, since one of the most hotly debated questions in the context of the data economy has been the "free flow of data",[12] and thus the issue of how to enable more access to data,[13] analysis of the economic theory of Adam Smith may reveal the downsides of such free flow of data by showing that it may be exactly the opposite that is needed for the data economy to function. After all, the role of creating and maintaining economic incentives for the operators in the markets not only in

---

rithms are often two sides of the same coin if we consider their broader role in the data economy.

[10] *Smith, A.*, An Inquiry into the Nature and Causes of the Wealth of Nations, Chicago: The University of Chicago Press 1976.

[11] *Smith, A.*, The Theory of Moral Sentiments, London: Henry G. Bohn, York Street, Covent Garden 1853.

[12] Communication from the Commission to the European Parliament, the Council, the European Economic and Social Committee and the Committee of the Regions "A Digital Single Market Strategy for Europe", Brussels, 6.5.2015, COM(2015) 192 final.

[13] See, for example, *Drexl, J.*, Designing Competitive Markets for Industrial Data – Between Propertisation and Access (31 October 2016). Max Planck Institute for Innovation & Competition Research Paper No. 16-13. Available at SSRN: https://papers .ssrn.com/sol3/papers.cfm?abstract_id=2862975; *Drexl, J.*, Data Access and Control in the Era of Connected Devices, Study on Behalf of the European Consumer Organisation BEUC (https://www.ip.mpg.de/fileadmin/ipmpg/content/aktuelles/aus_der_forschung/ beuc-x-2018-121_data_access_and_control_in_the_area_of_connected_devices.pdf).

terms of doing their business, but also in terms of innovating, should not be undermined. This may be even more important in light of an assumption that a large part of current competition in the data economy might be so-called Schumpeterian competition in terms of dynamic competition that takes place for future (emerging) AI markets. Thus, the purpose of delving into the economic theory of Adam Smith is also to better spotlight the issues of the data economy that may, indeed, be problematic, but which, owing to the attention of the regulators and academia sometimes being distracted by a focus on speculations related to artificial intelligence, risk remaining unexamined.

One of the most pressing issues in light of the development of AI technology is how to strike a balance between the interests that might be at stake, namely, creating incentives for AI developers, while at the same time protecting consumers who might also be data subjects. In light of this, the following issues beg for deeper analysis: trade secret protection for data that is a crucial input for AI, the reach of competition law in the algorithm-driven markets and the potential risks of so-called "algorithmic manipulation", which may raise a need to fill in potential legal gaps.

In fact, as regards the creation of economic incentives and solving the question of access to data in the business-to-business relationship, it is crucial to clarify the scope of legal protection that may be available for data and data sets. In this regard, trade secret protection comes into play (Chapter 3). Trade secret law protects information that is secret, has commercial value because it is kept secret and is subject to reasonable steps of the trade secret holder to protect its secrecy. Owing to the rather broad subject-matter of trade secrets, this might cover data (data sets) and algorithms. Should this be the case, trade secret protection may turn out to play a crucial role in the data economy. On the one hand, the beauty of trade secret protection may be the fact that it does not grant exclusive rights to trade secret holders. On the other hand, such protection may also raise legal questions, not least when it comes to the intersection of trade secret protection and the protection of personal data. If not only non-personal data may be eligible for trade secret protection, but also personal data, tensions may arise, for example, when it comes to the exercise of (at least some of) the rights of the data subjects enshrined in the EU General Data Protection Regulation (GDPR).[14] Thereby, it is crucial to clarify to what extent the GDPR would be applicable in such cases and how the potential tensions between trade secret and personal data protection should be solved.

---

[14]   Regulation (EU) 2016/679 of the European Parliament and of the Council of 27 April 2016 on the protection of natural persons with regard to the processing of personal data and on the free movement of such data, and repealing Directive 95/46/EC (General Data Protection Regulation), OJ [2016] L 119/1.

Moreover, although trade secrets can be reverse engineered, the effects of reverse engineering for the data economy need to be analysed deeper, bearing in mind the legitimacy of contractual restrictions to reverse engineer under the EU Trade Secrets Directive.[15] Also, the fact that industrial and humanoid robots may be eligible for trade mark protection under the Nice classification[16] raises the need to delve deeper into the intersection of trade secret protection and functional signs.

Furthermore, bearing in mind that, owing to the role of data, particularly for developing AI on the basis of "machine learning", companies compete fiercely over data, risks may arise of potential restrictions on competition. Although the issues related to "algorithmic collusion" may still be rather speculative, this fact does not yet mean that the increasing use of algorithms by business does not pose any risks to competition. In fact, real-life cases, where algorithms were used for restricting competition, have already been dealt with by the European Commission.[17] Indeed, the use of pricing algorithms by companies may need to be scrutinized more closely by competition authorities. After all, such algorithms may increase the likelihood of algorithmic price adjustments. Should algorithms act as the multipliers of the price fixed by, for example, a vertical agreement, horizontal price adjustments may follow with a result of higher prices in the markets. Thus, a need arises to scrutinize whether and how EU competition law may tackle competition law problems related to algorithms (Chapter 4).

EU competition law has tools for dealing with algorithmic price adjustments. Article 101 of the Treaty on the Functioning of the European Union (TFEU) condemns primarily anti-competitive agreements and concerted practices, whereas Article 102 TFEU prohibits abuse of a dominant position, including cases when such a dominant position is collective. The question is, however, how these legal tools have been interpreted, in particular in the case-law of the

---

[15] Directive (EU) 2016/943 of the European Parliament and of the Council of 8 June 2016 on the protection of undisclosed know-how and business information (trade secrets) against their unlawful acquisition, use and disclosure, OJ [2016] L 157/1.

[16] The Nice classification, which was established by the Nice Agreement (1957), is an international classification of goods and services applied for the registration of marks (see http://www.wipo.int/classifications/nice/en).

[17] Commission decision of 24.7.2018 relating to proceedings under Article 101 of the Treaty on the Functioning of the European Union, Case AT.40465 – ASUS; Commission decision of 24.7.2018 relating to proceedings under Article 101 of the Treaty on the Functioning of the European Union, Case AT.40469 – Denon & Marantz; Commission decision of 24.7.2018 relating to proceedings under Article 101 of the Treaty on the Functioning of the European Union, Case AT.40182 – Pioneer; Commission decision of 24.7.2018 relating to proceedings under Article 101 of the Treaty on the Functioning of the European Union, Case AT.40181 – Philips.

European Court of Justice (ECJ). Traditionally, parallel behaviour has been allowed under EU competition law. Algorithmic price adjustments may often be the result of such parallel behaviour. However, the guidance provided by the ECJ in the *E-Turas* case[18] seems to have broadened the EU competition law's concept of a concerted practice. In light of the use of pricing algorithms, the need thereby arises to analyse whether the concept of a concerted practice may capture the cases of algorithmic price adjustments and what implications the *E-Turas* case may have for the data economy.

Finally, it cannot be ruled out that algorithms may be used as a tool for manipulation. When it comes to the data economy, the question thus is whether there is a legal gap in this regard and whether it is therefore this area where any regulatory rules may be mostly needed for tackling the problem of algorithmic manipulation in the data economy (Chapter 5). In this regard, legal rules that restrict market abuses in the financial sector, including the prohibition of an algorithmic manipulation, may stand as an example.[19] Furthermore, bearing in mind the rise of private power and an increasing asymmetry of information between private companies and consumers, the question is whether a more robust state control of terms and conditions in the data economy may be needed, first and foremost, for the sake of consumer protection.

The importance of addressing the aforementioned issues in a timely manner should not be underestimated. Technological developments are progressing rapidly and the need for regulation may be immediate. Thereby, shifting the focus from speculations and loose terms such as artificial intelligence may be crucial in order not to lose sight of the problems that may need to be tackled for the overall benefits of a society that may be on the brink of the Fourth Industrial Revolution.

---

[18]   ECJ, Case C-74/14, *"Eturas" UAB and Others v. Lietuvos Respublikos konkurencijos taryba*, 21 January 2016, ECLI:EU:C:2016:42.

[19]   Directive 2014/65/EU of the European Parliament and of the Council of 15 May 2014 on markets in financial instruments and amending Directive 2002/92/EC and Directive 2011/61/EU (recast), OJ [2014] L 173/349; Regulation (EU) No. 596/2014 of the European Parliament and of the Council of 16 April 2014 on market abuse (market abuse regulation) and repealing Directive 2003/6/EC of the European Parliament and of the Council and Commission Directives 2003/124/EC, 2003/125/EC and 2004/72/EC; Directive 2014/57/EU of the European Parliament and of the Council of 16 April 2014 on criminal sanctions for market abuse, OJ [2014] L 173/179.

2. Digital economy: between human brains and artificial intelligence

The question of creating machines, which "carry out something which ought to be described as thinking but which is very different from what a man does" was raised by Alan Turing back in 1950 in his seminal article "Computing Machinery and Intelligence".[1] For decades, energy has been invested in developing artificial intelligence (AI).[2] The tip of the iceberg (at least, for the time being) may arguably be the creation of humanoids, one of them being the gynoid[3] Sofia – the robot that has human features and is the first one to have citizenship.[4] Yet, even in light of these – striking, but also much hyped – technological developments,[5] one crucial question remains: will machines be ever capable of being conscious and of "thinking" and acting completely autonomously? The fact that even artificial brains learn with data, which has been selected by those who created the machine, may seem to leave this question open. Yet it cannot be entirely ruled out that, at some point, machines may act completely on their own – and the hope remains that a human being will be able to spot that moment, but currently this remains a speculation. In fact, if AI is as smart as it is often claimed to be, a prediction of how it will develop should be almost impossible by definition.

For the purposes of the debate on AI in general and for a legal debate in particular, it is crucial to clarify what is meant by artificial intelligence in the first place.[6] After all, an analysis on the potential effects of AI can be started only when the definitions are set and clear.

---

[1]   *Turing, A.M.*, Computing Machinery and Intelligence, (1950) 59 Mind, A Quarterly Review of Psychology and Philosophy 433, 435.
[2]   For a more detailed analysis of the development of the AI technology see, for example, OECD (2017), Algorithms and Collusion: Competition Policy in the Digital Age (http://www.oecd.org/daf/competition/Algorithms-and-collusion-competition-pol icy-in-the-digital-age.pdf), pp. 8–11.
[3]   Although Sofia is often called a "humanoid", a more precise term is a gynoid – a female robot, as contrasted to an android – a male robot.
[4]   http://www.hansonrobotics.com/robot/sophia/.
[5]   An open question also remains whether technology such as humanoids (androids, gynoids), cyborgs, etc., will be accepted by the human society in the first place.
[6]   The importance of clarifying the definition of AI has also been stressed by the European Commission in the White Paper on Artificial Intelligence (European

2.1   INTELLIGENT MACHINES: AUTONOMY AND (THE LACK OF) CONSCIOUSNESS

The term "artificial intelligence" was coined by John McCarthy back in 1956 as "the science and engineering of making intelligent machines".[7] AI follows the architecture of human brains in artificial neural networks (ANNs). On the basis of "machine-learning" or "deep learning" algorithms,[8] intelligent systems are supposed to learn, and the learning material for such machines is data. The latter is processed in a number of layers of ANNs.[9]

The European Commission, in the Communication "Artificial Intelligence for Europe", issued in 2018, stated that "[a]rtificial intelligence (AI) refers to systems that display intelligent behaviour by analysing their environment and taking actions – with some degree of autonomy – to achieve specific goals".[10] It was furthermore explained that "AI-based systems can be purely software-based, acting in the virtual world (e.g. voice assistants, image analysis software, search engines, speech and face recognition systems) or AI can be

---

Commission, White Paper on Artificial Intelligence – A European approach to excellence and trust, Brussels, 19.2.2020, COM(2020) 65 final). According to the European Commission, "[i]n any new legal instrument, the definition of AI will need to be sufficiently flexible to accommodate technical progress while being precise enough to provide the necessary legal certainty" (*ibid.*, p. 16).

   [7]   See, for example, https://www.sciencedaily.com/terms/artificial_intelligence .htm; https://www.independent.co.uk/news/obituaries/john-mccarthy-computer-scien tist-known-as-the-father-of-ai-6255307.html. See also *The Economist*, Special Report: Artificial Intelligence, 25 June 2016, p. 3, http://www.economist.com/news/special -report/21700761-after-many-false-starts-artificial-intelligence-has-taken-will-it-cause -mass.

   [8]   On the difference between the "machine-learning" and "deep-learning" algorithms see, for example, OECD (2017), Algorithms and Collusion: Competition Policy in the Digital Age (http://www.oecd.org/daf/competition/Algorithms-and-colllusion -competition-policy-in-the-digital-age.pdf), p. 11.

   [9]   See, for example, *The Economist*, Special Report: Artificial Intelligence, 25 June 2016, p. 3 (http://www.economist.com/news/special-report/21700761-after-many-false -starts-artificial-intelligence-has-taken-will-it-cause-mass).

  [10]   European Commission, Communication from the Commission to the European Parliament, the European Council, the Council, the European Economic and Social Committee and the Committee of the Regions, "Artificial Intelligence for Europe", Brussels, 25.4.2018, COM(2018) 237 final, p. 1. Later on, this definition of AI was further specified: see European Commission, White Paper on Artificial Intelligence – A European approach to excellence and trust, Brussels, 19.2.2020, COM(2020) 65 final, p. 16 footnote 47.

embedded in hardware devices (e.g. advanced robots, autonomous cars, drones or Internet of Things applications)".[11]

Depending on the level of autonomy and on the range of tasks that can be carried out by a machine, AI can be divided into general AI and narrow AI. Whereas narrow AI "addresses specific application areas", such as e.g. language translation and self-driving vehicles, general AI "refers to a notional future AI system that exhibits apparently intelligent behavior at least as advanced as a person across the full range of cognitive tasks".[12] Although general AI is considered the final goal, it is still in the process of being developed (it is said it will "not be achieved for at least decades").[13] In contrast, narrow AI is pretty much a reality, as such intelligent systems may act as "helpers, assistants, trainers, and teammates of humans".[14] The advantages of the complementarity between human beings and AI systems have already been described.[15] AI may play an advantageous role in taking over some tasks, where human beings, owing to their nature, risk failing, for example, cases where extreme precision is required, in mining work, in nano-sized cells inside the body for diagnostics, etc.

Russell and Norvig, in their seminal work on AI,[16] distinguish between weak and strong AI and explain that the weak AI hypothesis means that "machines could act *as if* they were intelligent" (emphasis in original), whereas "the assertion that machines that do so are actually thinking (not just simulating

---

[11] European Commission, Communication from the Commission to the European Parliament, the European Council, the Council, the European Economic and Social Committee and the Committee of the Regions, "Artificial Intelligence for Europe", Brussels, 25.4.2018, COM(2018) 237 final, p. 1.

[12] Executive Office of the President of the United States, National Science and Technology Council Committee on Technology, "Preparing for the Future of Artificial Intelligence", October 2016 (https://obamawhitehouse.archives.gov/sites/default/files/whitehouse_files/microsites/ostp/NSTC/preparing_for_the_future_of_ai.pdf), p. 7.

[13] *Ibid.*, p. 7.

[14] *Ibid.*, p. 8.

[15] "While completely autonomous AI systems will be important in some application domains (e.g., underwater or deep space exploration), many other application areas (e.g., disaster recovery and medical diagnostics) are most effectively addressed by a combination of humans and AI systems working together to achieve application goals. This collaborative interaction takes advantage of the complementary nature of humans and AI systems" (Executive Office of the President of the United States, Office of Science and Technology Policy, The National Artificial Intelligence Research and Development Strategic Plan, October 2016 (https://www.nitrd.gov/PUBS/national_ai_rd_strategic_plan.pdf), p. 22).

[16] *Russell, S.J./Norvig, P.*, Artificial Intelligence: A Modern Approach, 3rd ed., Delhi: Pearson 2015.

thinking) is called the strong AI hypothesis".[17] Thus, the simulation of thinking translates into machines being programmed in a particular way and such
AI is considered to be weak AI, whereas, in the case of strong AI, machines
should be capable of acting (if not thinking) on their own, i.e. independently
of any program writers. The distinction between weak and strong AI may
have important consequences, including legal ones. First of all, if machines
are programmed to behave, or to "think", according to particular patterns, the
machines are not themselves behaving in a particular way, but rather fulfilling
the "orders" of those who programmed them. In terms of legal liability, this
circumstance may be highly important, since in such a case it is the program
writers who should be liable for the machines' behaviour and the machines
should not shield them from liability. After all, when machines simulate thinking, i.e. they act as if they were smart, just because they are programmed that
way, their capacity to act rather depends on the sequences of algorithms and on
the data that they are given.

In this regard, it could be recalled that the question – "Can machines think?"
– was analysed by Alan Turing back in 1950.[18] In his article "Computing
Machinery and Intelligence", he suggested that the latter question should
not be analysed on the basis of traditional definitions related to the terms
"machine" and "think", but rather in terms of the so-called "imitation game".[19]
Accordingly, the question was whether the interrogator (a human being), based
on communication in writing, could distinguish between the answers submitted by a human being and a machine, with a purpose of clarifying whether it
might be possible for a machine to outplay human brains, i.e. the interrogator
not being able to correctly identify whether the answers were provided by
a human being or by a machine. In his analysis, Turing referred to the machine
in terms of an "electronic" or a "digital computer",[20] pointing out that the idea
of a digital computer was "an old one" that went back to Charles Babbage, who
in the nineteenth century, suggested creating a machine called "the Analytical
Engine".[21] Thus, the question of whether machines can think, for Turing,

---

[17]   *Ibid.*, p. 1035.
[18]   *Turing, A.M.*, Computing Machinery and Intelligence, (1950) 59 Mind,
A Quarterly Review of Psychology and Philosophy 433.
[19]   *Ibid.*, at 433.
[20]   *Ibid.*, at 435–442.
[21]   *Ibid.*, at 439.

boiled down to the question whether a digital computer can perform well in the imitation game.[22] He stated:

> I believe that in about fifty years' time it will be possible, to programme computers, with a storage capacity of about 10^9, to make them play the imitation game so well that an average interrogator will not have more than 70 per cent chance of making the right identification after five minutes of questioning.[23]

Yet, as regards the question of "learning machines" (with regard to which Turing himself was rather cautious),[24] he stressed that a human mind consisted of three components: the initial state of mind (i.e. at the moment of birth), education and experience other than education.[25] In this regard, he suggested trying to produce a program to simulate a child's mind instead of that of an adult.[26] In his opinion, "[i]f this were then subjected to an appropriate course of education one would obtain the adult brain".[27]

Thus, the idea of Turing was to create a machine with a rather rudimentary knowledge with an expectation of developing it on the basis of further learning. Yet a learning process requires a teacher. In fact, Turing thoroughly described the process of teaching the "child machine".[28] However, he stressed the fact that teaching a machine did not mean that a teacher could be entirely sure of the outcome of the machine-learning process.[29] In his words:

> Intelligent behaviour presumably consists in a departure from the completely disciplined behaviour involved in computation, but a rather slight one, which does not give rise to random behaviour, or to pointless repetitive loops. Another important result of preparing our machine for its part in the imitation game by a process of teaching and learning is that "human fallibility" is likely to be omitted in a rather

---

[22] *Ibid.*, at 442: "It was suggested tentatively that the question, 'Can machines think?' should be replaced by 'Are there imaginable digital computers which do well in the imitation game?'"

[23] *Ibid.*, at 442.

[24] *Ibid.*, at 454: "The reader will have anticipated that I have no very convincing arguments of a positive nature to support my views. If I had I should not have taken so much pains to point out the fallacies in contrary views."

[25] *Ibid.*, at 455.

[26] *Ibid.*, at 456.

[27] *Ibid.*, at 456.

[28] *Ibid.*, at 456–460.

[29] *Ibid.*, at 458–459: "An important feature of a learning machine is that its teacher will often be very largely ignorant of quite what is going on inside, although he may still be able to some extent to predict his pupil's behaviour. This should apply most strongly to the later education of a machine arising from a child-machine of well-tried design (or programme). This is in clear contrast with normal procedure when using a machine to do computations."

natural way, i.e. without special "coaching". [...] Processes that are learnt do not produce a hundred per cent certainty of result; if they did they could not be unlearnt.[30]

This is a highly important passage. It explains that intelligent machines may be "born" with initial knowledge, but they will develop themselves on the basis of the learning–teaching process. The latter implies that, on the one hand, the behaviour of a machine may depend on how it was taught. On the other hand, however, uncertainty remains, since the behaviour of an intelligent machine may not be entirely predictable.

The latter insight raises the question of how rationally intelligent machines may be expected to behave. In this regard, Russell and Norvig explain the following:

> To the extent that an agent relies on the prior knowledge of its designer rather than on its own percepts, we say that the agent lacks **autonomy**. A rational agent should be autonomous – it should learn what it can to compensate for partial or incorrect prior knowledge. [...] So, just as evolution provides animals with enough built-in reflexes to survive long enough to learn for themselves, it would be reasonable to provide an artificial intelligent agent with some initial knowledge as well as an ability to learn. After sufficient experience of its environment, the behavior of a rational agent can become effectively *independent* of its prior knowledge. Hence, the incorporation of learning allows one to design a single rational agent that will succeed in a vast variety of environments.[31] (Emphasis in original)

It should, first of all, be noted that, although the word "agent" is used in the cited passage, it should not be understood in legal terms, i.e. someone acting on behalf of the principal. According to the authors, an agent "is just something that acts (*agent* comes from the Latin *agere*, to do)" (emphasis in original).[32] The cited passage clarifies the concept of "autonomy". The behaviour of a machine may depend on the extent of its autonomy. In the case when a machine relies completely on prior knowledge, such a machine lacks autonomy, because basically it relies on the information with which it was programmed. In the passage above, Russell and Norvig explain that a rational agent should be able to identify prior knowledge that was incorrect and should be able to correct it. This may, in fact, require a good portion of other knowledge, which a machine should be capable of gathering. In its essence, the concept of an (at least, partly) autonomous agent comes close to Turing's

---

[30]　*Ibid.*, at 459.
[31]　*Russell, S.J./Norvig, P.*, Artificial Intelligence: A Modern Approach, 3rd ed., Delhi: Pearson 2015, p. 39.
[32]　*Ibid.*, p. 4.

idea of creating brains (with a limited prior knowledge) that are capable of further development. So, only after "sufficient experience" (in the words of the passage above) will an agent become independent of its prior knowledge.

Thus, not all intelligent machines will stand in the same row as regards their autonomy. The key condition for machines to gain autonomy will be built on learning. Accessing large data sets[33] may be important for gaining initial knowledge. This circumstance, as it will be argued later,[34] may explain the incentive to protect such data sets as trade secrets. Yet any further developments of a machine may depend on the perception function,[35] which enables machines to gather additional knowledge by themselves and to learn from their environment. In this regard, it is noteworthy that the European Commission, in the White Paper on Artificial Intelligence, also explains that "[w]hile AI-based products can act autonomously by perceiving their environment and without following a pre-determined set of instructions, their behaviour is largely defined and constrained by its developers. Humans determine and programme the goals, which an AI system should optimise for."[36] Thus, any legal framework, including any legal norms on legal liability, will have to take into account the fact that AI technology, although it may seem to act autonomously from a technological point of view, may hardly be considered to be acting autonomously from a legal point of view.

Furthermore, Russel and Norvig point out that a rational agent "is one that acts so as to achieve the best outcome or, when there is uncertainty, the best expected outcome".[37] Hence, even for intelligent machines, it may be not always feasible to achieve perfect rationality. Russel and Norvig refer rather to limited rationality, which means "acting appropriately when there is not enough time to do all the computations one might like".[38] Thus, at the end of the day, perfect rationality, which may seem to be expected from intelligent machines, may boil down to "an appropriate behaviour", particularly, under spontaneous circumstances. Machines will act and deliver the best expected

---

[33] *Stucke, M.E./Grunes, A.P.*, Big Data and Competition Policy, Oxford: Oxford University Press 2016, p. 23.

[34] See *infra* Chapter 3.

[35] On the perception function of the machines in AI and the role of 3D see *Russell, S.J./Norvig, P.*, Artificial Intelligence: A Modern Approach, 3rd ed., Delhi: Pearson 2015, pp. 944–985.

[36] European Commission, White Paper on Artificial Intelligence – A European approach to excellence and trust, Brussels, 19.2.2020, COM(2020) 65 final, p. 16.

[37] *Russell, S.J./Norvig, P.*, Artificial Intelligence: A Modern Approach, 3rd ed., Delhi: Pearson 2015, p. 4. According to the authors, "rationality maximizes *expected* performance, while perfection maximizes *actual* performance" (emphasis in original) (*ibid.*, p. 38).

[38] *Ibid.*, p. 5.

outcome – the best under the circumstances. In this regard, it could be recalled that Turing, while analysing the question that "machines cannot make mistakes,"[39] distinguished between two types of errors, i.e. "errors of functioning" and "errors of conclusion". Whereas the former was said to relate to "some mechanical or electrical fault which causes the machine to behave otherwise than it was designed to do", the latter was said to "only arise when some meaning is attached to the output signals from the machine".[40] In the opinion of Turing, "abstract machines are mathematical fictions rather than physical objects", so that "[b]y definition they are incapable of errors of functioning".[41] However, as regards the errors of conclusion, he noted that:

> The machine might, for instance, type out mathematical equations, or sentences in English. When a false proposition is typed we say that the machine has committed an error of conclusion. There is clearly no reason at all for saying that a machine cannot make this kind of mistake. [...] To take a less perverse example, it might have some method for drawing conclusions by scientific induction. We must expect such a method to lead occasionally to erroneous results.[42]

Hence, it should not be expected that machines will always act perfectly rationally. At the end of the day, it may be that *errare humanum est* may need to be applied not only to human beings.

Finally, rationality of a machine should not be identified with its consciousness.[43] Although the moment of machines gaining consciousness may be difficult to spot with the human eye,[44] it could be argued that, as long as intelligent machines lack consciousness, they can hardly be an independent subject of legal liability. Bearing this in mind, it could be asked whether a debate such as that on Civil Rules on Robotics can effectively take place[45] when machines are

---

[39]   *Turing, A.M.*, Computing Machinery and Intelligence, (1950) 59 Mind, A Quarterly Review of Psychology and Philosophy 433, 448.

[40]   *Ibid.*, at 449.

[41]   *Ibid.*, at 449.

[42]   *Ibid.*, at 449.

[43]   On consciousness in the context of machines see *Russell, S.J./Norvig, P.*, Artificial Intelligence: A Modern Approach, 3rd ed., Delhi: Pearson 2015, p. 1048.

[44]   See also: *Nevejans, N.*, European Civil Law Rules in Robotics, 2016 (http://www.europarl.europa.eu/RegData/etudes/STUD/2016/571379/IPOL_STU(2016)571379_EN.pdf), p. 13: "It is already difficult to prove a human being's consciousness, so how might we detect its existence in a machine?"

[45]   Along these lines see also *ibid.*, p. 14: "When considering civil law in robotics, we should disregard the idea of autonomous robots having a legal personality, for the idea is as unhelpful as it is inappropriate." Furthermore, the author notes: "Once a robot is no longer controlled by another actor, it becomes the actor itself. Yet how can a mere machine, a carcass devoid of consciousness, feelings, thoughts or its own will, become an autonomous legal actor? How can we even conceive this reality as foresee-

not yet capable of being conscious. After all, the freedom of will (the ability to choose one's own behaviour) and self-determination, relevant for liability, might be missing, so that the question may boil down to the attribution of liability to the creators of machines rather than to machines themselves. Hence, from a legal point of view, it could be argued that, as long as intelligent machines lack consciousness, the liability for intelligent machines may have to be treated similarly to parental liability or pet liability.[46]

2.2 AUTOPOIETIC SYSTEMS: DOES AI LIVE UP TO A STANDARD OF A "LIVING MACHINE"?

The answer to the question whether intelligent machines may be held liable from a legal point of view may also depend on the question whether such machines may be considered as autopoietic systems.

Autopoietic systems were analysed by Maturana and Varela in their book "Autopoiesis and Cognition: the Realization of the Living".[47] Although the

---

able within 10 to 15 years [...]? From a scientific, legal and even ethical perspective, it is impossible today – and probably will remain so for a long time to come – for a robot to take part in legal life without a human being pulling its strings" (*ibid.*, p. 15).

[46]   In this regard, it is noteworthy that the risks related to the functioning of intelligent machines and thereto related (potential) liability of their developers may trigger a more intensive application of the insurance schemes. It should not be ruled out that such insurance schemes might, in addition to more "traditional" risks, also cover risks related to potential data or privacy breaches. In fact, the question of the safety and liability implications of AI has been addressed by the European Commission in the White Paper on Artificial Intelligence (European Commission, White Paper on Artificial Intelligence – A European approach to excellence and trust, Brussels, 19.2.2020, COM(2020) 65 final) and further analysed in the accompanying document, i.e. the Report on the safety and liability implications of AI (European Commission, Report from the Commission to the European Parliament, the Council and the European Economic and Social Committee, "Report on the Safety and Liability Implications of Artificial Intelligence, the Internet of Things and Robotics", Brussels, 19.2.2020, COM(2020) 64 final), where the European Commission, *inter alia*, discusses the strict liability schemes and considers the question of "coupling strict liability with a possible obligation to conclude available insurance" (*ibid.*, p. 16).

[47]   *Maturana, H.R./Varela, F.J.*, Autopoiesis and Cognition: The Realization of the Living, Dordrecht: D. Reidel 1972. As regards the notion of the "autopoiesis", the authors explain: "we wanted a word that would by itself convey the central feature of the organization of the living, which is autonomy. It was in these circumstances that one day, while talking with the friend (José Bulnes) about an essay of his Don Quixote de la Mancha, in which he analysed Don Quixote's dilemma of whether to follow the path of arms (*praxis*, action) or the path of letters (*poiesis*, creation, production), and his eventual choice of the path of *praxis* deferring any attempt at *poiesis*, I understood for the first time the power of the word 'poiesis' and invented the word that we needed: *autopoiesis*. This was a word without a history, a word that could directly mean what takes

word "autopoiesis" was used to define the autonomy that is inherent to living systems,[48] they also spoke about "living machines" and defined an autopoietic machine as follows:

> An autopoietic machine is a machine organized (defined as a unity) as a network of processes of production (transformation and destruction) of components that produces the components which: (i) through their interactions and transformations continuously regenerate and realize the network of processes (relations) that produced them; and (ii) constitute it (the machine) as a concrete unity in the space in which they (the components) exist by specifying the topological domain of its realization as such a network.[49]

Accordingly, an autopoietic machine (as a network of processes) not only consists of components – it also produces them. Firstly, it does so through interactions and transformations, and secondly, on this basis, these components (and, thereby, also the machine) continuously regenerate themselves. Furthermore, according to the passage, this process leads to an (independent) realization by a machine of the process, on the basis of which it was created. Finally, these regenerating components not only form a unity, but may also specify their placement as regards the network.

When it comes to the question whether AI machines may be considered autopoietic systems, the decisive factor for clarification would be their capability to regenerate, or to reproduce themselves and "realize the network of processes (relations) that produced them". In this regard, it should be recalled that the main components of intelligent machines are algorithms and data.[50] On the basis of self-learning algorithms, AI machines are capable of learning and developing themselves. Thus, the answer to the question whether AI machines may be autopoietic systems may, *inter alia*, depend on whether machines would be capable of rewriting their algorithms. After all, according to the passage above, a "living machine" is not only a "network of processes" – such a machine "continuously regenerates" (on the basis of interactions) the processes by which it was produced. Thereby, an autopoietic system in general and a "living machine" in particular is a creator, rather than just an imitator. Thereby, an example of an autopoietic machine may be a machine

---

place in the dynamics of the autonomy proper to living systems" (emphasis in original), p. xvii.

[48]   *Ibid.*, p. xviii.

[49]   *Ibid.*, pp. 78–79.

[50]   See also: European Commission, White Paper on Artificial Intelligence – A European approach to excellence and trust, Brussels, 19.2.2020, COM(2020) 65 final, p. 16.

that can write its own algorithms, a machine, which can – on its own – solve its dilemmas.

Accordingly, AI can hardly be considered as an autopoietic system. After all, such a system continuously regenerates itself through interactions and transformations – importantly though, completely autonomously. The fact that AI lacks features of an autopoietic system may be relevant for elaborating on the societal effects of AI in terms of the "systems theory" developed by Niklas Luhmann.[51]

According to the "systems theory", the subjects of a system organize themselves as systems, and it is only in this way that they realize themselves as well as face their limits.[52] Such systems are built on the basis of communication,[53] which leads to the emergence of the interaction systems.[54] According to Luhmann, interactions fulfil the "glueing function" (*Verleimungsfunktion*)[55] or "the linking function" (*Scharnierfunktion*)[56] of the society. Thereby, according to his theory, a social system is a system of individuals connected through (or "glued" by) their interactions. In other words, it is through the interactions that individuals, according to him, form a social system. In this regard, he criticized the "action theory" developed by Parson, who explained that actions refer only to individual people, and do not reflect the processes through which people may be connected.[57] Luhmann stressed the fact that the (Latin) roots of the word "an individual" ("das Wort 'Individuum'") and its use in earlier times show that the real meaning of the word was "anything that is indivisible" (*Unteilbares*); however, since the eighteenth century, the use of this term has been limited to "people" (*Menschen*).[58] In his "systems theory", Luhmann speaks about autopoietic systems, thus, such social systems that are capable of reproducing themselves. This basically means the reproduction of communications, which, in terms of Luhmann, does not mean a mere transfer and the receipt of information, but also includes the notion of "understanding".[59] Thus,

---

[51] *Luhmann, N.*, Systemtheorie der Gesellschaft, Berlin: Suhrkamp Verlag 2017 (edited by Johannes F.K. Schmidt and André Kieserling, under cooperation of Christoph Gesigora).

[52] *Ibid.*, pp. 16–17.

[53] *Ibid.*, p. 146.

[54] *Ibid.*, pp. 174–184.

[55] *Luhmann, N.*, Einführung in die Systemtheorie, Heidelberg: Carl-Auer-Systeme Verlag 2004 (edited by D. Baecker), p. 255.

[56] *Ibid.*, p. 256.

[57] *Ibid.*, pp. 250–251.

[58] *Ibid.*, pp. 247–248.

[59] See also *Seidl, D.*, Luhmann's theory of autopoietic social systems, Ludwig-Maximilians-Universität München, Munich School of Management, 2004 (https://www.zfog.bwl.uni-muenchen.de/files/mitarbeiter/paper2004_2.pdf).

Luhmann's "systems theory" is about autopoietic social systems, i.e. systems that are capable of reproducing themselves through communications.[60]

When it comes to AI technology, the question is whether such technology may fall under "an individual" in terms of the "social systems theory", or whether it rather fulfills the "glueing function", thus enabling the interaction of people and, in turn, helping them build social systems. Recalling the origins of the word "individual", i.e. anything that is indivisible, it could be argued that intelligent machines, i.e. a machine the functioning of which depends on the sequences of algorithms, which may determine the different functioning of the different parts of the machine, will not necessarily fulfil this requirement. Furthermore, to be considered an individual, the object would have to bear features based on which it could be identified. The latter feature will often be missing in the case of intelligent machines. This may be even more so owing to the fact that AI technology lacks consciousness, so that functioning based on algorithms may result in machines lacking their own identifiers. Thus, an intelligent machine could hardly be considered as "an individual" in terms of systems theory. Also, AI may hardly be considered to be an autopoietic system as long as it does not regenerate itself through interactions. In this regard, it does not suffice that a machine can learn on the basis of data – in order to be considered as an autopoietic system, an intelligent machine would need to be capable of producing components by itself, thus, it may need to be capable of rewriting its algorithms. As long as this is not the case, AI technology may merely be considered at the level of the interaction function. Thus, the question is what implications the AI technology may have for social systems consisting of people or, in other words, to what extent it may influence the building of autopoietic social systems. Such systems and their development would be based on the reproduction of communication. The question thereby is whether AI technology may help, or may rather hinder, building social systems.

On the one hand, and at first sight, it may seem to be almost stating the obvious to say that technology such as the Internet of Things (IoT) or a broader AI technology has increased the possibilities of people to interact. In this regard, it could be recalled that, back in 1996, Don Tapscott, while defining 12 themes for the digital economy, called it the "Age of Networked Intelligence".[61] At that time, he pointed out that:

> The Age of Networked Intelligence is an age of promise. It is not simply about the networking of technology but about *the networking of humans through technology*. It is not an age of smart machines but of humans who through networks can combine

---

[60]   See *Borch, C.*, Niklas Luhmann, London: Routledge 2011, pp. 26–28.
[61]   *Tapscott, D.*, The Digital Economy: Promise and Peril in the Age of Networked Intelligence, New York: McGraw-Hill 1996, pp. 1 et seq.

their intelligence, knowledge, and creativity for breakthroughs in the creation of wealth and social development.[62] (Emphasis added)

However, networked intelligence has turned out to be about both smart machines and people, so that it can no longer be confined to human beings only. Moreover, the developed technology may often cut the interactions of people, for example, self-driving cars and digital personal assistants.

Thus, the interaction, which, according to the "social systems theory" is the basis for building social systems through which society operates, may be disrupted by the increasing use of AI technology. In other words, such a technology, instead of fulfilling the "glueing function", may rather interrupt the interactions that form the basis for building social systems. In this regard, it might be "the interaction paradox" that may take place: on the surface, AI technology may seem to enable more interaction of people, thus helping them build social systems. On a closer look, however, it may turn out that such technology cuts, rather than enables, such interactions, thereby hindering the building of social systems. The result could be the fragmentation of society and, possibly, its estrangement.

In fact, in light of people's attention being more often devoted to smart technologies, it could already be observed that society has become increasingly individualistic.[63] Yet this should not lead to oversimplified conclusions that AI technology may step in and be better suited for knowing people. In fact, it has time and again been claimed that intelligent machines may, in the future, know people better than their human counterparts.[64] However, the question of "knowing" oneself and each other is a complex one and goes deep into the roots of philosophical recognition theory. It should not be expected that intelligent machines, although they may possess vast amounts of data, will be able to better (if at all) perceive people. In fact, machines can be the possessors of information, they can recognize particular patterns, draw parallels and make (limited) findings based on such information and their algorithms,[65]

---

[62] *Ibid.*, p. xiv.

[63] The question whether the society, the members of which are increasingly exhibiting themselves in the platforms of social media, has become narcissistic, can be left open.

[64] See, for example, *The Guardian*, "Your Computer Knows You Better Than Your Friends Do, Say Researchers", 13 January 2015 (https://www.theguardian.com/technology/2015/jan/13/your-computer-knows-you-researchers-cambridge-stanford-university).

[65] See, for example, Article 29 Data Protection Working Party, Guidelines on Automated individual decision-making and Profiling for the purposes of Regulation 2016/769, adopted on 3 October 2017, as last revised and adopted on 6 February 2018, 17/EN WP251rev.01, pp. 5, 12.

but it would be difficult for them to perceive people – a process that is not an easy one even for human beings. Hence, the vision of machines, which have vast amounts of data about people, being in a position to know people better than they know themselves or are known by other people remains highly speculative, since it would be an exaggeration to claim that being able to draw some insights from information possessed may lead to realizing a human being or perceiving them. This process is very complex and could hardly be based merely on the possession of (even vast) amounts of data.

2.3   THE THEORY OF ADAM SMITH FOR THE DATA- AND ALGORITHM-DRIVEN ECONOMY

As explained above, the impact of AI technology on the social relationships of people may be significant. Also, it could probably be claimed that AI technology has equally significantly affected the economy. Yet a pressing question is whether AI has indeed brought entirely new economic and legal questions. In order to provide an answer to this question, it may be helpful to go back to a very classic economic theory, i.e. that developed by Adam Smith. The analysis of his theory has been chosen not because he published *The Wealth of Nations* at the dawn of the First Industrial Revolution. Instead, Smith's theory has been chosen because some elements of it may help explain aspects of the data economy that have been considered as novel or unique, such as, for example, the "privacy paradox".

2.3.1   "Self-Interest"

The famous passage in Adam Smith's *The Wealth of Nations* reads:

> It is not from the benevolence of the butcher, the brewer, or the baker, that we expect our dinner, but from their regard to their *own interest*. We address ourselves, not to their humanity but to *their self-love*, and never talk to them of our own necessities but of their advantages.[66] (Emphasis added)

According to Adam Smith, the driver of economic behaviour is self-interest. It stimulates exchange to take place between human beings.[67] After all, in his words, it is not "our own necessities", but rather "their advantages", that count.

Speaking about human beings' "own interest" and "their self-love", Adam Smith refers to an (efficiency-creating) economic interest of human behaviour.

---

    [66]   *Smith, A.*, An Inquiry into the Nature and Causes of the Wealth of Nations, Chicago: The University of Chicago Press 1976, p. 18.
    [67]   *Ibid.*, p. 18.

Self-interest in his theory is said to be an economic form of self-love.[68] In the preface to the 1976 edition of Adam Smith's *The Wealth of Nations*, George J. Stigler writes that "the fundamental explanation of man's behavior, in Smith's view, is found in the rational, persistent pursuit of self-interest" – the concept which "the modern economist has labeled 'utility-maximizing behavior'".[69] Such individual behaviour, driven by self-interest, at the same time serves the overall interests of people.[70]

It should be stressed that self-interest, in the theory of Adam Smith, was attributable to human beings only. In his words, a propensity to exchange stimulated by self-interest can be found in people only: "it is common to all men, and to be found in no other race of animals, which seem to know neither this nor any other species of contracts".[71] However, bearing in mind the developments of AI technology, it could be asked whether the notion of self-interest may also be relevant in the case of intelligent machines. In fact, not only may an intelligent machine be programmed to increase utility,[72] but it also cannot be ruled out that self-interest of an intelligent machine may be developed through learning algorithms. In such a case, self-interest – the notion that was analysed by Adam Smith as the main economic driver of human behaviour – may have to be transposed into the context of economic behaviour of intelligent machines as well. Should intelligent machines become increasingly autonomous, the tricky part may turn out to be the limits of their self-interest, particularly bearing in mind that limits such as emotional feelings will not do in this regard.

According to Adam Smith, self-interest is one of the main driving factors for a propensity to exchange. In his words:

> But man has almost constant occasion for the help of his brethren, and it is in vain for him to expect it from their benevolence only. He will be more likely to prevail *if he can interest their self-love in his favour*, and show them that it is for their own advantage to do for him what he requires of them. Whoever offers to another

---

[68] *Recktenwald, H.C.*, Adam Smiths Paradigmen: Bewahrtes und Unvollendetes, Stuttgart: Steiner 1986, p. 27.

[69] *Stigler, G.J.*, Preface, in: Smith, A., An Inquiry into the Nature and Causes of the Wealth of Nations, Chicago: The University of Chicago Press 1976, at xi.

[70] See *Viner, J.*, Adam Smith und Laissez-faire, in: H.C. Recktenwald (Ed.), Ethik, Wirtschaft und Staat: Adam Smiths politische Ökonomie heute, Darmstadt: Wissenschaftliche Buchgesellschaft 1985, pp. 82–83.

[71] *Smith, A.*, An Inquiry into the Nature and Causes of the Wealth of Nations, Chicago: The University of Chicago Press 1976, p. 17.

[72] On utility in AI, see, for example, *Russell, S.J./Norvig, P.*, Artificial Intelligence: A Modern Approach, 3rd ed., Delhi: Pearson 2015, p. 1061, pp. 1 et seq. The authors distinguish four types of agents: simple reflex agents, model-based reflex agents, goal-based agents and utility-based agents (*ibid.*, pp. 47–54).

a bargain of any kind, proposed to do this. Give me that which I want, and you shall have this which you want, is the meaning of every such offer; and it is in this manner that we obtain from one another the far greater part of those good offices which we stand in need of.[73] (Emphasis added)

Thus, in the case of a human behaviour, self-interest, although it is a strong economic driver, at the same time provides room for bargaining. In the case of a machine, however, where self-interest may be written into algorithms (or worse, may be developed by machines themselves through the process of self-learning), it may be much more difficult to haggle. Thus, the self-interest of intelligent machines may result in the statement "give me that which I want, and you shall have this which you want" boiling down to the obedience of people to the machines rather than their bargain. This risk should probably be kept in mind by the developers of AI technology.

Coming back to a human behaviour, self-interest may possibly help "crack the nut" when it comes to the phenomenon of the data economy, namely, the so-called "privacy paradox". The latter defines the situation when individuals share or give away their personal information in exchange for services that are granted, allegedly "for free" (yet, in fact, in exchange for their data), in spite of their concerns regarding privacy.[74] Hence, the "privacy paradox" means that individuals are, on the one hand, aware of the (potential) risks related to their personal data, but on the other hand they still share such data in exchange for some kind of a commercial benefit (for example, a particular service, for which they do not need to pay with money).

At first sight, the notion of "privacy paradox" may seem to imply that the attitude towards privacy might be changing. It has, in fact, been argued that societal developments bring changes as regards the notion of privacy.[75] Indeed,

---

[73] *Smith, A.*, An Inquiry into the Nature and Causes of the Wealth of Nations, Chicago: The University of Chicago Press 1976, p. 18.

[74] Competition & Markets Authority, The commercial use of consumer data. Report on the CMA's call for information, June 2015 (https://www.gov.uk/government/uploads/system/uploads/attachment_data/file/435817/The_commercial_use_of_consumer_data.pdf), pp. 129–130. This study also analyses how much the users of the Internet value different types of data (*ibid.*, at pp. 110 et seq.). On the empirical research of the value that the Internet users place on their privacy see, for example, *Acquisti, A./John, L.K./Loewenstein, G.*, What Is Privacy Worth?, (2013) 42 The Journal of Legal Studies 249; *Chakraborty, R./Vishik, C./Rao, H.R.*, Privacy Preserving Actions of Older Adults on Social Media: Exploring the Behavior of Opting Out of Information Sharing, (2013) 55 Decision Support Systems 948; *Tucker, C.E.*, The Economics of Advertising and Privacy, (2012) 30 International Journal of Industrial Organization 326.

[75] See, for example, *Richard, N.M./King, J.*, Big Data Ethics, (2014) 49 Wake Forest Law Review 393 ("Notions of privacy are changing with society as they always have" (*ibid.*, at 395)).

on the one hand, it should not be ruled out that the attitude towards privacy may to some extent have been changing. On the other hand, however, broader conclusions as regards privacy should probably not be drawn too quickly. Although currently it may seem that the attitude towards the notion of privacy has been changing, it may still be that the pendulum will swing to the other side. For good reasons, privacy as a notion does not seem to be disappearing.

Yet, the "privacy paradox" could possibly be explained on the basis of self-interest. Bearing in mind that, in the data economy, goods and services are often offered in exchange for data, self-interest will often exist on both sides, i.e. those who offer goods and services and those who offer data. Thus, the exchange of goods and services for data may be triggered not only by the self-interest of the companies, but also by the self-interest of data subjects who give away their data in order to get something which they often consider to be received "for free". Hence, since people are increasingly offered goods and services based on their data, they, while recognizing the risks involved, may still exchange their data, because it might be in their "self-interest" to do so. So it is not necessarily a "paradox" that happens here, but rather the meeting of different sides driven by their "self-interest", in other words, mutual self-interest.

In fact, in the data economy, the role of individuals is no more confined to the demand side (for a good or service), but also extends to the supply side. After all, companies which demand data may be interested in extracting from individuals as much data as possible. Hence, it is the self-interest of the latter that may often need to be attracted by the companies. In light of this, the role of the psychological effects of the offering of goods and services based on the processing of personal data, including the role that the use of psychological effects may play in competition,[76] may become increasingly important. After all, it is no longer only companies that play an important role in the economy, but also each individual, since they are the carriers of their data.

The fact that companies in the data economy may appeal to the emotions of individuals is not entirely new. It has been stressed that companies in data markets may possess data about consumers' preferences, purchasing habits, etc. Attention has been drawn to the fact that "[a]n algorithm-fueled environment will provide firms with unparalleled information about our desires, behavior, interests, search patterns, and willingness and ability to pay".[77] Thus,

---

[76] See *Surblytė, G.,* Competition Law at the Crossroads in the Digital Economy: is it all About Google?, (2015) 4 EuCML 170 (Max Planck Institute for Innovation & Competition Research Paper No. 15-13 (7 December 2015); http://papers.ssrn.com/sol3/papers.cfm?abstract_id=2701847).

[77] *Ezrachi, A./Stucke, M.E.,* Virtual Competition: The Promise and Perils of the Algorithm-Driven Economy, Cambridge, MA: Harvard University Press 2016, p. 105.

in order to increase their demand, consumers' biases may be exploited, since companies "will likely appeal to our emotional wants".[78]

In this regard, the demand-pull hypothesis for data markets has been suggested. According to Mehra:

> the nascent field of demand chain optimization is trying to use software and mathematical algorithms to proactively manage the pull of consumer demand and its effects on a firm and its suppliers.[79]

However, a word of caution has to be spoken in this regard. Companies may need to attract individuals' self-interest in order to get their data. Yet, when it comes to the demand for goods or services (even if offered in relation to the processed data of individuals), the economic principles do not seem to have changed in the data economy. The unknown effects on demand of targeted advertising may stand as an example. In simple words, there is no guarantee that a bargain will take place, even if the company has all the knowledge about the (potential) demand.

Nevertheless, the demand-pull hypothesis may be important for explaining the competitive process when it comes to the demand for data. In this regard, it could be recalled that the demand-pull hypothesis was analysed by Jacob Schmookler back in 1966.[80] In his book *Invention and Economic Growth*, he analysed the question whether innovations were knowledge-induced or demand-induced[81] and noted that an inducing factor for an invention was knowledge about its usefulness.[82] Thus, knowledge about the (potential) demand for the companies may be very valuable. In his words:

> in static economics [...] it is consumer preferences which govern the allocation of economic resources among alternative uses. [...] When we shift from the static context to developmental phenomena, the only necessary amendments to this framework are those which result from *a recognition of knowledge itself as an economic*

---

[78]   *Ibid.*, p. 105.

[79]   *Mehra, S.K.*, Antitrust and the Robo-Seller: Competition in the Time of Algorithms (2015–2016) 100 Minn. L. Rev. 1323, at 1337.

[80]   *Schmookler, J.*, Invention and Economic Growth, Cambridge, MA: Harvard University Press 1966.

[81]   *Ibid.*, p. 12: "In short, *are inventions mainly knowledge-induced or demand-induced?* In the parlance of economics, are they primarily the outgrowth of changes in the conditions of their supply, or do they largely reflect changes in the demand for them?" (emphasis in original). See also *ibid.*, p. 166: "For if we ask not *how* the inventions are made, or which industry makes the invented product, but why inventions directed toward the given effect are invented at all, the answer is, demand" (emphasis in original).

[82]   *Ibid.*, pp. 12–13.

good, the production of knowledge as an economic process, and the interaction of changes in knowledge, resources, and preferences. [...] now, preferences, the state of knowledge, and resources endowment *determine the allocation of resources in the production of knowledge and other kinds of goods*, and more specifically, they guide their allocation in the production of different kinds of knowledge.[83] (Emphasis added)

Hence, knowledge about a (potential) demand, or information, which enables the prediction of demand, may be an economic good and the production of such knowledge may form part of an economic process. Whereas, in traditional markets, the allocation of resources is governed mostly by consumer preferences, an additional factor in light of the demand-pull hypothesis is that knowledge – or to be more precise, the production of knowledge – forms part of an economic process. In other words, the allocation of resources no longer covers only the production of goods, but the production of such knowledge as well. Thus, the beauty of the demand-pull hypothesis is the acknowledgement of the (potential) economic value of information about demand.

2.3.2   Data as a Commodity

Bearing in mind that, in the data economy, goods and services are often offered in exchange for data, it has been discussed whether data may be considered as a commodity.[84]

A particular good may be considered as a commodity if it has particular features, such as durability and divisibility. In this regard, Kenneth Arrow, for example, saw difficulties in treating information as a commodity. According to him, information could be considered a commodity to "a limited extent".[85] He pointed out two features of information that may complicate its treatment as a commodity: firstly, the indivisibility in the use of information, and secondly, the difficulty of appropriating it.[86]

---

[83]   *Ibid.*, p. 185.

[84]   See, for example, *Zech, H.*, A Legal Framework for a Data Economy in the European Digital Single Market: Rights to Use Data, (2016) 11(6) Journal of Intellectual Property Law & Practice 460, 461 ("Raw data becomes a 'commodity' which is traded in a data economy" (footnote omitted)); *Vestager, M.*, "Making Data Work for Us", Speech, 9 September 2016 (https://ec.europa.eu/competition/speeches/index_2016.html) ("personal data has become a valuable commodity"); *Lohsse, S./ Schulze, R./Staudenmayer, D.* (Eds.), Trading Data in the Digital Economy: Legal Concepts and Tools, Baden-Baden: Nomos Verlagsgesellschaft 2017.

[85]   *Arrow, K.J.*, Information and Economic Behavior, reprinted in: Collected Papers of Kenneth J. Arrow, The Economics of Information, Vol. 4, Cambridge, MA: The Belknap Press of Harvard University Press 1984, pp. 136–152, at p. 142.

[86]   *Ibid.*, p. 142.

The question of the instruments of commerce was also analysed by Adam Smith, who explained that the "[d]ifficulties of barter system lead to the selection of one commodity as money" and gave other examples such as "cattle, salt, shells, cod, tobacco, sugar, leather and nails".[87] Salt was given by Adam Smith as an example of earlier times, when the latter was a valuable commodity and thus an instrument of commerce.[88] He also noted that metals were a preferable exchange tool due to the fact that they were, firstly, durable, and secondly, divisible.[89] Thus, they could be further used. Thereby, Smith outlined the problem, related to weighing the rude bars of metal, so that what followed was stamping them in order "to show quantity and fineness".[90] It was public offices which were "meant to ascertain, by means of a public stamp, the quantity and uniform goodness of those different commodities when brought to market",[91] for example, coins used to express weight.[92] With regard to money, Adam Smith noted that:

> Money is said to have had its origin in the fact that men naturally fell upon one commodity with which to compare the value of all other commodities. When this commodity was once selected it became the medium of exchange.[93]

Thereby, one of the key issues when considering a commodity as an instrument of commerce is its value. Hence, when it comes to data, it could be argued that, while loose data may lack the relevant features of a commodity, particular data sets that may be exchanged in business may be considered a commodity, as long as they have at least a potential value.

For example, Adam Smith distinguished between two types of value of a commodity:

> The word VALUE, it is to be observed, has two different meanings, and sometimes expresses the utility of some particular object, and sometimes the power of purchasing other goods which the possession of that object conveys. The one may be called "value in use"; the other, "value in exchange". The things which have the greatest value in use have frequently little or no value in exchange; and on the contrary, those which have the greatest value in exchange have frequently little or no value in use.[94] (Emphasis in original)

---

[87] *Smith, A.,* An Inquiry into the Nature and Causes of the Wealth of Nations, Chicago: The University of Chicago Press 1976, pp. 26–27.

[88] *Ibid.,* pp. 26–27.

[89] *Ibid.,* pp. 27–28.

[90] *Ibid.,* p. 28.

[91] *Ibid.,* p. 29.

[92] *Ibid.,* p. 30.

[93] *Ibid.,* p. 32, footnote 3.

[94] *Ibid.,* p. 32.

Although the distinction by Adam Smith between the value in exchange and the value in use was subject to some criticism,[95] such a distinction may, possibly, be valid for the data economy. The question of the value of data is a tricky one. In many cases data will not have immediate value, since the latter may depend upon any further use of data, to be more precise, upon its intended use.[96] Thus, the value of data may be merely hypothetical. Often, the value of data will derive from data analytics.[97] Hence, the value of data may often be undetermined and context-specific.[98] Hence, in many cases, data may have (merely) the value in use.

And yet it cannot be ruled out that data (sets) may also have value in exchange. The latter value may often be merely potential. In other words, a precise value of data may not necessarily be determined at the point of time when the exchange takes place, since such value might be measured in hypothetical terms. Importantly though, potential economic value of data would be sufficient to protect data, for example, as a trade secret.[99] Hence, although loose data may lack the features of a commodity, in particular, the value, data sets may be not only a commodity, but under the circumstances may also form part of the instruments of commerce.

2.3.3   The Implications of AI for People's Employment

In light of the increasing abilities of AI technologies to manage a wide range of tasks, the question is whether the developments of such technology may have any implications for the employment of people. In other words, it could be asked whether people risk losing their jobs owing to intelligent machines being capable of doing them. Although fears in this regard have often been expressed, they do not seem to have been fulfilled, yet.[100]

---

[95] See *Stigler, G.J.*, The Development of Utility Theory, (1950) 58 Journal of Political Economy 307, 308.

[96] *Stucke, M.E./Grunes, A.P.*, Big Data and Competition Policy, Oxford: Oxford University Press 2016, p. 43.

[97] *Ibid.*, p. 43: "data's value is not absolute, but relative to how much other data the company has, and the *intended use* of the data" (emphasis added).

[98] *Ibid.*, p. 44.

[99] See *infra* Chapter 3.

[100] See, for example, *The Economist*, "The Rich World is Enjoying an Unprecedented Jobs Boom", 23 May 2019 (https://www.economist.com/leaders/2019/05/23/the-rich-world-is-enjoying-an-unprecedented-jobs-boom); *The Economist*, "Across the Rich World, an Extraordinary Jobs Boom is Under Way", 23 May 2019 (https://www.economist.com/briefing/2019/05/23/across-the-rich-world-an-extraordinary-jobs-boom-is-under-way).

The efficiencies deriving from the division of labour are very much based on the expertise, or, in other words, the specialization of a person. Adam Smith, who developed the notion of the division of labour (on the basis of the example of a pin factory[101]), explained that:

> the certainty of being able to exchange all that surplus part of the produce of his own labour, which is over and above his own consumption, for such parts of the produce of other men's labour as he may have occasion for, encourages every man to apply himself to a particular occupation, and to cultivate and bring to perfection whatever talent or genius he may possess for that particular species of business.[102]

Since the division of labour is based on the skills and knowledge, one of the results to which the employment of machines may lead is hyper-specialization.[103] However, the extent to which machines may be employed depends on how much machines may be capable of "learning by doing".

The concept of "learning by doing" (as applied to people) was developed in more detail by Kenneth Arrow.[104] According to him, "[l]earning is the product of experience. [...] To have steadily increasing performance, then, implies that the stimulus situations must themselves be steadily evolving rather than merely repeating".[105] Hence, for the development of skills based on "learning by doing", it is essential that the situation (or the occupation) does not only repeat itself, but that such a situation (or occupation) constantly evolves. Only then, as explained by Kenneth Arrow, would it be possible to develop expertise on the basis of "learning by doing".

Transferred to intelligent machines this means that the scope of "learning by doing" in the case of machines will depend not only on their algorithms, but also on data. Thus, although it cannot be ruled out that intelligent machines may be capable of "learning by doing" on an equal footing with people,[106] the

---

[101] *Smith, A.*, An Inquiry into the Nature and Causes of the Wealth of Nations, Chicago: The University of Chicago Press 1976, pp. 8–9.

[102] *Ibid.*, p. 19.

[103] This idea is not entirely new. The fact that the developments of the technology may lead to hyper-specialization was discussed in *The Economist* years ago quoting Thomas Malone (the MIT Sloan School of Management), who "argued that computer technology is producing an age of hyper-specialisation, as the process that Adam Smith observed in a pin factory in the 1760s is applied to more sophisticated jobs" (*The Economist*, "There's an App for That", 30 December 2014 (https://www.economist .com/briefing/2014/12/30/theres-an-app-for-that)).

[104] *Arrow, K.J.*, The Economic Implications of Learning by Doing, 29 (1962) Review of Economic Studies 155.

[105] *Ibid.*, at 155–156.

[106] Along these lines see also *Ezrachi, A./Stucke, M.E.*, Virtual Competition: The Promise and Perils of the Algorithm-Driven Economy, Cambridge, MA: Harvard University Press 2016, pp. 153–154.

implications of such "learning by doing" by intelligent machines may depend on the context and the sector where the intelligent machine would be employed as well as on its access to the data relevant for such learning. However, intelligent machines will not be capable of taking over all tasks from people: after all, machines may have limited capabilities to perform tasks that require consciousness, for example, making evaluation decisions, which may require morality.

Finally, it could be recalled that, back in 1996, Don Tapscott noted that:

> In the old economy, individuals learned a skill, trade, or profession, and they simply kept up with changes in that field. In the new economy, individuals can expect to fundamentally change their knowledge base and skill set several times throughout their working lives.[107]

The increasing employment of intelligent machines may raise the need for people to requalify their skills. Hence, although the requalification of skills and knowledge of people may be needed, the possibility of machines taking over all tasks from people remains unlikely, at least as long as machines lack consciousness. After all, tasks that require moral capacity and evaluation judgements will remain at the discretion of human beings.

2.3.4 Moral Standards: A Dilemma for Machines or for Their Creators?

In 2016, the IEEE Standards Association introduced a Global Initiative for Ethical Considerations in the Design of Autonomous Systems.[108] According to Konstantinos Karachalios, the managing director for IEEE-SA, "as machines increasingly assist humans in a multitude of critical and sensitive tasks, it is important to prioritize the use of ethical considerations in the design of these emergent systems, and this new Initiative will help ensure that we are working to advance technology for humanity under principled disciplines".[109]

Similarly, "Moral Machine",[110] the project launched by the Massachusetts Institute of Technology, is devoted to clarifying the question how to solve the problems of self-driving cars. The machines will often face dilemmas, the answers to which are provided by people, so that these solutions can further be programmed in the machines. In fact, since self-driving cars are not capable of

---

[107] *Tapscott, D.*, The Digital Economy: Promise and Peril in the Age of Networked Intelligence, New York: McGraw-Hill 1996, p. 299.
[108] http://standards.ieee.org/news/2016/ieee_autonomous_systems.html.
[109] *Ibid.*
[110] http://moralmachine.mit.edu/.

writing their own algorithms and thereby solving dilemmas on their own, the solutions have to be programmed by way of sequences of algorithms by those who create such machines.

The examples illustrated above show how topical the question of ethical standards is in the light of AI technology. Yet, as explained, although the dilemmas are or will be faced by intelligent machines, the solutions for solving machines' dilemmas will be provided by people. After all, machines not only lack consciousness; they also lack morality and the ability to feel. Indeed, the fact that machines are not capable (and can hardly be imagined to be capable) of feeling and making independent decisions on the basis of moral standards shows that it will be the moral standards of people that will count.

In this regard, one of the moral standards, i.e. sympathy, may come into play. In *The Theory of Moral Sentiments*,[111] Adam Smith talks about sympathy or, in other words, "fellow-feeling".[112] In the words of Adam Smith:

> In every passion of which the mind of man is susceptible, the emotions of the bystander always correspond to what, *by bringing the case home to himself*, he imagines should be the sentiments of the sufferer.[113] (Emphasis added)

Accordingly, sympathy is "bringing the case home to himself". As fellow-feeling, sympathy means that the situation of the other will be perceived as one's own. However, according to Adam Smith, even when empathizing, the situation will be judged by a person from their own perspective.[114] Hence, sympathy, for Adam Smith, is perceiving the situation of the other as one's own, but judging on that situation according to one's own standards. Importantly though, Adam Smith speaks of "mutual sympathy"[115] and "the correspondence of the sentiments"[116] and explains:

> Mankind, though naturally sympathetic, never conceive, for what has befallen another, that degree of passion which naturally animates the person principally concerned. That imaginary change of situation, upon which their sympathy is founded, is but momentary. [...] What they feel will, indeed, always be in some respects different from what he feels, and compassion can never be exactly the same with original sorrow; [...]. *These two sentiments, however, may, it is evident, have such a correspondence with one another, as is sufficient for the harmony of society.*

---

[111] Smith, A., The Theory of Moral Sentiments, London: Henry G. Bohn, York Street, Covent Garden 1853.

[112] *Ibid.*, pp. 4 et seq.

[113] *Ibid.*, p. 5.

[114] *Ibid.*, p. 18.

[115] *Ibid.*, pp. 10 et seq.

[116] *Ibid.*, p. 10 ("this correspondence of the sentiments of others with our own appears to be a cause of pleasure" (*ibid.*, p. 11)).

Though they will never be unisons, they may be concords, and this is all that is wanted or required.[117] (Emphasis added)

Accordingly, although an absolute correspondence of sentiments can hardly be achieved, it should suffice that the decisions made take place in light of "mutual sympathy", so that a level of the correspondence of sentiments can be achieved that is necessary for the harmony of society.

Transferred to the context of intelligent machines, it is, first of all, note-worthy that "fellow-feeling", as explained by Adam Smith, is an ability to empathize, which can be attributed to human beings (only). Sympathy, as a moral category, could hardly be transferred to machines. After all, senti-ments – as feelings – apply to human beings. Although it might be possible to program algorithms in such a way that a machine expresses sympathy, it will still not be equal to the senses and emotions that human beings are capable of. Hence, when it comes to intelligent machines, values such as sympathy may be written into them with the help of algorithms, but they will never be capable of having this ability by themselves. One of the examples is gynoid Sofia, which keeps repeating that she respects human values, including sympathy.[118] Yet such programmed language stands as an example of a machine with algorithm-prescribed values.

In fact, since ethical standards are closely related to morality, it should be kept in mind that morality can be attributed to people, but it can hardly be attributed to machines. As stated by Nevejans, "we should not confuse ethics in robotics with machine ethics, which oblige the robots themselves to adhere to ethical rules. Today, machine ethics is still in a theoretical state since even autonomous robots are incapable of taking moral decisions."[119] Hence, given the fact that it is human beings who create intelligent machines, the question of ethical standards boils down to such standards as they are applied by people, since it is them who write machines' algorithms. Considering that currently machines do not yet act consciously (i.e. machine ethics, as explained, remains speculation), the ethical standards to be set for intelligent machines are rather a reflection of ethical standards of the members of the society, who are human beings (i.e. ethics in robotics). In other words, discussion of setting ethical standards for intelligent machines boils down to the question of what standards we apply in our society. At the end of the day, it will be these standards that will be reflected in machines.

---

[117] *Ibid.*, pp. 22–23.

[118] http://www.hansonrobotics.com/robot/sophia/.

[119] *Nevejans, N.*, European Civil Law Rules in Robotics, 2016 (http://www.europarl.europa.eu/RegData/etudes/STUD/2016/571379/IPOL_STU(2016)571379_EN.pdf), p. 20.

In light of the fact that absolute "mutual sympathy" can hardly be achieved, it could be asked how a consensus could be reached when setting ethical standards for intelligent machines. On the basis of the "moral machine" example, it is clear that the decision whether to sympathize with the young, the old, the human being, the animal, the child, etc., is not an easy one. It could even be an illusion that a perfect consensus could be reached with regard to all of the issues. Yet a correspondence of sentiments that "would be sufficient for the harmony of the society" could be achieved. Therefore, moral standards should not be set from one's own point of view (the "I" perspective). The standard of an "impartial spectator" in terms of Smith "is neither of the 'I' nor of the 'you'. It is […] the 'I with you in mind'".[120] It is this latter point that should be borne in mind when setting ethical standards for machines.

Thus, it could be argued that sympathy, as a fundamental moral principle, should play a role in ethics in robotics, i.e. when it comes to setting ethical standards of machines. This may be even more so if we rely on the concept of "mutual sympathy", as explained by Adam Smith. When designing ethics in robotics, standards are set by people through their decisions on how to solve the dilemmas of machines, which are not capable of solving them on their own. By setting such standards, people rely on their moral categories. Sympathy, or "fellow-feeling" as described by Adam Smith, may be highly relevant in this regard. This moral category requires empathy with others, but allows the situation to be judged from one's own perspective. Most importantly, it is the effort of "bringing the situation home to himself" that counts, so that correspondence of sentiments can be achieved. Such correspondence does not need to be perfect, but should be such that is "sufficient for the harmony of the society".

At first sight, sympathy stands in stark contrast to Adam Smith's other concept, i.e. self-interest, the notion which he elaborated on in *The Wealth of Nations*.[121] A possible collision between the two concepts was particularly discussed by some German scholars who tried to interpret both works of Adam Smith in a consistent manner – triggering the so-called "Adam Smith problem".[122] It was argued that, if treated separately, the two concepts are

---

[120]   *Wilson, D./Dixon, W.*, Das Adam Smith Problem: A Critical Realist Perspective, (2006) 5 Journal of Critical Realism 251, 268. "These are standards that are not external at all but, according to Smith's lights, inhere in me: they are my norms; norms that are somehow taken into myself. Better, this 'man within' is the 'me'" (*ibid.*).

[121]   *Smith, A.*, An Inquiry into the Nature and Causes of the Wealth of Nations, Chicago: The University of Chicago Press 1976.

[122]   The term was coined by the German scholars as "das Adam-Smith-Problem". For more see, for example, *Viner, J.*, Adam Smith und Laissez-faire, in: H.C. Recktenwald (Ed.), Ethik, Wirtschaft und Staat: Adam Smiths politische Ökonomie heute, Darmstadt: Wissenschaftliche Buchgesellschaft 1985, p. 75.

completely contradictory, so that it was suggested that they should be aligned by reading Adam Smith's writings in a systemic view of his overall works (*Gesamtwerk/Gesamtschau*).[123] Also, a word of caution was spoken with regard to a potential misunderstanding of *The Wealth of Nations* if it were read without *The Theory of Moral Sentiments*.[124] The risk of a "narrow reading of Adam Smith" was pointed out.[125]

However, it could be questioned whether the economic and the moral theory of Adam Smith should indeed be read together. Contradictory as they are, both concepts (self-interest and sympathy) were explained by Adam Smith in different contexts. Whereas sympathy was analysed by him as a moral category, self-interest was considered as a driving factor of economic human behaviour. So, it could be argued that, instead of reading both theories in a consistent manner, it could be exactly the opposite that may be needed, i.e. reading and explaining them separately. Aligning the two concepts, which were meant for different contexts, may raise the risk of changing the meaning attributed to them by Adam Smith.

In fact, some scholars, like Viner, have argued that the two books have to be treated and interpreted separately.[126] In particular, it was stressed that the metaphysical grounds, on which the *Theory of Moral Sentiments* rests, are not found in *The Wealth of Nations*.[127] Also, George J. Stigler in the preface to *The Wealth of Nations* notes that:

> This is not to say that Smith believed men to be guided only by self-interest. Indeed his first book, *The Theory of Moral Sentiments*, is devoted to the exploration of the sentiment of sympathy [...]. Nevertheless Smith believed that the most persistent, the most universal, and therefore the most reliable of man's motives was the pursuit of his own interests.[128]

---

[123] *Recktenwald, H.C.*, Einleitung, in: H.C. Recktenwald (Ed.), Ethik, Wirtschaft und Staat: Adam Smiths politische Ökonomie heute, Darmstadt: Wissenschaftliche Buchgesellschaft 1985, p. 2.

[124] For a more detailed analysis see *Viner, J.*, Adam Smith und Laissez-faire, in: H.C. Recktenwald (Ed.), Ethik, Wirtschaft und Staat: Adam Smiths politische Ökonomie heute, Darmstadt: Wissenschaftliche Buchgesellschaft 1985, pp. 75 et seq.

[125] *Wells, T.*, Adam Smith on Morality and Self-Interest, in: C. Luetge (Ed.), Handbook of the Philosophical Foundations of Business Ethics, Dordrecht/Heidelberg/New York/London: Springer 2013, p. 283; see also at p. 295.

[126] *Viner, J.*, Adam Smith und Laissez-faire, in: H.C. Recktenwald (Ed.), Ethik, Wirtschaft und Staat: Adam Smiths politische Ökonomie heute, Darmstadt: Wissenschaftliche Buchgesellschaft 1985, pp. 75 et seq.

[127] *Ibid.*, pp. 81 et seq.

[128] *Stigler, G.J.*, Preface, in: Smith, A., An Inquiry into the Nature and Causes of the Wealth of Nations, Chicago: The University of Chicago Press 1976, p. xii.

Hence, bearing in mind that self-interest and sympathy have been analysed by Adam Smith in different contexts, it could be argued that self-interest should not necessarily be read along the lines of his moral categories. Indeed, his two books address different contexts, so that a rather artificial convergence of, in fact, two different categories could actually lead to imprecise interpretations. For Adam Smith, self-interest was an economic (not a moral) driver of human behaviour, giving rise to a propensity to exchange goods and, in turn, leading to the division of labour.

2.3.5   The Implications of Revisiting the Theory of Adam Smith for the Data Economy

The results of the analysis above are twofold: first of all, such analysis shows that the data economy, despite the fact that it has been claimed to be revolutionary, has not brought any drastic changes. Instead, it functions on the same classic economic principles. Secondly, although concepts such as "privacy paradox" have been considered to be a phenomenon of the data economy, the analysis of "self-interest" as developed by Adam Smith reveals that such a "privacy paradox" can be explained by the existence of mutual self-interest. Furthermore, the fact that the value of a commodity may be distinguished into value in use and value in exchange shows that it might be sufficient for data to have a potential value (thus, value in exchange) in order for it to be considered a commodity. Moreover, the concept of the division of labour as developed by Adam Smith shows that the requalification of the skills and knowledge of people might be needed in light of an increasing employment of intelligent machines. However, not all tasks might be taken over by machines, bearing in mind that for the fulfilment of some of them consciousness and moral evaluation may be required. Finally, since setting ethical standards for intelligent machines has become increasingly important, sympathy, as a moral standard, may be of the utmost importance for human beings when judging the implementation of ethical standards of machines.

2.4   "FREE FLOW OF DATA"

Although, as shown above, the data economy has not brought any fundamental economic changes that would beg for drastic changes in the law, it can hardly be contested that the economic role of data has increased dramatically. After all, data has become a key asset for developing data-based technology. Thus, in light of the fact that data is one of the key conditions for the development of AI technology, it is not surprising that the question of access to data arose in the industry. What may seem to be more surprising though, is the enthusiasm with which this question was picked up by the European Commission and by some members of academia. Whereas the European Commission proposed the "free flow of data initiative" (as described below), some scholars have actively pleaded for data access.[129]

However, the question of access to data is more nuanced and requires a thorough analysis, first and foremost raising the need to dig deeper into concepts related to economic incentives. Also, when it comes to data, a distinction has to be made not only with regard to different types of data, but also as regards the context in which such data is processed, i.e. in the public or in the private sector. The incentives for processing data in these two contexts may be very different.

2.4.1 The (Mis)conception of the "Free Flow of Data"

In 2015, the European Commission announced its Digital Single Market Strategy, part of which was the goal of building the European data economy.[130] In the Digital Single Market Strategy the European Commission stated that it would propose "the 'free flow of data' initiative that tackles restrictions on the free movement of data for reasons other than the protection of personal data within the EU and [...] address the emerging issues of ownership, interoperability, usability and access to data in situations such as business-to-business, business to consumer, machine generated and machine-to-machine data"[131] (emphasis added). Thus, the "free flow of data" initiative was supposed to clarify issues such as data ownership and access to data related to, *inter alia*, the business-to-business relationship.[132] Business-to-business data sharing and access to data form part of the focus of the European strategy for data

---

[129] See, for example, *Drexl, J.*, Designing Competitive Markets for Industrial Data – Between Propertisation and Access (31 October 2016). Max Planck Institute for Innovation & Competition Research Paper No. 16-13. Available at SSRN: https://papers .ssrn.com/sol3/papers.cfm?abstract_id=2862975; *Drexl, J.*, Data Access and Control in the Era of Connected Devices, Study on Behalf of the European Consumer Organisation BEUC (https://www.ip.mpg.de/fileadmin/ipmpg/content/aktuelles/aus_der_forschung/ beuc-x-2018-121_data_access_and_control_in_the_area_of_connected_devices.pdf).

[130] Communication from the Commission to the European Parliament, the Council, the European Economic and Social Committee and the Committee of the Regions "A Digital Single Market Strategy for Europe", Brussels, 6.5.2015, COM(2015) 192 final.

[131] *Ibid.*, p. 15.

[132] These questions were addressed by the European Commission also in its earlier documents, see, for example: European Commission, Communication from the Commission to the European Parliament, the Council, the European Economic and Social Committee and the Committee of the Regions, "Towards a Thriving Data-Driven Economy", Brussels, 2.7.2014, COM(2014) 442 final, p. 12.

published by the European Commission in February 2020.[133] In the aforementioned strategy, the European Commission speaks about "a data access right", saying that such a right "should only be sector-specific and only given if a market failure in this sector is identified/can be foreseen, which competition law cannot solve".[134]

In light of such a debate on data ownership and access to data, it should be stressed that it is of utmost importance to take into account economic incentives. In this regard, it could be recalled that, back in 1945, von Hayek, in *The Use of Knowledge in Society*, wrote that:

> The economic problem of society is thus not merely a problem of how to allocate "given" resources – if "given" is taken to mean given to a single mind which deliberately solves the problem set by these "data." It is rather a problem of how to secure the best use of resources known to any of the members of society, for ends whose relative importance only these individuals know. Or, to put it briefly, it is a problem of the utilization of knowledge which is not given to anyone in its totality.[135]

---

[133]   European Commission, Communication from the Commission to the European Parliament, the Council, the European Economic and Social Committee and the Committee of the Regions, "A European Strategy for Data", Brussels, 19.2.2020, COM(2020) 66 final.

[134]   *Ibid.*, p. 13 footnote 39.

[135]   *von Hayek, F.A.*, The Use of Knowledge in Society, (1945) 35(4) American Economic Review 519, 519. In fact, by this passage he was giving an answer to the original question, i.e. "What is the problem we wish to solve when we try to construct a rational economic order? On certain familiar assumptions the answer is simple enough. *If* we possess all the relevant information, *if* we can start out from a given system of preferences, and *if* we command complete knowledge of available means, the problem which remains is purely one of logic. [...] the economic calculus which we have developed to solve this logical problem, though an important step toward the solution of the economic problem of society, does not yet provide an answer to it. The reason for this is that the 'data' from which the economic calculus starts are never for the whole society 'given' to a single mind which could work out the implications and can never be so given" (emphasis in original) (*von Hayek, F.A.*, The Use of Knowledge in Society (1945) 35(4) American Economic Review 519, 519). The latter passage has also been quoted by Ezrachi and Stucke, yet, stating that "[w]ith the advancement in Big Data and Big Analytics, our ability to amass information has progressed far beyond what Hayek envisaged in the mid-twentieth century. [...] Is Hayek's 'knowledge problem' less problematic today?" (footnote omitted) (*Ezrachi, A./Stucke, M.E.*, Virtual Competition: The Promise and Perils of the Algorithm-Driven Economy, Cambridge, MA: Harvard University Press 2016, p. 208). Yet a precise reading of von Hayek's passage reveals that the question posed by Ezrachi and Stucke should probably be answered in the negative. After all, von Hayek spoke about the construction of a rational economic order, the notion that is broader than competition. In this context, von Hayek was not referring to private companies, but rather to conceptual issues related to the creation of a rational economic order.

Thus, the economic question is not merely confined to how to allocate resources, but is rather a question of how to secure the best use of resources. Transferred to the data economy, the question should probably be not simply one of how to enable access to data (i.e. the allocation of resources in the society). Instead, a more complex issue to consider would be how to create incentives for the best use of resources. After all, incentives should be created and maintained not only for allocating data, but also for making the best use of it. Thus, the question is more complex and more nuanced, i.e. how to increase the economic incentives of those who rely in their business on the commercialization of data without undermining the other interests that might be at stake, first and foremost, those of the individuals (data subjects).

In this regard, it could also be recalled that, according to Coase, it is possible to modify initial entitlements by way of transactions. In 1960, in *The Problem of Social Cost*, R.H. Coase stated that:

> [I]it has to be remembered that the immediate question faced by the courts is *not* what shall be done by whom *but* who has the legal right to do what. It is always possible to modify by transactions on the market the initial legal delimitation of rights. And, of course, if such market transactions are costless, such a rearrangement of rights will always take place if it would lead to an increase in the value of production.[136] (Emphasis in original)

Accordingly, in the case of no transaction costs, the initial entitlement may not matter and can be modified by the parties based on their bargain. As regards the data economy, it could, at first sight, be argued that, since the users of data-related services do not pay any monetary payment, there are no monetary transaction costs. Hence, the argument could go, it should be possible for the market players to modify their transactions by themselves. However, the transaction costs in the data economy may be expressed by the (hypothetical) value of data. Such value is often undetermined and context-specific. Thus, the transactions in the data economy will not always be costless, with a result that the modification of the initial entitlements by way of transactions may not always so easily take place.

Thereby, the question is which current regulatory tools may be most suitable in the data economy for preserving the aforementioned economic incentives and how a regulatory framework may strike a balance between creating the incentive mechanisms for the business and protecting the rights of individuals.

---

[136] *Coase, R.H.*, The Problem of Social Cost, (1960) 3 The Journal of Law & Economics 1, at p. 15.

In this regard, the scope of legal protection for data in terms of trade secret protection may be most important.[137]

Yet one of the options considered by the European Commission for enabling access to data was the creation of the "data producer's right". In the Communication on "Building a European Data Economy" announced on 10 January 2017,[138] the European Commission explained that:

> In some cases manufacturers or service providers may become the *de facto* "owners" of the data that their machines or processes generate, even if those machines are owned by the user. A *de facto* control of this data can be a source of differentiation and competitive advantage for manufacturers. However, this can be problematic, because the user is often prevented by the manufacturer from authorising usage of the data by another party.[139]

Thereby, the European Commission is concerned about the fact that manufacturers and service providers may own data that would actually be generated by their machines. The problem that the European Commission sees in this context is that a manufacturer of the machine may be reluctant to share such data with the manufacturer of the device, whereas the users of machines would be helpless in this regard, since they may be deprived of their right to authorize the usage of their data by a party other than the manufacturer of the machine. Thus, for example, if the car manufacturer integrates sensors in their cars, the concern of the European Commission is that the car manufacturer may benefit from the data generated by the sensor, thereby depriving the manufacturer of the sensor of benefit from the data, which was actually generated by the latter's devices. The users of the car, since they could not interfere in such a relationship, could also not authorize the usage of such data.

Thus, according to the European Commission:

> A right to use and authorise the use of non-personal data could be granted to the "data producer", i.e. the owner or long-term user (i.e. the lessee) of the device. This approach would aim at clarifying the legal situation and giving more choice to the

---

[137] See *infra* Chapter 3.

[138] European Commission, Communication from the Commission to the European Parliament, the Council, the European Economic and Social Committee and the Committee of the Regions, Brussels, 10.1.2017, COM(2017) 9 final. This Communication was accompanied by the Staff Working Document (European Commission, Commission Staff Working Document on the free flow of data and emerging issues of the European data economy, Brussels, 10.1.2017, SWD(2017) 2 final).

[139] European Commission, Communication from the Commission to the European Parliament, the Council, the European Economic and Social Committee and the Committee of the Regions, Brussels, 10.1.2017, COM(2017) 9 final, p. 10.

data producer, by opening up the possibility for users to utilise their data and thereby contribute to unlocking machine-generated data.[140]

As the passage shows, the European Commission, while considering a regulatory approach interfering within the relationship between the manufacturers of machines and the manufacturers of the devices in terms of reallocating data, speaks about non-personal data only. However, conclusions on what may be considered non-personal data should not be drawn too quickly. Although a distinction between personal and non-personal data may seem to be clear at first sight, it may not always be easy to distinguish them in practice, in particular, if they form part of a data set. Yet the distinction between personal and non-personal data will have important legal consequences: whereas the protection of personal data falls under the framework of the GDPR, non-personal data, in contrast, remains "outside the scope of GDPR".[141]

In more general terms, it is noteworthy that the focus on non-personal data while analysing the issue of access to data may be too narrow. In fact, reacting to the "free flow of data" initiative of the European Commission and picking up on the approach of the European Commission to focus on non-personal data, some scholars have stressed the role of "industrial data" – basically as non-personal data – and looked for ways to solve the issue of data ownership and data access in the data economy.[142] However, this academic debate, while looking at "industrial data" from a non-personal data point of view only, overlooked the fact that personal data remains highly important in the data economy.[143] As will be shown in the following sub-section, a large portion of data, although it may seem to be non-personal, may turn out to be personal. This insight cannot be left out of the debate related to the data economy.

---

[140] *Ibid.*, p. 13.

[141] See European Commission, Commission Staff Working Document on the free flow of data and emerging issues of the European data economy, Brussels, 10.1.2017, SWD(2017) 2 final, p. 10.

[142] See, for example, *Drexl, J.*, Designing Competitive Markets for Industrial Data – Between Propertisation and Access (31 October 2016). Max Planck Institute for Innovation & Competition Research Paper No. 16-13. Available at SSRN: https://papers.ssrn.com/sol3/papers.cfm?abstract_id=2862975; *Wiebe, A.*, Protection of industrial data – a new property right for the digital economy? (2016) 65 GRUR Int. 877.

[143] Later on, Drexl, to some extent, analysed the impact of the data economy for personal data as well (*Drexl, J.*, Data Access and Control in the Era of Connected Devices, Study on Behalf of the European Consumer Organisation BEUC (https://www.ip.mpg.de/fileadmin/ipmpg/content/aktuelles/aus_der_forschung/beuc-x-2018-121_data_access_and_control_in_the_area_of_connected_devices.pdf)).

2.4.2   Types of Data: Personal v. Non-Personal Data

In the Communication, the European Commission states that:

> One common theme linking the free flow of data with the emerging issues of access
> and transmission of data is that *enterprises and actors in the data economy will be
> dealing with both personal and non-personal data, and that data flows and datasets
> will regularly contain both types.* Any policy measure must take account of this eco-
> nomic reality and of the legal framework on the protection of personal data, while
> respecting the fundamental rights of individuals.[144] (Emphasis added)

Thereby, the European Commission acknowledges that both types of data (personal and non-personal data) may be important in the data economy and that
the rules of the protection of personal data should be respected when it comes
to assessing questions such as, for example, access to data. In fact, various
types of data are processed in the data economy, so that particular attention has
to be drawn to the fact that it will be not only non-personal data, but often also
personal data that may come into play.

Furthermore, bearing in mind an increasing trend towards digitaliza-
tion in the data economy, machine-generated data may often be produced.
Machine-generated data is defined by the European Commission as data that
"is created without the direct intervention of a human by computer processes,
applications or services, or by sensors processing information received from
equipment, software or machinery, whether virtual or real".[145] According to
the European Commission, such data can be both personal (if such data allows
the identification of a natural person, e.g. location data of mobile applications)
and non-personal.[146]

However, although the European Commission stresses that data sets may
consist of both personal and non-personal data, the focus of its analysis
in the "free flow of data" initiative (and, thus, related questions of data
ownership and data access) is basically on non-personal data. In the Staff

---

[144] European Commission, Communication from the Commission to the European
Parliament, the Council, the European Economic and Social Committee and the
Committee of the Regions, "Building a European Data Economy", Brussels, 10.1.2017,
COM(2017) 9 final, Section 3.1, p. 9.

[145] *Ibid.*, p. 9, Section 3.1.

[146] *Ibid.*, p. 9, Section 3.1.

Working Document,[147] which accompanies the Communication, the European Commission says that:

> In light of the adoption of the General Data Protection Regulation (GDPR) which provides a comprehensive and complete legal framework on the processing of personal data, *the scope of this examination is limited to non-personal or personal data that have been anonymised.*[148] (Footnotes omitted; emphasis added)

Accordingly, the European Commission not only confines its analysis to non-personal data, but also considers that anonymized data would belong to the latter category. However, firstly, such a conclusion should not be drawn too quickly, and secondly, the scope of such an analysis may be too narrow and based on an oversimplified approach towards the notions of personal and non-personal data.

2.4.2.1 Personal v. non-personal data

The idea that data can be of at least two types, i.e. personal or non-personal, was discussed in academia even before the Communication of the European Commission came out.[149] In the Communication, the European Commission noted that:

> In general, data can be personal or non-personal. [...] Personal data can be turned into non-personal data through the process of anonymisation. Where data qualifies as personal data, the data protection framework, in particular the GDPR, will apply. (Footnote omitted)[150]

---

[147] European Commission, Commission Staff Working Document on the free flow of data and emerging issues of the European data economy, Brussels, 10.1.2017, SWD(2017) 2 final.

[148] *Ibid.*, p. 11.

[149] See, for example, *Surblytė, G.*, Data Mobility at the Intersection of Data, Trade Secret Protection and the Mobility of Employees in the Digital Economy, (2016) 65 GRUR Int. 1121, at 1122–1123 (Max Planck Institute for Innovation & Competition Research Paper No. 16-03 (11 May 2016), (http://papers.ssrn.com/sol3/papers.cfm?abstract_id=2752989)); *Surblytė, G.*, Data-Driven Economy and Artificial Intelligence: Emerging Competition Law Issues, (2017) 67 WuW 120 (first made available as the Max Planck Institute for Innovation & Competition Research Paper No. 16-08 (5 August 2016), (http://papers.ssrn.com/sol3/papers.cfm?abstract_id=2819873)).

[150] European Commission, Communication from the Commission to the European Parliament, the Council, the European Economic and Social Committee and the Committee of the Regions, "Building a European Data Economy", Brussels, 10.1.2017, COM(2017) 9 final, p. 9, Section 3.1.

According to the European Commission, "data generated by home temperature sensors may be personal in nature if it can be related to a living person, while data on soil humidity is not personal".[151]

At first sight, the line between personal and non-personal data may seem to be clear-cut: personal data relates to a natural living person, whereas other data may be non-personal. In fact, a similar definition is provided in the Regulation on the free flow of non-personal data (Regulation 2018/1807),[152] Article 3(1) of which stipulates that "[f]or the purposes of this Regulation [...] 'data' means data other than personal data as defined in point (1) of Article 4 of Regulation (EU) 2016/679". Yet such a distinction, clear as it may sound on paper, may be highly complicated in practice.

To start with, some data may, indeed, be purely non-personal, for example, weather data, data on soil conditions, traffic data, etc. The development of intelligent technologies, such as e.g. self-driving cars, has raised the need for companies to process this type of data. For a big portion of data, however, a distinction between personal and non-personal data may be more nuanced.

According to Article 4(1) GDPR, personal data "means any information relating to an identified or identifiable natural person ('data subject')". Thereby, the core requirement for data to be considered personal data is the ability to directly identify a natural person or for such a person to be identifiable. Thus, the definition of personal data is rather broad, since it relates to any information based on which a natural person can be identified or can be identifiable.

As regards the question whether a natural person is "identifiable", recital 26 GDPR explains that "account should be taken of all the means reasonably likely to be used, such as singling out, either by the controller or by another person to identify the natural person directly or indirectly". In the case-law of the European Court of Justice (ECJ), it was, for example, held that the users' IP addresses "are protected personal data because they allow those users to be precisely identified".[153] Furthermore, in *Google Spain*, the ECJ noted that "the data found, indexed and stored by search engines and made available to their users include information relating to identified or identifiable natural persons and thus 'personal data'".[154]

---

[151] *Ibid.*, p. 9, Section 3.1.

[152] Regulation (EU) 2018/1807 of the European Parliament and of the Council of 14 November 2018 on a framework for the free flow of non-personal data in the European Union, OJ [2018] L 303/59.

[153] ECJ, Case C-70/10, *Scarlet Extended SA v. Société belge des auteurs, compositeurs et éditeurs SCRL (SABAM)*, 24 November 2011, ECLI:EU:C:2011:771, para. 51.

[154] ECJ, Case C-131/12, *Google Spain SL, Google Inc. v. Agencia Española de Protección de Datos (AEPD), Mario Costeja González*, 13 May 2014, ECLI:EU:C: 2014:317, para. 27.

Hence, personal data will cover not only data from which a natural person can be identified, but also data on the basis of which such a person may be (merely) identifiable. The latter part of the definition of personal data may be crucial when considering whether data is personal or non-personal data in general and in the data economy, which is characterized by the processing of vast amounts of data, in particular.

Although the European Commission considers anonymized data as non-personal data, the question whether personal data that has been anonymized could, in fact and in all cases, be considered as non-personal data is a tricky one. According to recital 26 GDPR:

> The principles of data protection should therefore not apply to anonymous information, namely information which does not relate to an identified or identifiable natural person or to personal data *rendered anonymous in such a manner that the data subject is not or no longer identifiable*. This Regulation does not therefore concern the processing of such anonymous information, including for statistical or research purposes. (Emphasis added)

Thereby, the protection of personal data does not apply to anonymous data or anonymized data. The latter is data, that was previously personal data, but was subsequently rendered anonymous. Importantly though, the anonymization process should be such that a data subject can no longer be not only identified, but also not identifiable. The latter concept, as it was explained, is rather broad. Furthermore, as regards data sets, the Article 29 Data Protection Working Party noted that "the creation of a truly anonymous dataset [...] is not a simple proposition",[155] and explained that:

> anonymisation results from processing personal data in order to *irreversibly* prevent identification. In doing so, several elements should be taken into account by data controllers, having regard to *all the means "likely reasonably" to be used* for identification (*either by the controller or by any third party*).[156] (Emphasis added)

Hence, anonymization, should, first of all, be irreversible,[157] i.e. anonymized data is data which can by no means be traced back either directly or indirectly to a natural person. Secondly, not only direct identification, but also potential

---

[155] Article 29 Data Protection Working Party, Opinion 05/2014 on Anonymisation Techniques, adopted on 10 April 2014, 0829/14/EN WP216, p. 5. Furthermore, it was stressed that the risk of identification may "increase over time and depends also on the development of information and communication technology" (*ibid.*, p. 9).

[156] *Ibid.*, p. 3.

[157] See also *ibid.*, p. 5 ("An important factor is that the processing must be irreversible").

identifiability[158] should be prevented as regards not only the controller, but also any third party. An open question is whether identification should be rendered completely impossible, reasonably impossible[159] or (merely) more difficult. Bearing all this in mind, not all anonymized data could automatically be treated as non-personal, so that a big portion of such data may remain personal and, thus, may fall under the personal data protection rules, such as GDPR.

Anonymized data should be distinguished from pseudonymized data.[160] According to Article 4(5) GDPR, pseudonymization is "the processing of personal data in such a manner that the personal data can no longer be attributed to a specific data subject without the use of additional information, provided that such additional information is kept separately and is subject to technical and organisational measures to ensure that the personal data are not attributed to an identified or identifiable natural person". Furthermore, recital 26 GDPR explains that "[p]ersonal data which have undergone *pseudonymisation*, which could be attributed to a natural person by the use of additional information should be considered to be information on *an identifiable natural person*" (emphasis added). Hence, in contrast to anonymized data, which, if rendered irreversibly anonymous, may constitute non-personal data, pseudonymized data is said to be data on an identifiable natural person, and, thereby, should be personal data.

However, depending on the circumstances and bearing in mind a rather broad test of the means reasonably likely to be used by a data controller or any third party to render such data identifiable, it could be asked whether situations may arise when pseudonymized data may, in fact, be considered to be non-personal data.[161] On the one hand, pseudonymized data would be personal data when not only direct identification, but also potential identifiability would

---

[158] *Ibid.*, p. 10: "It must be clear that 'identification' not only means the possibility of retrieving a person's name and/or address, but also includes *potential identifiability* by singling out, linkability and inference. Furthermore, for data protection law to apply, it does not matter what the intentions are of the data controller or recipient. As long as the data are identifiable, data protection rules apply" (emphasis added).

[159] The Article 29 Data Protection Working Party has pointed out that the criterion of the "means 'reasonably likely' to be used" should "be applied in order to assess whether the anonymisation process is sufficiently robust, i.e. whether identification has become 'reasonably' impossible" (Article 29 Data Protection Working Party, Opinion 05/2014 on Anonymisation Techniques, adopted on 10 April 2014, 0829/14/EN WP216, p. 8). For a more detailed analysis on national legal provisions in this regard see *ibid.*, p. 6 footnote 3.

[160] See Article 29 Data Protection Working Party, Opinion 05/2014 on Anonymisation Techniques, adopted on 10 April 2014, 0829/14/EN WP216, p. 10 ("A specific pitfall is to consider pseudonymised data to be equivalent to anonymised data"), also pp. 20–23.

[161] Along these lines see also *Mourby, M./Mackey, E./Elliot, M./Gowans, H./ Wallace, S.E./Bell, J./Smith, H./Aidinlis, S./Kaye, J.*, Are "pseudonymised" data always

be possible. In this regard, owing to the existence of additional data that may enable such identifiability, pseudonymized data would be treated as personal data. On the other hand, however, pseudonymized data may be considered personal data only as long as the means are reasonably likely to be used for identification. Bearing in mind that, in the case of pseudonymized data, the identification (or potential identifiability) of a natural person may be enabled only by the use of additional data, it could be asked whether, in the cases when it is impossible or disproportionately difficult to use such means, such data may fall under the category of non-personal data. The latter argument may be even stronger in the case where the portion of data that might enable identification is protected under trade secret law and reverse engineering of such a trade secret turns out to be impossible. In fact, as it will be shown,[162] the test of "identifiability" comes very close to the test of reverse engineering a trade secret. Bearing in mind that pseudonymized data may be rendered personal data by the use of additional information, for example, using a key in order to "decrypt" data, it could be that pseudonymized data might be non-personal if such data is, for example, key-coded, and it is impossible to get access to it (for example, by failing to reverse engineer it). Thereby, protecting the portion of pseudonymized data as a trade secret may hinder identifiability, rendering the relevant data (or a data set) non-personal data. After all, if personal data in the data set is pseudonymized, it may be impossible (or disproportionately difficult) for a third party to reverse engineer a data set if the key for decrypting the data is in the hands of, for example, the data controller. In such a case, pseudonymized data would not necessarily include data based on which a natural person may be rendered identifiable.

2.4.2.2 Identifiable data sets

One of the most pressing questions in the data economy may be related to "identifiable" data sets. This may be particularly so if we bear in mind that, in the data economy, it will predominantly be data sets (i.e. combinations of data) that will be most important. Therefore, the question is whether, or under what circumstances, such data sets may be considered "identifiable" and therefore subject to personal data protection.

An identifiable data set may be created not only in the cases where a data set consists of both types of data (personal and non-personal data). In fact, a data set, even if it consists of non-personal data, may be rendered an identifiable data set when it is combined with other data. In the case of a data set, situations

---

personal data? Implications of the GDPR for administrative research in the UK, (2018) 34 Computer Law & Security Review 322.

[162] See *infra* Chapter 3.

may arise when data, which, if taken separately, would be non-personal, may be rendered personal if pooled together with other data. For example, the Article 29 Data Protection Working Party noted that "a dataset considered to be anonymous may be combined with another dataset in such a way that one or more individuals can be identified".[163] Hence, various combinations of data may result in (at least parts of) a data set being rendered "identifiable". This may be particularly so if we recall that, according to recital 26 GDPR, the word "identifiable" means that a natural person can be identified directly or indirectly by a data controller or any third party.

The ECJ, in the *Patrick Breyer* case,[164] held that the word "indirectly" suggests that, "in order to treat information as personal data, it is not necessary that that information alone allows the data subject to be identified".[165] It was explained that, owing to the fact that the means reasonably likely to be used for the purposes of identifiability may be used not only by a data controller, but also by a third party, "it is not required that all the information enabling the identification of the data subject must be in the hands of one person".[166] It was thus held by the ECJ that it was possible to consider as personal data a dynamic IP address registered by the online media services provider even if the additional data necessary for the identification of the user of a website is not held by that online media services provider, but rather by that user's internet service provider.[167] Importantly though, the ECJ said that, in order to consider such data as personal, "it must be determined whether the possibility to combine a dynamic IP address with the additional data held by the internet service provider constitutes a means likely reasonably to be used to identify the data subject".[168] This was considered not to be the case if the identification of the data subject was, for example, prohibited by law or "practically impossible on account of the fact that it requires a disproportionate effort in terms of time, cost and man-power, so that the risk of identification appears in reality to be insignificant".[169]

---

[163] Article 29 Data Protection Working Party, Opinion 05/2014 on Anonymisation Techniques, adopted on 10 April 2014, 0829/14/EN WP216, p. 5.

[164] ECJ, Case C-582/14, *Patrick Breyer v. Bundesrepublik Deutschland*, 19 October 2016, ECLI:EU:C:2016:779. On the comment of the case see, for example, *Richter, H.*, Anmerkung (EuGH, C-582/14 (*Breyer/Deutschland*)), (2016) 27 Europäische Zeitschrift für Wirtschaftsrecht 912.

[165] ECJ, Case C-582/14, *Patrick Breyer v. Bundesrepublik Deutschland*, 19 October 2016, ECLI:EU:C:2016:779, para. 41.

[166] *Ibid.*, para. 43.

[167] *Ibid.*, para. 44.

[168] *Ibid.*, para. 45.

[169] *Ibid.*, para. 46.

Hence, the test for "identifiability" is rather broad and may depend on the "means reasonably likely to be used" – importantly though, not only by the data controller, but also by "another person". Moreover, such identifiability may be merely hypothetical or potential, and may not necessarily depend only upon the data controller. Instead, it may be a third party that may render such data identifiable. Furthermore, the question whether the means are reasonably likely to be used may depend on the question of how much effort may be needed to render such data identifiable. Such effort may be measured in terms of time, cost or man-power. Recital 26 GDPR says that account should be taken of "the available technology at the time of the processing and technological developments".

It follows that the criterion of the "means reasonably likely to be used" implies a rather broad test for "identifiability". After all, it includes situations when identifiability may be merely hypothetical. Thereby, a big portion of data, even if considered non-personal at first sight, may, at the end of the day, turn out to be personal.

The analysis above shows that a distinction between personal and non-personal data may not always be an easy one. The fact that personal data is defined broadly under the EU data protection legal framework may result in data protection rules often coming into play even in the cases where non-personal data may, at first sight, seem to be processed. This analysis also shows that straightforward conclusions as regards non-personal data should not be drawn too quickly. In the data economy, it will often be both sides of the coin that will need to be taken into account.

However, considerations on non-personal data – without taking account of the relevance of possibly related personal data – have already found their way not only into some of the academic writings, as it was said before,[170] but also into EU legislation. For example, Regulation 2018/1807,[171] which "aims to ensure the free flow of data other than personal data within the Union" (Article 1), explains in recital 9 that "[t]he expanding Internet of Things, artificial intelligence and machine learning, represent major sources of non-personal data, for example as a result of their deployment in automated industrial production processes" and mentions that "[s]pecific examples of non-personal data include aggregate and anonymised datasets used for big data analytics,

---

[170] See note 142.

[171] Regulation (EU) 2018/1807 of the European Parliament and of the Council of 14 November 2018 on a framework for the free flow of non-personal data in the European Union, OJ [2018] L 303/59. See also: Communication from the Commission to the European Parliament and the Council, Guidance on the Regulation on a framework for the free flow of non-personal data in the European Union, Brussels, 29.5.2019, COM(2019) 250 final.

data on precision farming that can help to monitor and optimise the use of pesticides and water, or data on maintenance needs for industrial machines". It, finally, says that "[i]f technological developments make it possible to turn anonymised data into personal data, such data are to be treated as personal data, and Regulation (EU) 2016/679 is to apply accordingly".

However, Article 2(2) of the Regulation 2018/1807 stipulates that:

> In the case of a data set composed of both personal and non-personal data, this Regulation applies to the non-personal data part of the data set. Where personal and non-personal data in a data set are inextricably linked, this Regulation shall not prejudice the application of Regulation (EU) 2016/679.

Apart from the fact that such a rule may be difficult to apply in practice in terms of the integrity of one data set, it could be asked how the free flow of non-personal data could affect cases of identifiable data sets, including situations when data sets may be combined with other data (or other data sets). As explained, situations may arise where a data set may render a natural person identifiable even if such a set consists of data that could be considered non-personal data if taken separately. Such "identifiable" data sets, as it was argued, may be most problematic in the data economy, and the free flow of data, as claimed to be ensured by the Regulation 2018/1807, may therefore pose serious risks when it comes to the protection of personal data of individuals. The vague formulation of the passage above "shall not prejudice the application of Regulation (EU) 2016/679" hardly brings clarity to the extent needed when a fundamental right to protect personal data may be at stake.

2.4.3   Public v. Private Sector

With the rise of the data economy, data has increasingly been processed not only by the public, but also by the private sector. In contrast to the public sector, which usually processes data for the purposes of the public interest, the private sector processes data for commercial purposes. Before analysing the different incentives behind the data processing, the question is whether the legal framework adequately addresses the distinction between the public and the private sectors.

The primary EU law, Article 286 TEC (the Treaty establishing the European Community[172]), paragraph 1, addressed the application of data protection laws to EU institutions and bodies ("the institutions and bodies set up by, or on the basis of, this Treaty"). The aforementioned legal provision formed, for

---

[172]   Consolidated version, OJ [2006] C 321 E/37.

example, the legal basis for Regulation No. 45/2001.[173] The Lisbon Treaty introduced an explicit legal basis for legislating on data protection,[174] namely, Article 16 TFEU (Treaty on the Functioning of the European Union[175]). In Article 16 TFEU (the legal provision that succeeded Article 286 TEC), paragraph 2, it is said that:

> The European Parliament and the Council, acting in accordance with the ordinary legislative procedure, shall lay down the rules relating to the protection of individuals with regard to the processing of personal data by Union institutions, bodies, offices and agencies, and by the Member States when carrying out activities which fall within the scope of Union law, and the rules relating to the free movement of such data.

Thereby, Article 16(2) TFEU does not mention the processing of personal data by private parties. Instead, it entitles the EU institutions (namely, the European Parliament and the Council) to legislate on the processing and on the free movement of personal data.

The Explanatory Memorandum of the Proposal for the General Data Protection Regulation[176] notes that Article 16 TFEU constitutes a legal basis for the GDPR and explains that this legal provision "allows the adoption of rules relating to the free movement of personal data, including personal data processed by Member States or *private parties*"[177] (emphasis added). Thus, the rights and obligations with regard to the processing of personal data, including such processing by private parties, are not stipulated in the primary EU law, but are enshrined in the EU secondary law,[178] such as, for example, the

---

[173] Regulation (EC) No. 45/2001 of the European Parliament and of the Council of 18 December 2000 on the protection of individuals with regard to the processing of personal data by the Community institutions and bodies and on the free movement of such data, OJ [2001] L 8/1. This Regulation was repealed in 2018 by Regulation (EU) 2018/1725 of the European Parliament and of the Council of 23 October 2018 on the protection of natural persons with regard to the processing of personal data by the Union institutions, bodies, offices and agencies and on the free movement of such data, and repealing Regulation (EC) No. 45/2001 and Decision No. 1247/2002/EC, OJ [2018] L 295/39.

[174] For more detail see *Lynskey, O.*, The Foundations of EU Data Protection Law, Oxford: Oxford University Press 2015, pp. 14 et seq.

[175] Consolidated version, OJ [2016] C 202/1.

[176] European Commission, Proposal for a Regulation of the European Parliament and of the Council on the protection of individuals with regard to the processing of personal data and on the free movement of such data (General Data Protection Regulation), Brussels, 25.1.2012, COM(2012) 11 final.

[177] *Ibid.*, Section 3.1, p. 5.

[178] *Kokott, J./Sobotta, C.*, The Distinction between Privacy and Data Protection in the Jurisprudence of the CJEU and the ECtHR, (2013) 3 International Data Privacy Law 222, at 225.

GDPR, which replaces the EU Data Protection Directive,[179] and the ePrivacy Directive[180] (to be replaced by the (proposed) ePrivacy Regulation[181]).

Historically, the addressees of the data protection rules have been the actors of both the public and the private sector. In the Convention 108[182] – the first binding international instrument for personal data protection – a data controller was defined as "a natural or legal person, public authority, agency or any other body" (Article 2(d)). The modernized Convention, the so-called Convention 108+,[183] broadened this definition to some extent, but, in the essence, it reflects the same idea. A similar definition of a data controller was included in the EU Data Protection Directive (Article 2(d)) and may also be found in the GDPR (Article 4(7)).

Neither the GDPR nor the EU Data Protection Directive makes a clear distinction between data protection rules applicable for the processing of personal data in the public sector and in the private sector. In fact, the rules of the GDPR apply almost[184] equally to both sectors.

Interestingly though, in the original proposal of the EU Data Protection Directive,[185] the European Commission made a distinction between the processing of personal data in the public and in the private sectors. The public sector was defined as "all the authorities, organizations and entities of a Member State that are governed by public law, with the exception of those which carry on an industrial or commercial activity, and bodies and entities

---

[179] Directive 95/46/EC of the European Parliament and of the Council of 24 October 1995 on the protection of individuals with regard to the processing of personal data and on the free movement of such data, OJ [1995] L 281/31.

[180] Directive 2002/58/EC of the European Parliament and of the Council of 12 July 2002 concerning the processing of personal data and the protection of privacy in the electronic communications sector (Directive on privacy and electronic communications), OJ [2002] L 201/37.

[181] European Commission, Proposal for a Regulation of the European Parliament and of the Council concerning the respect for private life and the protection of personal data in electronic communications and repealing Directive 2002/58/EC (Regulation on Privacy and Electronic Communications), Brussels, 10.1.2017, COM(2017) 10 final.

[182] Council of Europe, Convention for the Protection of Individuals with regard to Automatic Processing of Personal Data, ETS No. 108, open for signature in 1981, entry into force in 1985.

[183] Council of Europe, Modernised Convention for the Protection of Individuals with regard to the Processing of Personal Data, 18 May 2018.

[184] For a more detailed analysis on the practical nuances, which may, to some extent, distinguish the application of data protection rules between these two sectors see *Lynskey, O.*, The Foundations of EU Data Protection Law, Oxford: Oxford University Press 2015, pp. 16–23.

[185] Commission of the European Communities, Proposal for a Council Directive concerning the protection of individuals in relation to the processing of personal data, COM(90) 314 final – SYN 287, OJ [1990] C 277/3.

governed by private law where they take part in the exercise of official authority" (Article 2(g)), whereas a private sector included "any natural or legal
person or association, including public sector authorities, organizations and
entities in so far as they carry on an industrial or commercial activity" (Article
2(h)). Hence, the line was drawn between these two sectors as regards carrying
on "an industrial or commercial activity". Accordingly, Chapter II of the original proposal for the directive elaborated on the lawfulness of the processing in
the public sector, whereas Chapter III provided rules for such processing with
regard to the private sector. The European Commission explained that "[t]he
definitions of public sector and private sector are justified in the Directive as
some of its provisions are specific to one or other sector [...]. These definitions
are based on the nature of the service provided by the body concerned, regardless of its private or public status. The body will have to apply the rules specific
to the private sector or to the public sector according as to whether it carries
on commercial activities or performs public-service duties."[186] In the amended
proposal for the directive,[187] however, this distinction was dropped with the
result that the same data protection rules were provided for both sectors.

A number of years later, the same concerns may be found in the preparatory
materials of the GDPR. In fact, a similar discussion, i.e. whether data protection rules should be the same for the public and the private sector, took place
also during the legislative process of this legal act: during the negotiations, an
opinion was expressed that "a Regulation might be appropriate for the private
sector, but not for the public sector",[188] and it was also said that "the Regulation
should distinguish more clearly between the public and private sectors".[189]

---

[186] Commission of the European Communities, Proposal for a Council Directive
concerning the protection of individuals in relation to the processing of personal data,
SYN 287 in: Commission of the European Communities, COM(90) 314 final – SYN
287 and 288, Brussels, 13 September 1990, pp. 10–70 (https://eur-lex.europa.eu/legal
-content/EN/TXT/PDF/?uri=CELEX:51990DC0314&from=EN), p. 20, Discussion of
the provisions, Article 2.

[187] Amended proposal for a Council Directive on the protection of individuals with
regard to the processing of personal data and on the free movement of such data, OJ
[1992] C 311/30.

[188] Council of the European Union, Working Party on Information Exchange and
Data Protection (DAPIX) on 23–24 February 2012: "Summary of Discussions",
Brussels, 8 March 2012, 7221/12 DAPIX 22 (https://data.consilium.europa.eu/doc/
document/ST-7221-2012-INIT/en/pdf), p. 4. For a more detailed analysis see *Lynskey,
O.*, The Foundations of EU Data Protection Law, Oxford: Oxford University Press
2015, pp. 20–23.

[189] Council of the European Union, Working Party on Information Exchange and
Data Protection (DAPIX) on 23–24 February 2012: "Summary of Discussions",
Brussels, 8 March 2012, 7221/12 DAPIX 22 (https://data.consilium.europa.eu/doc/
document/ST-7221-2012-INIT/en/pdf), p. 5.

However, in the final text of the GDPR, data protection rules apply almost in the same way to both sectors without making a distinction between them.

Yet, bearing in mind the gap that has increasingly been widened between the public and the private sectors, in particular, when it comes to the amount, the speed and the goals of the processing of personal data in the context of a commercial activity, it could be asked whether the original distinction included in the proposal of the EU Data Protection Directive concerning the different data protection rules for the private and the public sectors depending on whether a commercial activity is carried on, could be valid in the data economy. After all, technological developments have not only triggered the interest of private parties to process increasing amounts of personal data for commercial purposes, but have also enabled them to do this by providing technological tools. The public sector, however, processes such data mostly for the sake of the public interest. Thus, the gap between the public and the private sectors as regards the scope and the purpose of the processing of personal data seems to have been widening. So, it could be asked whether the idea of having equal rules for the processing of personal data by the public and the private sector is still wholly valid for the age of the rapid technical developments. For example, the exercise of the rights of data subjects or data processing principles such as "data minimization" could be highly relevant for the private sector, but may risk overburdening the public sector. Although it is true that the restriction of particular rights and obligations is possible pursuant to Article 23(1) GDPR, such restrictions should be made on the basis of the national law provisions and are subject to the requirements of Article 23(2) GDPR. The risk, therefore, may be that divergent rules among the Member States may exist as regards issues of such a high importance as the rights of the data subjects and the principles of data processing. Thus, it could be asked whether, for the sake of more uniform rules, which was, after all, one of the aims of the GDPR, it would have been reasonable to include more flexible rules on data processing when it comes to the public sector as compared with stricter rules for the private one, bearing in mind that the decisive factor for such different rules would be the processing of personal data for the purpose of carrying on a commercial activity.

2.5   INTERMEDIATE CONCLUSION

When speaking about any economic, social or legal impact that may be brought by AI technology, precision is needed while defining what AI is in the first place. Therefore, a distinction has to be made between the general and the narrow AI. Whereas general AI would come close to the capabilities of a human being and is yet to be developed, narrow AI is capable of performing more specific tasks that may not only complement, but to some extent, also substitute for the actions performed by people. Furthermore, the fact that most intelligent machines are programmed by people means that it should be human beings who have to be held liable for the actions of (intelligent) machines. As long as machines lack consciousness we cannot speak about their legal liability, since such machines cannot be the subject of legal relationships.

The technology of AI may have implications for the social relationships of people. Although, at first glance, intelligent machines seem to enable more interactions among people, on closer inspection, they may often interrupt, rather than encourage, the communication of human beings. On the basis of the "social systems" theory developed by Luhmann, where autopoietic systems develop themselves through interactions, it could be argued that the development of AI technology may hinder, rather than help, building social systems of people. Thus, instead of fulfilling the "glueing function" of the society in terms of the "social systems" theory, the impact of the AI technology on human society could rather be the fragmentation of the society, if not its estrangement.

Although the economic impact of AI technology cannot be underestimated, it can hardly be stated that the AI technology has drastically changed the fundamental economic principles based on which the data economy functions. Equally so, the development of AI technology has hardly raised entirely new legal questions that would beg for revolutionary changes to be made in the law. In fact, many of the allegedly new concepts of the data economy may be explained on the basis of classic economic theories, such as the economic theory developed by Adam Smith. For example, the answer to the so-called "privacy paradox" problem, that has frequently been considered as an unsolved feature of the data economy, may be found in the mutual "self-interest" – the notion that was considered by Adam Smith as the main driver of economic behaviour. Also, based on the economic theory of Adam Smith, it could be argued that data sets can be a commodity – or, under some circumstances, form part of an instrument of commerce – even if they have (merely) value in exchange, instead of value in use.

Yet, despite the fact that no drastic changes may be needed in the law, the question that has become acute with the development of AI technology is how to strike a balance between the economic incentives while developing AI and the protection of consumers who may also be data subjects. In the academic debate as well as in the European Commission's "free flow of data" initiative, this question has often been overshadowed by the focus on non-personal data as an allegedly new type of data and the issue of access to data in the business-to-business relationship. However, bearing in mind that companies in the data economy often process data sets that, at the end of the day, may turn out to be "identifiable", a big portion of data that might, at first sight, be considered to be non-personal data, may turn out to be personal data and will thus have to be processed in compliance with data protection laws. The fact that it might be not only non-personal, but also personal data that forms part of a data set may be highly important not only for considering whether a data set may be protected as a trade secret – a legal tool that might be highly relevant in the data economy. In fact, it may be highly relevant for clarifying what implications such trade secret protection may have for the rights of the data subjects. Thus, a deeper analysis of this question may be crucial for searching for the right balance between the economic incentives of AI developers on the one hand, and the protection of consumers who might also be data subjects on the other.

3. Trade secret protection for data

Trade secrets, a legal tool that protects information, may be highly relevant in the data economy for protecting both data (data sets) and algorithms. As such, trade secret protection is not new. In fact, the first cases on trade secrets date back to the nineteenth century in the US,[1] and so do some of the legislative provisions on trade secret protection in Europe.[2] However, just as in earlier times, so in modern ones, trade secrets seem to be doomed to play the role of "Cinderella".[3] When the European Commission's "free flow of data" initiative was announced, the discussion, including the scholarly one, on the role of the EU Trade Secrets Directive,[4] which entered into force in 2016, was rather modest. If at all, it was argued that the EU Trade Secrets Directive was "out-dated" and did not reflect the issues of the data economy, so that its suitability for the data economy was strongly questioned.[5]

It is however noteworthy that, even before the European Commission's "free flow of data" initiative and the academic debate that followed, the question of trade secret protection in the intersection with data was analysed by some members of academia, in fact, pleading for the eligibility of trade secret protection for data. For example, it was explained that "while factual data about users such as their age, gender and occupation can hardly qualify as secret information, data relating to the interests they have expressed on a par-

---

[1] *Vickery v. Welch*, 36 Mass. 523 (1837).

[2] For example, Art. 418 Code Pénal in France (1810) or the Law Against Unfair Competition (UWG) in Germany (1896).

[3] Alluding to the comparison originally made by Sharon K. Sandeen (*Sandeen, S.K.*, The Cinderella of Intellectual Property Law: Trade Secrets, in: Peter K. Yu (ed.), Intellectual Property and Information Wealth: Issues and Practices in the Digital Age, Vol. 2, Westport 2007, pp. 399–420). Along similar lines, see also *Ann, C.*, Know-how – Stiefkind des Geistigen Eigentums?, (2007) GRUR 39.

[4] Directive (EU) 2016/943 of the European Parliament and of the Council of 8 June 2016 on the protection of undisclosed know-how and business information (trade secrets) against their unlawful acquisition, use and disclosure, OJ [2016] L 157/1.

[5] See, for example, *Drexl, J.*, Designing Competitive Markets for Industrial Data – Between Propertisation and Access (31 October 2016). Max Planck Institute for Innovation & Competition Research Paper No. 16-13. Available at SSRN: https://papers.ssrn.com/sol3/papers.cfm?abstract_id=2862975, p. 22; *Wiebe, A.*, Protection of industrial data – a new property right for the digital economy?, (2016) 65 GRUR Int. 877.

ticular online platform, information about their online behaviour or the online purchasing history of users may not be generally known and thus qualify for trade secret protection".[6] Also, it was argued that data (data sets) could fall under trade secret protection with a note that this fact may be highly relevant for the data economy.[7]

In fact, trade secrets may turn out to be one of the most suitable tools for the protection of data (data sets) in the data economy, so that, in the following, a deeper analysis of the definition of a trade secret with a focus on data is provided. Furthermore, should data be eligible for trade secret protection, a deeper analysis is needed as regards the implications of such trade secret protection for the data economy.

3.1   EU TRADE SECRETS DIRECTIVE: A DEBATE OVER TRADE SECRET PROTECTION FOR DATA

The European Commission addressed the question of the eligibility of data for trade secret protection in the Communication published in January 2017 as part of its "free flow of data" initiative. In the Communication, the European Commission stated that:

> Raw machine-generated data are not protected by existing intellectual property rights since they are deemed not to be the result of an intellectual effort and/or have any degree of originality. [...] For data to qualify as a "trade secret", measures have to be taken to protect the secrecy of information, which represents the "intellectual capital of the company".
>
> Under the law of different Member States, legal claims are applied to data only when that data meets specific conditions for it to qualify, for instance, as an intellectual property right, database right or a trade secret. However, as at EU level, raw machine-generated data as such would not generally meet the relevant conditions.[8]

---

[6]   *Graef, I.*, Market Definition and Market Power in Data: The Case of Online Platforms, (2015) 38(4) World Competition Law and Economic Review 473, 481.

[7]   See *Surblytė, G.*, Data-Driven Economy and Artificial Intelligence: Emerging Competition Law Issues, (2017) 67 WuW 120 (first made available as the Max Planck Institute for Innovation & Competition Research Paper No. 16-08 (5 August 2016), (http://papers.ssrn.com/sol3/papers.cfm?abstract_id=2819873)); *Surblytė, G.*, Data as a Digital Resource, Max Planck Institute for Innovation & Competition Research Paper No. 16-12 (6 October 2016), https://papers.ssrn.com/sol3/papers.cfm?abstract_id= 2849303.

[8]   European Commission, Communication from the Commission to the European Parliament, the Council, the European Economic and Social Committee and the Committee of the Regions, Brussels, 10.1.2017, COM(2017) 9 final, p. 10, Section 3.3. It is noteworthy that, in the European strategy for data issued in February 2020, the European Commission foresees "a possible clarification of the application of the

Accordingly, raw machine-generated data, in the view of the European Commission, could hardly be protected as a trade secret. As regards the quoted passage, however, it should, first of all, be noted that, although the European Commission speaks about trade secrets as "the intellectual capital of the company", trade secrets, by law, cover a wide spectrum of information, which is not required to amount to information of high quality. In contrast to intellectual property rights such as patents, which grant protection to inventions, trade secrets provide protection for information. Such information may range from rather simple information to patentable inventions.[9] Hence, trade secrets could be called a valuable asset of the company, but not necessarily intellectual capital. Furthermore, the European Commission says that raw machine-generated data is not covered by intellectual property rights owing to the lack of intellectual effort in creating it. Yet again, although this insight is true as regards intellectual property rights, intellectual efforts are not necessarily required for the creation of trade secrets.[10] Trade secret protection does not depend on intellectual efforts. Therefore, trade secrets may represent the "capital of the company", but not necessarily "the intellectual one". Finally, the European Commission draws a conclusion that raw machine-generated data will not meet the relevant requirements of trade secret protection without giving a more detailed explanation why this should be the case.

Interestingly though, in the Staff Working Document, which, in fact, is an accompanying document to the aforementioned Communication, the European Commission as regards the EU Trade Secrets Directive says that "[i]t is doubtful that individual data generated by interconnected machines and devices could be regarded as 'trade secret' in the sense of this Directive, mostly because of its lack of commercial value as individual data; however, combination of data (datasets) can be trade secrets under this Directive if all the criteria are met".[11]

Trade Secrets Protection Directive as an enabling framework" (footnote omitted) (see: European Commission, Communication from the Commission to the European Parliament, the Council, the European Economic and Social Committee and the Committee of the Regions, "A European Strategy for Data", Brussels, 19.2.2020, COM(2020) 66 final, p. 13).

9   For a more detailed analysis see *Surblytė, G.*, The Refusal to Disclose Trade Secrets as an Abuse of Market Dominance – *Microsoft* and Beyond, Berne: Stämpfli 2011, pp. XLVII + 263 (Munich Series on European and International Competition Law, Volume 28), pp. 19–88.

10   *Ibid.*, pp. 19–88.

11   European Commission, Commission Staff Working Document on the free flow of data and emerging issues of the European data economy, Brussels, 10.1.2017, SWD(2017) 2 final, p. 20.

Accordingly, the European Commission, although it has doubts with regard to the eligibility of individual data for trade secret protection – first and foremost, owing to the concern that such data might lack commercial value, which is, in fact, one of the requirements for a trade secret, says that the sets of data may be eligible for trade secret protection upon the condition that all of the requirements for such protection are fulfilled. However, when speaking of such individual data, the European Commission basically refers to interconnected machines and devices.

Several remarks have to be made in this regard. The European Commission basically considers that trade secret protection could apply to data sets, mostly in the context of interconnected machines. In the data economy, however, the relevance of trade secrets may be broader and may, possibly, go beyond the data sets of interconnected machines. After all, as explained before,[12] the developments of AI technology range from the narrow to general AI, so that connected technology (the Internet of Things, IoT) may form part of AI, but AI should not be confined to the IoT only. Bearing in mind that data is key for learning algorithms, based on which AI technology is developed, the training sets of AI may, in fact, be valuable trade secrets. Hence, the importance of trade secrets in the data economy should not be underestimated and confined to the data sets of IoT, but may, in fact, be much broader. Furthermore, it should also be recalled that the European Commission's "free flow of data" initiative focuses on non-personal data only,[13] so that the analysis in the Communication and the Staff Working Document lacks an important, yet complex, question of how trade secret protection may intersect with personal data. The latter question may be of utmost importance, particularly bearing in mind "identifiable" data sets.[14] Thus, a deeper analysis may be needed in order to clarify the requirements for a trade secret and whether, and to what extent, data (data sets) may qualify for trade secret protection.

3.2 ELIGIBILITY OF DATA FOR TRADE SECRET PROTECTION

The definition of a trade secret is provided in Article 2(1) of the EU Trade Secrets Directive and is identical to the definition of undisclosed information as enshrined in Article 39(2) TRIPS,[15] which resembles the US model act – the

---

12   See *supra* Chapter 2, Section 2.1.
13   See *supra* Chapter 2, Section 2.4.1.
14   See *supra* Chapter 2, Section 2.4.2.2.
15   Agreement on Trade-Related Aspects of Intellectual Property Rights (TRIPS) of 15 April 1994 (Annex to the Agreement Establishing the World Trade Organization (WTO)) as amended on 23 January 2017.

Uniform Trade Secrets Act (UTSA).[16] A similar, yet not identical, trade secret definition can be found in the US federal piece of legislation on trade secret protection, i.e. the Defend Trade Secrets Act.[17]

A trade secret definition consists of a number of cumulative requirements. The question thereby is how these legal requirements intersect with data.

3.2.1   A Subject Matter of a Trade Secret

According to the trade secret definition, a subject matter of a trade secret is "information". As regards the data economy, the question, first of all, is whether information may cover data, and secondly, how the subject matter of a trade secret intersects with personal data.

3.2.1.1   Data v. information

According to the wording of the definition of a trade secret, its subject matter is information. The question thereby is whether this includes data.

In the academic debate, opinions have been expressed arguing that data and information are different concepts, particularly for the purposes of the question whether data could fall under trade secret protection. Zech, for example, noted that "in its simplest meaning, the term data can be defined as machine-readable encoded information" (footnote omitted).[18] When it comes to data and information, he suggested distinguishing three levels: a syntactic level (i.e. signs and characters), a semantic level (i.e. a meaning) and a carrier level (a carrier/a medium where the information is embodied).[19] According to him, "[t]rade secrets are another example of semantic information as an object of legal protection. Trade secrets are basically defined by their semantic connection with a company that can be embodied as a file (syntactic information) or a sheet of paper (structural information)".[20] So, "[a]s a legal object,

---

[16]   National Conference of Commissioners on Uniform State Laws, Uniform Trade Secrets Act, 1979, as amended in 1985.

[17]   An Act to amend Chapter 90 of title 18, United States Code, to provide Federal jurisdiction for the theft of trade secrets, and for other purposes (Defend Trade Secrets Act of 2016), Public Law 114–153, 11 May 2016.

[18]   *Zech, H.*, A legal framework for a data economy in the European Digital Single Market: rights to use data, (2016) 11(6) Journal of Intellectual Property Law & Practice 460, 462.

[19]   *Zech, H.*, Information as Property, (2015) 6 JIPITEC 192, 194. According to Zech, "legal ownership of information ought to be constructed according to the bundle of rights theory, as the exclusive attribution of certain aspects or activities dealing with specific information (defined as an object, i.e. as semantic, syntactic or structural information)" (*ibid.*, at 195).

[20]   *Ibid.*, at 196.

sequences of 'zeros' and 'ones' would be protected, either as a file or as a data stream".[21] In a similar vein, Drexl notes that "[a]ccording to the definition of trade secrets, the subject-matter of protection is information. This clearly locates trade secrets protection on the semantic level of data. This means that a set of raw data as such, namely, as an aggregation or sequence of bits and bytes, cannot be considered trade secrets".[22]

Yet although a precise distinction of information into different levels may be attractive from a theoretical point of view, the question is how, if at all, it might be implemented in practice. In this regard, it may particularly be questioned whether the distinction between the syntactic and the semantic level of information may always be feasible. After all, data will often carry in it information, so that a distinction between data and information may turn out to be rather artificial. In such a way, it should probably not be ruled out that even raw data, which carries in it particular information, may never be considered a trade secret.

In fact, the European Commission, in the Staff Working Document, which accompanies the Communication, notes that "information (*this can include data*) qualifies as a 'trade secret' if it meets the following three requirements" (emphasis added).[23] In this regard, the European Commission seems to accept that data, as long as it carries in it information, can be a trade secret. It could also be noted that the Federal German Cartel Office (Bundeskartellamt) and the French competition authority, in their common study on competition law and data, explained that the term data "in a wider sense is used to refer to (any) information, or to the representation of such information, often in combina-

---

[21] *Zech, H.*, A Legal Framework for a Data Economy in the European Digital Single Market: Rights to use Data, (2016) 11(6) Journal of Intellectual Property Law & Practice 460, 463.

[22] *Drexl, J.*, Data Access and Control in the Era of Connected Devices, Study on Behalf of the European Consumer Organisation BEUC (https://www.ip.mpg .de/fileadmin/ipmpg/content/aktuelles/aus_der_forschung/beuc-x-2018-121_data _access_and_control_in_the_area_of_connected_devices.pdf), p. 92. See also *Drexl, J.*, Designing Competitive Markets for Industrial Data – Between Propertisation and Access (31 October 2016). Max Planck Institute for Innovation & Competition Research Paper No. 16-13. Available at SSRN: https://papers.ssrn.com/sol3/papers.cfm ?abstract_id=2862975, where he, when analysing "what we mean by data and big data", notes that: "For data protection, the distinction between the syntactic and the semantic level is key. The syntactic level regards the representation of information in particular signs, for instance as a text, a photograph or a video. In contrast, the semantic level relates to the meaning" (at p. 12).

[23] European Commission, Commission Staff Working Document on the free flow of data and emerging issues of the European data economy, Brussels, 10.1.2017, SWD(2017) 2 final, p. 20.

tion with it being stored on a computer".[24] Thereby, it is accurately pointed out that data, in fact, represents information and could hardly be artificially distinguished from it. Thus, digital data could be said to carry information represented by digits and stored in a digital form.

In comparison, for example, with the US, the EU definition of a trade secret does not provide any examples of information that could be considered a trade secret. According to the definition of a trade secret in the UTSA, a trade secret "means information, including a formula, pattern, compilation, program, device, method, technique, or process" (§ 1(4)). Furthermore, the Defend Trade Secrets Act of 2016, which is a federal piece of the US trade secret legislation, says that "the term 'trade secret' means all forms and types of financial, business, scientific, technical, economic, or engineering information, including patterns, plans, compilations, program devices, formulas, designs, prototypes, methods, techniques, processes, procedures, programs, or codes, whether tangible or intangible, and whether or how stored, compiled, or memorialized physically, electronically, graphically, photographically, or in writing" (18 U.S.C. §1839(3)). Accordingly, a trade secret may consist of a program or a code.

Finally, it should be noted that recital 14 of the EU Trade Secrets Directive stipulates that "[t]he definition of a trade secret excludes trivial information". The recital, however, does not further explain what such trivial information means. The latter sentence, however, may be relevant for the data economy. On the one hand, the argument could go that data could be considered as trivial information (in particular, if one considers a syntactic level of information, i.e. data in a form of 1s and 0s) and should thus fall outside trade secret protection. On the other hand, however, it could be recalled that trade secrets protect information of any quality. For example, the UK High Court of Justice, Chancery Division, held in *Coco v. A.N. Clark (Engineers) Ltd*[25] that:

> the mere simplicity of an idea does not prevent it being confidential. [...] Indeed, the simpler an idea, the more likely it is to need protection.[26] (References omitted)

---

[24] Bundeskartellamt/Autorité de la concurrence, Competition Law and Data, 10 May 2016, p. 4.

[25] *Coco v. A.N. Clark (Engineers) Ltd* [1968] F.S.R. 415.

[26] *Ibid.*, at 420.

The question of what can be considered as trivial may be subjective and may need to be decided on a case-by-case basis. For example, it was explained by academia that:

> Unfortunately, the assessment of "trivia", like one's grasp of "general knowledge" in quiz programmes, or one's evaluation of whether a belief is merely a delusion, is apt to be influenced by subjectivity. [...] And when pieces of information are put together the sum might be greatly more significant than the parts.[27]

The cited passage neatly fits into the context of the data economy: even if individual pieces of data could (under the circumstances) be considered as trivial, it might be that their combination would be not. In contrast, such combination may even have economic value.[28]

Hence, if we consider that particular data or data sets represent information within them, it may be difficult to make a clear-cut distinction between the semantic and the syntactic level, so that the discussion on whether the information on a semantic or a syntactic level should be protected as a trade secret may be interesting in theory, but its relevance in practice, not to speak of its practical applicability, may be questioned. As explained, syntactic information in the form of digital data may actually carry in it semantic information, which – importantly – may be also personal information. In fact, the debate focusing on the distinction between the syntactic and the semantic level of information overlooks a more nuanced picture of the data economy and that a more important, yet a more difficult, question in the data economy is the issue of whether personal data may form part or the whole of a data set. Hence, what may be more important in the data economy for the purposes of trade secret protection might be not necessarily the – rather artificial – distinction between the syntactic and the semantic level of information, but, instead, a distinction between different types of data, in particular as regards the (need for) protection of personal data included in digital data sets. So, instead of focusing on an artificial distinction between the syntactic and semantic level, at least not at the stage of a subject matter of a trade secret, what should matter more – in particular for a legal discussion – is how legal norms can strike a balance among different interests, which, bearing in mind the personal data involved, may be particularly at stake in the data economy.

---

[27]   *Chandler, A./Holland, J.A.*, Information: Protection, Ownership and Rights, London: Blackstone Press Limited 1993, p. 38.
[28]   See *infra* in this chapter, Section 3.2.3.

3.2.1.2 Personal data as a subject matter of a trade secret

The question whether personal data may form part of a trade secret is not entirely new. A customer list is a classical example of a trade secret. Such a customer list would normally contain information about clients, possibly including their personal data.

Thus, neither personal data nor the processing of personal data is a feature that should be considered new or very particular in the context of the data economy. In fact, data was processed in the offline industries as well. Rapid technological developments, however, have enabled companies to collect and to further process vast amounts of data (often referred to by the – rather flawed – term "Big Data"[29]). Such possibilities for processing data, including data analytics, have turned data into a commercial asset.[30] Thereby, the question of the intersection of trade secrets with personal data has become acute. After all, in contrast to earlier times, vast amounts of personal data may now be processed by companies – importantly, for commercial purposes.

In fact, it was during the process of the drafting of the EU Trade Secrets Directive when the European Data Protection Supervisor (EDPS) strongly advised the European Commission to consider the relationship of personal

---

[29] For a description of various definitions of "Big Data" see, for example, Preliminary Opinion of the European Data Protection Supervisor, "Privacy and Competitiveness in the Age of Big Data: The Interplay Between Data Protection, Competition Law and Consumer Protection in the Digital Economy", March 2014, p. 6 footnote 1 (https://edps.europa.eu/sites/edp/files/publication/14-03-26_competitition_law_big_data_en.pdf). The European Commission, for example, explains that "[t]he term 'big data' refers to large amounts of different types of data produced with high velocity from a high number of various types of sources. Handling today's highly variable and real-time datasets requires new tools and methods, such as powerful processors, software and algorithms" (footnote omitted) (European Commission, Communication from the Commission to the European Parliament, the Council, the European Economic and Social Committee and the Committee of the Regions, "Towards a Thriving Data-Driven Economy", Brussels, 2.7.2014, COM(2014) 442 final, p. 4).

[30] In fact, this possibility has not only enabled companies to extract value from the analysis of data, but has also helped them to personalise their services. The benefits of the latter are often linked with targeted advertising. For a more detailed analysis see *Surblytė, G.*, Competition Law at the Crossroads in the Digital Economy: is it all About Google?, (2015) 5 EuCML 170 (Max Planck Institute for Innovation & Competition Research Paper No. 15-13 (7 December 2015), http://papers.ssrn.com/sol3/papers.cfm?abstract_id=2701847). On behavioural advertising see, for example, FTC Staff Report: Self-regulatory Principles For Online Behavioral Advertising, February 2009 (https://www.ftc.gov/sites/default/files/documents/reports/federal-trade-commission-staff-report-self-regulatory-principles-online-behavioral-advertising/p085400behavadreport.pdf).

data and trade secrets. The EDPS issued an opinion,[31] in which it highlighted "the need for the proposal to consider in particular the rights to privacy and to the protection of personal data of data subjects whose personal data may form part or whole of the trade secrets in question".[32] The EDPS stressed the fact that, when personal data is part of a trade secret, a trade secret holder becomes a data controller and "as such has a number of obligations towards data subjects".[33] So, the EDPS, assuming that trade secrets can cover personal data and in the light of the business models of the companies in the data economy, stated that "[t]he relevance of *personal data*, which is defined in Article 2(a) of Directive 95/46/EC, to the concept of trade secrets, should therefore be more explicitly acknowledged in the proposal"[34] (emphasis in original). Hereby, the EDPS stressed the importance of personal data protection, in particular in the intersection with trade secrets. This is an important insight, which has not been addressed fully and in more detail in the EU Trade Secrets Directive.

The final text of the EU Trade Secrets Directive does not explicitly mention whether personal data can be the subject matter of a trade secret. The definition of a trade secret provided in Article 2(1) of the EU Trade Secrets Directive is silent on this issue. Recital 14 of the EU Trade Secrets Directive stipulates that "[i]t is important to establish a homogenous definition of a trade secret" and that "such a definition should [...] be constructed so as to cover know-how, business information and technological information". Furthermore, recital 2 of the EU Trade Secrets Directive explains that trade secrets may relate to "a diverse range of information that extends beyond technological knowledge to commercial data such as information on customers and suppliers, business plans, and market research and strategies". It could be noted in this regard that, although recital 2 does not explicitly mention personal data, the cited passage differs from the text of the Directive that was proposed by the Council of the European Union. In fact, the passage was almost identical, but for one part of the sentence: namely, that trade secrets may cover "a diversified range of information, which extends beyond technological knowledge to commercial data such as information on customers and suppliers (*which may involve personal data*), business plans or market research and strategies" (emphasis added).[35]

---

[31]   European Data Protection Supervisor, Opinion of the European Data Protection Supervisor on the proposal for a directive of the European Parliament and of the Council on the protection of undisclosed know-how and business information (trade secrets) against their unlawful acquisition, use and disclosure, 12 March 2014.

[32]   *Ibid.*, para. 7.

[33]   *Ibid.*, para. 6.

[34]   *Ibid.*, paras 13–14.

[35]   Council of the European Union, Proposal for a Directive of the European Parliament and of the Council on the protection of undisclosed know-how and busi-

Thereby, the proposed text of the Directive by the Council of the European Union explicitly mentioned personal data as a subject matter of a trade secret. This specification, which did not exist in the initial proposal of the EU Trade Secrets Directive by the European Commission,[36] cannot be found in the final text of the Directive.

Furthermore, two other recitals of the EU Trade Secrets Directive address the intersection of personal data and trade secrets. Namely, recital 34 stipulates that "[t]his Directive respects the fundamental rights and observes the principles recognized in particular by the Charter, notably the right to respect for private and family life, the right to protection of personal data", whereas recital 35 stipulates that "[i]t is important that the rights to respect for private and family life and to protection of personal data of any person *whose personal data may be processed by the trade secret holder when taking steps to protect a trade secret*, or of any person involved in legal proceedings concerning the unlawful acquisition, use or disclosure of trade secrets under this Directive, and whose personal data are processed, be respected" (emphasis added). Furthermore, according to recital 35, the EU Trade Secrets Directive, "should not affect the rights and obligations laid down in Directive 95/46/EC", such as the rights of the data subjects to access their data, to have their data erased, etc.

Thereby, the EU Trade Secrets Directive does not clearly explain whether personal data may be a subject matter of a trade secret, but it is acknowledged that the actions of the processing of personal data may take place "when taking steps to protect a trade secret". Bearing in mind that "processing" is defined broadly in Article 4(2) GDPR, the aforementioned formulation in the quoted passage may, for example, illustrate cases of anonymization with the purpose of protecting a data set as a trade secret. However, it does not provide an answer – not to speak of any guidance – on whether personal data could "form part or whole of a trade secret", in the parlance of the EDPS, as mentioned above.[37] In other words, it is not explained how situations should be solved

---

ness information (trade secrets) against their unlawful acquisition, use and disclosure, 9870/14, Brussels, 19 May 2014, recital 1.

[36] European Commission, Proposal for a Directive of the European Parliament and of the Council on the protection of undisclosed know-how and business information (trade secrets) against their unlawful acquisition, use and disclosure, Brussels, 28.11.2013, COM(2013) 813 final (2013/0402 (COD)), recital 1: "Businesses, irrespective of their size, value trade secrets as much as patents and other forms of intellectual property right and use confidentiality as a business and research innovation management tool, covering a diversified range of information, which extends beyond technological knowledge to commercial data such as information on customers and suppliers, business plans or market research and strategies."

[37] As said above, the EDPS highlighted "the need for the proposal to consider in particular the rights to privacy and to the protection of personal data of data subjects

when a company might be willing to protect as a trade secret an "identifiable" data set,[38] for example, a data set consisting of both types of data (i.e. personal and non-personal data) or a data set consisting of non-personal data, but which could render particular individuals identifiable if it were pooled with other data. The EU Trade Secrets Directive does not provide clarification in this regard. Furthermore, although it speaks of respecting fundamental rights such as the right to personal data protection, at the same time, the cited passage shows that the tension may arise between trade secret protection and the rights of the data subjects. In fact, there is a high potential for conflict between trade secret protection and the exercise of (at least, some of) the rights of the data subjects in the data economy.[39] However, the EU Trade Secrets Directive provides no further guidance on how such a tension should be solved.

The preparatory materials of the EU Trade Secrets Directive on this matter are controversial and do not provide much guidance either.

The European Commission's Impact Assessment for the Proposal of the EU Trade Secrets Directive,[40] in Annex 21, which elaborates on the impact of the protection of trade secrets on fundamental rights, stipulates that policy option 3 (i.e. the prohibition of acts of misappropriation of trade secrets) would have "indirect beneficial effects as regards personal data protection (Article 8)".[41] It is further stated that:

> Information kept as trade secrets (such as list of clients/customers; internal datasets containing research data or other) may include personal data. The protection of trade secrets against misappropriation therefore reinforces the protection of personal data from unauthorised used by third parties. In addition, this option is likely to reduce

whose personal data may form part or whole of the trade secrets in question" (European Data Protection Supervisor, Opinion of the European Data Protection Supervisor on the proposal for a directive of the European Parliament and of the Council on the protection of undisclosed know-how and business information (trade secrets) against their unlawful acquisition, use and disclosure, 12 March 2014, para. 7).

[38]   On "identifiable" data sets see *supra* Chapter 2, Section 2.4.2.2.

[39]   See *infra* in this chapter, Section 3.4.

[40]   European Commission, Commission Staff Working Document. Impact Assessment. Accompanying the document: Proposal for a Directive of the European Parliament and of the Council on the protection of undisclosed know-how and business information (trade secrets) against their unlawful acquisition, use and disclosure, Brussels, 28.11.2013, SWD(2013) 471 final.

[41]   *Ibid.*, Annex 21, p. 254. The same impact is said to remain when the European Commission analyses policy option 4 (i.e. the prohibition of acts of misappropriation of trade secrets and convergence of national civil law remedies), which is said to integrate policy option 3 (*ibid.*, Annex 21, p. 257), and policy option 5 (i.e. the prohibition of acts of misappropriation of trade secrets and convergence of national civil law remedies and criminal law remedies against the misappropriation of trade secrets), which is said to integrate policy options 3 and 4 (*ibid.*, Annex 21, p. 260).

the need for the use of extraordinary protective measures, thus reducing the risk of intrusion in the privacy sphere of employees and of disproportionate personal data processing.[42] ["Unauthorised used" should probably be "unauthorised use" (author's remark)]

It goes from what is said in the passage above that personal data may form part or the whole of a trade secret and that the European Commission sees benefits arising from such protection, first and foremost, the fact that trade secret protection would reinforce the protection of personal data by preventing third parties from unlawfully or disproportionately processing such data.

However, in Annex 4 of the aforementioned Impact Assessment, which elaborates on trade secrets and their scope, personal data is left out from the scope of trade secret protection. In this regard, the European Commission, while elaborating on the various terminology that is used when it comes to trade secrets,[43] explains that:

> A large overlap exists with the term "confidential business information" which is also often used as interchangeable with "trade secret". Not all the information generated or kept by a company is or should be confidential. [...] confidential information may refer to personal information (e.g. journals, pictures), professional information (e.g. information supplied in the course of professional duties) and information in the context of business, commerce or trade (e.g. trade secrets or secret know-how).[44] (A footnote and a reference omitted)

Accordingly, a trade secret would cover information related to the business, commerce or trade and would fall under a broader category of confidential information, which would encompass not only trade secrets, but also personal and professional information. Thereby, personal data could be treated as confidential information, but would not necessarily be a trade secret.

The analysis above shows that it is not entirely clear whether personal data could be a subject matter of a trade secret. Whereas the Impact Assessment of the European Commission at one place seems to confirm it, in another place, it states exactly the opposite.

3.2.1.3 Personal information: confidential information or a trade secret?

The fact that not all confidential information may be a trade secret is not entirely new. In fact, companies may possess a good amount of confidential information, yet not all of it will necessarily constitute trade secrets.

---

[42] *Ibid.*, Annex 21, p. 254.
[43] *Ibid.*, Annex 4, pp. 107–108.
[44] *Ibid.*, Annex 4, p. 108.

Bearing in mind that the European Commission, in the Impact Assessment, allocated personal information under both confidential information and trade secrets, the question is whether personal information should indeed be considered merely confidential information, instead of being a trade secret, or should it be possible for it to, in fact, form part or the whole of a trade secret of a company.

The roots of protecting personal confidences under the law of confidentiality can be found in the common law jurisdictions, such as the UK and the US. In the common law system, privacy protection, in fact, emerged from the law of confidentiality, so that in the UK, as in the US, the right to privacy finds its roots in the law of confidentiality.

It was two authors – *Warren* and *Brandeis* – who gave the beginning to the right to privacy in the US,[45] arguably, crystallizing it from the law of confidentiality.[46] In their seminal article, discussing the protection of private facts with regard to the content of a diary, *Warren* and *Brandeis* asked:

> What is the thing which is protected? Surely, not the intellectual act of recording the fact that the husband did not dine with his wife, but that fact itself. It is not the intellectual product, but the domestic occurrence.[47]

Accordingly, the protection of privacy, firstly, does not require any intellectual creations, and secondly, it protects (mere) facts.

Whereas the right to privacy may be considered as the right against the world, the right to confidentiality is basically a relative right, i.e. a right that derives from a relationship. Hence, privacy is an absolute right against everybody and is protected through confidentiality, the obligation of which arises from the relationship. In fact, according to *Warren* and *Brandeis*:

> We must therefore conclude that the rights, so protected, whatever their exact nature, are not rights arising from contract or from special trust, but are rights as against the world; [...] the principle which has been applied to protect these rights is in reality not the principle of private property. [...] The principle which protects personal writings and any other productions of the intellect or of the emotions, is the right to privacy, and the law has no new principle to formulate when it extends this protection to the personal appearance, sayings, acts, and to personal relation, domestic or otherwise.[48] (Footnote omitted)

---

[45]   *Warren, S.D./Brandeis, L.D.*, The Right to Privacy, (1890–1891) 4 Harv. L. Rev. 193.

[46]   *Richards, N.M./Solove, D.J.*, Privacy's Other Path: Recovering the Law of Confidentiality, (2007–2008) 96 Geo. L. J. 123.

[47]   *Warren, S.D./Brandeis, L.D.*, The Right to Privacy, (1890–1891) 4 Harv. L. Rev. 193, 201.

[48]   *Ibid.*, at 213.

Thus, whereas privacy is an absolute right, which protects an individual against anybody, confidentiality, in contrast, is a relative right, and a duty of confidentiality arises on the basis of a relationship. In fact, it is also noted by *Richards* and *Solove* that "then as now, confidentiality is about protecting information from disclosure in the context of relationships".[49] Furthermore, they point out that "'[p]rivacy' has often been understood to mean total secrecy. [...] Confidentiality is more nuanced, as it involves the sharing of information with others and the norms by which people within relationships handle each other's personal information"[50] (footnote omitted).

It is interesting to note that, while in the US the "independent" right to privacy has crystallized out of the law of confidentiality (bearing in mind that the right to privacy is an absolute right), in England the right to privacy still forms part of the law of confidentiality. It is explained that, when the English Human Rights Act was passed in 1998 and came into effect in 2000, "English courts responded to Article 8 not by endorsing a new action for privacy, but by further stretching the law of confidence".[51] Hence, "[i]n contrast to Warren and Brandeis's individualistic conception of privacy, the English law of confidentiality focuses on relationships rather than individuals. Far from a right to be left alone, confidentiality focuses on the norms of trust within relationships".[52] Thereby, while the right to privacy is the right "to be left alone" in the US, private confidences remained a protectable subject matter of the law of confidentiality in the UK. Importantly though, "while American privacy law has centered around the individual's inviolate personality, English privacy law has focused on social relationships".[53]

Furthermore, with regard to trade secret protection, it could be noted that Justice Goulding, in the landmark *Faccenda Chicken* case, decided by the High Court of Justice – Chancery Division,[54] distinguished among three types of information: firstly, trivial or non-confidential information, which cannot be protected; secondly, confidential information, which becomes part of the employee's skills and knowledge and which can be protected after the end

---

[49] *Richards, N.M./Solove, D.J.*, Privacy's Other Path: Recovering the Law of Confidentiality, (2007–2008) 96 Geo. L. J. 123, 132.

[50] *Ibid.*, at 174.

[51] *Ibid.*, at 168. The authors note that "[t]he English experience is instructive, for it demonstrates how the concept of confidentiality can develop into a powerful protection of personal information" (*ibid.*, at 172).

[52] *Ibid.*, at 174.

[53] *Ibid.*, at 127 ("Rather than protecting the information we hide away in secrecy, confidentiality protects the information we share with others based upon our expectations of trust and reliance in relationships" (*ibid.*, at 125)).

[54] *Faccenda Chicken Ltd v. Fowler and Others*, High Court of Justice – Chancery Division, 8 November 1983, [1985] F.S.R. 105.

of the employment only by way of a restrictive covenant; and thirdly, trade secrets, which cannot be used after the term of the employment "for anyone's benefit but the employer's".[55] Justice Golding held that the sales information, which was at the core of the dispute in the case at hand, belonged to his second category, so that it could not be protected "in the absence of an express restrictive stipulation".[56] The Court of Appeal,[57] although it confirmed the outcome of the judgement of the High Court of Justice (i.e. information in that case could not be protected after the end of the employment), did not uphold Justice's Goulding finding that "an employer can protect the use of information in his second category, even though it does not include either a trade secret or its equivalent, by means of a restrictive covenant".[58] According to the Court of Appeal, "a restrictive covenant will not be enforced unless the protection sought is reasonably necessary to protect a trade secret or to prevent some personal influence over customers being abused in order to entice them away".[59] The *Faccenda Chicken* case was related to a particular type of cases, in the words of Justice Goulding – the "cases of master and servant"[60] (i.e. in the employment and post-employment context). However, the distinction of information between confidential information and "real" trade secrets may, in fact, be relevant for the data economy as well.

In fact, cases may exist where personal data may form part or the whole of a (real) trade secret. As it was explained, before the technological developments, which enabled the processing of vast amounts of data for commercial purposes, this question was not so acute. In contrast, now companies have tools to process vast amounts of personal data – importantly, for commercial purposes. For example, the European Data Protection Supervisor, while, in their preliminary opinion, elaborating on "big personal data as an asset", explained that:

> Information on subscribers to a given online service which is collected include names, gender, personal preferences, location, email addresses, IP addresses and surfing history. This is used to invest in existing client relations and to acquire new clients.[61]

---

[55]   *Ibid.*, at 114–116.

[56]   *Ibid.*, at 116.

[57]   *Faccenda Chicken Ltd v. Fowler and Others*, Court of Appeal, 5 December 1985, [1987] Ch. 117.

[58]   *Ibid.*, at 137.

[59]   *Ibid.*, at 137.

[60]   *Faccenda Chicken Ltd v. Fowler and Others*, High Court of Justice – Chancery Division, 8 November 1983, [1985] F.S.R. 105, at 114.

[61]   Preliminary Opinion of the European Data Protection Supervisor, "Privacy and Competitiveness in the Age of Big Data: The Interplay between Data Protection, Competition Law and Consumer Protection in the Digital Economy", March 2014, p. 9

Furthermore, as it was explained in the previous chapter,[62] given a broad definition of personal data, a good portion of data, even if it may seem to be non-personal, may, at the end of the day, turn out to be personal. The question thereby is whether any limitations could be found in the EU Trade Secrets Directive that could restrict the ability of the companies to protect personal data as forming part or the whole of their trade secrets.

In this regard, it is noteworthy that recital 14 of the EU Trade Secrets Directive stipulates that a definition of a trade secret should be constructed "to cover know-how, business information and technological information where there is *both a legitimate interest* in keeping them confidential and *a legitimate expectation* that such confidentiality will be preserved" (emphasis added). Although these two additional elements, i.e. a legitimate interest and a legitimate expectation, are not included in the trade secret definition enshrined in Article 2(1) of the EU Trade Secrets Directive, their stipulation in the aforementioned recital means that they will stand in support for interpreting the trade secret definition in Article 2(1). The question is whether such a legitimate interest and a legitimate expectation could serve the purpose of limiting the trade secret definition to (purely) non-personal data.

It is noteworthy that the two aforementioned elements, although they are not found in the definition of undisclosed information of Article 39(2) TRIPS, are not entirely new. In fact, they were known in the national trade secret protection. Namely, in Germany, where the definition of a trade secret was not included in the legislative provisions, but was rather developed by the case-law, the definition of a trade secret consisted of the following elements: information relating to a particular business; known to a narrowly limited number of persons, thus, being secret; under the express or identifiable (as a rule, commercial) owner's will, based on a legitimate interest, is intended to be kept secret.[63] Thereby, in addition to the requirements of TRIPS, the German definition of a trade secret consisted of two additional requirements, i.e. a legitimate interest (*Geheimhaltungsinteresse*) and an intent to keep particular information secret (*Geheimhaltungswille*). According to the com-

---

(https://edps.europa.eu/sites/edp/files/publication/14-03-26_competition_law_big_data_en.pdf).

[62] See *supra* Chapter 2, Section 2.4.2.

[63] See, for example, Federal Supreme Court of Germany, 15 March 1955 (*Möbelwachspaste*), (1995) GRUR 424, at 425; Federal Supreme Court of Germany, 1 July 1960 (*Wurftaubenpresse*), (1961) GRUR 40, at 43; Federal Supreme Court of Germany, 27 April 2006 (*Kundendatenprogramm*), 2006 GRUR 1044, at 1046. For a more detailed analysis of trade secret protection in Germany see *Surblytė, G.*, The Refusal to Disclose Trade Secrets as an Abuse of Market Dominance – *Microsoft* and Beyond, Berne: Stämpfli 2011, pp. XLVII + 263 (Munich Series on European and International Competition Law, Volume 28), pp. 49–60.

mentators, a justifiable commercial interest could, for example, be considered to exist in the cases when the information is of high importance for the competitiveness of a company with the result that its disclosure would be capable of causing damage or providing a free ride to competitors.[64] Whereas a legitimate interest is an objective element of a trade secret, an intent is a subjective one. However, in the cases of an existence of an objective commercial interest, such an intent would often be presumed.[65]

The EU Trade Secrets Directive does not explain what a legitimate interest is supposed to mean. Yet, on the basis of what was said above with regard to the legal framework of Germany, it should not be ruled out that such an interest might be confirmed in cases when the information in question (for example, a particular data set) may enhance the competitiveness of a company. In such a way, the requirement of a legitimate interest could not be relied on when arguing that personal data should not be protected as a trade secret.

When it comes to the requirement of legal expectations, it is noteworthy that this requirement, as enshrined in the aforementioned recital of the EU Trade Secrets Directive, differs from the requirement in the German definition of a trade secret. After all, the latter speaks about the intent of a trade secret holder to keep particular information secret. Such an intent, as explained above, could be presumed under the German law if a legitimate interest exists. Although both an intent to preserve secrecy and the expectation that confidentiality will be preserved are the requirements of a subjective nature, the EU Trade Secrets Directive speaks about legal expectations, which, in fact, may be not necessarily those of a trade secret holder, but rather of any third party. As regards the legal expectations requirement, as enshrined in the EU Trade Secrets Directive, it may be more difficult to presume them. In fact, the EU Trade Secrets Directive does not specify whose legal expectations recital 14 talks about. It should not be ruled out, however, that such expectations may be those of natural persons whose data is processed forming part or the whole of a trade secret. Hence, the lack of legal expectations that confidentiality will be preserved may be used as one of the arguments when challenging trade secret protection for data, which may include personal data. This may in particular be so if it is recalled that trade secrets can be shared.

---

[64]   *Köhler, H./Bornkamm, J.*, Gesetz gegen den unlauteren Wettbewerb, München: Verlag C.H. Beck 2008, 29. Auflage: § 17, para. 9; *Westermann, I.*, Handbuch Know-how-Schutz, München: Verlag C.H. Beck 2007, p. 21; *Wodtke, C./Richter, S.*, Schutz von Betriebs- und Geschäftsgeheimnissen, Berlin: Erich Schmidt Verlag 2004, p. 24.

[65]   *Köhler, H./Bornkamm, J.*, Gesetz gegen den unlauteren Wettbewerb, München: Verlag C.H. Beck 2008, 29. Auflage: § 17, para. 10.

The analysis above shows that it may actually be both non-personal and personal data that may form part or the whole of a trade secret. Such a trade secret may cover the whole data set or, under the circumstances, even smaller portions of data. Hence, the focus of the debate on non-personal data only is not only incomplete, but, more importantly, carries risks and may lead to unintended consequences. After all, a too simple approach of non-personal data in general and with regard to trade secret protection in particular overlooks the impact that trade secret protection may have for personal data. The latter may be at stake not only in the cases when the portions of personal data form part or the whole of a trade secret, but also in the cases of "identifiable" data sets. Although such data sets may, at first sight, seem to consist of non-personal data, additional precautions may be needed as regards the protection of data based on which particular individuals, may, if not identified, be at least rendered identifiable.

3.2.2 Secrecy

The second requirement for a trade secret is secrecy: if there is no secrecy, there is no trade secret.

According to Article 2(1)(a) of the EU Trade Secrets Directive, a trade secret covers information, which is "secret in the sense that it is not, as a body or in the precise configuration and assembly of its components, generally known among or readily accessible to persons within the circles that normally deal with the kind of information in question". In light of the data economy, the question is whether or when this requirement may be fulfilled.

In trade secret law, it is not absolute secrecy that is required, but rather relative secrecy.[66] This means that information, which is kept as a trade secret, can be shared – as long as secrecy is not destroyed, such information will be considered secret. The question thereby is when such secrecy can be destroyed, in particular in the context of the data economy.

In this regard, it could, first of all, be noted that even those trade secrets that appear on the Internet are not always considered to lose secrecy. For example, the US scholar Elisabeth A. Rowe has suggested applying the "sequential preservation model" when deciding on whether trade secrets that have appeared on the Internet should be considered as destroyed. According to this model, three factors would be relevant: firstly, how long a trade secret was available on the Internet and how prompt the reaction of a trade secret holder was; secondly,

---

[66]   As noted by some scholars, "secrecy is never absolutely guaranteed, neither does it need to be" (*Psaroudakis, G.*, Trade Secrets in the Cloud, (2016) 38(6) E.I.P.R. 344, 346).

whether a trade secret had "essentially entered the public domain as a result of the disclosure"; and thirdly, the good faith of the recipient.[67]

Also, legal issues that might be related to trade secret protection as regards trade secrets stored in the "cloud" were identified a while ago by the US scholar Sharon K. Sandeen.[68] In particular, the issue was analysed as regards the terms and conditions of cloud service provider agreements and their duty of confidentiality. In this regard, Sandeen proposed a four-step model for distinguishing between trade secret-destroying disclosure and non-trade secret-destroying mere transfers of information.[69] The latter distinction may, however, be highly relevant not only for the cases when trade secrets would be stored in the "cloud", but also for the data economy as a whole. In fact, bearing in mind an increasing use of the connected technology (the IoT) and the use of data in the context of machine learning, it may be crucial – when analysing the secrecy requirement of a trade secret definition – to make a distinction between communication (including communication that takes place without an intervention of human beings, i.e. among machines) that results in the disclosure of information and may thus be considered as secrecy-destroying and communication that amounts merely to the transfer of information without such a disclosure taking place.

3.2.2.1 Machine-to-machine communication: how to preserve secrecy

Technological developments have increased machine-to-machine communication. In light of the fact that information may need to go through a number of networks with regard to the use of AI technology, it may be asked whether it is at all possible to preserve secrecy.

Confidentiality of electronic communications data, including confidentiality of machine-to-machine communication, is addressed in the proposed ePrivacy Regulation,[70] which is meant to replace the ePrivacy Directive (Directive

---

[67] *Rowe, E.A.*, Saving Trade Secret Disclosures on the Internet Through Sequential Preservation, (2007) 42 Wake Forest L. Rev. 1, at 31. For a detailed description of the suggested "sequential preservation model" see *ibid.*, at 29–37.

[68] *Sandeen, S.K.*, Lost in the Cloud: Information Flows and the Implications of Cloud Computing for Trade Secret Protection, (2014) 19 Virginia Journal of Law and Technology 1.

[69] *Ibid.*, at 78–98.

[70] European Commission, Proposal for a Regulation of the European Parliament and of the Council concerning the respect for private life and the protection of personal data in electronic communications and repealing Directive 2002/58/EC (Regulation on Privacy and Electronic Communications), Brussels, 10.1.2017, COM(2017) 10 final. As of writing this manuscript, the latest version of the draft ePrivacy Regulation provided by the Council of the European Union was the draft ePrivacy Regulation as of 6 March 2020 (Council of the European Union, Brussels, 6 March 2020, 6543/20

2002/58/EC).[71] According to Article 5 of the proposed ePrivacy Regulation, which elaborates on the confidentiality of electronic communications data:

> Electronic communications data shall be confidential. Any interference with electronic communications data, including listening, tapping, storing, monitoring, scanning or other kinds of interception, surveillance and processing of electronic communications data, by anyone other than the end-users concerned, shall be prohibited, except when permitted by this Regulation.[72]

Thereby, Article 5 does not mention machine-to-machine communication. However, recital 12 of the proposed ePrivacy Regulation explains that:

> The use of machine-to-machine and Internet of Things services, that is to say services involving an automated transfer of data and information between devices or software-based applications with limited or no human interaction, is emerging. In order to ensure full protection of the rights to privacy and confidentiality of communications, and to promote a trusted and secure Internet of Things in the digital single market, this Regulation, in particular the requirements relating to the confidentiality of communications, should apply to the transmission of such services. […] This Regulation should apply to the provider of the transmission service if that transmission is carried out via a publicly available electronic communications service or network.[73]

Thereby, confidentiality of machine-to-machine communication should be guaranteed, firstly, for the machine-to-machine electronic communications in transmission, and, secondly, when the transmission service is carried out via an electronic communications service that is publicly available. As regards the former, recital 12 explains that "the transmission of machine-to-machine or Internet of Things services regularly involves the conveyance of signals via an electronic communications network" and thus "constitutes an electronic communication service".[74] The criterion that the electronic communications service has to be publicly available was added in the draft version of the ePri-

---

(Interinstitutional File: 2017/0003 (COD))). According to Article 1(3) of the proposed ePrivacy Regulation, the latter will "particularise and complement" the GDPR (Council of the European Union, Brussels, 6 March 2020, 6543/20 (Interinstitutional File: 2017/0003 (COD))).

[71] Directive 2002/58/EC of the European Parliament and of the Council of 12 July 2002 concerning the processing of personal data and the protection of privacy in the electronic communications sector (Directive on privacy and electronic communications), OJ [2002] L 201/37.

[72] Council of the European Union, Brussels, 6 March 2020, 6543/20 (Interinstitutional File: 2017/0003 (COD)).

[73] *Ibid.*

[74] *Ibid.*

vacy Regulation as of 8 November 2019.[75] It basically means that the ePrivacy Regulation would not capture "data processed by services or networks used for purely internal communications purposes" (recital 13).[76] Importantly, in the earlier versions of the proposed ePrivacy Regulation, recital 12 explained that a distinction should be drawn between the services provided at the application layer of machine-to-machine services and the transmission services: whereas, pursuant to recital 12, the latter was said to qualify for electronic communication services, and thus to fall under the ePrivacy Regulation, the former did not.[77] In the draft ePrivacy Regulation of 6 March 2020, the latter rule was further refined stating that the providers of machine-to-machine and the Internet of Things services typically operate at the application layer, so that they as well as their customers "benefit from the protection of confidentiality of their electronic communications data".[78] However, such a statement does not change the essence of the idea included in the previous versions of the proposed ePrivacy Regulation, so that the services provided at the application layer would still not fall under the ePrivacy Regulation.

The confidentiality of machine-to-machine communication seems to have been a point of discussion. It should be noted that, in the version that was provided by the Council of the European Union in September 2017,[79] Article 5(2) was included in the square brackets and stipulated that "[Confidentiality of electronic communications data in machine-to-machine communications shall only apply when such communication is related to the end-user]". It was

---

[75] Council of the European Union, Brussels, 8 November 2019, 13808/19 (Interinstitutional File: 2017/0003 (COD)), p. 3.

[76] Recital 13 further explains that "[a]s soon as electronic communications data is transferred from a closed group network to a public electronic communications network, this Regulation applies to such data, including when it is M2M/IoT and personal/home assistant data" (Council of the European Union, Brussels, 8 November 2019, 13808/19 (Interinstitutional File: 2017/0003 (COD))); see also Council of the European Union, Brussels, 6 March 2020, 6543/20 (Interinstitutional File: 2017/0003 (COD)).

[77] See, for example, Council of the European Union, Brussels, 18 November 2019, 14068/19 (Interinstitutional File: 2017/0003 (COD)); Council of the European Union, Brussels, 30 October 2019, 13632/2019 (Interinstitutional File: 2017/0003 (COD)).

[78] Council of the European Union, Brussels, 6 March 2020, 6543/20 (Interinstitutional File: 2017/0003 (COD)), recital 12: "Typically, providers of machine-to-machine or Internet of Things services operate at the application layer (on top of electronic communications services). These service providers and their customers who use IoT devices services are in this respect end-users, and not providers of the electronic communication service and therefore benefit from the protection of confidentiality of their electronic communications data."

[79] Council of the European Union, Brussels, 8 September 2017, 11995/17 (Interinstitutional File: 2017/0003 (COD)).

explained that the legal provision was included in order "to start the discussion" and invite "delegations to express their view on how to approach and further clarify the issue of machine-to-machine communications".[80] However, in the later draft version the latter provision was amended and stated that "[Confidentiality of electronic communications data shall apply to the transmission of machine-to-machine electronic communications where carried out via an electronic communications service]".[81] However, in the draft version as of 13 April 2018,[82] Article 5(2) was deleted.[83] Thereby, Article 5 no longer mentions this issue. Instead, the clarification as regards confidentiality of machine-to-machine communication found its way into the recitals part of the proposed ePrivacy Regulation, namely, recital 12.

It should, however, be stressed that, according to the proposed ePrivacy Regulation, confidentiality of machine-to-machine communication should be guaranteed for data in transmission. In this regard, it could be noted that the European Data Protection Supervisor, in their opinion as of 5 October 2017, while strongly supporting the confidentiality of machine-to-machine communication, stated that "[t]he confidentiality of communications should also be ensured when data are stored in the cloud rather than only in transmission"[84] (emphasis in original omitted).

In this regard, it is noteworthy that recital 15, as it was originally proposed by the European Commission, stipulated that:

> Electronic communications data should be treated as confidential. This means that any interference with *the transmission* of electronic communications data, whether

---

[80] *Ibid.*, p. 5.

[81] Council of the European Union, Brussels, 6 October 2017, 12955/17 (Interinstitutional File: 2017/0003 (COD)).

[82] Council of the European Union, Brussels, 13 April 2018, 7820/18 (Interinstitutional File: 2017/0003 (COD)).

[83] In the *travaux préparatoires* of the ePrivacy Regulation, it is stated that: "During the discussion on doc. 5165/18 most delegations seemed to support to keep the transmission services used for the provision of M2M services in the scope of the ePR. The Presidency is also of the view that the issue of distinction between the transmission and application layers is sufficiently addressed in the European Electronic Communications Code (EECC) at the level of definitions. While the transmission layer constitutes an electronic communications service, the application layer is out of the scope. Bearing in mind that the ePR specifically refers to the EECC definitions, there seems to be no need for the ePR to specifically address this issue in the operative part of the ePR. The Presidency has therefore proposed to delete **art. 5(2)**" (emphasis in original) (Council of the European Union, Brussels, 7 March 2018, 6726/18 (Interinstitutional File: 2017/0003 (COD)), p. 3).

[84] European Data Protection Supervisor (EDPS), EDPS recommendations on specific aspects of the proposed ePrivacy Regulation, 5 October 2017, p. 1.

directly by human intervention or through the intermediation of automated processing by machines, without the consent of all the communicating parties should be
prohibited. (Emphasis added)[85]

Thereby, the recital explained that confidentiality had to be ensured when
electronic communications data were in transmission. However, during the
preparatory process, the text of this passage has been changed, so that the
recital states that:

> Electronic communications data should be treated as confidential. This means that
> any *interference of electronic communications data*, whether directly by human
> intervention or through the intermediation of automated processing by machines,
> without the consent of the communicating parties should be prohibited.[86] (Emphasis
> added)

Although such a passage could imply that the confidentiality obligation in
the proposed ePrivacy Regulation has been broadened, it is not entirely clear
how it would comply with recital 12, which, as explained above, states that
the requirements relating to the confidentiality of communications, should
apply to the transmission of electronic communication services. Thus, it
might be that the confidentiality obligation as regards the machine-to-machine
communication under ePrivacy Regulation may be applied only to data in
transmission.[87]

The scope of such obligation may nevertheless be important from a legal
point of view. The obligation of confidentiality, under the proposed ePrivacy
Regulation, extends to the protection of trade secrets. Recital 3 stipulates that:

> Electronic communications data may also reveal *information concerning legal
> entities*, such as *business secrets or other sensitive information that has economic
> value* and the protection of which *allows legal persons to conduct their business,*

---

[85]   European Commission, Proposal for a Regulation of the European Parliament
and of the Council concerning the respect for private life and the protection of personal
data in electronic communications and repealing Directive 2002/58/EC (Regulation on
Privacy and Electronic Communications), Brussels, 10.1.2017, COM(2017) 10 final.

[86]   Council of the European Union, Brussels, 6 March 2020, 6543/20
(Interinstitutional File: 2017/0003 (COD)).

[87]   This insight is further supported by recital 15a of the proposed ePrivacy
Regulation, which stipulates that "[t]he prohibition of interception of electronic communications content under this Regulation should apply until receipt of the content of
the electronic communication by the intended addressee, i.e. during the end-to-end
exchange of electronic communications content between end-users" (*ibid.*). See also
Article 2(2)(e): "This Regulation does not apply to electronic communications data processed after receipt by the end-user concerned" (*ibid.*).

supporting among other *innovation*. Therefore, the provisions of this Regulation should in principle apply to both natural and legal persons.[88] (Emphasis added)

Bearing in mind that the proposed ePrivacy Regulation, according to Article 1 and Article 1a, lays down rules regarding the protection of fundamental rights and freedoms of not only natural persons, but also legal persons, it might be that the duty of confidentiality, as enshrined in Article 5, would also cover trade secrets. Thereby, the obligation of confidentiality would be broader and would serve for protecting both the right to privacy and the right to personal data protection of natural persons as well as the confidentiality of electronic communications of legal persons. In fact, according to recital 15aa of the proposed ePrivacy Regulation, trade secrets should be protected in accordance with the EU Trade Secrets Directive.[89] However, should such an obligation exist only in the cases of mere transmissions of information, this would still not solve the problem of secrecy-destroying disclosure in the cases of their storage. After all, it is the latter fact that might be highly relevant for preserving secrecy in general and in the case of machine-to-machine communication in particular.

In the meantime, while the final scope of the ePrivacy Regulation is not yet clear, it might be that not only contractual, but also technical precautions (such as the encryption of information) may be needed. This may be so in order not only to protect privacy and personal data of natural persons, but also to avoid the secrecy-destroying disclosure of trade secrets.

3.2.2.2 Secrecy of data sets
As regards the secrecy of data sets, it is first of all noteworthy that the EU Trade Secrets Directive, Article 2(1), just as Article 39(2) TRIPS, stipulates that information is considered secret "in the sense that it is not, *as a body or in the precise configuration and assembly of its components*, generally known among or readily accessible to persons within the circles that normally deal with the kind of information in question" (emphasis added). Hence, trade secrets – by definition – do not necessarily consist of only individual pieces of information, but may also comprise different categories of information in one set.

The fact that, in order to be protected as a trade secret, information would have to be secret in terms of the "precise configuration and assembly of its components" may be relevant for the data economy. A careful reading of this requirement reveals that secrecy is required in terms of a data set as a whole,

---

[88] Council of the European Union, Brussels, 6 March 2020, 6543/20 (Interinstitutional File: 2017/0003 (COD)).

[89] *Ibid.*

not the individual parts of such a combination.[90] Thus, and this may be highly relevant for the data economy, different pieces of information in the data set may be publicly available, but as long as their compilation or the data extracted from them, for example, in the course of data analytics, is secret, a data set may constitute a trade secret.[91] Hence, even when parts of a data set are publicly available, it may be a trade secret. In fact, a data set consisting of solely public information may be considered a trade secret.[92]

In this regard, a comparison could be made with the US, where, according to the statutory provisions as well as case-law, the combinations of different components (of even public information) may be considered a trade secret. For example, the Federal Court of Appeals (Second Circuit) held that:

> a trade secret can exist in a combination of characteristics and components, *each of which, by itself,* is in the public domain, but *the unified process*, design and operation of which, in *unique combination*, affords a competitive advantage and is a protectable secret.[93] (Emphasis added)

Accordingly, a data set that consists of information, all of which is publicly available, may be considered a trade secret, if the combination of such information is unique. This is a very important insight in the context of the data

---

[90]   A different opinion, yet based merely on the interpretation of the language in translation of the EU Trade Secrets Directive and ignoring the fact that the latter, in fact, follows the definition of a trade secret enshrined in Article 39 TRIPS in *Drexl, J.*, Data Access and Control in the Era of Connected Devices, Study on Behalf of the European Consumer Organisation BEUC (https://www.ip.mpg.de/fileadmin/ipmpg/content/aktuelles/aus_der_forschung/beuc-x-2018-121_data_access_and_control_in_the_area_of_connected_devices.pdf), p. 93: "secrecy should not only be related to the each and every piece of information in isolation but also to its entirety or to how individual pieces of information relate to each other" (footnote with a reference to the French and the German translation of the relevant legal provision of the EU Trade Secrets Directive omitted).

[91]   Another opinion by Drexl in *Drexl, J.*, Designing Competitive Markets for Industrial Data – Between Propertisation and Access (31 October 2016). Max Planck Institute for Innovation & Competition Research Paper No. 16-13. Available at SSRN: https://papers.ssrn.com/sol3/papers.cfm?abstract_id=2862975, p. 23: "while the secrecy could be confirmed for data that is produced by the machines inside a factory, data collected by smart cars on freely accessible roads could be collected by the cars of many manufacturers and, hence, will not fulfil this requirement".

[92]   See, for example, *Richards, N.M./Solove, D.J.*, Privacy's Other Path: Recovering the Law of Confidentiality, (2007–2008) 96 Georgetown Law Journal 123, 165: "English confidence law also protects collections of data even where the individual pieces of data are each drawn from the public domain."

[93]   *Imperial Chemical Industries Limited v. National Distillers and Chemical Corporation*, 342 F.2d. 737, 742 (2nd Cir. 1965).

economy, where the role of unique data sets has time and again been stressed, for example, by the EU Commissioner for Competition Margrethe Vestager.[94] Moreover, the circumstance that particular data may be capable of rendering a particular data set unique, as compared with the data sets possessed by competitors, may be important for the data economy. In contrast to the considerations of the European Commission that it may be merely data sets (not the individual pieces of data) that may be eligible for trade secret protection,[95] it should probably not be ruled out that cases may exist when also smaller portions of data may fall under trade secret protection.

Furthermore, the combination of data in a data set may have implications for a legal assessment of secrecy-destroying disclosure. For example, in *Servo Corporation of America v. General Electric Company*, the United States Court of Appeals, Fourth Circuit, held that:

> it does not follow that public disclosure of the working combination may be accomplished only through a single integrated document. That doctrine is a defense of anticipation in the field of patent law. [...] It has no necessary application to a trade secrets case where the question is whether, taking into account *all* of the plaintiff's relevant disclosures, it is reasonable to conclude that a competitor could have ascertained the working combination from an examination of those disclosures.[96]
> (References to case-law omitted; emphasis in original)

The passage clearly illustrates that, even if parts of a data set were disclosed, this would not necessarily amount to destroying a trade secret. It would be important to clarify whether a data set, in its precise combination, had been disclosed. This may be particularly so where data are combined in a data set and may have value only in connection to other data. In other words, to destroy the secrecy of an interconnected data set may be even more difficult, since such a disclosure is more sophisticated than the disclosure of an individual piece of data.

Finally, it could be recalled that the Federal Supreme Court of Germany in *Möbelwachspaste*,[97] a case that was decided back in 1955, acknowledged

---

[94] *Vestager, M.*, "Making Data Work for Us", Speech, 9 September 2016 (https://ec.europa.eu/competition/speeches/index_2016.html). As of 2019, Margrethe Vestager serves also as the Executive Vice President of the European Commission for a Europe Fit for the Digital Age.

[95] See *supra* in this chapter Section 3.1.

[96] *Servo Corporation of America v. General Electric Company*, 393 F.2d. 551 (4th Cir. 1968), 554. See also *Patel, A.B./Pade, J.A./Cundiff, V./Newman, B.*, The Global Harmonisation of Trade Secret Law: The Convergence of Protection for Trade Secret Information in the US and EU, (2016) 38(12) E.I.P.R. 738, 739.

[97] Federal Supreme Court of Germany, 15 March 1955 (*Möbelwachspaste*), (1995) GRUR 424.

as a trade secret a manufacturing process used by a company, although the process as such was widely known. The Federal Supreme Court of Germany held that a "process that as such is widely known may constitute a subject-matter of a trade secret of a particular company as long as it is secret that that particular company is using that process and, through such a use, it possibly gains particular benefits".[98] The Court thereby explained that the Court of Appeals could confirm the existence of a trade secret notwithstanding the question whether that particular process, which formed the subject matter of a trade secret, was not necessarily secret in objective terms (*nicht "objektiv geheim"*).[99] Transferred to the data economy, this means that the particular use of data (which, as such, may be publicly available) may form part of a trade secret of a company. This is an important insight, since companies often process data that is publicly available. Thus, despite the fact that data may be publicly available, particular uses of such data collected by the company may form part of their trade secret. In other words, data/data sets could be considered a trade secret if a company is gathering/using for particular purposes particular (types of) data that may even be publicly available. Moreover, information related to the fact that a company collects particular types of data and (or) uses such data for particular purposes could be a trade secret should such information provide a competitive advantage for the company.

3.2.3   Economic Value

The third requirement of a trade secret definition is commercial value (Article 2(1)(b) of the EU Trade Secrets Directive). Economic value of information covered by a trade secret basically translates into a competitive advantage. A careful reading of the definition of a trade secret reveals that economic value of information may (merely) derive from the fact that such information is kept secret.

3.2.3.1   Actual or potential economic value
According to the EU Trade Secrets Directive, the value of a trade secret can be actual or merely potential. Although this is not directly stated in Article 2(1)(b) of the EU Trade Secrets Directive, recital 14 stipulates that "information should have a commercial value, whether actual or potential".

---

[98]   *Ibid.*, at 425. See also: Federal Supreme Court of Germany, 1 July 1960 (*Wurftaubenpresse*), (1961) GRUR 40, 43.

[99]   Federal Supreme Court of Germany, 15 March 1955 (*Möbelwachspaste*), (1995) GRUR 424, at 425.

The fact that the economic value (a competitive advantage) of a trade secret can be actual or merely potential may be highly relevant for the data economy, where the value of data (data sets) may be context-specific and hypothetical.[100] After all, such value may depend upon the information to be extracted from the data sets.

The "potential value" criterion was not included in the definition of undisclosed information under Article 39(2) TRIPS. Also, potential value, as part of a trade secret definition, was not mentioned in the European Commission's proposal of the EU Trade Secrets Directive.[101] Yet, in the text proposed by the Council of the European Union it was noted that "[s]uch information or know-how should furthermore have commercial value, whether actual or potential" (recital 8).[102] The requirement has been included in the final version of the EU Trade Secrets Directive and is now anchored in recital 14.

From a comparative point of view, it is noteworthy that the requirement of actual and potential economic value can be found in the US trade secret law. Both the definition of a trade secret in the UTSA and the Defend Trade Secrets Act of 2016 mention potential economic value among the requirements of a trade secret definition. For example, the UTSA (§ 1(4)(i)) stipulates that a trade secret covers information, which "derives independent economic value, actual or potential, from not being generally known to, and not being readily ascertainable by proper means by, other persons who can obtain economic value from its disclosure or use". Thereby, firstly, information should derive independent economic value. Secondly, such value can be either actual or merely potential. Thirdly, economic value derives from the fact that the information is either not generally known or easily accessible to such persons who could obtain economic value from the disclosure of the information in question. Thereby, the economic value criterion is closely related to another requirement of a trade secret definition, i.e. reasonable steps of a trade secret holder to keep the information secret. This requirement strikes the balance between the efforts of a trade secret holder and those of any third party that may try to access the information under a trade secret by fair means such as, for example, reverse engineering. After all, according to the UTSA's definition

---

[100] See *supra* Chapter 2, Section 2.3.2.

[101] European Commission, Proposal for a Directive of the European Parliament and of the Council on the protection of undisclosed know-how and business information (trade secrets) against their unlawful acquisition, use and disclosure, 2013/0402 (COD) (COM(2013) 813 final, 28.11.2013).

[102] Council of the European Union, Proposal for a Directive of the European Parliament and of the Council on the protection of undisclosed know-how and business information (trade secrets) against their unlawful acquisition, use and disclosure, 9870/14, Brussels, 19 May 2014, p. 15.

of a trade secret, economic value derives from information "not being readily ascertainable by proper means". The latter reflects the efforts of both any third party trying to access information and a trade secret holder hindering such access.

The EU Trade Secrets Directive, in contrast, is not that specific when elaborating on the commercial value of information. After all, Article 2(1)(b) of the EU Trade Secrets Directive states that information has commercial value because it is secret. Furthermore, in contrast to the economic value requirement in the US legal provisions, which construct such a requirement from the perspective of economic value that the disclosure or use of a trade secret could have for third parties (for example, competitors), the EU Trade Secrets Directive speaks about such value in relation to the potential harm to the interests of the trade secret holder. Recital 14 of the EU Trade Secrets Directive stipulates that:

> [s]uch know-how or information should be considered to have a commercial value, for example, where its unlawful acquisition, use or disclosure is likely to harm the interests of the person lawfully controlling it, in that it undermines that person's scientific and technical potential, business or financial interests, strategic positions or ability to compete.

Thereby, economic value, as it is formulated in the EU Trade Secrets Directive, is constructed more from the perspective of a trade secret holder.[103] Thereby, economic value might be measured by the likelihood of harm that could be suffered by a trade secret holder, for example as regards their ability to compete, rather than by the economic value of a trade secret vis-à-vis third parties, including (potential) competitors, and thus their efforts to access the information that is kept secret, for example by way of reverse engineering. However, any harm that could be suffered by a trade secret holder because of a trade secret infringement should be relevant when calculating damages rather than when assessing the economic value of a trade secret, so that defining the economic value requirement from the perspective of a competitive (dis)advantage as regards third parties, as provided by the relevant US legal provisions, seems to be more convincing.

---

[103] See also *Wennakoski, A.A.*, Trade Secrets under Review: A Comparative Analysis of the Protection of Trade Secrets in the EU and in the US, (2016) 38(3) E.I.P.R. 154, 157.

Finally, it is noteworthy that economic value may derive also from so-called negative information. As pointed out by the European Commission in the Impact Assessment of the EU Trade Secrets Directive:

> Even negative information that certain applications or commercial strategies are technically or commercially unfeasible may be of economic value. (Footnote omitted)[104]

In the US, for example, the explanation that the information under a trade secret may cover negative information was included in the Uniform Trade Secrets Act. According to the Comment on Section 1:

> The definition of "trade secret" contains a reasonable departure from the Restatement of Torts (First) definition which required that a trade secret be "continuously used in one's business". The broader definition in the proposed Act extends protection to a plaintiff who has not yet had an opportunity or acquired the means to put a trade secret to use. The definition includes information that has commercial value from a negative viewpoint, for example the results of lengthy and expensive research which proves that a certain process will **not** work could be of great value to a competitor.[105] (Emphasis in original)

The fact that the value of information to be protected as a trade secret may be confirmed even in cases when such a trade secret has not yet been put to use may be highly important for the data economy. In the latter, it may often be that the particular market does not yet exist, so that the requirement of the "use of a trade secret" and the commercial value deriving from the use of such a trade secret would unjustifiably narrow down the definition of a trade secret.

Bearing in mind a broad formulation of the economic value requirement for a trade secret definition, the question is whether or how this criterion may be fulfilled in the case of data (data sets).

---

[104] European Commission, Commission Staff Working Document. Impact Assessment. Accompanying the document: Proposal for a Directive of the European Parliament and of the Council on the protection of undisclosed know-how and business information (trade secrets) against their unlawful acquisition, use and disclosure, Brussels, 28.11.2013, SWD(2013) 471 final, Annex 4, p. 109.

[105] National Conference of Commissioners on Uniform State Laws, Uniform Trade Secrets Act, 1979, as amended in 1985, p. 7. In fact, according to the Restatement (First) of Torts, § 757, comment b, "[a] trade secret may consist of any formula, pattern, device or compilation of information which is used in one's business, and which gives him an opportunity to obtain an advantage over competitors who do not know or use it".

3.2.3.2   Economic value of data and data sets

As mentioned above,[106] a potential lack of commercial value when it comes to data has been one of the main reasons why the European Commission seemed to have doubts as regards trade secret protection for data. In the Staff Working Document, the European Commission noted that "it is doubtful that individual data generated by interconnected machines and devices could be regarded as 'trade secret' in the sense of this Directive, mostly because of its lack of commercial value as individual data; however, combination of data (datasets) can be trade secrets under this Directive if all the criteria are met".[107]

However, the fact that pieces of particular data may have economic value was acknowledged back in 1973. At that time, Kenneth J. Arrow, in his analysis of the Information Economy,[108] elaborated on the question whether weather data could be considered as a trade secret "in the economy of gatherers of different kinds of food".[109] In his analysis, Arrow stressed the importance of private demand for such information, calling it information, which "is socially useless but privately valuable".[110] He explained that:

> it has been a classic position that a competitive world will underinvest in research and development, because the information acquired will become general knowledge and cannot be appropriated by the firm financing the research. [...] But Hirshleifer (1971) has pointed out that, if secrecy is possible, there may be overinvestment in information gathering; each firm may secretly get the same information, either on nature or on each other, although it would of course consume less of society's resources if they were collected once and disseminated to all.[111]

Hence, commercial value of information, which may even be publicly available, may derive from the (particular) use of that information in one's business. In other words, the "private demand" may increase the value of information, which is otherwise publicly available. Although Arrow's main point – made in 1973 – was not meant in terms of the data economy, it may be highly valid now when the discussion is back on the table. Apart from the fact that it was as long ago as 1973 that he elaborated on non-personal data (namely, weather data), it is important to stress that data such as weather data, data on soil conditions,

---

[106]   See *supra* in this chapter Section 3.1.

[107]   European Commission, Commission Staff Working Document on the free flow of data and emerging issues of the European data economy, Brussels, 10.1.2017, SWD(2017) 2 final, p. 20.

[108]   *Arrow, K.J.*, Information and Economic Behavior, in: Collected Papers of Kenneth J. Arrow, The Economics of Information, Vol. 4, Cambridge, MA: The Belknap Press of Harvard University Press 1984, pp. 136–184.

[109]   *Ibid.*, p. 143.

[110]   *Ibid.*, p. 143.

[111]   *Ibid.*, pp. 142–143.

temperature, etc., is not only publicly available, but may often be considered as "socially useless". Yet, the example provided by Arrow explains why such data could be "privately valuable" for particular industry circles: namely, this may be due to the fact that the possession of this data may grant competitive advantage.

In fact, in the data economy, it is not merely the volume of data sets (i.e. "big" data sets) that might be important, but rather what can be done with the data. The question whether data or a data set may have commercial value may thus often depend on factual circumstances. Moreover, the Bundeskartellamt and the French competition authority, in their paper on competition law and data, point out that an economic value of data may depend on whether data is structured or unstructured, since "unstructured data [...] usually needs to be processed by different and more recent algorithms in order to become of commercial value".[112]

Data sets, although they could not be completely identified with customer lists, bear some resemblance to them, and though often consisting of various data that is publicly available, they may be protected as a trade secret. For example, the Federal Supreme Court of Germany in 2006 held in *Kundendatenprogramm*[113] that:

> As long as a customer list does not consist merely of the list of addresses that can be easily, i.e. without a particular effort, found in public sources, it can be protected as a trade secret despite a low price for which such a customer list was obtained. [...] Trade secrets do not necessarily feature as such property value. It suffices that negative consequences might arise for the plaintiff in the case when third parties, particularly competitors, get knowledge about the relevant data.[114]

In another case the Federal Supreme Court of Germany stated that no unfair competitive behaviour could be found in the case of the use made of the customers' addresses that remained in the memory of a departing commercial agent or the use of the addresses of such customers who did not have a long-term commercial relationship to the company.[115]

Hence, economic value should not necessarily be directly related to data that forms part of a trade secret. Such value may, instead, derive from the potential of such data to grant a competitive advantage to the company. This may be an

---

[112] Bundeskartellamt/Autorité de la concurrence, Competition Law and Data, 10 May 2016, p. 6.

[113] Federal Supreme Court of Germany, 27 April 2006 (*Kundendatenprogramm*), 2006 GRUR 1044.

[114] *Ibid.*, at 1046.

[115] Federal Supreme Court of Germany, 14 January 1999 (*Kundenanschriften*), 1999 WRP 912, at 914.

important insight with regard to the data economy. Although individual pieces of data, according to the European Commission, would lack economic value, it could be asked whether smaller accumulations of data or, under some circumstances, even individual pieces of data may create economic value of a whole data set, for example, in cases where they render such a data set unique. Should the economic value of a data set be related to personal information, it might be that the "key data" that may enable the identification of natural persons in the cases of pseudonymized data could be protected as a trade secret.

Finally, the value of data sets may also derive from data analytics, so that information extracted from data should be eligible for trade secret protection as well. In fact, the increasing importance of data analytics may also raise the need for the use of related patents – which can lead to the issues known under FRAND licensing[116] (i.e. fair, reasonable and non-discriminatory licensing). Although the European Commission addresses FRAND licensing in terms of access to data sets,[117] the questions related to FRAND licensing in the data economy may rather boil down to the "old" issues, i.e. the licensing of patents (or standard-essential patents), in the case of data analytics.

3.2.4   Reasonable Steps

The fourth requirement of a trade secret definition is reasonable steps taken by a trade secret holder to protect information kept as a trade secret (Article 2(1)(c) of the EU Trade Secrets Directive). A reasonable steps requirement strikes a balance between the interests of a trade secret holder and third parties, since it requires efforts from both a trade secret holder taking steps to protect particular information as a trade secret and a third party willing to access information under trade secret protection by way of fair means, such as, for example, reverse engineering.

In the Staff Working Document, the European Commission explains that "the condition of the Trade Secrets Protection Directive that efforts must have been made to keep 'information' 'secret' (article 2) may need requalification when applied to 'data' so as to account for the fact that in many scenarios, data needs to be shared with a wider range of business partners in interconnected settings, while there remains a need to keep the data protected against any other third party".[118]

---

[116]   See, for example, ECJ, C-170/13, *Huawei Technologies Co. Ltd v. ZTE Corp, ZTE Deutschland GmbH*, 16 July 2015, ECLI:EU:C:2015:477.

[117]   European Commission, Commission Staff Working Document on the free flow of data and emerging issues of the European data economy, Brussels, 10.1.2017, SWD(2017) 2 final, p. 38.

[118]   *Ibid.*, p. 35.

In this regard, it should, first of all, be recalled that owing to the requirement of relative secrecy, the information under a trade secret can be shared – as long as secrecy is not destroyed, a trade secret will not be lost. Hence, the question is, firstly, what reasonable steps should be taken to preserve secrecy when sharing it, and secondly, whether such steps may also raise a risk that natural persons, whose data may be included in a data set, may be rendered identifiable.

It should be noted at the outset that, with the rise of digitization, information has become more vulnerable. Hence, when it comes to the data economy in general and to the reasonable steps requirement of a trade secret in particular, better precautions may be needed on the side of trade secret holders to safeguard their trade secrets given the increasing vulnerability of data theft.[119] In this regard, the Cybersecurity directive[120] and, thereby, the standardization of security requirements,[121] may be very important.

Trade secret law, which protects information, knows different ways of preserving secrecy. Reasonable steps taken by a trade secret holder can be of various natures, for example, contractual, technical restrictions ("i.e. confidentiality agreements with parties acquiring access to the information on the one hand and passwords, encryption, physical security, etc. on the other"[122]), etc. When it comes to the data economy, one of the reasonable measures to protect information under a trade secret could be the use of encryption technology. Thus, the encryption of information may be one of the possible solutions that might help avoid secrecy-destroying disclosure.[123] For example, as regards pseudonymized data, there are several techniques of pseudonymization,[124] one of them being the "encryption with secret key", in case of which, decryption

---

[119] See *Rowe, E.A.*, Contributory Negligence, Technology, and Trade Secrets, (2009) 17 Geo. Mason L. Rev. 1, 15.

[120] Directive (EU) 2016/1148 of the European Parliament and of the Council of 6 July 2016 concerning measures for a high common level of security of network and information systems across the Union, OJ [2016] L 194/1. See also Regulation (EU) 2019/881 of the European Parliament and of the Council of 17 April 2019 on ENISA (the European Union Agency for Cybersecurity) and on information and communications technology cybersecurity certification and repealing Regulation (EU) No. 526/2013 (Cybersecurity Act), OJ [2019] L 151/15.

[121] Directive (EU) 2016/1148 of the European Parliament and of the Council of 6 July 2016 concerning measures for a high common level of security of network and information systems across the Union, OJ [2016] L 194/1, recital 66, Art. 19(1).

[122] *Psaroudakis, G.*, Trade Secrets in the Cloud, (2016) 38(6) E.I.P.R. 344, 346.

[123] See, for example, *Psaroudakis, G.*, Trade Secrets in the Cloud, (2016) 38(6) E.I.P.R. 344, 346.

[124] For more detail see Article 29 Data Protection Working Party, Opinion 05/2014 on Anonymisation Techniques, adopted on 10 April 2014, 0829/14/EN WP216, pp. 20–21.

is normally possible only with knowledge of the key.[125] Thereby, reasonable steps to protect the encrypted data set may boil down to securing the "key".[126]

Yet, one particular feature of protecting data under trade secrets is that the reasonable steps requirement may serve a twofold purpose, particularly, when it comes to data sets, which include personal data. If a data set, which includes personal data, is protected as a trade secret, it might be that reasonable steps taken in order to hinder access to such data, as a requirement of trade secret law, will simultaneously hinder the ability of third parties to enable the identifiability of natural persons whose data may be involved. This may in particular be so if we bear in mind that the test for reverse engineering comes very close to the test for identifiability.[127] Hence, not only the secrecy of a data set, but also the identifiability of natural persons whose data may be included in such a data set may be secured.

Such a dual role of the reasonable steps requirement does not yet mean that trade secret law reinforces the protection of personal data. Although the European Commission, when assessing the impact of the EU Trade Secrets Directive on the fundamental rights, including the right to protect personal data, stated that the protection of trade secrets "reinforces the protection of personal data",[128] such an approach is oversimplified, if not incorrect. In fact, trade secret law, firstly, does not deal with the protection of personal data, and does not contain any guarantees in this regard. Moreover and secondly, it protects information against access by third parties, namely, on the basis of the reasonable steps taken by a trade secret holder. Yet, thirdly, such a protection neither guarantees that a trade secret will not be misappropriated nor does it presume that any access by third parties will be unauthorized. On the contrary, third parties may access a trade secret by way of fair means such as reverse engineering, which is allowed under trade secret law. Thus, trade secrets, although they have to fulfil the requirements as regards the protection of information kept under a trade secret, are not meant to reinforce personal data protection. Quite to the contrary, tensions may arise in the intersection of trade

---

[125]   *Ibid.*, p. 20.

[126]   *Ibid.*, p. 22: "if the secret key is stored alongside the pseudonymised data, and the data are compromised, then the attacker may be able to trivially link the pseudonymised data to their original attribute. The same applies if the key is stored separately from the data but not in a secure manner".

[127]   See *infra* in this chapter, Section 3.7.

[128]   European Commission, Commission Staff Working Document. Impact Assessment. Accompanying the document: Proposal for a Directive of the European Parliament and of the Council on the protection of undisclosed know-how and business information (trade secrets) against their unlawful acquisition, use and disclosure, Brussels, 28.11.2013, SWD(2013) 471 final, Annex 21, p. 254.

secret and personal data protection, not the least when it comes to the exercise of the rights of the data subjects under the GDPR.[129]

3.3 THE PROTECTION OF KNOW-HOW UNDER THE EU TRADE SECRETS DIRECTIVE

The legal framework provided by the EU Trade Secrets Directive should be applicable not only to the "classical" trade secrets, but also to the concept of "know-how". Moreover, according to the EU Trade Secrets Directive, know-how seems to form part of a trade secret.[130]

Even before the EU Trade Secrets Directive was issued, the term "know-how" could be (and can still be) found in other EU legal acts, for example, in the block exemption regulations (BER),[131] one of which is the Technology Transfer Block Exemption Regulation (TTBER).[132] Article 1(1)(i) TTBER defines "know-how" as "a package of practical information, resulting from experience and testing, which is: (i) secret, that is to say, not generally known or easily accessible; (ii) substantial, that is to say, significant and useful for the production of the contract products; and (iii) identified, that is to say, described in a sufficiently comprehensive manner so as to make it possible to verify that it fulfils the criteria of secrecy and substantiality".[133] The latter definition differs from the definition of a trade secret that is provided in the EU Trade Secrets Directive. Yet it is BER-specific and would be applied in the framework of technology transfer agreements.

From a more general perspective, it could be noted that a precise terminology used in the case of trade secrets may be important. For example, Article 39 TRIPS[134] – the international legal provision for trade secret protection – delib-

---

[129]   See *infra* in this chapter, Section 3.4.

[130]   See, for example, recitals 2, 14.

[131]   Block exemption regulations provide a legal exemption from the application of Article 101 TFEU for particular categories of agreements. For more information on the block exemption regulations under EU competition law see, for example, *Jones, A./Sufrin, B.*, EU Competition Law: Texts, Cases, and Materials, Oxford: Oxford University Press 2014, pp. 263–266.

[132]   Commission Regulation (EU) No. 316/2014 of 21 March 2014 on the application of Article 101(3) of the Treaty on the Functioning of the European Union to categories of technology transfer agreements, [2014] OJ L 93/17.

[133]   These requirements are further explained in the Guidelines on the application of Article 101 of the Treaty on the Functioning of the European Union to technology transfer agreements ([2014] OJ C/89), para. 45.

[134]   Agreement on Trade-Related Aspects of Intellectual Property Rights (TRIPS) of 15 April 1994 (Annex to the Agreement Establishing the World Trade Organization (WTO)), as amended on 23 January 2017.

erately uses the term "undisclosed information". The selection of this term was a compromise solution during the negotiations of TRIPS in order to choose a neutral term for a "trade secret" owing to the variety of terms used in the Member States (for example, a trade secret, know-how, confidential information, business information, enterprise secrets, manufacturing secrets, etc.) and possibly different legal consequences for the infringement of the different types of secrets (for example, for a disclosure of a manufacturing secret in France).[135] In fact, the terminology that was used in the European countries with regard to a trade secret differed[136] – the circumstance, which was also taken into account by the European Commission while preparing the EU Trade Secrets Directive.[137]

In comparison with the US, it could be noted that the UTSA defines a trade secret as "information, including a formula, pattern, compilation, program, device, method, technique, or process, that: (i) derives independent economic value, actual or potential, from not being generally known to, and not being readily ascertainable by proper means by, other persons who can obtain economic value from its disclosure or use, and (ii) is the subject of efforts that are reasonable under the circumstances to maintain its secrecy". The Comment to Section 1 of the UTSA explains that, in the aforementioned definition of a trade secret, "[t]he words 'method, technique' are intended to include the concept of 'know-how'".[138]

The fact that the legal framework provided by the EU Trade Secrets Directive is identical to both know-how and trade secrets may have important legal consequences, not the least, when it comes to the data economy in general and to the developments of the AI technology in particular. As it was explained,[139] AI technology usually develops on the basis of algorithms learning with data ("learning algorithms"). "Cumulative learning" in AI is based on prior knowledge and improves the learning ability of the agents as they acquire

---

[135] For a more detailed analysis see *Surblytė, G.*, The Refusal to Disclose Trade Secrets as an Abuse of Market Dominance – *Microsoft* and Beyond, Berne: Stämpfli 2011, pp. XLVII + 263 (Munich Series on European and International Competition Law, Volume 28), pp. 20–21, 60–66.

[136] For a more detailed analysis see *ibid.*, pp. 49–85.

[137] See European Commission, Commission Staff Working Document. Impact Assessment. Accompanying the document: Proposal for a Directive of the European Parliament and of the Council on the protection of undisclosed know-how and business information (trade secrets) against their unlawful acquisition, use and disclosure, Brussels, 28.11.2013, SWD(2013) 471 final, Annex 4.

[138] National Conference of Commissioners on Uniform State Laws, Uniform Trade Secrets Act, 1979, as amended in 1985, Comment to Section 1 of the UTSA, p. 6.

[139] See *supra* Chapter 2, Section 2.1.

more knowledge.[140] In this regard, even historic data could be valuable in light of the learning processes of AI technology. Hence, data sets may be relevant for the developments of AI technology, which "learns" on the basis of their training sets. This fact explains why it can be of utmost importance for the companies to protect training sets used for machine-learning in AI as a trade secret (or, under the circumstances, as a "know-how" related to intelligent machines). If current competition is competition for future AI markets,[141] such data sets are crucial for conquering these future markets. Thus, the method, technique, not to speak of data, based on which the AI technology learns (or, to be more precise, is taught) may fall under the notion of know-how, and thereby, under a trade secret. The question whether machine-generated knowledge may amount to "know-how" and may thus be protected under the EU Trade Secrets Directive, may remain open, at least for the time being, without ruling out that such protection may be possible.

3.4 TRADE SECRET PROTECTION AND THE RIGHTS OF DATA SUBJECTS

The fact that data and (or) data sets may be protected as trade secrets begs for a deeper analysis of potential implications of such protection for the data economy. In light of the fact that data, including personal data, can be protected as a trade secret, tensions may arise between the companies' interest in protecting their trade secrets and the interests of the data subjects in protecting their personal data, including while exercising the data subjects' rights under the GDPR such as, for example, the right to access data, the right to data portability and the right not to be subject to automated decision-making.

3.4.1 The Right of Access

According to Article 8(2) of the EU Charter of Fundamental Rights,[142] "[e]veryone has the right of access to data which has been collected concerning him or her". Thereby, the right of access is a fundamental right enshrined in the EU Charter, so that strict conditions for its limitation should apply.

According to Article 15 GDPR, a data subject, while exercising their right of access, has a right not only "to obtain from the controller confirmation as to whether or not personal data concerning him or her are being processed, and,

---

[140] *Russell, S.J./Norvig, P.*, Artificial Intelligence: A Modern Approach, 3rd ed., Delhi: Pearson 2015, p. 812. On learning see *ibid.*, pp. 706–816.

[141] See *infra* Chapter 4, Section 4.6.1.

[142] Charter of the Fundamental Rights of the European Union, OJ [2016] C 202/389.

where that is the case, access to the personal data" and thereto related relevant information (Article 15(1)), but also to get from the data controller "a copy of the personal data undergoing processing" (Article 15(3)). Bearing in mind that data (a data set) may form part or the whole of a trade secret, the interests of a trade secret holder and those of a data subject may stand in a sharp conflict in the case where a data subject may be willing to exercise the right to access data, which forms part or the whole of a trade secret of a company. The GDPR does not elaborate in more detail on how such potential conflicts should be solved. Nevertheless, Article 15(4) GDPR provides an exception for the exercise of the right of access stating that "[t]he right to obtain a copy referred to in paragraph 3 shall not adversely affect the rights and freedoms of others".

In the GDPR, the right of access (Article 15 GDPR) is the only right of the data subjects with regard to which the relationship with trade secret protection is addressed. Recital 63 GDPR explains that the right of access "should not adversely affect the rights or freedoms of others, *including trade secrets* or intellectual property and in particular *the copyright protecting the software.* However, the result of those considerations should not be a refusal to provide all information to the data subject" (emphasis added). Thereby, the recital specifies the exception foreseen in Article 15(4) by stipulating that the rights or freedoms of others, as foreseen in the aforementioned legal norm, may cover the protection of trade secrets. Accordingly, the exercise of the right to access personal data should not interfere with trade secret protection. However, the recital, although it addresses the relationship between personal data and trade secrets, does not explain how the exercise of the data subject's right to access their data should be balanced with the trade secrets. It merely says that, on the one hand, the exercise of the right to access data "should not adversely affect" the protection of trade secrets, and that, on the other hand, the protection of trade secrets should not lead to situations where provision of all the relevant information to the data subject would be refused. However, these statements are rather open and leave room for interpretation.

It is noteworthy that, during the preparatory process of the EU Trade Secrets Directive, the European Data Protection Supervisor provided the comments on the proposal of the EU Trade Secrets Directive and noted that:

> The proposal should also, therefore, take account of the obligations of the holders of trade secrets as data controllers towards the individuals where their personal information is considered to be a trade secret.[143]

---

[143] European Data Protection Supervisor, Opinion of the European Data Protection Supervisor on the proposal for a directive of the European Parliament and of the Council on the protection of undisclosed know-how and business information (trade secrets) against their unlawful acquisition, use and disclosure, 12 March 2014, para. 19.

The EDPS gave an example of existing situations when a request of a data subject to access personal data was rejected "on grounds that disclosures would 'adversely affect trade secrets or intellectual property'".[144] The EDPS proposed that, in the case of a conflict between the right to protect trade secrets and the right to access personal data, "it may be advisable to provide for an adjudication process involving the relevant supervisory authorities including the national data protection authority".[145] The EU Trade Secrets Directive does not elaborate on such a possibility. On the one hand, strengthening the enforcement of the supervisory authorities in this regard may be one of the solutions for solving conflicts between trade secret holders and data subjects, while exercising their right to access data. On the other hand, however, the question may be whether these cases should rather be left for the courts to solve.

3.4.2 The Right to Data Portability

A potential area of tension as regards data and trade secret protection is the "new" right enshrined in the GDPR – the right to the portability of personal data. The relationship between the portability of personal data (Article 20 GDPR) and trade secrets is not clear in the EU Trade Secrets Directive.[146] Although this right comes close to the right of access, the right of access and the right to data portability are two independent rights listed separately in the GDPR.[147]

It should, first of all, be noted that the right to data portability, according to Article 20(1) GDPR, applies in a rather limited number of cases, i.e. when processing is based on a consent (Article 6(1)(a), Article 9(1)(a) GDPR) or on a contract (Article 6(1)(b) GDPR) and is carried out by automated means. According to recital 68 GDPR, the right to data portability "should not apply where processing is based on a legal ground other than consent or contract". A consent and a contract are two out of several legal bases for a lawful processing of data listed in Article 6 GDPR. Importantly, the right to data portability would not be applied when the processing is based on the balancing of the legitimate interests of the data controller or of any third party and the fundamental rights of the data subjects (Article 6(1)(f) GDPR). The latter provision

---

[144] *Ibid.*, para. 20.

[145] *Ibid.*, para. 22.

[146] See also *Surblytė, G.*, Data Mobility at the Intersection of Data, Trade Secret Protection and the Mobility of Employees in the Digital Economy, (2016) 65 GRUR Int. 1121, at 1125–1126.

[147] See also Article 29 Data Protection Working Party, Guidelines on the right to data portability, adopted on 13 December 2016 (last revised and adopted on 5 April 2017), 16/EN WP 242 rev.01, p. 3.

provides a margin of discretion for a data controller to decide on the processing of data.

In order to discuss the scope of the right to data portability and its intersection with trade secrets, the scope of data covered by this right should, first of all, be clarified. For this purpose, it may be helpful to analyse the proposal of the General Data Protection Regulation. Article 18(2) of the proposed General Data Protection Regulation provided the right to a data subject to transmit the provided personal data "and any other information provided by the data subject". Accordingly, the right to data portability (or, to be more precise, the right to transmit data), was meant to apply to the transfer of "personal data and any other information *provided* by the data subject" (emphasis added). Hereby, the spectrum of the data that was eligible to be transferred was rather broad: the information provided could have gone beyond the personal data of the data subject only. In fact, a careful reading of the proposed legal provision reveals that it would have been possible to request the transfer of not only of the personal data provided by the data subject, but also of any other information provided by the data subject. One possible explanation for such formulation could be found in recital 55 of the proposed General Data Protection Regulation, which revealed that the right to data portability was partly written with social networks in mind:

> The data subject should also be allowed to transmit those data, *which they have provided*, from one automated application, *such as social network*, into another one. This should apply where the data subject provided the data to the automated processing system, based on their consent or in the performance of a contract. (Emphasis added)

Yet, common as it may be to upload not only one's own personal data, but also other data in a social network, formulating the right to data portability with such a wide scope of data could have been highly problematic. It has to be kept in mind that data records in social networks are usually related and linked, so that information about one individual can be shared by other individuals.[148] Digital platforms such as social networks enable the sharing of personal data of the individuals other than the data subject. According to Article 18(2) in the proposed GDPR, the right to data portability could have covered such data that went beyond the personal information of the data subject, i.e. any information that was (merely) provided by them. It could be doubtful whether such a wide

---

[148] See *Mortazavi, M./Salah, K.*, "Privacy and Big Data", in: S. Zeadally and M. Badra (eds), Privacy in a Digital, Networked World: Technologies, Implications and Solutions, Berlin: Springer 2015, p. 53.

right to data portability could have been desired from the point of view of protecting personal information.

Moreover, Article 18(2) in the proposed GDPR did not explain what *any other information* meant. One possible interpretation could have been that "any other information" could have gone beyond personal information and could have extended to information of legal persons, even to their trade secrets. The problem in such a case could have arisen with the employees sharing their employer's trade secrets in their social media accounts.[149] Although the portability of such information would not be desired, it could have been made possible through the formulation of the right to data portability in Article 18(2) of the proposed General Data Protection Regulation. In this regard, access to data (for example, through a social media account) could have amounted to access to trade secrets – a circumstance that would have been too far-fetched as regards the right to data portability. The broad scope of the right to data portability did not take this risk into account and could have compromised companies in cases when their trade secrets were uploaded onto social networks. Indeed, the proposed text was not included in the same form in the final version of the GDPR.

According to the current legal norm enshrined in Article 20(1) GDPR, data that is eligible for data portability is personal data concerning the data subject provided by him or her. What is meant by the word "concerning" is not yet entirely clear. In the strictest sense, such personal data would be data *about* a natural person. Data portability should thereby be applicable to data about a natural person, who – knowingly and actively[150] – provides that data to a data controller. As regards the word "provided", the Article 29 Data Protection Working Party explains that:

> data "provided by" the data subject also result from the observation of his activity. As a consequence, the WP29 considers that to give its full value to this new right, "provided by" should also include the personal data that are *observed* from the

---

[149] It is, of course, true that making a trade secret available in a social network could result in the disclosure of a trade secret, so that, the argument could go, such a trade secret would be gone with the result that there would be no trade secret to be ported. However, it should be recalled that, firstly, not all trade secrets made available on the Internet would always be considered to be disclosed (see *supra* in this chapter Section 3.2.2), and, secondly, that the question whether a trade secret disclosure took place would depend on the factual question of how wide was a circle that got to know about such a trade secret. After all, users can control the number of persons who may see particular information in their social media accounts.

[150] Article 29 Data Protection Working Party, Guidelines on the right to data portability, adopted on 13 December 2016 (last revised and adopted on 5 April 2017), 16/EN WP 242 rev.01, p. 3.

activities of users such as raw data processed by a smart meter or other types of connected objects, activity logs, history of website usage or search activities. This latter category of data *does not include data that are created by the data controller* (using the data observed or directly provided as input) such as a user profile created by analysis of the raw smart metering data collected.[151] (Footnote omitted; emphasis added)

Accordingly, the right to data portability should also cover data generated by the data subject's activity,[152] but the right do data portability should not extend so far as to apply to the data created by the data controllers. To some extent, a balance thereby would be struck between data and trade secrets, since data created by a data controller can, in fact, amount to their trade secrets. Such data would not be subject to data portability. The Article 29 Data Protection Working Party suggests that only data provided by the data subject should fall under the right to data portability, whereas other data, such as "derived data", "inferred data", etc., should not.[153] Since the GDPR does not touch upon the relationship of trade secrets and data in the case of data portability, such an explanation should be particularly helpful in clarifying the intersection of data and trade secrets when it comes to the exercise of the right to data portability. However, the question is still left open as regards trade secret protection for the portions of data that go beyond the data created by the data controller (e.g. by way of data analytics), for example, data generated by the data subject's acivity and obtained by the data controller, for example, by way of observing.

With regard to the scope of the right to data portability, it is noteworthy that, in contrast to Article 18(2) of the proposed GDPR, which formulated the right to data portability as the right to transmit data, current Article 20 GDPR foresees that the right to data portability covers the right of the data subject to receive personal data concerning him or her and to transmit or, where technically feasible, to have it transmitted directly from one controller to another. Thereby, the right to data portability consists of two parts, i.e. the right to receive data and the right to transmit it or to have it transmitted. The GDPR does not explain whether these two sub-rights are cumulative or whether they can be exercised as alternatives. For example, the Article 29 Data Protection Working Party has suggested that the right to data portability should be interpreted in terms of the right to receive and "to store those data for further personal use [...] on a private device or on a private cloud, without necessarily transmitting the data to another data controller".[154] Thereby, it would be at the

---

[151]   *Ibid.*, pp. 9–10.
[152]   *Ibid.*, p. 3.
[153]   *Ibid.*, pp. 10–11.
[154]   *Ibid.*, p. 4.

discretion of the data subject to decide whether to transmit such data/to have it transmitted. However, in this regard, the question could arise on how the right to data portability would differ from the right to access data, which basically also means the right to receive a copy of personal data by the data subject (Article 15(3) GDPR). So, bearing in mind the essence of the right to data portability, it could possibly be argued that the core of this right is the right to transmit data/to have it transmitted.

In any case, the GDPR does not explain how these two sub-rights of the right to data portability should correlate with the protection of trade secrets. In light of the fact that data can be covered by a trade secret and given that such data may be requested to be received and/or transmitted, it is not clear whether any limitations should apply from the perspective of trade secret protection.

In contrast to the right of erasure (Article 17 GDPR), the right to data portability does not imply that the data that is transferred has to be deleted. Although, pursuant to Article 20(3) GDPR, both rights can be exercised together,[155] in the case where the data is not requested to be erased, even if it is transferred, it will remain in the original source.[156] Since transferred data, on the one hand, stays with the previous data controller, but on the other hand, may also appear with a new data controller, the question of how the right to data portability may affect trade secrets in this regard remains open. It could be argued that, as long as data that is transmitted does not compromise the remaining data set in terms of a trade secret, a trade secret should not be considered as disclosed. However, this question will be context-specific, depending on the facts, in particular, whether the remaining data set, without the transmitted data, may still qualify as a trade secret, particularly bearing in mind the requirements of a trade secret definition such as secrecy and commercial value (thus, providing a competitive advantage to the company). Arguably, protection of trade secrets in the case of data portability may get even more complicated in the cases of the joint controllership[157] of data.

---

[155] Article 20(3) GDPR reads: "The exercise of the right referred to in paragraph 1 of this Article shall be without prejudice to Article 17". See also recital 68 GDPR: "that right should not prejudice the right of the data subject to obtain the erasure of personal data".

[156] A limitation to the right of erasure, while exercising the right to data portability, can be found in recital 68, which explains that the right to data portability "should, in particular, not imply the erasure of personal data concerning the data subject which have been provided by him or her for the performance of a contract to the extent that and for as long as the personal data are necessary for the performance of that contract".

[157] For more detail see Article 29 Data Protection Working Party, Guidelines on the right to data portability, adopted on 13 December 2016 (last revised and adopted on 5 April 2017), 16/EN WP 242 rev.01, in particular, p. 6: "In case of a joint controller-

As regards trade secrets and the right to data portability, issues may also arise with regard to the format in which data has to be transmitted. Article 20(1) GDPR stipulates that a data subject should have a right to receive data in "a structured, commonly used, machine-readable format". In this regard, the Article 29 Data Protection Working Party, for example, noted that:

> data controllers should provide personal data using commonly used open formats [...] along with useful metadata at the best possible level of granularity, while maintaining a high level of abstraction. As such, suitable metadata should be used in order to accurately describe the meaning of exchanged information. This metadata should be enough to make the function and reuse of the data possible *but, of course, without revealing trade secrets.*[158] (Emphasis added)

Yet, finding a middle path between the right to data portability and not revealing trade secrets may not always be easy, so that it remains to be seen how the aforementioned requirement will be implemented in practice.

Furthermore, although Article 20 GDPR does not mention interoperability, recital 68 GDPR refers to interoperable formats and states that "[d]ata controllers should be encouraged to develop interoperable formats that enable data portability". Yet, it is also explained in recital 68 GDPR that "[t]he data subject's right to transmit or receive personal data concerning him or her should not create an obligation for the controllers to adopt or maintain processing systems which are technically compatible". However, the lack of interoperability may make the exercise of the right to data portability very difficult, if not impossible. After all, the exercise of the right to data portability may hinge on interoperability. If there is no interoperability, transfer of data may be hindered. The intersection of trade secrets and the right to data portability may be highly problematic when it comes to interoperability. In fact, the "problem" with interoperability in the digital economy is not new. This question was raised in the *Microsoft* case.[159] In that case, Microsoft kept the information that was needed for software interfaces as a trade secret and refused to grant access to this information for its competitors. The EU General Court decided that Microsoft, as a dominant company, abused its dominant position by refusing to grant such access (Article 102 TFEU), so that Microsoft was forced to provide

---

ship, a contract should allocate clearly the responsibilities between each data controller regarding the processing of data portability requests."

[158] Article 29 Data Protection Working Party, Guidelines on the right to data portability, adopted on 13 December 2016 (last revised and adopted on 5 April 2017), 16/EN WP 242 rev.01, p. 18. See also *ibid.*, p. 12.

[159] General Court, Case T-201/04, *Microsoft v. Commission*, 17 September 2007, [2007] E.C.R. II-3601 (ECLI:EU:T:2007:289).

interoperability information to its competitors.[160] Yet, in light of the potential issues of interoperability that may arise with regard to the right to data portability, it should be recalled that compulsory access based on Article 102 TFEU can be granted only in cases where a company has a dominant position in the relevant market, so that a good number of cases will not be covered.

Finally, according to Article 20(4) GDPR, "[t]he right referred to in paragraph 1 shall not adversely affect the rights and freedoms of others". This stipulation highly resembles Article 15(4) GDPR. Hence, on the one hand, it could be argued that, since the right to access data and the right to data portability, although they are separate rights, are related, the explanation to Article 15(4) as provided in recital 63, i.e. that the rights and freedoms of others also cover the trade secrets of data controllers, should be applied also in the case of the right to data portability as enshrined in Article 20 GDPR. On the other hand, however, recital 68, which explains Article 20 GDPR, states that "[w]here, in a certain set of personal data, more than one data subject is concerned, the right to receive the personal data should be without prejudice to the rights and freedoms of *other data subjects* in accordance with this Regulation" (emphasis added). Hence, the effect on the rights and freedoms of others while exercising the right to data portability, as enshrined in Article 20 GDPR, seems to be rather meant in terms of the rights and freedoms of other data subjects, not those of the data controller. In such a way, it remains unclear how a potential conflict between the interests of a data controller to protect their trade secrets and those of the data subject while exercising the right to data portability should be resolved.

Bearing in mind that the right to data portability consists of two sub-rights, one of which is the right to receive data, which highly resembles the right to access, it could be tempting to argue that the logic behind the right to access data (namely, that the exercise of such a right should not adversely affect trade secrets) should also apply in the case of the right to data portability. In this way, it could, by analogy, be explained that, as in the case of the right to access data, so in the case of the right to data portability, the rights and freedoms of others, including the protection of trade secrets, should not be adversely affected. Aligning these two rights as regards their intersection with trade secrets and filling in the gap that seems to exist in the GDPR in this regard, an argument could go that, bearing in mind the resemblances of these two rights, it would be illogical to apply different interpretations when it comes to the

---

[160] For a more detailed analysis of the case see *Surblytė, G.*, The Refusal to Disclose Trade Secrets as an Abuse of Market Dominance – *Microsoft* and Beyond, Berne: Stämpfli 2011, pp. XLVII + 263 (Munich Series on European and International Competition Law, Vol. 28), pp. 115–141.

exercise of these rights and the protection of trade secrets. In fact, preserving the protection of trade secrets in the case of the right to data portability may be crucial, also recalling that the right to data portability consists not only of the right to receive data, but also of the right to transmit it or to have it transmitted. Thus, the exercise of the right to data portability may result in that data having to be transmitted between competitors, so that – not least from a competition law point of view – it may be highly important that trade secrets are not transmitted along with such data.

A narrow application of the right to data portability and technical difficulties in implementing it as well as potential issues with interoperability may have to be borne in mind when it comes to the enthusiasm that has been expressed with regard to the right to data portability and competition. Claiming that the right to data portability is meant to enhance competition, the argument went that, on the basis of this right, lock-in effects may be weakened and more companies enabled to obtain access to data.[161] Yet a deeper analysis of the right to data portability shows, firstly, that the scope of the application of this right is rather narrow (i.e. a consent or a contract), secondly, that the implementation of this right depends upon technical feasibility,[162] and thirdly, that competition law issues may arise when it comes to the interoperability of the transmission of data. So, the effect of this right as regards competition, although it may be relevant, should not be overestimated.[163] Also, since the right to data portability is exercised by data subjects, the effect of this right on competition will highly depend on the data subject's decisions with the result that the effect on

---

[161] See, for example, Monopolkommission (German Monopolies Commission), "Competition Policy: The Challenge of Digital Markets", Special Report No. 68, 2015, para. 302: "A lack of data portability may thus increase users' switching costs and heighten any lock-in effect."

[162] Concerns as regards technical feasibility of the data subjects' rights such as the right to data portability and the right to be forgotten were also raised on the Member States' side during the negotiations of the GDPR. (See: Council of the European Union, Working Party on Information Exchange and Data Protection (DAPIX) on 23–24 February 2012: "Summary of Discussions", Brussels, 8 March 2012, 7221/12 DAPIX 22, p. 6: "Some delegations expressed concerns as to the technical feasibility of concepts such as the right to be forgotten and the right to data portability.")

[163] A similar opinion was expressed by the Article 29 Data Protection Working Party: "Whilst the right to personal data portability may also enhance competition between services (by facilitating service switching), the GDPR is regulating personal data and not competition. In particular, article 20 does not limit portable data to those which are necessary or useful for switching services" (footnote omitted) (Article 29 Data Protection Working Party, Guidelines on the right to data portability, adopted on 13 December 2016 (last revised and adopted on 5 April 2017), 16/EN WP 242 rev.01, p. 4).

competition may rather be a spin-off of the data subject's decisions to exercise their right to data portability.

Finally, since the right to data portability covers personal data only, it has been suggested that a right, similar to the right to data portability, should be created for non-personal data as well: for example, the portability of non-personal data is addressed by the European Commission in its Communication on Building a European Data Economy.[164] In this regard, it should, first of all, be recalled that the purpose of the right to data portability is to strengthen the data subject's control over their data (recital 68 GDPR). Such a purpose is missing when it comes to non-personal data. Instead, the logic behind the portability of non-personal data rests mostly (if not solely) on economic interests. In fact, the exercise of such a right may simply translate into claiming access to data collected by competitors on their own capacity (i.e. the "free-riding" problem). Moreover, the right to data portability, as explained above, applies to data provided by the data subject. The question hereby is how the right to the portability of non-personal data should be applied in this regard. Furthermore, for the exercise of this right, interoperability issues may arise, just as in the case of the right to the portability of personal data. So, instead of the purpose of enhancing competition, the introduction of such a right may, in fact, defeat the purpose by stifling it. Finally, the suggestion to introduce such a right does not take proper account of the fact that data sets may be identifiable, so that the portability of such "non-personal" data may also raise issues when it comes to the protection of personal data.

3.4.3 Automated Decision-Making, Including "Profiling"

Automated decision-making, including "profiling", makes the potential tension between algorithmic machines and human beings particularly visible. As pointed out by the Article 29 Data Protection Working Party:

> Advances in technology and the capabilities of big data analytics, artificial intelligence and machine learning have made it easier to create profiles and make

---

[164] European Commission, Communication from the Commission to the European Parliament, the Council, the European Economic and Social Committee and the Committee of the Regions, Brussels, 10.1.2017, COM(2017) 9 final, at p. 15; European Commission, Commission Staff Working Document on the free flow of data and emerging issues of the European data economy, Brussels, 10.1.2017, SWD(2017) 2 final, pp. 46–49. See also *Drexl, J.*, Designing Competitive Markets for Industrial Data – Between Propertisation and Access (31 October 2016). Max Planck Institute for Innovation & Competition Research Paper No. 16-13. Available at SSRN: https://papers.ssrn.com/sol3/papers.cfm?abstract_id=2862975, p. 57 ("data portability rules should also be considered for industrial relations").

automated decisions with the potential to significantly impact individuals' rights and freedoms.[165]

Article 22(1) GDPR states that a data subject has a right "not to be subject to a decision based solely on automated processing, including profiling, which produces legal effects concerning him or her or similarly significantly affects him or her". Accordingly, the GDPR, although it frames it as a data subject's right, simultaneously includes an obligation for data controllers as regards their abilities to make decisions based solely on automated decisions.

The aforementioned legal provision lists several conditions. First of all, it speaks only of the decisions that would be based *solely* on automated processing. In general terms and as explained by the Article 29 Data Protection Working Party, "[s]olely automated decision-making is the ability to make decisions by technological means without human involvement".[166] However, it is not further clarified in the GDPR what "a decision based solely on automated processing" is. Although, at first sight, it may seem to be self-explanatory, difficulties may arise in practice when deciding what scope of human intervention at which stage of the decision-making may be needed in order to draw a conclusion that a decision was no longer based solely on automated processing,[167] with the result that the conditions listed in Article 22(1) GDPR will not apply. This may be particularly so when an algorithm makes a decision and a human being only implements it. It is argued in this regard that a decisive factor when assessing whether a solely automated decision was made should be the question to what extent a human being had influence on the content of the decision.[168] Secondly, a data subject has a right not to be subject to the aforementioned decisions if such decisions produce legal effects concerning data subjects or similarly significantly affecting them. Recital 71 GDPR gives an example of an "automatic refusal of an online credit application or e-recruiting practices without any human intervention". Thirdly, although Article 22(1) GDPR mentions both automated decision-making and profiling, automated decision-making and "profiling" do not necessarily overlap,[169] yet

---

[165] Article 29 Data Protection Working Party, Guidelines on Automated individual decision-making and Profiling for the purposes of Regulation 2016/769, adopted on 3 October 2017, as last revised and adopted on 6 February 2018, 17/EN WP251rev.01, p. 5.

[166] *Ibid.*, p. 8.

[167] For more detail see, for example, *Martini, M.* in: Paal, B.P./Pauly, D.A., Datenschutz-Grundverordnung, München: C.H. Beck 2017, Art. 22, pp. 256–259.

[168] *Martini, M.* in: Paal, B.P./Pauly, D.A., Datenschutz-Grundverordnung, München: C.H. Beck 2017, Art. 22, p. 256, para. 17.

[169] Profiling, as defined in Article 4(4) GDPR, is broader in that the definition refers to *any* form of automated processing, whereas Article 22 GDPR speaks about a decision-making based *solely* on automated processing.

"[s]omething that starts off as a simple automated decision-making process could become one based on profiling, depending upon how the data is used".[170]

Although Article 22(1) GDPR states that a data subject has a right not be subject to decision-making based solely on automated processing, Article 22(2) GDPR provides a list of exceptions.[171] According to Article 22(2) GDPR, the aforementioned right does not apply if the decision "is necessary for entering into, or performance of, a contract between the data subject and a data controller" (Article 22(2)(a) GDPR), if it "is authorised by Union or Member State law to which the controller is subject and which also lays down suitable measures to safeguard the data subject's rights and freedoms and legitimate interests" (Article 22(2)(b) GDPR) or if it "is based on the data subject's explicit consent" (Article 22(2)(c) GDPR). Thereby, the GDPR provides for a list of cases when decision-making based solely on automated processing may be allowed. Such a list is broader than, for example, some national legal provisions. For instance, the UK Data Protection Act of 2018 states in Section 49(1) that "a controller may not take a significant decision based solely on automated processing unless that decision is required or authorised by law". Thereby, exceptions to the solely automated decision-making can be made only on the basis of the law, which is but only one case when such decision-making would be allowed by the GDPR. Notably, whereas Article 22(3) GDPR, as explained below, entitles an individual to request human intervention in cases where the decision is made on the basis of necessity to enter into or to perform a contract or on the basis of a data subject's consent, the data subject in such cases has no right not to be subject to the decision-making based solely on automated processing in the first place.

Article 22(3) GDPR stipulates that when decision-making based solely on automated processing takes place because the decision is necessary for entering into or for the performance of a contract (Article 22(2)(a)) or when it is based on the data subject's consent (Article 22(2)(b) GDPR), "the data controller shall implement suitable measures to safeguard the data subject's rights and freedoms and legitimate interests, at least the right to obtain human intervention on the part of the controller, to express his or her point of view and to contest the decision". Article 22 GDPR, however, does not explain what such "suitable measures" are. To some extent, such an explanation is provided in recital 71, which says that, when decision-making is based on solely auto-

---

[170] Article 29 Data Protection Working Party, Guidelines on Automated individual decision-making and Profiling for the purposes of Regulation 2016/769, adopted on 3 October 2017, as last revised and adopted on 6 February 2018, 17/EN WP251rev.01, p. 8.

[171] Exceptions to the exceptions listed in Article 22(2) GDPR are provided in Article 22(4) GDPR with regard to special categories of personal data.

mated processing, "such processing should be subject to suitable safeguards, which *should include specific information to the data subject* and the right to obtain human intervention, to express his or her point of view, *to obtain an explanation of the decision reached after such assessment* and to challenge the decision" (emphasis added). Accordingly, a data subject has a right to receive "specific information" and to get "an explanation of the decision reached". These terms are rather abstract and are not further specified in the legal framework of Article 22 GDPR.

However, Article 15 GDPR, which speaks about the right to access data, stipulates that, a data subject, while exercising their right to access data, has a right to get information about "the existence of automated decision-making, including profiling, referred to in Article 22(1) and (4) and, at least in those cases, *meaningful information about the logic involved*, as well as the significance and the envisaged consequences of such processing for the data subject" (Article 15(1)(h) GDPR) (emphasis added).[172] Hence, the data subject has a right not only to get information about the existence and the consequences of decision-making based on solely automated processing, but is also entitled to receive "meaningful information about the logic involved".[173] It is here where the tension between personal data protection and trade secrets may come into play.

It might be that the "information about the logic involved" may be closely related to a company's trade secret. For example, in the former UK Data Protection Act of 1998 (which was replaced by the Data Protection Act 2018), Section 7(1)(d), it was stated that a person had the right to be informed about the logic involved in the decision-taking based on profiling, except for cases "if, and to the extent that, the information constitutes a trade secret".[174]

Also, in Germany, for example, the Federal Supreme Court of Germany[175] confirmed that the relevant content of the scoring formula could be protected

---

[172] Similar provisions may be found in Articles 13 and 14 GDPR, which elaborate on the obligations of data controllers to provide information to data subjects. An obligation to provide information related to automated decision-making, in a similar formulation as it is enshrined in Article 15(1)(h), could be found respectively in Article 13(2)(f) and Article 14(2)(g) GDPR.

[173] See also Article 29 Data Protection Working Party, Guidelines on Automated individual decision-making and Profiling for the purposes of Regulation 2016/769, adopted on 3 October 2017, as last revised and adopted on 6 February 2018, 17/EN WP251rev.01, p. 25.

[174] On the comment of the provision see also *Malgieri, G., Trade Secrets v. Personal Data*: a possible solution for balancing rights, (2016) 6(2) International Data Privacy Law 102, at 107.

[175] Federal Supreme Court of Germany, 28 January 2014 (VI ZR 156/13).

as a trade secret.[176] The disclosure of the scoring formula was not considered by the Court to be captured by the right of the data subject to get the explanation on the scoring values.[177] Specifically, it was explained that the right to know the logic behind the scoring values did not extend to the information about the comparison groups built for the purposes of scoring and covered by the formula or the emphases of the scoring formula; instead, it was said that the aforementioned right was solely related to personal data and how it influenced the reaching of the particular scoring result. Yet the latter information was said not to cover the scoring formula and its elements themselves.[178] Importantly, it was noted by the Court that, although the right to know the logic behind the scoring result did not extend to information about the comparison groups (the circumstance, which made it more difficult for the data subject to assess/check the correctness of the result), this limitation was said to be based on the intention of the legislator to find a balance between the transparency requirement, on the one hand, and the protection of trade secrets, on the other, with the result that the right to know the logic behind the scoring result covered personal data, but not (the disclosure of) the scoring formula.[179] The Court stressed that scoring was rather an automated data evaluation, based on which the decision was made, since the decision itself was still made by a human being (hence, it was not a completely automated decision-making).[180]

The judgement of the Federal Supreme Court of Germany was criticized by academia,[181] in particular with regard to the relationship between the transparency requirements and the protection of trade secrets. The argument went that the balance, in the way suggested by the Court, raised constitutional concerns, in particular with regard to the right to informational self-determination (*informationelle Selbstbestimmung*), which was said to cover the right to obtain information. Hence, an academic suggestion was that milder tools could be implemented in this regard, for example, the covenant on the side of the recipient of information not to disclose particular information, instead of a complete refusal to grant information based on the protection of a trade secret.[182]

In fact, finding a neat balance between providing information "about the logic involved" without, at the same time, disclosing company's trade secrets may be challenging in practice. It seems to be clear that the fact that the deci-

---

176 *Ibid.*, para. 27.
177 *Ibid.*, para. 28.
178 *Ibid.*, para. 29.
179 *Ibid.*, para. 32.
180 *Ibid.*, para. 34.
181 *Gärtner, S.*, Anmerkung (BGH, VI ZR 156/13), (2014) Zeitschrift für Bank- und Kapitalmarktrecht 197.
182 *Ibid.*, at 198.

sion is made based on the calculations done by an algorithm and that such an algorithm could be protected by a trade secret should not lead to the situations where an individual is entirely deprived of their right to know why, how and based on what criteria that particular decision was made. Hence, although information such as, for example, a scoring formula, could be protected as a trade secret, ways should exist of explaining to the data subject the criteria based on which the decision was made. For example, the Article 29 Data Protection Working Party explains that:

> The growth and complexity of machine-learning can make it challenging to understand how an automated decision-making process or profiling works. The controller should find *simple ways* to tell the data subject *about the rationale behind*, or *the criteria* relied on in reaching the decision. The GDPR requires the controller to provide meaningful information about the logic involved, *not necessarily a complex explanation of the algorithms used or disclosure of the full algorithm.* [...] The information provided should, however, be sufficiently comprehensive for the data subject to understand the reasons for the decision.[183] (Footnote omitted; emphasis added)

On the one hand, it should be possible to provide criteria or to explain other factors related to the logic behind the decision made, even if the latter was made with the help of algorithms. On the other hand, however, it may be asked whether this may indeed always be possible in the case of solely automated-decision-making, i.e. without any involvement of human beings.[184] Bearing in mind the developments of AI, it remains to be hoped that human beings will remain capable of providing an explanation of the decisions made by automated processing, which would be in the hands of the (intelligent)

---

[183] Article 29 Data Protection Working Party, Guidelines on Automated individual decision-making and Profiling for the purposes of Regulation 2016/769, adopted on 3 October 2017, as last revised and adopted on 6 February 2018, 17/EN WP251rev.01, p. 25.

[184] Opacity ("black box-effect") as one of the features of AI technologies has been stressed in the White Paper on Artificial Intelligence issued in February 2020 by the European Commission (European Commission, White Paper on Artificial Intelligence – A European approach to excellence and trust, Brussels, 19.2.2020, COM(2020) 65 final, p. 12: "The specific characteristics of many AI technologies, including opacity ('black box-effect'), complexity, unpredictability and partially autonomous behaviour, may make it hard to verify compliance with, and may hamper the effective enforcement of, rules of existing EU law meant to protect fundamental rights. Enforcement authorities and affected persons might lack the means to verify how a given decision made with the involvement of AI was taken and, therefore, whether the relevant rules were respected"; see also *ibid.*, p. 14).

machines, which – by definition – become increasingly more and more intelligent (and, thus, also more autonomous).[185]

3.5 TRADE SECRETS AS PART OF THE RIGHT TO CONDUCT BUSINESS

Trade secrets may be a valuable asset of the company and may thus form part of a broader right, i.e. the right to conduct business. The fact that data sets are often a valuable asset of the companies that do business in the economy, which is strongly driven by data and algorithms, has time and again been pointed out by the European Commission, according to which, "data have a value as a business asset [...]".[186] The role of data sets as a valuable asset of the companies has also been stressed by the EU Commissioner for Competition – Margrethe Vestager.[187]

In this regard, trade secret protection for data (data sets) may need to be considered in a broader context, i.e. the right to conduct business.

For example, trade secrets – as part of the right to conduct business – are protected by tort law in Germany. Here, trade secrets – as an asset, not as property[188] – are protected under Section 823(1) of the German Civil Code (BGB).[189] According to this norm, the "right which extends to the establishment and exercise of a business" (*das Recht am eingerichteten und ausgeübten Gewerbebetrieb*) forms part of "a special right" (*sonstiges Recht*), protected under Section 823(1) of the German Civil Code. In 1955, The Federal Supreme Court of Germany explained in *Schwermetall-Kokillenguß* that trade secrets, although they are not protected as exclusive rights, can be protected as part of

---

[185] See *supra* Chapter 2, Section 2.1.

[186] European Commission, Commission Staff Working Document on the free flow of data and emerging issues of the European data economy, Brussels, 10.1.2017, SWD(2017) 2 final, p. 37.

[187] *Vestager, M.*, "Making Data Work for Us", Speech, 9 September 2016 (https://ec .europa.eu/competition/speeches/index_2016.html).

[188] For an analysis see also *Surblytė, G.*, The Refusal to Disclose Trade Secrets as an Abuse of Market Dominance – *Microsoft* and Beyond, Berne: Stämpfli 2011, pp. XLVII + 263 (Munich Series on European and International Competition Law, Vol. 28), pp. 55–56.

[189] Section 823(1) of the German Civil Code (BGB) reads: "A person who, either willfully or negligently, wrongfully interferes with or injures the life, body, health, freedom, property, or special right (sonstiges Recht) of another is bound to compensate him for any damage arising from said injury." (Translation from *Knospe, M.*, Chapter 15: Germany, in: Melvin F. Jager (ed.), Trade Secrets Throughout the World, Volume 2, Eagan, MN: Thomson Reuters 2014–2015, p. 96.)

the right to conduct business.[190] The Federal Constitutional Court of Germany further held in 1961 that the right which extends to the establishment and exercise of a business falls under the "property guarantee" of Article 14 of the German Constitution, although only to the extent that the business is treated as a factual and legal entirety, so that protection is granted against interference with the substance of such an entirety, but not with the separate parts of it.[191] Hence, as part of the right to the establishment and exercise of a business, trade secrets may be protected under Section 823(1) of the German Civil Code and, thereby, may also fall under the Constitutional "property guarantee".

In the data economy, data sets processed by the company and protected as their trade secrets may often form part of the business conducted by the company. In fact, bearing in mind that business models have increasingly been based on the processing of vast amounts of data, (unique) data sets may constitute a substantial part of the assets related to a company's business operations. Thus, the fact that trade secrets, as a valuable asset of the company, may form part of the right to conduct business may be highly relevant. This begs the question of balancing the right to data protection with the right to conduct business. Thus, instead of the "free flow of data" advocated by the European Commission,[192] it may rather be a "balanced" flow of data that may need to be spoken of. This may, first and foremost, be due to the fundamental rights involved.

The fact that trade secrets, as a valuable asset of the company, may form part of the right to conduct business may beg the question of how to balance fundamental rights such as the right to data protection and the right to privacy, on the one hand, and the freedom to conduct a business, on the other. In other words, the protection of personal data in the data economy may need to be weighed against the right to conduct business in general and the protection of trade secrets in particular. It should be recalled that the right to privacy is enshrined in Article 8(1) of the European Convention of Human Rights.[193] In

---

[190]   Federal Supreme Court of Germany, 18 March 1955 (*Schwermetall-Kokillenguß*), (1955) GRUR 468, at 472. See also Federal Supreme Court of Germany, 9 March 1989 (*Forschungskosten*), (1990) GRUR 221, at 222.

[191]   Federal Constitutional Court of Germany, 29 November 1961, 13 BVerfGE 225, at 229. See also *Surblytė, G.*, The Refusal to Disclose Trade Secrets as an Abuse of Market Dominance – *Microsoft* and Beyond, Berne: Stämpfli 2011, pp. XLVII + 263 (Munich Series on European and International Competition Law, Vol. 28), p. 56.

[192]   See *supra* Chapter 2, Section 2.4.1.

[193]   Convention for the Protection of Human Rights and Fundamental Freedoms, which entered into force on 3 September 1953, with amendments that entered into force on 1 June 2010 (https://www.echr.coe.int/Documents/Convention_ENG.pdf).

the EU Charter of Fundamental Rights,[194] the right to personal data protection (Article 8(1)) is an independent fundamental right enshrined separately from the right to privacy (Article 7). The right to personal data protection is also stipulated in Article 16(1) TFEU. Yet the EU Charter of Fundamental Rights also speaks about the freedom to conduct a business (Article 16).

In fact, the Explanatory Memorandum of the Proposal for the EU Trade Secrets Directive notes that:

> This initiative does not negatively affect fundamental rights. In particular, the initiative will promote the right to property and the right to conduct a business.[195]

However, the EU Trade Secrets Directive does not explain how different fundamental rights would have to be balanced. Recital 34 of the EU Trade Secrets Directive merely stipulates that "this Directive respects the fundamental rights and observes the principles recognized in particular by the Charter, notably the right to respect for private and family life, the right to protection of personal data, [...] the freedom to conduct a business".

According to the GDPR, the right to personal data protection is not an absolute right. Recital 4 GDPR explains that:

> The processing of personal data should be designed to serve mankind. The right to the protection of personal data *is not an absolute right*; it must be considered in relation to its *function in society and be balanced against other fundamental rights*, in accordance with *the principle of proportionality*. This Regulation respects all fundamental rights and observes the freedoms and principles recognised in the Charter as enshrined in the Treaties, in particular [...] *freedom to conduct a business*. (Emphasis added)

---

[194] Charter of Fundamental Rights and Freedoms of the European Union, OJ [2016] C 202/389.

[195] European Commission, Proposal for a Directive of the European Parliament and of the Council on the protection of undisclosed know-how and business information (trade secrets) against their unlawful acquisition, use and disclosure, Brussels, 28.11.2013, COM(2013) 813 final (2013/0402 (COD)), Explanatory Memorandum, Section 2.2., p. 6. For a more detailed analysis by the European Commission of the (potential) impact of the EU Trade Secrets Directive on fundamental rights see: European Commission, Commission Staff Working Document. Impact Assessment. Accompanying the document: Proposal for a Directive of the European Parliament and of the Council on the protection of undisclosed know-how and business information (trade secrets) against their unlawful acquisition, use and disclosure, Brussels, 28.11.2013, SWD(2013) 471 final, Annex 12, pp. 248–262.

Thereby, a functional approach as regards the right to personal data protection is enshrined, stressing the importance of such right to be balanced against other fundamental rights and freedoms, including the freedom to conduct a business.

The exercise of the fundamental rights and freedoms may be limited only upon strict conditions listed in Article 52 of the EU Charter of Fundamental Rights. According to Article 52(1) of the EU Charter, any limitations of the rights and freedoms enshrined in the EU Charter shall be subject to five cumulative conditions. Any such limitation must, first and foremost, be provided for by law. Secondly, such limitations must respect the essence of the fundamental rights and freedoms. Thirdly, such limitations are subject to the principle of proportionality. Fourthly, such limitations must be necessary. Fifthly, such limitations must meet the objectives of general interest recognized by the Union or the need to protect the rights and freedoms of others.

These conditions were explained by the ECJ in the *Digital Rights Ireland* case[196] where the ECJ was requested a preliminary ruling on the validity of Directive 2006/24/EC on the retention of data generated or processed in connection with the provision of publicly available electronic communications services or of public communications networks.

As regards the first condition, i.e. that the limitations have to be provided for by law, it could be noted that, according to the Advocate General in *Digital Rights Ireland*, "the interference with the right to privacy which the directive constitutes must be regarded as being formally provided for by law".[197] With regard to trade secret protection for data sets (which may involve personal data) and the freedom to conduct a business, two EU legal acts are mostly relevant, namely, the GDPR and the EU Trade Secrets Directive. Although a directive is not an EU legal act that is directly applicable in the Member States, following the explanations of the Advocate General in *Digital Rights Ireland*, it would fulfil the first requirement as regards the limitations of fundamental rights, i.e. that such limitations have to be enshrined in the law.

With regard to the second condition, i.e. the respect of the essence of the fundamental rights, the ECJ, in *Digital Rights Ireland*, stated that the retention of data, although it was held to constitute "a particularly serious interference" with the right to privacy, was "not such as to adversely affect the essence" of this right given that the directive did "not permit the acquisition of knowledge of the content of the electronic communications as such".[198] With regard to the

---

[196]   ECJ, Joined Cases C-293/12 and C-594/12, *Digital Rights Ireland Ltd*, 8 April 2014, ECLI:EU:C:2014:238.

[197]   Opinion of Advocate General Cruz Villalón delivered on 12 December 2013 in Case C-293/12 and Case C-594/12, ECLI:EU:C:2013:845, para. 108.

[198]   ECJ, Joined Cases C-293/12 and C-594/12, *Digital Rights Ireland Ltd*, 8 April 2014, ECLI:EU:C:2014:238, para. 39.

right to personal data protection, the ECJ held that the retention of data did not "adversely affect the essence" of this fundamental right:

> because Article 7 of Directive 2006/24 provides [...] that [...] certain principles of data protection and data security must be respected by providers of publicly available electronic communications services or of public communications networks. According to those principles, Member States are to ensure that appropriate technical and organizational measures are adopted against accidental or unlawful destruction, accidental loss or alteration of the data.[199]

When it comes to trade secrets that may involve personal data, the EU Trade Secrets Directive states in recital 35 that "[i]t is important that the rights to respect for private and family life and to protection of personal data of any person whose personal data may be processed by the trade secret holder when taking steps to protect a trade secret [...] be respected". However, it does not contain any specific provisions on how these rights should be respected. Yet, in the case of trade secrets, it will often be that such data will not only be acquired by trade secret holders, but may also be further processed. Bearing in mind the "reasonable steps" requirement for the protection of a trade secret, it could be that measures will often be in place protecting the security of such data, which would form part of a trade secret. Whether such measures will always be sufficient may have to be decided on a case-by-case basis. In other words, the question whether trade secret protection for personal data may interfere with and adversely affect the essence of the fundamental rights of individuals may depend on how (to what extent, in which context and what circumstances, based on what conditions, etc.) personal data, forming part or the whole of a trade secret may be processed.

The third condition is the principle of proportionality. In this regard, the ECJ, in *Digital Rights Ireland*, stipulated that:

> according to the settled case-law of the Court, the principle of proportionality requires that acts of the EU institutions be appropriate for attaining the legitimate objectives pursued by the legislation at issue and do not exceed the limits of what is appropriate and necessary in order to achieve those objectives.[200] (References to the cited cases omitted)

One of the primary aims of the EU Trade Secrets Directive was to harmonize trade secret protection in the EU. When the European Commission published

---

[199] *Ibid.*, para. 40.
[200] *Ibid.*, para. 46.

a proposal for the EU Trade Secrets Directive back in November 2013,[201] the Explanatory Memorandum of the aforementioned Proposal said that:

> experience in this field shows that even when Member States are coordinated to a certain extent, e.g. by the TRIPS Agreement, a sufficient degree of substantive harmonisation of national rules is not achieved. Hence, the necessary scale and effects of the proposed action are at EU level.[202]

Indeed, although TRIPS,[203] which entered into force in 1995, contained one legal provision (Article 39) on undisclosed information, it was possible for the Members of the aforementioned agreement to go beyond this legal provision in their national laws owing to the fact that TRIPS provided minimum harmonization (Article 1(1) TRIPS). Thus, recital 6 of the EU Trade Secrets Directive stipulates that "[n]otwithstanding the TRIPS Agreement, there are important differences in the Member States' legislation as regards the protection of trade secrets". Yet the EU Trade Secret Directive provides a legal framework for harmonized rules "on the protection against the unlawful acquisition, use and disclosure of trade secrets" (Article 1(1) of EU Trade Secrets Directive), but allows the Member States to provide a more far-reaching protection (minimum harmonization[204]). Owing to the fact that the aforementioned Directive speaks only of minimum harmonization, it remains to be seen to what extent the harmonization of trade secret law in the EU will be achieved. It is noteworthy that the purpose of such harmonization was to encourage cross-border economic activities and to promote innovation by improving the conditions for such innovation to take place.[205] In the data economy, the achievement of this goal may be closely related to the processing of data, which may also include personal data.

The fourth condition requires that limitations should be necessary. In *Digital Rights Ireland*, the ECJ held that, whereas the fight against serious crime was

---

[201] European Commission, Proposal for a Directive of the European Parliament and of the Council on the protection of undisclosed know-how and business information (trade secrets) against their unlawful acquisition, use and disclosure, Brussels, 28.11.2013, COM(2013) 813 final (2013/0402 (COD)).

[202] *Ibid.*, Explanatory Memorandum, Section 3, p. 7.

[203] Agreement on Trade-Related Aspects of Intellectual Property Rights (TRIPS) of 15 April 1994 (Annex to the Agreement Establishing the World Trade Organization (WTO)), as amended on 23 January 2017.

[204] Article 1(1), recital 10 of the EU Trade Secrets Directive.

[205] European Commission, Proposal for a Directive of the European Parliament and of the Council on the protection of undisclosed know-how and business information (trade secrets) against their unlawful acquisition, use and disclosure, Brussels, 28.11.2013, COM(2013) 813 final (2013/0402 (COD)), Explanatory Memorandum, Section 1, p. 2.

one of the objectives for data retention, "such an objective of general interest, however fundamental it may be, does not, in itself, justify a retention measure such as that established by Directive 2006/24 being considered to be necessary for the purpose of that fight".[206] Furthermore, it was stated that:

> the EU legislation in question must lay down clear and precise rules governing the scope and application of the measure in question and imposing minimum safeguards so that the persons whose data have been retained have sufficient guarantees to effectively protect their personal data against the risk of abuse and against any unlawful access and use of that data. [...] The need for such safeguards is all the greater where, as laid down in Directive 2006/24, personal data are subjected to automatic processing and where there is a significant risk of unlawful access to those data.[207] (References to the case-law of the European Court of Human Rights omitted)

The ECJ noted that the retention of data pursuant to the Directive interfered with "the fundamental rights of practically the entire European population",[208] since it covered "in a generalized manner, all persons and all means of electronic communication as well as all traffic data without any differentiation, limitation or exception being made in the light of the objective of fighting against serious crime".[209] Thus, the ECJ held that "Directive 2006/24 did not provide for sufficient safeguards, as required by Article 8 of the Charter, to ensure effective protection of the data retained against the risk of abuse and against any unlawful access and use of that data".[210] The ECJ said that "by adopting Directive 2006/24, the EU legislature has exceeded the limits imposed by compliance with the principle of proportionality in the light of Articles 7, 8 and 52(1) of the Charter"[211] and considered Directive 2006/24 to be invalid.[212]

When it comes to trade secret protection for personal data, it could, in fact, be questioned whether limitations of the fundamental rights of individuals are necessary. On the one hand, it could be argued that the objective of promoting innovation is very broad and unspecified, so that, the argument could go, the limitation of the fundamental right to personal data protection should not be considered as necessary to achieve this goal. On the other hand, however, the EU Trade Secrets Directive provides a legal framework against unlawful

---

[206] ECJ, Joined Cases C-293/12 and C-594/12, *Digital Rights Ireland Ltd*, 8 April 2014, ECLI:EU:C:2014:238, para. 51.

[207] *Ibid.*, paras 54–55.

[208] *Ibid.*, para. 56.

[209] *Ibid.*, para. 57.

[210] *Ibid.*, para. 66.

[211] *Ibid.*, para. 69.

[212] *Ibid.*, para. 71.

acquisition, use and disclosure of trade secrets, so that it could be argued that, at least to some extent, it strikes a balance between the limitations of the fundamental rights of individuals and the interest of the business to protect their trade secrets that may include personal data.

With regard to the fifth condition, i.e. that the limitations must meet the objective of the general interest or the need to protect the rights and freedoms of others, the ECJ, in *Digital Rights Ireland*, held that "the retention of data for the purpose of allowing the competent national authorities to have possible access to those data, as required by Directive 2006/24, genuinely satisfies an objective of general interest".[213] In this regard, it could be recalled that the limitations, which were discussed by the ECJ in *Digital Rights Ireland*, were analysed in the case of access to data by public bodies. In the data economy, however, there is a rising need for private parties to access, and often to further process, vast amounts of personal data – importantly, for commercial purposes. Thus, in the case of trade secrets, it may often be that it will be the rights of others that may need to be protected, specifically, the right to conduct business. Therefore, this right may have to be balanced against the right to protect personal data.

In the case-law of the ECJ, the right to data protection and the right to conduct business was, for example, balanced against intellectual property rights, such as copyright.[214] It was held that the request to install a filtering system in order to monitor potential copyright infringements did not strike "a fair balance" as regards the right to conduct business by the Internet service providers (ISPs) and the protection of copyright.[215] Moreover, it was said that "the contested filtering system may also infringe the fundamental rights of that ISP's customers, namely their right to protection of their personal data".[216]

As regards the free movement of data, the ECJ held in the *Max Schrems* case that "the national supervisory authorities must, in particular, ensure *a fair balance* between, on the one hand, observance of the fundamental right to privacy and, on the other hand, the interests requiring free movement of personal data" (reference omitted; emphasis added).[217] Also, in *Lindqvist*, the ECJ stated that: "the harmonization of those national rules must seek to ensure not

---

[213] *Ibid.*, para. 44.

[214] ECJ, Case C-275/06, *Promusicae v. Telefónica de España SAU*, 29 January 2008, ECLI:EU:C:2008:54, paras 62–68; ECJ, Case C-70/10, *Scarlet Extended SA v. SABAM*, 24 November 2011, ECLI:EU:C:2011:711, paras 42–50.

[215] ECJ, Case C-70/10, *Scarlet Extended SA v. SABAM*, 24 November 2011, ECLI: EU:C:2011:711, para. 49.

[216] *Ibid.*, para. 50.

[217] ECJ, Case C-362/14, *Maximillian Schrems v. Data Protection Commissioner*, 6 October 2015, ECLI:EU:C:2015:650, para. 42.

only the free flow of such data between Member States but also the safeguard-ing of the fundamental rights of individuals. Those objectives may of course be inconsistent with one another".[218]

Finally, balancing may have to be done by data controllers themselves before starting to process personal data. Legitimate interests of a data control-ler, which override the fundamental rights of a data subject, form one of the legal bases for the lawful processing of personal data. Article 6(1)(f) GDPR includes balancing and stipulates that processing shall be lawful if such "pro-cessing is necessary for the purposes of the legitimate interests pursued by the controller or by a third party, except where such interests are overridden by the interests or fundamental rights and freedoms of the data subject which require protection of personal data, in particular where the data subject is a child". According to this legal provision, the legitimate interests that may have to be balanced against the fundamental rights of a data subject may be related not only to the data controllers themselves, but also to a third party. Recital 47 GDPR explains that, while considering whether the legitimate interests of a data controller may override the fundamental rights of the data subjects, account should be taken of "the reasonable expectations of data subjects based on their relationship with the controller", for example, "where the data subject is a client or in the service of the controller". Furthermore, the aforementioned recital stipulates that:

> the existence of a legitimate interest would need careful assessment including whether a data subject can reasonably expect at the time and in the context of the collection of the personal data that processing for that purpose may take place. The interests and fundamental rights of the data subject *could in particular override* the interest of the data controller where personal data are processed in circumstances *where data subjects do not reasonably expect further processing*. (Emphasis added)

Accordingly, the limitations to the free flow of data are included in the legal framework for personal data protection by, on the one hand, allowing the pro-cessing of such data, yet, on the other hand, requiring the balancing of the busi-ness's interests against the fundamental rights of the data subjects. However, the criteria for such balancing, although provided in the GDPR, remain rather abstract. Although they may be clearer in the case of data processing by a data controller (for example, on the basis of a relationship between a data controller and a data subject), this may not necessarily be the case when it comes to a third party.

---

[218] ECJ, Case C-101/01, *Lindqvist*, 6 November 2003, ECLI:EU:C:2003:569, para. 79.

Hence, although, in the case of the processing of personal data for commercial purposes by private parties, it may be a "balanced" flow of data rather than a "free" flow of data that may take place, the question of how (or based on what criteria) the balancing of the right to data protection and the right to conduct business should be done, remains open. Based on the principle of proportionality, such balancing remains to be solved on a case-by-case basis.

Yet, it is noteworthy that, even if the EU Trade Secrets Directive were considered to be compatible with Article 8(1) of the EU Charter of Fundamental Rights, the right to conduct business may need to be balanced not only against the right to data protection, but also against the right to privacy (Article 7 of the EU Charter of Fundamental Rights). In *Digital Rights Ireland*, the Advocate General held that:

> the fact that Directive 2006/24 may satisfy fully the requirements of Article 8(2) and (3) of the Charter and be considered not to be incompatible with Article 8 of the Charter in no way means that it is fully compatible with the requirements resulting from the right to privacy guaranteed by Article 7 of the Charter. [...] Since the "private sphere" forms the core of the "personal sphere", it cannot be ruled out that legislation limiting the right to the protection of personal data in compliance with Article 8 of the Charter may nevertheless be regarded as constituting a disproportionate interference with Article 7 of the Charter.[219]

Accordingly, even if legislation complies with the fundamental right of data protection, it might be that it interferes with the right to privacy. For example, the Advocate General held that:

> the fact remains that the collection and, above all, the retention, in huge databases, of the large quantities of data generated or processed in connection with most of the everyday electronic communications of citizens of the Union constitute a serious interference with the privacy of those individuals, even if they only establish the conditions allowing retrospective scrutiny of their personal and professional activities. The collection of such data establishes the conditions for surveillance which, although carried out only retrospectively when the data are used, none the less constitutes a permanent threat throughout the data retention period to the right of citizens of the Union to confidentiality in their private lives. The vague feeling of surveillance created raises very acutely the question of the data retention period.[220]
> (Footnotes omitted)

In light of this, the question whether trade secret protection for personal data does not unjustifiably interfere with the right to privacy may be very topical

---

[219] Opinion of Advocate General Cruz Villalón delivered on 12 December 2013 in Case C-293/12 and Case C-594/12, ECLI:EU:C:2013:845, paras 60–61.

[220] *Ibid.*, para. 72.

indeed. It remains to be seen to what extent this question may have to be solved by the courts.

3.6 TRADE SECRETS AS A FORM OF "DATA OWNERSHIP"?

In light of the debate by the European Commission and academia on data ownership and access to data, it should be noted that trade secrets are not a typical form of ownership. The EU Trade Secrets Directive explicitly states that trade secret holders are not granted exclusive rights.[221] Instead, trade secrets are protected within the legal framework against unfair competition. Such a – weaker – protection of trade secrets, as compared with the intellectual property rights such as, for example, patents,[222] was a compromise solution when including the protection of trade secrets in the international agreement, i.e. TRIPS.[223]

In the context of the data economy, the lack of exclusivity has been considered by some scholars, for example, Zech, as a drawback of trade secret protection for data.[224] Furthermore, Zech, as explained before,[225] suggested distinguishing between the semantic and the syntactic level of information. According to him, "semantic information as a property causes greater losses to the public domain than syntactic information. Having an exclusive right to use semantic information (e.g. certain knowledge) gives a greater range of exclusive competences than having an exclusive right to use syntactic information (e.g. a certain text)".[226] He therefore argued that "some good reasons exist for creating a new exclusive right to use data (defined as syntactic information generated by machines with automated sensors) for big data analyses pertaining to the person economically maintaining the machine".[227]

---

[221] Directive (EU) 2016/943 of the European Parliament and of the Council of 8 June 2016 on the protection of undisclosed know-how and business information (trade secrets) against their unlawful acquisition, use and disclosure, OJ [2016] L 157/1, recital 16.

[222] For a more detailed analysis on the nature of trade secret protection, also from a comparative perspective, see, for example, *Surblytė, G.*, The Refusal to Disclose Trade Secrets as an Abuse of Market Dominance – *Microsoft* and Beyond, Berne: Stämpfli 2011, pp. XLVII + 263 (Munich Series on European and International Competition Law, Volume 28), pp. 19–88.

[223] For a more detailed analysis see *ibid.*, pp. 23–28.

[224] *Zech, H.*, A legal framework for a data economy in the European Digital Single Market: rights to use data, (2016) 11(6) Journal of Intellectual Property Law & Practice 460, 466: "the information is not protected against any use, but only against certain attacks on the secret" (for a more detailed analysis see *ibid.*, pp. 465–466).

[225] See *supra* in this chapter Section 3.2.1.1.

[226] *Zech, H.*, Information as Property, (2015) 6 JIPITEC 192, 196.

[227] *Ibid.*, at 197.

However, it has already been explained that, in practice, it might be difficult to always make a clear-cut distinction between the semantic and the syntactic level of information.[228] Nevertheless, the point is (and this is what Zech also seems to be saying) that, in the data economy, protection may be needed when it comes to mere data (data sets). It is questionable, however, whether such protection should necessarily be in a form of exclusive rights, as suggested by Zech.

In fact, as argued before, protection for both the semantic and the syntactic levels of information can be granted by trade secret protection.[229] Such protection does not amount to the exclusive rights of the trade secret holders that would be similar to, for example, the rights of patent owners. However, this circumstance does not yet mean that a trade secret cannot be treated as property. For example, in a number of the US cases, a trade secret was considered to be property.[230] The limits to the right to exclude, in the case of a trade secret, were most clearly drawn in the comment to the *Restatement (First) of Torts*. It was stated that "the suggestion that one has a right to exclude others from the use of his trade secret because he has a right of property in the idea has been frequently advanced and rejected. The theory that has prevailed is that the protection is afforded only by a general duty of good faith and that the ability rests upon breach of this duty; that is, breach of contract, abuse of confidence or impropriety in the means of procurement".[231] In illustrative terms, Milgrim called trade secret rights as "disappearing property rights".[232] However, this was mainly due to the fact that a trade secret itself is gone once it is disclosed.

In this regard, it is also noteworthy that the EU Trade Secrets Directive provides a definition of a "trade secret holder". Article 2(2) stipulates that a "'trade secret holder' means any natural or legal person lawfully controlling a trade secret". The definition of a trade secret owner is not provided, although, in the Impact Assessment of the EU Trade Secrets Directive, the European Commission uses the terms "trade secret owner" and a "trade secret holder" interchangeably.[233] In the Explanatory Memorandum, it is pointed out that

---

[228] See *supra* in this chapter Section 3.2.1.1.

[229] See *supra* in this chapter Section 3.2.1.1.

[230] For a more detailed analysis see *Surblytė, G.*, The Refusal to Disclose Trade Secrets as an Abuse of Market Dominance – *Microsoft* and Beyond, Berne: Stämpfli 2011, pp. XLVII + 263 (Munich Series on European and International Competition Law, Volume 28), pp. 36–42.

[231] *Restatement (First) of Torts*, § 757 comment a.

[232] *Milgrim, R.M.*, Milgrim on Trade Secrets, Vol. 1, New York: LexisNexis 2008, Ch. 2, pp. 20–23.

[233] See, for example, European Commission, Commission Staff Working Document. Impact Assessment. Accompanying the document: Proposal for a Directive of the European Parliament and of the Council on the protection of undisclosed know-how

"[t]he definition of 'trade secret holder' incorporates, also following the TRIPS Agreement, the concept of lawfulness of control of the trade secret as a key element. It therefore ensures that not only the original owner of the trade secret but also licensees can defend the trade secret".[234] In this regard, several remarks have to be made.

First of all, it is true that Article 39(2) TRIPS stipulates that "natural and legal persons shall have the possibility of preventing information lawfully within their control from being disclosed to, acquired by, or used by others without their consent in a manner contrary to honest commercial practices". Such a formulation, however, does not mean to say that there is no trade secret owner in the first place, but rather it reflects the compromise that was made during the TRIPS negotiations to protect trade secrets against unfair competition and to expand the circle of persons who may protect a trade secret against the acts of unfair competition. Namely, such persons are not only trade secret owners, but also any other person who is in a lawful control of a trade secret, for example, licensors.

Secondly, although the EU Trade Secrets Directive, as the Explanatory Memorandum claims, overtakes the concept of the lawfulness of control from TRIPS, it should be borne in mind that the EU Trade Secrets Directive, in contrast to Article 39(2) TRIPS, not only elaborates on the unlawful acts, but also speaks about, for example, remedies for a trade secret infringement. In this regard, a trade secret owner should be the first person in the line, in particular when it comes to the enforcement of trade secrets, including the remedies.

From a comparative point of view, it could be noted that, in the US, both the Uniform Trade Secrets Act and the Defend Trade Secrets Act of 2016 speak only about a "trade secret owner". In fact, this is precise from a legal point of view, bearing in mind that a trade secret owner will be the first addressee of the rights and obligations under trade secret law.

In the EU, it is only the Explanatory Memorandum that mentions a trade secret owner, not the EU Trade Secrets Directive itself. This may have important legal consequences in general and for the data economy in particular. In fact, by having missed including the term of a trade secret owner, the EU Trade Secrets Directive turns out to speak only of the – subsequent – trade secret holders. Such persons may, for example, be licensees. Important as they

---

and business information (trade secrets) against their unlawful acquisition, use and disclosure, Brussels, 28.11.2013, SWD(2013) 471 final.

[234] European Commission, Proposal for a Directive of the European Parliament and of the Council on the protection of undisclosed know-how and business information (trade secrets) against their unlawful acquisition, use and disclosure, Brussels, 28.11.2013, COM(2013) 813 final (2013/0402 (COD)), Explanatory Memorandum, Section 5.1, p. 7.

are, it is still crucial to know who the initial trade secret owner may be. In the data economy, there may be a number of persons who may be involved in the creation of a data set. Although, following the concept of the lawfulness of control in TRIPS, they would be all entitled to protect a trade secret against unfair commercial actions, it would not be clear which of them would be the owner of a trade secret, given the fact that the EU Trade Secrets Directive does not elaborate on this concept. It may thus be for the Member States to clarify this in their national laws. However, such national legal provisions may differ and thereby bring legal uncertainties with regard to the notion of a "trade secret owner". Thus, a too straightforward, if not a mistaken, application of the TRIPS concept of the lawfulness of control in the EU Trade Secrets Directive may be a major drawback for the data economy.[235]

Thus, the fact that trade secret law does not grant exclusive rights does not mean that trade secrets cannot be considered as a company's property. However, the fact that exclusive rights are not granted means that the scope of protection in the case of trade secrets is weaker than it is, for example, in the case of patents. After all, as the US Supreme Court said in the landmark *Kewanee Oil* case,[236] "[t]rade secret law provides far weaker protection in many respects than the patent law. [...] Where patent law acts as a barrier, trade secret law functions relatively as a sieve".[237] Indeed, some types of behaviour, such as, for example, reverse engineering, are allowed and are considered to be lawful.

Recital 16 of the EU Trade Secrets Directive stipulates that:

> In the interest of innovation and to foster competition, the provisions of this Directive should not create any exclusive right to know-how or information protected as trade secrets. Thus, the independent discovery of the same know-how or information should remain possible. Reverse engineering of a lawfully acquired product should be considered as a lawful means of acquiring information, except when otherwise contractually agreed. The freedom to enter into such contractual arrangements can, however, be limited by law.

---

[235] Another opinion by Drexl who elaborates on the notion of "a trade secret holder" in the context of the right of access to data, yet mostly focusing on the issue of the "co-holders of the trade secret" (see *Drexl, J.*, Data Access and Control in the Era of Connected Devices, Study on Behalf of the European Consumer Organisation BEUC (https://www.ip.mpg.de/fileadmin/ipmpg/content/aktuelles/aus_der_forschung/beuc-x-2018-121_data_access_and_control_in_the_area_of_connected_devices.pdf, pp. 95–96).

[236] *Kewanee Oil Co. v. Bicron Co.*, 416 U.S. 470 (1974).

[237] *Ibid.*, at 489–490.

Thus, in the case of a trade secret, an independent creation of the same trade secret as well as reverse engineering is allowed. Trade secrets are thus not a typical form of ownership, first and foremost, owing to the fact that one of the fair means of accessing the information covered by a trade secret is reverse engineering. Although trade secrets are protected against unlawful acquisition, use and disclosure, two means of acquiring a trade secret are considered lawful, i.e. an independent creation of the information covered by a trade secret and reverse engineering. Both ways are important in the data economy. The independent creation of a similar data set would not amount to an infringement of a trade secret. Furthermore, the use of the same data set by a number of companies does not mean that a trade secret will be destroyed. As long as secrecy and commercial value are maintained, a trade secret is not gone. These flexibilities may, on the one hand, be the beauty of trade secret law in the data economy. After all, trade secret law, firstly, protects information without any requirements for the quality of such information, and secondly, it protects information that is kept secret, but thirdly, at the same time allows for sharing of such information (relative secrecy) within certain limits. On the other hand, however, the aforementioned flexibilities of trade secret law may also have their drawbacks.

The fact that an independent creation of the same trade secret is considered to be lawful behaviour is important for the data economy, but may also have its limitations. It means that, even if a number of (independent) companies gather the same data and create their data sets, such data sets may be eligible for trade secret protection even if they are the same. However, this will hold true only, firstly, as long as the latter fact is unknown, and, secondly, to the extent that such data still provides a competitive advantage to the company as compared with its competitors. Hence, different companies can possess the same trade secrets (and, thus, data sets) as long as the trade secret is not disclosed and commercial value (a competitive advantage) is not lost.[238] Furthermore, concerns may arise when it comes to reverse engineering a data set, which may also include personal data.

---

[238] For example, *de Carvalho* suggests that secrecy could be preserved until the last person (or even the last competitor) in the circle that normally deals with the information gets that information (*de Carvalho, N.P.*, The TRIPS Regime of Antitrust and Undisclosed Information, Alphen aan den Rijn: Kluwer Law International 2008, p. 233). However, the question thereby may be whether such information would still provide a competitive advantage if a trade secret were possessed by almost all competitors (see also *Surblytė, G.*, Enhancing TRIPS: Trade Secrets and Reverse Engineering, in: Ullrich, H./Hilty, R.M./Lamping, M./Drexl, J. (eds), TRIPS plus 20, Berlin: Springer 2016, pp. 725–760, at p. 737).

3.7 REVERSE ENGINEERING

In trade secret law, one of the legal means of acquiring a trade secret is reverse engineering. Reverse engineering is defined as "starting with the known product and working backward to find the method by which it was developed".[239] Reverse engineering provides a compromise in trade secret law for protecting information: the information may be kept secret, but the possibility remains to get access to such information on the basis of one's own efforts.

Article 3(1)(b) of the EU Trade Secrets Directive stipulates that reverse engineering is a lawful means of obtaining a trade secret. According to this legal provision, however, the lawfulness of reverse engineering is not unlimited: firstly, Article 3(1)(b) refers to the reverse engineering of a "product or object"; secondly, such a product or object has either to be made publicly available or be in the lawful possession of the acquirer of information, such as, for example, may be the case with a software licence, and thirdly, there should be no valid restriction (e.g. a contractual restriction) to acquire a trade secret by means of reverse engineering.[240] These factors, or limitations, may be important for the data economy, in particular, in the light of the complexity of AI technology. In fact, bearing in mind that data may need to go through a number of layers of artificial neural networks or taking account of a number of devices that may be connected in IoT technology, it may be difficult to reverse engineer data. Moreover, difficulties as regards reverse engineering may arise if we recall that most of the data may be stored on servers and will not necessarily be directly embedded in the product that is made available in the market and that may thus be subject to reverse engineering. Furthermore, in light of the validity of contractual restrictions to reverse engineer pursuant to Article 3(1)(b), cases may exist when reverse engineering would be restricted by way of a contract clause.

And yet, reverse engineering may be important for AI technology, for example, if we consider the production of robotics. Owing to the fact that such robotics may also be eligible for trade mark protection, the question arises as regards the intersection of the protection of trade secrets and functional signs.

---

[239] National Conference of Commissioners on Uniform State Laws, Uniform Trade Secrets Act, 1979, as amended in 1985, Comment to Section 1, p. 5.

[240] For a more detailed analysis of these requirements see *Surblytė, G.*, Enhancing TRIPS: Trade Secrets and Reverse Engineering, in: Ullrich, H./Hilty, R.M./Lamping, M./Drexl, J. (eds), TRIPS plus 20, Berlin: Springer 2016, pp. 725–760.

3.7.1 Reverse Engineering in the Intersection of Trade Secrets and Functional Signs

Reverse engineering may be important not only for trade secrets, but also in the case of functional signs, i.e. the signs that consist of a shape of a product, which is necessary to obtain a technical result.

AI technology may be registered as a trade mark. According to the Nice classification,[241] Class 7, which covers machines, machine tools, motors and engines, includes "industrial robots",[242] whereas Class 9 includes "humanoid robots with artificial intelligence".[243] Hence, industrial robots as well as humanoid robots may be eligible for trade mark protection.

Bearing this in mind and given the role of the multi-dimensionality for the perception function of the AI machines,[244] the intersection may have to be analysed between trade marks and trade secrets. At first sight, such an intersection may seem surprising. After all, trade mark law is basically about the visual appearances of a product, whereas trade secret law protects information that is kept secret. Yet such an intersection may be highly important in the case of functional signs. Bearing in mind that the multi-dimensional shape of industrial or humanoid robots may be intrinsically linked to their functionality, the question may arise whether access to technical solutions (for example, by way of reverse engineering) remains available under both trade mark and trade secret law.

3.7.1.1 Functional signs under EU trade mark law
According to the Regulation on the European Union trade mark,[245] Article 4 and the case-law of the ECJ,[246] a trade mark may consist of the shape of goods.

---

[241] The Nice classification, which was established by the Nice Agreement (1957), is an international classification of goods and services applied for the registration of marks (see http://www.wipo.int/classifications/nice/en).

[242] Nice Classification, 11th edition, Version 2020, Class 7.

[243] Nice Classification, 11th edition, Version 2020, Class 9.

[244] On the perception function of the machines in AI and the role of 3D see *Russell, S.J./Norvig, P.*, Artificial Intelligence: A Modern Approach, 3rd ed., Delhi: Pearson 2015, pp. 944–985.

[245] Regulation (EU) 2017/1001 of the European Parliament and of the Council of 14 June 2017 on the European Union trade mark, OJ [2017] L 154/1. This Regulation repealed the Council Regulation (EC) No. 207/2009 of 26 February 2009 on the Community trade mark, OJ [2009] L 78/1, and amended Regulation 2015/2424, OJ [2015] L 341/21.

[246] For example, ECJ, Case C-48/09 P, *Lego Juris v. OHIM*, 14 September 2010, ECLI:EU:C:2010:516, para. 39; ECJ, Case C-218/01, *Henkel KGaA*, 12 February 2004, ECLI:EU:C:2004:88, para. 29.

The registration of three-dimensional signs as trade marks was the subject matter of several cases of the ECJ.[247] For example, although it was acknowledged that the shape of the Lego brick did not lack a distinctive character,[248] it was disputed whether it could be registered as a trade mark owing to the functionality features.[249]

The question of the validity of a three-dimensional trade mark was addressed by the ECJ also in the *Simba Toys* case.[250] In this case, the ECJ set aside the judgement of the General Court[251] and annulled the decision of the European Union Intellectual Property Office (EUIPO) with regard to registering as a trade mark the shape of the Rubik's Cube. At the core of the proceedings was the issue of the functionality of the sign, which was registered as a trade mark, and the question whether granting such protection did not impede the ability of competitors to access technical solutions.

Whereas trade mark law basically relates to the visual appearance of the product, the question in the *Simba Toys* case was whether "the invisible elements of the functionality of the essential characteristics of the contested mark" have to be taken into account when registering a trade mark.[252] In this regard, the ECJ explained that:

> the General Court should have defined the technical function of the actual goods at issue, namely a three-dimensional puzzle, and it should have taken this into account when assessing the functionality of the essential characteristics of that sign. [...] While it was necessary [...], for the purpose of that analysis, *to proceed on the basis of the shape* at issue, *as represented graphically, that analysis could not be*

---

[247] For example, ECJ, Case C-30/15 P, *Simba Toys GmbH & Co. KG v. European Union Intellectual Property Office (EUIPO)*, 10 November 2016, ECLI:EU:C:2016: 849; ECJ, Case C-48/09 P, *Lego Juris v. OHIM*, 14 September 2010, ECLI:EU:C: 2010:516; ECJ, Case C-205/13, *Hauck GmbH & Co. KG v. Stokke A/S and Others*, 18 September 2014, ECLI:EU:C:2014:2233.

[248] ECJ, *Lego Juris*, *supra* note 247, para. 40.

[249] The ECJ pointed out that "even if a shape of goods which is necessary to obtain a technical result has become distinctive in consequence of the use which has been made of it, it is prohibited from being registered as a trade mark" (ECJ, *Lego Juris*, *supra* note 247, para. 47).

[250] ECJ, Case C-30/15 P, *Simba Toys GmbH & Co. KG v. European Union Intellectual Property Office (EUIPO)*, 10 November 2016, ECLI:EU:C:2016:849. On the comment of the case see, for example, *Kur, A.*, Rubik's Cube – Würfelzauber am Ende?, (2017) GRUR 134. Owing to the timeframe of the facts, the dispute in the *Simba Toys* case was governed by the Regulation No. 40/94 (ECJ, *Simba Toys*, para. 3), which was replaced by Council Regulation (EC) No. 207/2009.

[251] General Court, Case T-450/09, *Simba Toys GmbH & Co. KG v. European Union Intellectual Property Office (EUIPO)*, 25 November 2014, ECLI:EU:T:2014:983.

[252] *Ibid.*, para. 59.

made without taking into consideration, where appropriate, the additional elements relating to the function of the actual goods at issue.[253] (Emphasis added)

Hence, according to the ECJ, the analysis of the functionality of a sign should take account of the shape and of any additional elements, which may be important for the technical functionality of the good, even if such elements are invisible. In *Simba Toys*, the ECJ further explained that:

the General Court rejected the appellant's arguments relating to the rotating capability of the individual elements of the cube at issue [...] by pointing out [...] that those arguments were essentially based on knowledge of the rotating capability of the vertical and horizontal lattices of the "Rubik's Cube" and that *that capability cannot result from the characteristics of the shape presented but, at most, from an invisible mechanism internal to that cube.* The General Court held that the Board of Appeal was right not to include that invisible element in its analysis of the functionality of the essential characteristics of the contested mark. In that context, the General Court took the view that inferring the existence of an internal rotating mechanism from the graphic representations of that mark would not have been consistent with the requirement that any inference must be drawn as objectively as possible from the shape in question, as represented graphically, and with sufficient certainty. (Emphasis added)[254]

Hence, the opinion of the General Court was that the technical capability did not derive from the shape of the good, but was rather related to "an invisible mechanism internal to that cube". The ECJ, however, held that the General Court erred in law[255] in that it took the view that "the grid structure on each surface of the cube at issue did not perform any technical function since the fact that that structure had the effect of dividing visually each surface of that cube into nine equal square elements could not constitute a technical function for the purposes of the relevant case-law".[256]

In fact, one of the absolute grounds for a refusal to register a sign as a trade mark is related to a shape of good, which is necessary to obtain a technical result. Article 7(1)(e)(ii) of the Trade Mark Regulation No. 207/2009 stipulated that "signs which consist exclusively of the shape of goods which is necessary to obtain a technical result shall not be registered". A similar provision had also been included in Article 7(1)(e)(ii) of the Community Trade Mark

---

[253] ECJ, *Simba Toys*, *supra* note 247, paras 47–48.

[254] ECJ, *Simba Toys*, *supra* note 247, para. 43; in this regard, see also the GC, *Simba Toys*, *supra* note 251, paras 57–59.

[255] ECJ, *Simba Toys*, *supra* note 247, para. 45.

[256] ECJ, *Simba Toys*, *supra* note 247, para. 44.

Regulation No. 40/94²⁵⁷ and in Article 3(1)(e) of the Trade Mark Directive.²⁵⁸ These legal provisions were explained in a number of ECJ cases,²⁵⁹ including the aforementioned *Simba Toys* case.

However, the legal grounds for a refusal to register a trade mark were expanded when the Community Trade Mark Regulation was amended in 2015.²⁶⁰ In contrast to the previous text of Article 7(1)(e)(ii), according to which one of the absolute grounds for a refusal to register a sign as a trade mark was the fact that the sign consists "exclusively of the shape of goods which is necessary to obtain a technical result", the new text of this provision addresses signs that consist "exclusively of the shape, or *another characteristic*, of goods which is necessary to obtain a technical result" (emphasis added). Thereby, a sign cannot be registered as a trade mark if it exclusively consists *of the shape of the good or of another characteristic*, either of which (hence the word "or" in the provision) is necessary to obtain a technical result. Thereby, the legal grounds for a refusal to register a trade mark have been broadened. Although the Regulation No. 207/2009, together with the amendment of 2015,

---

²⁵⁷ Council Regulation (EC) No. 40/94 of 20 December 1993 on the Community trade mark, OJ [1994] L 11/1. Article 7(1)(e)(ii) of this Regulation is identical to Article 7(1)(e)(ii) of the Community Trade Mark Regulation No. 207/2009.

²⁵⁸ First Council Directive 89/104/EEC of 21 December 1988 to approximate the laws of the Member States relating to trade marks, OJ [1989] L 40/1, which was repealed by Directive 2008/95/EC of the European Parliament and of the Council of 22 October 2008 to approximate the laws of the Member States relating to trade marks, OJ [2008] L 299/25. The latter Directive was repealed by Directive (EU) 2015/2436 of the European Parliament and of the Council of 16 December 2015 to approximate the laws of the Member States relating to trade marks, OJ [2015] L 336/1.

²⁵⁹ For example, on Article 7(1)(e)(ii) of the Community Trade Mark Regulation No. 40/94 see: ECJ, Case C-30/15 P, *Simba Toys GmbH & Co. KG v. European Union Intellectual Property Office (EUIPO)*, 10 November 2016, ECLI:EU:C:2016:849; ECJ, Joined Cases C-337/12 P to C-340/12 P, *Pi-Design AG and Others v. Yoshida Metal Industry Co. Ltd and OHIM*, 6 March 2014, ECLI:EU:C:2014:129; ECJ, Case C-48/09 P, *Lego Juris v. OHIM*, 14 September 2010, ECLI:EU:C:2010:516; on Article 3(1)(e)) of the Trade Mark Directive see: ECJ, Case C-205/13, *Hauck GmbH & Co. KG v. Stokke A/S and Others*, 18 September 2014, ECLI:EU:C:2014:2233; ECJ, Case C-218/01, *Henkel KGaA*, 12 February 2004, ECLI:EU:C:2004:88; ECJ, Case C-299/99, *Koninklijke Philips Electronics NV v. Remington Consumer Products Ltd.*, 18 June 2002, ECLI:EU:C:2002:377.

²⁶⁰ Regulation (EU) 2015/2424 of the European Parliament and of the Council of 16 December 2015 amending Council Regulation (EC) No. 207/2009 on the Community trade mark and Commission Regulation (EC) No. 2868/95 implementing Council Regulation (EC) No. 40/94 on the Community trade mark, and repealing Commission Regulation (EC) No. 2869/95 on the fees payable to the Office for Harmonization in the Internal Market (Trade Marks and Designs), OJ [2015] L 341/21.

was repealed in July 2017,[261] the aforementioned legal provision remained unchanged.

In this regard, it could, first of all, be noted that, while explaining the previous legal provision and highlighting the words "exclusively" and "necessary", the ECJ stressed that the legal grounds for a refusal to register a functional sign were meant to be narrow. According to the ECJ:

> the legislature duly took into account that any shape of goods is, to a certain extent, functional and that it would therefore be *inappropriate* to refuse to register a shape of goods as a trade mark *solely on the ground that it has functional characteristics.* By the terms "exclusively" and "necessary", that provision ensures that *solely shapes of goods which only incorporate a technical solution, and whose registration as a trade mark would therefore actually impede the use of that technical solution by other undertakings, are not to be registered.*[262] (Emphasis added)

In the *Philips* case, the ECJ explained that "[Article 3(1)(e), second indent, of the Directive] is intended to preclude the registration of shapes whose *essential characteristics perform a technical function*" (emphasis added).[263] Referring to the essential (yet, not exclusive) characteristics of the shape, the passage implied that these (functional) characteristics of the sign, although they had to be essential, did not need to be the sole ones. For example, according to the Advocate General in the *Philips* case, the "[u]se of the phrase 'essential features' means that a shape containing an arbitrary element which, from a functional point of view, is minor, such as its colour, does not escape the prohibition".[264]

In contrast to the previous legal provision though, the current legal provision also excludes the registration of the signs, which exclusively consist of the characteristic, other than a shape, if such a characteristic is necessary to achieve a technical result. According to the wording of the provision, "another characteristic" is not related to the shape of the goods. In line with the case-law of the ECJ on the previous legal provision,[265] it could be argued that such a characteristic should relate to the essential characteristics of a product and such characteristics should be properly identified.

---

[261] Regulation (EU) 2017/1001 of the European Parliament and of the Council of 14 June 2017 on the European Union trade mark, OJ [2017] L 154/1.

[262] ECJ, Case C-48/09 P, *Lego Juris v. OHIM*, 14 September 2010, ECLI:EU:C: 2010:516, para. 48.

[263] ECJ, *Philips*, *supra* note 259, para. 79.

[264] Opinion of Advocate General Ruiz-Jarabo Colomer delivered on 23 January 2001 in Case C-299/99, *Koninklijke Philips Electronics NV v. Remington Consumer Products Ltd.* (ECLI:EU:C:2001:52), para. 28.

[265] See, for example, ECJ, *Simba Toys*, *supra* note 247, para. 40 (with further references).

Yet it could be asked whether a broader formulation of the legal grounds for a refusal to register a trade mark will not have unintended legal consequences when it comes to registering as a trade mark AI technology, such as, for example, industrial or humanoid robots. In fact, it might be that their functionality will often be intrinsically linked to some type of a characteristic other than a shape. Since the EU Trade Mark Regulation does not explain what such other characteristics should mean, it will remain for the ECJ to clarify this in the case-law. However, it should not be ruled out that the word "characteristic" may be interpreted broadly. In the case of the AI technology, it could, arguably, include even algorithms. Yet, in this regard, the intersection of functional signs and trade secrets may be at its peak.

3.7.1.2   Functional signs and trade secrets

Although invisible elements may contribute to the functionality features of the sign, it may be asked whether this may be exactly where trade secrets come into play and have to be aligned with the logic of trade mark law as regards functional signs.

As explained, it might be that the technical functions may stem not solely from a shape, but also (or even rather) from other characteristics of a sign. Such characteristics may be invisible and could, arguably, form part of a trade secret. The amendment of Article 7(1)(e)(ii), by including another characteristic in addition to the shape of the product, has broadened the absolute legal grounds for a refusal to register a functional sign. Thereby, signs, the technical functionality of which may be conditioned upon the invisible elements rather than their shapes, would not be registered as trade marks. Yet such invisible elements may rather be protected as a trade secret. Such broad legal grounds for a refusal to register a functional sign may have unintended consequences for AI technology, the technical functionality of which may often be related to the invisible part of the product. It remains to be hoped that it will not lead to a rejection of such a registration becoming a rule rather than an exception.

However, trade mark and trade secret law, although the former basically protects the visible part of the product, whereas the latter protects the invisible part of it, have in common that both of them have as their goal the idea that technical solutions underlying the product remain accessible. The rationale behind a refusal to register such signs as trade marks, the shape or another characteristic of which is necessary for achieving a technical solution, is to maintain the ability of competitors to access such technical solutions. The rationale of maintaining access to technical solutions may also be found in trade secret law. One of the legal means of acquiring a trade secret is reverse engineering. The latter is meant to strike a balance in trade secret law by allowing the protection of the information based on secrecy, thereby leaving the door open for (potential) competitors to find it out by way of reverse engineering. Hence, the grounds for refusing trade mark registration and the protection of a technical solution by a trade secret may become inextricably linked.

In the case-law of the ECJ, the boundaries of trade mark law in the case of functional signs have been explained mostly by comparing trade marks with industrial patents and designs. For example, in the *Lego* case, the ECJ held that:

> When the shape of a product merely incorporates the technical solution developed by the manufacturer of that product and patented by it, protection of that shape as a trade mark once the patent has expired would considerably and permanently reduce the opportunity for other undertakings to use that technical solution. In the system of intellectual property rights developed in the European Union, technical solutions are capable of protection only for a limited period, so that subsequently they may be freely used by all economic operators.[266]

Indeed, in the case of a patent, a compromise for granting exclusive rights to a patent owner is that patent applications are made publicly available, so that competitors, although they cannot imitate, can "invent around" a patent. Yet technical solutions can be protected by both patents and trade secrets. At the end of the day, it is upon the decision of an inventor whether to patent an invention (in the case where a subject matter is patentable) or to keep it secret.[267] In contrast to patents, trade secret protection, although it does not grant exclusive rights, is not limited in time – it lasts as long as the subject matter of a trade secret remains secret. Access to the information covered by a trade secret remains possible through means such as, for example, reverse engineering.

---

[266] ECJ, *Lego Juris, supra* note 247, para. 46. Similarly, Advocate General *Ruiz-Jarabo Colomer* explained in *Philips*: "it is clear that Community legislature sought to delimit the scope of protection of a trade mark from that of an industrial patent. Likewise, it distinguishes between the scopes of patents and designs respectively. [...] a trade mark seeks to protect the identity of the origin of the goods and, therefore, indirectly, the *goodwill* which the goods attract, whereas designs – like patents – seek to protect the goods, in their own right, as an economic factor: their substantial value (in the case of designs) or the value which derives from their technical performance (in the case of patents)" (emphasis in original) (Opinion of AG in *Philips, supra* note 264, paras 32, 37). In *Philips*, the ECJ held: "In refusing registration of such signs, Article 3(1)(e), second indent, of the Directive reflects the legitimate aim of not allowing individuals to use registration of a mark in order to acquire or perpetuate exclusive rights relating to technical solutions" (ECJ, *Philips, supra* note 259, para. 82).

[267] On the assessment of strategic decisions between patenting and keeping secret in terms of "an incentive to invent" and "an incentive to disclose" see *Strandburg, K.J.,* What does the public get? Experimental use and the patent bargain, (2004) Wisconsin Law Review 81, at 100–118.

Reverse engineering, as a fair means of acquiring information that is the subject matter of a trade secret, is included in the EU Trade Secrets Directive. Article 3(1)(b) states that "[t]he acquisition of a trade secret shall be considered lawful when the trade secret is obtained by [...] observation, study, disassembly or testing of a product or object that has been made available to the public or that is lawfully in the possession of the acquirer of the information *who is free from any legally valid duty to limit the acquisition of the trade secret*" (emphasis added). Hence, pursuant to Article 3(1)(b) of the EU Trade Secrets Directive, the acquisition of a trade secret by means of reverse engineering is lawful, except for cases when there is "a legally valid duty to limit the acquisition of a trade secret". A systemic analysis of the Directive reveals that reverse engineering can be restricted by way of a contract.[268]

Although restrictions to reverse engineer imposed by a contract do not, as such, amount to exclusive rights, the question is, firstly, what effect they may have for accessing technical solutions, and secondly, whether their validity under the EU Trade Secrets Directive complies with the logic and the goal of the legal grounds for a refusal to register a trade mark.

The rationale behind refusing to register as a trade mark a sign, which consists of a shape of goods that is necessary to achieve a technical result, is the need to avoid the perpetuation of exclusive rights as regards technical solutions. This has time and again been stressed in the case-law of the ECJ. For example, the ECJ in *Lego* explained that:

> the inclusion in Article 7(1) of Regulation No 40/94 of the prohibition on registration as a trade mark of any sign consisting of the shape of goods which is necessary to obtain a technical result ensures that undertakings may not use trade mark law in order to perpetuate indefinitely, exclusive rights relating to technical solutions.[269]

Also, in the *Simba Toys* case, with regard to marks that represent the shape of the goods themselves, Advocate General *Szpunar* said that:

> the issue surrounding this type of mark is specific in nature on account of the risk that the exclusive right arising from registration of the trade mark will be extended to the functional characteristics of a product expressed in its shape.[270]

---

[268] For a more detailed analysis on contractual restrictions to reverse engineer see *Surblytė, G.*, Enhancing TRIPS: Trade Secrets and Reverse Engineering, in: Ullrich, H./Hilty, R.M./Lamping, M./Drexl, J. (eds), TRIPS plus 20, Berlin: Springer 2016, pp. 725–760. See also *Surblytė, G.*, Data-Driven Economy and Artificial Intelligence: Emerging Competition Law Issues, (2017) 67 WuW 120, at 126.

[269] ECJ, *Lego Juris*, *supra* note 247, para. 45.

[270] Opinion of Advocate General Szpunar delivered on 25 May 2016 in Case C-30/15 P, *Simba Toys GmbH & Co. KG v. European Union Intellectual Property Office (EUIPO)*, ECLI:EU:C:2016:350, para. 4.

Finally, in *Philips*, the ECJ noted that the grounds for refusal of registration are intended "to prevent the protection conferred by the trade mark right from being extended, beyond signs which serve to distinguish a product or service from those offered by competitors, so as to form an obstacle preventing competitors from freely offering for sale products incorporating such technical solutions or functional characteristics in competition with the proprietor of the trade mark".[271]

Restricting reverse engineering by contract does not, as such, grant exclusive rights to its holder. Yet, a cumulative effect of such contractual restrictions, when a product is sold in the market, may have to be considered. With regard to trade marks, a cumulative effect of registering similar functional signs was addressed by the ECJ. In trade mark law, a refusal to register a functional sign is based on the idea that a registration of a purely functional product shape could lead to the situation where a trade mark would prevent competitors from using not only the same shape, but also similar shapes.[272] As explained by the ECJ in *Lego*, "that would be particularly so if various purely functional shapes of goods were registered at the same time, which might completely prevent other undertakings from manufacturing and marketing certain goods having a particular technical function".[273] Hence, it was said that, even if other shapes were available, this did not mean that the registration of a functional sign would not be refused.[274] According to the Advocate General in *Philips*:

> If we were to accept Philips' argument, which consists in accepting evidence of the existence of other shapes capable of achieving the same technical performance with the aim of preventing the exclusion of a merely functional mark, nothing would stop an undertaking from registering as trade marks *all* imaginable shapes which achieved such a result, thus obtaining a permanent monopoly over a particular technical solution.[275] (Emphasis in original)

---

[271] ECJ, *Philips*, *supra* note 259, para. 78.

[272] ECJ, *Lego Juris*, *supra* note 247, para. 56.

[273] ECJ, *Lego Juris*, *supra* note 247, para. 57.

[274] "As to the question whether the establishment that there are other shapes which could achieve the same technical result can overcome the ground for refusal or invalidity contained in Article 3(1)(e), second indent, there is nothing in the wording of that provision to allow such a conclusion. [...] Where the essential functional characteristics of the shape of a product are attributable solely to the technical result, Article 3(1)(e), second indent, precludes registration of a sign of that shape, even if that technical result can be achieved by other shapes" (ECJ, *Philips*, *supra* note 259, paras 81, 83). Cited in ECJ, *Lego Juris*, *supra* note 247, para. 58. (See also ECJ, *Philips*, *supra* note 259, para. 84: "the ground for refusal or invalidity of registration imposed by that provision cannot be overcome by establishing that there are other shapes which allow the same technical result to be obtained".)

[275] Opinion of AG in *Philips*, *supra* note 264, para. 39.

Although contractual restrictions to reverse engineer a trade secret do not restrict the ability of competitors to develop their own technical solutions, it may hinder them from accessing information that might, for example, be needed for the development of compatible products. Thus, in the case of contractual restrictions to reverse engineer, it might be that their cumulative effect may be similar to that described by the ECJ. On the one hand, it could be argued that trade secret law leaves the door open to access technical solutions by way of reverse engineering. On the other hand, however, such a possibility may be restricted, rendering reverse engineering – legally, not technically – impossible. Hence, restricting reverse engineering of a trade secret, in particular in terms of a cumulative effect of such restrictions on the basis of a contract, may have similar consequences to those that trade mark law tries to avoid. In other words, although the effect of preventing competitors from accessing information on technical solutions seems to be neatly avoided by trade mark law, such an effect may be achieved by the companies using the legal tools provided by the EU Trade Secrets Directive. Restricting reverse engineering may block access to technical solutions, not only for a limited period of time, but rather perpetually.

Hence, the systemic analysis of the relevant provisions of trade mark and trade secret law reveals a potential tension between the two areas of law in the case of functional signs. Whereas, under the EU trade mark law, the shape or other characteristic of the good that is necessary for achieving a technical solution is one of the absolute legal grounds for a refusal to register a functional sign as a trade mark, such a technical solution could be protected by trade secret law. In the case of the latter, reverse engineering should serve as a tool for accessing technical solutions that are kept as a trade secret. Yet the validity of contractual restrictions to reverse engineer, as enshrined in the EU Trade Secrets Directive, may lead to the opposite result.

It is not argued here that contractual restrictions to reverse engineer should be considered as invalid in all cases. In fact, they may be important and may serve as an incentive for the companies not only to do business, but also to innovate. What may need to be considered though, is a cumulative effect of such contractual restrictions in the market. With regard to AI technology, reverse engineering may be mostly important in order to enable interoperability. In such cases in particular, contractual restrictions to reverse engineer should be assessed with caution.

3.7.2   Reverse Engineering and Identifiability

If personal data may form part or the whole of a trade secret, the question is whether reverse engineering may result in natural persons being identified or rendered identifiable. In other words, the implications of reverse engineering for personal data protection have to be analysed.

Reverse engineering rests upon the efforts of competitors to obtain the information covered by a trade secret. In such a way, the reasonable efforts of a trade secret holder to protect secrecy are placed on the one hand and the efforts of (potential) competitors to acquire such information are placed on the other. The rationale behind considering reverse engineering as a fair means of obtaining a trade secret is thereby based on the balance between the requirement for reasonable steps to be taken by the trade secret holder to protect a trade secret and the efforts of a reverse engineer to obtain the information covered by a trade secret. Such efforts may include costs and time spent on reverse engineering. The logic behind allowing reverse engineering is thereby the time, costs and other efforts invested in reverse engineering the information by (potential) competitors and the advantage of the head-start of a trade secret holder.

Bearing in mind that a trade secret may consist of personal data, the question is whether reverse engineering a trade secret by any third party may raise risks with regard to the protection of personal data included in a data set.

As regards personal data, one of the main criteria when deciding whether a natural person may be (rendered) identifiable is the "means reasonably likely to be used" – importantly though, not only by the data controller, but also by any third party. According to recital 26 GDPR:

> To determine whether a natural person is *identifiable*, account should be taken of *all the means reasonably likely to be used*, such as singling out, either by the controller or by another person to identify the natural person directly or indirectly. *To ascertain whether means are reasonably likely to be used to identify the natural person, account should be taken of all objective factors, such as the costs of and the amount of time required for identification, taking into consideration the available technology at the time of the processing and technological developments.* (Emphasis added)

Accordingly, the "legal test" for identifiability sounds very similar to the efforts requested for reverse engineering. After all, in the case of both reverse engineering and the test for identifiability account is taken of the efforts in terms of costs, time, etc., as well as the possibilities provided by the technology that is available at the time of processing.

Reverse engineering could lead to the identifiability of natural persons in the case of both anonymized and pseudonymized data. As regards anonymized data, risks related to the "differential privacy" anonymization technique[276] stand

---

[276] Article 29 Data Protection Working Party, Opinion 05/2014 on Anonymisation Techniques, adopted on 10 April 2014, 0829/14/EN WP216, pp. 15–16. It is noted

as an example. With regard to pseudonymized data, it can be recalled that, as it was explained by the Article 29 Data Protection Working Party, "pseudonymization is not a method of anonymization. It merely reduces the linkability of a dataset with the original identity of a data subject, and is accordingly a useful security measure".[277] Thus, it could be argued that, if such linkability is made impossible or is disproportionately difficult, it may be that efforts of reverse engineering might fail with the result that not only is the secrecy of a data set secured, but also the identifiability of natural persons whose data is involved in the data set may be prevented with the result that such data could possibly be even considered to be non-personal.[278] In fact, in the case of an encrypted data set (for example, pseudonymized data), the identifiability of natural persons by third parties may depend on the question whether such data can be decrypted. Bearing in mind that identifiability is determined by the "means reasonably likely to be used", including the efforts of a third party, it could possibly be argued that such a data set may be non-identifiable as long as it is impossible (or disproportionately difficult) for any third party to decrypt it.

In this regard, it could be noted that, for example, the proposal by the European Commission for the EU Data Protection Directive[279] – the first EU legal act on personal data protection[280] – included the concept of depersonalized data. Article 2(b) of the proposed directive explained that "'depersonalize' means modify personal data in such a way that the information they contain can no longer be associated with a specific individual or an individual capable of being determined except *at the price of an excessive effort in terms of staff, expenditure and time*" (emphasis added). The European Commission

---

that one of the failures of differential privacy arises when treating each query independently: "A combination of query results may allow disclosing information which was intended to be secret. If a query history is not retained, then an attacker may engineer multiple questions to a 'differential privacy' database that progressively reduce the amplitude of the outputted sample until a specific character of a single data subject or a group of data subjects might emerge, deterministically or with very high likelihood. Furthermore, an additional caveat is to avoid the mistake of thinking the data are anonymous for the third party, while the data controller can still identify the data subject in the original database taking into account all the means likely reasonably to be used" (*ibid.*, p. 16).

[277]   See Article 29 Data Protection Working Party, Opinion 05/2014 on Anonymisation Techniques, adopted on 10 April 2014, 0829/14/EN WP216, p. 3.

[278]   See *supra* Chapter 2, Section 2.4.2.1.

[279]   Commission of the European Communities, Proposal for a Council Directive concerning the protection of individuals in relation to the processing of personal data, COM(90) 314 final – SYN 287, OJ [1990] C 277/3.

[280]   Directive 95/46/EC of the European Parliament and of the Council of 24 October 1995 on the protection of individuals with regard to the processing of personal data and on the free movement of such data, OJ [1995] L 281/31.

explained that this concept was "designed to permit the exclusion from the scope of certain provisions of the Directive of data which are no longer identifiable. An item of data can be regarded as depersonalized even if it could theoretically be repersonalized with the help of disproportionate technical and financial resources".[281] Thereby, the notion of "depersonalized" data means that data, even if it could – in theory – enable the identifiability of natural persons, could be regarded as non-personal as long as such an identifiability would be possible only upon efforts of time, costs, etc., that would be excessive.

Furthermore, bearing in mind that, in the data economy, data sets will often be created on the basis of combinations of data, it might be that a trade secret, in the case where it covers a data set, could be reverse engineered not by way of "working backwards" – as the classical definition of reverse engineering suggests,[282] but, instead, of working forwards, i.e. by pooling the relevant data together. Also, in such a case, the same risks with regard to identifiability may arise.

The ECJ, in the *Patrick Breyer* case,[283] held that the question whether data can be considered personal data depends on the question whether it is reasonably likely that different data, which would enable identification, would be combined. In the words of the ECJ:

> it must be determined whether the possibility to combine a dynamic IP address with the additional data held by the internet service provider *constitutes a means likely reasonably to be used to identify the data subject*. […] that would not be the case if the identification of the data subject was […] *practically impossible* on account of the fact that *it requires a disproportionate effort in terms of time, cost and man-power*, so that the risk of identification appears in reality to be insignificant.[284] (Emphasis added)

Hence, if reverse engineering occurs on the basis of the combination of such data, it could reveal both a trade secret and the identifiability of natural persons. In fact, through reverse engineering the "missing" part of the data set could become available and this could increase the likelihood of identifi-

---

[281] Commission of the European Communities, Proposal for a Council Directive concerning the protection of individuals in relation to the processing of personal data, SYN 287 in: Commission of the European Communities, COM(90) 314 final – SYN 287 and 288, Brussels, 13 September 1990, pp. 10–70 (https://eur-lex.europa.eu/legal-content/EN/TXT/PDF/?uri=CELEX:51990DC0314&from=EN), at p. 19, Discussion of the legal provisions, Article 2.

[282] See *supra* in this section, note 239.

[283] ECJ, Case C-582/14, *Patrick Breyer v. Bundesrepublik Deutschland*, 19 October 2016, ECLI:EU:C:2016:779.

[284] *Ibid.*, paras 45–46.

ability. Thereby, in the data economy, reverse engineering can have twofold implications: it can destroy secrecy and it can also enable the identifiability of a natural person.

The fact that data sets can be kept as trade secrets, which, in turn, can be reverse engineered, may raise questions when it comes to personal data protection and privacy. In fact, owing to a rather broad definition of processing as enshrined in Article 4(2) GDPR, it could be asked whether the act of reverse engineering a trade secret, which may cover personal data, may be considered as processing. In turn, it could be asked whether data protection laws may provide limitations to such reverse engineering. After all, it may be that, while reverse engineering a data set, which is protected as a trade secret, access may be gained by a third party to personal data, which would form part of such a data set. Thus, it could be asked whether any safeguards are available in order to protect such data. In particular, the question in the cases related to reverse engineering a data set, which may consist of personal data, may be whether any further processing of such data may be considered lawful.

Legal grounds for legitimate processing of personal data are enshrined in Article 6 GDPR. One of the legal grounds listed there may merit attention, i.e. Article 6(1)(f) GDPR. The latter provision stipulates that the processing shall be lawful if "processing is necessary for the purposes of the legitimate interests pursued by the controller or by a third party, except where such interests are overridden by the interests or fundamental rights and freedoms of the data subject which require protection of personal data, in particular where the data subject is a child". Such a legal ground is an alternative to other legal grounds for lawful processing of personal data, including the data subject's consent (Article 6(1)(a) GDPR). Hence, reverse engineering a trade secret, which may consist of personal data, may rest on this legal basis. Furthermore, relying on this legal basis, further processing of personal data that was reverse engineered from the data set, may be legitimate if the data controller may demonstrate the overriding interest of the controller or any third party. This is a rather broad legitimate ground to process personal data. Recital 47 GDPR explains that "[t]he interests and fundamental rights of the data subject could in particular override the interest of the data controller where personal data are processed in circumstances where data subjects do not reasonably expect further processing". However, the question whether a data subject may "reasonably" expect further processing is rather subjective and will have to be answered on a case-by-case basis.

Furthermore, Article 6(4) GDPR foresees the possibility of the processing of personal data by a data controller for purposes other than those for which the personal data was initially collected if the processing for another purpose is compatible with these initial purposes. Such processing can take place in the absence of consent from a data subject. Hence, based on Article 6(4) GDPR, further processing of personal data gained through reverse engineering would be possible if the purpose of such processing, although it is not the same, is not incompatible with the purpose for which initial data was collected.

What is more, the aforementioned legal provision stipulates that, when ascertaining whether processing for another purpose may be compatible with the purpose for which data was initially collected, account should be taken by the data controller of factors such as any link between these purposes, the context, in which data was initially collected, the question of whether any special categories of data may be involved, the possible consequences of the intended further processing and "the existence of appropriate safeguards, which may include encryption and pseudonymisation". Hence, should the purposes of reverse engineering and further data processing be linked, it may be possible to lawfully further process such personal data pursuant to Article 6(4) GDPR.

What may be troubling though is the fact that Article 4(2) GDPR, as mentioned, provides a rather broad definition of processing, which may include acts such as "disclosure by transmission, dissemination or otherwise making available". Thus, such information may be not only further shared, but may also go through a number of networks of machine-to-machine communication. Confidentiality, as explained based on the example of the proposed ePrivacy Regulation,[285] may be ensured for data in transmission, yet not necessarily further. Thereby, safeguards such as encryption or pseudonymization may play a crucial role in this regard.

In light of what was said above, it could be questioned whether additional safeguards should have been included in the GDPR when it comes to reverse engineering data sets. On the one hand, one theoretical consideration could be that it should have been stated that any further processing of personal data gained by way of reverse engineering a data set shall be lawful only upon an (explicit) consent of a data subject. Consent is one of the legal bases for a lawful processing of personal data under Article 6(1)(a) GDPR, whereas explicit consent is required in the case of the processing of special categories of data (Article 9(2)(a) GDPR). On the other hand, however, if such a clause had been included, it would probably have resulted in an unjustified burden for economic operators bearing in mind that they would have had to ask for a consent each time they processed personal data gained by reverse engineering.

---

[285] See *supra* in this chapter Section 3.2.2.1.

3.8   PECUNIARY COMPENSATION

In the data economy, in particular in the light of the networked technology, the question may arise as regards the reach of third party liability for the use of information that may be covered by a trade secret. According to Article 4(4) of the EU Trade Secrets Directive, the acquisition, use or disclosure of a trade secret shall be considered unlawful "whenever a person, at the time of the acquisition, use or disclosure, knew or ought, under the circumstances, to have known that the trade secret had been obtained directly or indirectly from another person who was using or disclosing the trade secret unlawfully within the meaning of paragraph 3".

In the case of a trade secret infringement, Article 12 and Article 14 of the EU Trade Secrets Directive list remedies such as an injunction and/or corrective measures (the latter mostly relating to infringing goods) as well as damages. Yet, in Article 13(3), the EU Trade Secrets Directive provides for a relatively novel measure, i.e. pecuniary compensation.[286] Owing to the fact that, based on this measure, a possibility may exist to substitute an injunction and/or a corrective measure with a royalty thereby enabling a trade secret's further use, the question is what effects the application of the aforementioned alternative remedy may have for the data economy.

3.8.1   Conditions for the Application of a Pecuniary Compensation

Article 13(3) of the EU Trade Secrets Directive stipulates that:

> Member States shall provide that, *at the request of the person liable to be subject to the measures provided for in Article 12*, the competent judicial authority may order pecuniary compensation to be paid to the injured party *instead of applying those measures* if all the following conditions are met. (Emphasis added)

---

[286] It is noteworthy that before the EU Trade Secrets Directive the legal provision on pecuniary compensation could be found in the EU Directive on the enforcement of IP rights (Directive 2004/48/EC of the European Parliament and of the Council of 29 April 2004 on the enforcement of intellectual property rights, OJ [2004] L 157/45). Pursuant to Article 12 of the latter directive, pecuniary compensation could be applied as an alternative remedy to an injunction or corrective measures ("Member States may provide that, in appropriate cases and at the request of the person liable to be subject to the measures provided for in this Section, the competent judicial authorities may order pecuniary compensation to be paid to the injured party instead of applying the measures provided for in this Section if that person acted unintentionally and without negligence, if execution of the measures in question would cause him disproportionate harm and if pecuniary compensation to the injured party appears reasonably satisfactory").

Thereby, in the case of a trade secret infringement, pecuniary compensation, firstly, may be applicable only upon the request of a trade secret infringer, and, secondly, may serve as an alternative measure for an injunction and corrective measures listed in Article 12 of the EU Trade Secrets Directive.

Three cumulative conditions have to be fulfilled for a pecuniary compensation to be applied pursuant to Article 13(3) of the EU Trade Secrets Directive: "a) the person concerned at the time of use or disclosure neither knew nor ought, under the circumstances, to have known that the trade secret was obtained from another person who was using or disclosing the trade secret unlawfully; b) execution of the measures in question would cause that person disproportionate harm; and c) pecuniary compensation to the injured party appears reasonably satisfactory".

As regards the first condition, i.e. the fact that the person, while using or disclosing a trade secret, did not know and ought not to have known that the acquired trade secret was related to the unlawful behaviour, it may, at first sight, be not entirely clear how the wording of Article 13(3) letter (a) correlates with Article 4(4) of the EU Trade Secrets Directive, which stipulates no third-party liability for a trade secret infringement if the person at the time of the acquisition, use or disclosure of a trade secret did not know or ought not to have known about the unlawful behaviour involved. After all, if a person – at the time of the acquisition, use or disclosure of a trade secret – did not know or ought not to have known "that the trade secret had been obtained directly or indirectly from another person who was using or disclosing the trade secret unlawfully" (Article 4(4)), liability for such an acquisition, use or disclosure of a trade secret should not arise in the first place. In turn, there should be no question as regards the remedy. So, recalling that a pecuniary compensation is an alternative measure to the remedy such as an injunction, it may be asked how this remedy should be applied if there should be no liability in the first place.

Recital 29 of the EU Trade Secrets Directive explains that:

> A person could have originally acquired a trade secret in good faith, but *only become aware at a later stage, including upon notice served by the original trade secret holder*, that that person's knowledge of the trade secret in question derived from sources using or disclosing the relevant trade secret in an unlawful manner. In order to avoid, under those circumstances, the corrective measures or injunctions provided for causing disproportionate harm to that person, Member States should provide for the possibility, in appropriate cases, of pecuniary compensation being awarded to the injured party as an alternative measure. (Emphasis added)

Hence, it might be that the person who had acquired a trade secret lawfully (i.e. without knowledge about the unlawful behaviour related to the obtained trade secret), in the course of time, for example, while using a trade secret, becomes aware of the fact that the acquired trade secret was used or disclosed unlawfully (including the situation when such awareness occurs upon the notice of a trade secret holder). It is from that point of time, i.e. when a lawful trade secret holder becomes aware of the unlawful behaviour related to a trade secret, that the person can be held liable. It might thus be that a trade secret was acquired in good faith, but in the course of its use or at the moment of its disclosure, the person became aware of the unlawful conduct. In such a case, such person may be liable for a trade secret infringement. However, bearing in mind that a trade secret may already be put into use, an injunction may be too severe a remedy, for example, in cases where a person has been using that trade secret for a long period of time. Thus, the application of pecuniary compensation as an alternative remedy to an injunction and/or corrective measures is subject to an important condition, i.e. the acquisition of a trade secret by a third party was in good faith. In fact, the whole purpose of this remedy is to protect such good faith acquirers of information from remedies such as an injunction and/or corrective measures (that are rather severe as regards infringing goods) in cases where a trade secret has, for example, already been put into use. Hence, while liability should not arise as long as a third party acts in good faith (i.e. does not know and ought not to have known about the unlawful behaviour related to the acquired trade secret), at the moment when this situation changes, i.e. a third party becomes aware of such an unlawful conduct, such a third party may, in fact, be considered to be using or disclosing a trade secret unlawfully, so that such a person might be held liable for the unlawful use or disclosure of a trade secret.

Article 13(3)(a) of the EU Trade Secrets Directive, however, should have been more precise in this regard. As shown, Article 13(3)(a) itself does not speak of a good faith acquisition, since this explanation can be found only in the recitals part of the EU Trade Secrets Directive, namely, recital 29. A lack of clarity may arise when the legal provision on pecuniary compensation is directly compared with Article 4(4) of the EU Trade Secrets Directive. Whereas, pursuant to Article 13(3)(a), "the person *at the time of use or disclosure* neither knew nor ought, under the circumstances, to have known" about the unlawful behaviour involved, Article 4(4) of the EU Trade Secrets Directive stipulates exactly the opposite, i.e. that a third party will be held liable when "a person, *at the time of the [...] use or disclosure*, knew or ought, under the circumstances, to have known" about the unlawful behaviour related to that particular trade secret. This analysis shows that the wording of Article 13(3)(a) of the EU Trade Secrets Directive not only lacks clarity (as the explanation about a good faith acquirer is provided in recital 29), but also does not entirely conform with Article 4(4) of the EU Trade Secrets Directive. In order to align both legal provisions in terms of third-party liability, Article 13(3)(a) should have been formulated in a clearer way, saying that a trade secret was acquired lawfully by the person concerned, but at the time of use or disclosure such a person *became aware or ought, under the circumstances, to have become aware* of the unlawful conduct involved. In such a way, it would have been clearer that Article 13(3)(a) speaks of good faith acquirers who obtain knowledge about the unlawful behaviour after the acquisition of a trade secret. In other words, it should have been specified that, although at the time of the acquisition, the third party did not know about the unlawful behaviour and thus acquired a trade secret lawfully, in the course of time the situation changed and that third party became aware of these circumstances while using or disclosing a trade secret. In order to extract the full potential of this remedy, it would have been helpful if this condition had at least been specified in the national laws of the Member States in the framework of the implementation of the EU Trade Secrets Directive.[287] Otherwise, a lack of clarity as regards the conditions of this remedy may lead to misinterpretations and, possibly, to its limited application by the national courts.

The purpose of a pecuniary compensation is to serve as a remedy striking a balance between the interests of a third party that acquired the trade secret in good faith and a trade secret holder. The balance is meant in terms of weighing, on the one hand, the disproportionate harm that the third party may suffer in the case of an injunction of the trade secret already employed in the business and, on the other hand, the interests of a trade secret holder. In fact, this is where two other conditions listed in Article 13(3) letters (b) and (c) come into play, i.e. a likelihood of disproportionate harm to the person who uses the trade secret and a reasonable satisfaction by a pecuniary compensation to a trade secret holder. What a "disproportionate harm" and a compensation, which is "reasonably satisfactory" might be will be subject to interpretation and will have to be decided on a case-by-case basis.

Finally, it should be noted that there is one more condition that may limit the application of a pecuniary compensation. Recital 29 of the EU Trade Secrets Directive, which speaks of pecuniary compensation, stipulates that "where the unlawful use of the trade secret would constitute an infringement of law other than that provided for in this Directive or would be likely to harm consumers,

---

[287] This is, however, not the case in all EU Member States. For example, in the Trade Secrets Act of the Republic of Lithuania (Law on the Legal Protection of Trade Secrets of the Republic of Lithuania as of 26 April 2018, No. XIII-1125), the wording of Article 13 of the EU Trade Secrets Directive was overtaken directly (Article 7(7) of the Lithuanian Trade Secrets Act), with the result that, in the absence of the clarification, which is provided in recital 29 of the EU Trade Secrets Directive, the wording of this national legal provision stands in some conflict with the wording of the legal provision, which implemented Article 4(4) of the EU Trade Secrets Directive, i.e. on third-party liability (Article 4(3) of the Lithuanian Trade Secrets Act).

such unlawful use should not be allowed". Hence, even if all the conditions of Article 13(3) of the EU Trade Secrets Directive were satisfied, pecuniary compensation, and thus further use of a trade secret, may not be applied if the use of a trade secret could infringe other laws or would be likely to harm consumers. Safety requirements of the products or rules on personal data or privacy protection may stand as an example.

In terms of its legal construction, pecuniary compensation comes close to the remedy known in the US trade secret law, i.e. the so-called "royalty order injunction". Therefore, it may be helpful to have a closer look at the latter and then to analyse the similarities and differences of these remedies on both sides of the Atlantic and what implications this may have for the application of these remedies in practice.

3.8.2   A "Royalty Order Injunction" in the US

A "royalty order injunction" is enshrined in the Uniform Trade Secrets Act (UTSA).[288] Section 2(b) UTSA reads:

> In exceptional circumstances, an injunction may condition future use upon payment of reasonable royalty for no longer than the period of time for which use could have been prohibited. Exceptional circumstances include, but are not limited to, a material and prejudicial change of position prior to acquiring knowledge or reason to know of misappropriation that renders a prohibitive injunction inequitable.

According to the passage, a "royalty order injunction" may be applied in lieu of an (ordinary) injunction in a form of a payment of a "reasonable royalty". Such a royalty may be applied for a limited period of time, which is basically meant in the passage as the period of a "head start", i.e. "the period of time for which use could have been prohibited".

Importantly though, the application of this remedy is limited to exceptional circumstances, one of them being related to "a change in the position" of the third party before the acquisition of knowledge about the unlawful behaviour related to a trade secret. Also, a "royalty order injunction" may be applicable in exceptional circumstances such as the public interest.[289]

---

[288]   National Conference of Commissioners on Uniform State Laws, Uniform Trade Secrets Act, 1979, as amended in 1985.

[289]   See the comment of Section 2 of the UTSA (National Conference of Commissioners on Uniform State Laws, Uniform Trade Secrets Act, 1979, as amended in 1985). See also *Rowe, E.A./Sandeen, S.K.*, Trade Secrecy and International Transactions. Law and Practice, Cheltenham: Edward Elgar 2015, pp. 119–120: "the second reasonable royalty scenario under the UTSA concerns rare situations where the grant of injunctive relief (either preliminary or permanent) would originally be called

For example, in *Progressive Products, Inc. v. Swartz*,[290] the Supreme Court of Kansas pointed out that "there are no set rules for what constitutes 'exceptional circumstances'".[291] In that case, the Court of Appeal of Kansas[292] did not consider "society's general interest in fostering competition to rise to the level of an overriding public interest requiring the court to withhold injunctive relief".[293] It was pointed out by the Court of Appeal of Kansas that this case was not such "where the public will be prohibited from accessing the product if Appellees are enjoined from manufacturing and selling it".[294] However, owing to the incomplete findings of the district court, the case was remanded to the district court by the Supreme Court of Kansas and the opinion of the Court of Appeals reversing the remedy (a "royalty order injunction") ordered by the district court[295] was itself reversed.[296]

According to the comment in the UTSA, a "royalty order injunction" should be distinguished from damages, so that these remedies cannot be applied together:

> The reasonable royalty alternative measure of damages for a misappropriator's past conduct under Section 3(a) is readily distinguishable from a Section 2(b) royalty order injunction, which conditions a misappropriator's future ability to use a trade secret upon payment of a reasonable royalty. A Section 2(b) royalty order injunction is appropriate only in exceptional circumstances; whereas a reasonable royalty measure of damages is a general option. Because Section 3(a) damages are awarded for a misappropriator's past conduct and a Section 2(b) royalty order injunction regulates a misappropriator's future conduct, both remedies cannot be awarded for the same conduct.[297]

---

for except for overriding public interest concerns. [...] The public policy interests that may justify the grant of a so-called 'royalty injunction' in lieu of a regular injunction are not well developed or defined in the United States, but the provision (and its associated comments) represents one place in the UTSA where the public interest is explicitly mentioned."

[290]   *Progressive Products, Inc. v. Swartz*, 258 P.3d 969 (2011).

[291]   *Ibid.*, at 979.

[292]   *Progressive Products, Inc. v. Swartz*, 205 P.3d 766 (2009).

[293]   *Ibid.*, at 778. The Court specified that "[a]lthough we acknowledge society's general interest in fostering competition is a matter of public concern, there is simply no evidence to establish a substantial probability that the public will be prejudiced if the misappropriators here are enjoined" (*ibid.*).

[294]   *Ibid.*, at 778.

[295]   *Ibid.*, at 778.

[296]   *Progressive Products v. Swartz*, 258 P.3d 969, 980 (2011).

[297]   National Conference of Commissioners on Uniform State Laws, Uniform Trade Secrets Act, 1979, as amended in 1985, Comment to Section 3, p. 11.

Thereby, since a "royalty order injunction" – as a remedy applicable in exceptional circumstances – is directed towards the use of a trade secret in the future, it is said to be not compliant with – a more ordinary remedy – damages, which can normally be applied together with a prohibitive injunction as a remedy for past behaviour. In this regard, a "royalty order injunction" comes close to compulsory licensing of a trade secret.

3.8.3 Pecuniary Compensation v. a "Royalty Order Injunction"

The analysis above shows that, by their nature, a pecuniary compensation and a "royalty order injunction" come close to each other. After all, the goal of both remedies is to enable further use of a trade secret upon a payment. Both of them serve as an alternative to a remedy such as a (prohibitive) injunction thereby seeking for a balance between the interests of a trade secret holder and a third party. Yet the purpose of the "royalty order injunction" is broader. It incorporates scenarios when the public interest may be involved, so that a "material change in a position" in terms of a good faith acquirer is one of the exceptional circumstances when the "royalty order injunction" could be applied. An alternative exceptional circumstance is the public interest, which, as shown, will not always be considered by the US courts to involve competition-related matters.

In fact, there are further important differences between these two remedies, not the least when it comes to the conditions of when they may be applied.

Contrary to a "royalty order injunction", the application of which is limited to exceptional circumstances, including the public interest, Article 13(3) of the EU Trade Secrets Directive does not entail such a requirement. The EU Trade Secrets Directive does not mention the public interest among the conditions for the application of pecuniary compensation. The latter can be applied upon the request of a person liable for the trade secret infringement.

Whereas a "material change in position" is one of the exceptional circumstances when the "royalty order injunction" could be applied for pecuniary compensation under the EU Trade Secrets Directive, this is one of the cumulative conditions, even if, as argued, Article 13(3)(a) of the EU Trade Secrets Directive could have been better formulated in this regard.

Furthermore, whereas a "royalty order injunction" may substitute an ordinary injunction (only), pecuniary compensation, according to the EU Trade Secrets Directive, is a remedy that may be an alternative not only to an injunction, but also to corrective measures. According to the EU Trade Secrets Directive, Article 12(1)(c), corrective measures may be adopted with regard to the so-called "infringing goods". Article 2(4) of the EU Trade Secrets Directive defines infringing goods as "goods, the design, characteristics, functioning, production process or marketing of which significantly benefits from trade secrets unlawfully acquired, used or disclosed". Such a definition is not only broad, it is also unclear. For example, a good may be considered an infringing good if the latter "significantly benefits from a trade secret", whereas it is not clear what a "significant benefit" is supposed to mean. Article 4(5) of the EU Trade Secrets Directive elaborates on the third-party liability as regards infringing goods by stipulating that "[t]he production, offering or placing on the market of infringing goods, or the importation, export or storage of infringing goods for those purposes, shall also be considered an unlawful use of a trade secret where the person carrying out such activities knew, or ought, under the circumstances, to have known that the trade secret was used unlawfully within the meaning of paragraph 3". Furthermore, Article 12(1) of the EU Trade Secrets Directive requires Member States to ensure that "where a judicial decision taken on the merits of the case finds that there has been unlawful acquisition, use or disclosure of a trade secret, the competent judicial authorities may, at the request of the applicant, order one or more of the following measures against the infringer". Accordingly, in addition to "the cessation of or, as the case may be, the prohibition of the use or disclosure of the trade secret" (Article 12(1)(a) of the EU Trade Secrets Directive), Article 12(1)(b) lists "the prohibition of the production, offering, placing on the market or use of infringing goods, or the importation, export or storage of infringing goods for those purposes". Finally, Article 12(1)(c) enables "the adoption of the appropriate corrective measures with regard to the infringing goods",[298] whereas Article 12(2) of the EU Trade Secrets Directive specifies that such corrective measures shall include recalling the infringing good from the market, depriving the infringing good of their infringing quality, or ordering the destruction of the infringing good or, where appropriate, their withdrawal from the market. Although recital 28 of the EU Trade Secrets Directive states that "[h]aving regard to the principle of proportionality, corrective measures should not necessarily entail the destruction of the goods if other viable options are present, such as depriving the good of its infringing quality or the disposal of the goods outside the market, for example, by means of donations to charitable organisations", this does not necessarily provide much comfort in the light of what was explained above. In this regard, pecuniary compensation may sound as a big relief indeed.

Finally, according to Article 13(3) of the EU Trade Secrets Directive, "[w]here pecuniary compensation is ordered instead of the measures referred to in points (a) and (b) of Article 12(1), it shall not exceed the amount of

---

[298] According to Article 12(4) of the EU Trade Secrets Directive, such corrective measures shall be "carried out at the expense of the infringer, unless there are particular reasons for not doing so".

royalties or fees which would have been due, had that person requested authorisation to use the trade secret in question, for the period of time for which use of the trade secret could have been prohibited".[299] In this regard, pecuniary compensation comes close to a "royalty order injunction", which may also be applicable for a limited period of time (i.e. "the period of time for which use could have been prohibited"). Such a period of time, as explained, could be considered in terms of a "head start". However, in contrast to the "royalty order injunction", which cannot be applied together with damages, pecuniary compensation is an alternative to an injunction and/or corrective measures only. However, not only an injunction, but also corrective measures, may be applied together with damages. Article 12(4) of the EU Trade Secrets Directive states that measures such as corrective remedies "shall be without prejudice to any damages that may be due to a trade secret holder" by reason of a trade secret infringement. The EU Trade Secrets Directive does not mention that a pecuniary compensation, which is an alternative to an injunction and/or corrective remedies, cannot be applied together with damages. Hence, it might be that pecuniary compensation (Article 13) and damages (Article 14) could be applied cumulatively.

The analysis above shows that, although a pecuniary compensation bears resemblance to a "royalty order injunction", which has for a long time been known under the US trade secret law as a remedy alternative to an injunction, these two remedies also have important differences. The question thereby is what role a pecuniary compensation may play in the data economy.

3.8.4   Pecuniary Compensation as a Compulsory Licensing?

In light of a broad range of remedies that are listed in the EU Trade Secrets Directive for a trade secret infringement, pecuniary compensation stands out as an attractive alternative. After all, it offers a possibility to substitute not only an injunction, but also a range of corrective measures that might be applicable in the case of a rather problematic concept of the EU Trade Secrets Directive, i.e. infringing goods. Therefore, pecuniary compensation seems to be offering a balance of the severe effects that may be caused by the aforementioned remedies, in particular bearing in mind that it would be applicable in the cases of a good faith acquirer.

---

[299] Points (a) and (b) of Article 12(1) of the EU Trade Secrets Directive foresee measures such as respectively "the cessation of or, as the case may be, the prohibition of the use or disclosure of the trade secret" and "the prohibition of the production, offering, placing on the market or use of infringing goods, or the importation, export or storage of infringing goods for those purposes".

In the data economy in general and in the light of the AI technology in particular, such an alternative remedy may be relevant. After all, bearing in mind not only the numerous chains of the connected technology, but also the role of the training sets (which may be protected as a trade secret) for machine learning, it may often be that the condition of an infringing good in terms of such a good significantly benefiting from a trade secret (even if it is not entirely clear what such a benefit is supposed to mean) might be fulfilled. In this regard, pecuniary compensation may seem to be a remedy that could serve the purpose.

Pecuniary compensation, similarly to the "royalty order injunction", comes close to a compulsory licensing scheme. In contrast to the "royalty order injunction", however, such a compulsory licensing in a form of a pecuniary compensation under the EU Trade Secrets Directive would be applicable upon the request of a trade secret infringer. Differently from the UTSA as regards the "royalty order injunction", the EU Trade Secrets Directive does not mention the public interest among the relevant conditions for the application of a pecuniary compensation.

In cases where, on the basis of the application of this alternative remedy, further use of a trade secret is allowed (for example, when a pecuniary compensation substitutes the cessation or the prohibition of the use or disclosure of a trade secret (Article 12(1)(a) of the EU Trade Secrets Directive) or the prohibition of the production, offering, placing on the market or use of infringing goods, or the importation export or storage of such goods as stated in Article 12(1)(b)), the amount of royalty will have to be determined as required by Article 13(3) of the EU Trade Secrets Directive.

Whereas in the case of a "royalty order injunction", the UTSA speaks about a reasonable royalty,[300] the EU Trade Secrets Directive (Article 13(3)) does not mention this. It is rather said that the amount of such royalties should be that which would have been in the case if the person concerned had requested authorization to use the trade secret. Moreover, such an amount should cover the period of time for which the use of the trade secret could have been pre-

---

[300] National Conference of Commissioners on Uniform State Laws, Uniform Trade Secrets Act, 1979, as amended in 1985, Comment to Section 3, p. 11. The concept of a "reasonable royalty" resembles the criterion known under the "(F)RAND licensing", i.e. licensing on (fair), reasonable and non-discriminatory terms. In the EU, the issue of FRAND licensing was addressed by the ECJ in the *Huawei* case (ECJ, Case C-170/13, *Huawei Technologies Co. Ltd v. ZTE Corp. and ZTE Deutschland GmbH*, 16 July 2015, ECLI:EU:C:2015:477). However, in that case, the ECJ did not have to explain what a reasonable royalty could be, but rather had to provide guidance (in a form of a preliminary ruling) on when the actions of a company in terms of not honouring their commitment given to a standard setting organization to grant licenses on FRAND terms might be considered an abuse of a dominant position in the framework of Article 102 TFEU.

vented by the original trade secret holder.[301] Yet, finally, it says that such an amount "shall not exceed" the amount of royalties calculated on the aforementioned criteria, implying that the amount of a royalty determined in a particular case may, in fact, be lower.

It is noteworthy that a compulsory licensing scheme, including compulsory access to a trade secret, is known under EU competition law. It was used in the *Microsoft* case[302] where compulsory access to a trade secret was granted on the basis of Article 102 TFEU. The latter legal provision prohibits an abuse of a dominant position. The EU compulsory licensing scheme is based on the so-called "exceptional circumstances" test, which was created in the *Magill* case[303] and was further explained in two other cases, i.e. *IMS Health*[304] and *Microsoft*. The four requirements of the "exceptional circumstances" test after *Microsoft* are as follows: firstly, access to a particular input is indispensable; secondly, there is a risk of the elimination of effective competition in the related markets; thirdly, technical development is hindered to the prejudice of consumers; and fourthly, there is no objective justification as regards the refusal to grant access to the input requested.[305]

Accordingly, a compulsory licence on the basis of competition law may be possible only in a limited number of cases. First and foremost, an important requirement for Article 102 TFEU to be applied is that there is a dominant position in the relevant market in the first place. In the absence of such a position neither Article 102 TFEU in general nor the "exceptional circumstances" test in particular may be applied. Furthermore, although the requirements of the "exceptional circumstances" test were broadened in the *Microsoft* case as compared with the original requirements of the "exceptional circumstances" created in *Magill*,[306] for example, regarding "economic" indispensability, hindering technical development as contrasted to the "new product" rule, or

---

[301] See also recital 29 of the EU Trade Secrets Directive.

[302] General Court, Case T-201/04, *Microsoft v. Commission*, 17 September 2007, [2007] E.C.R. II-3601 (ECLI:EU:T:2007:289).

[303] ECJ, Joined cases C-241/91 P and C-242/91 P, *Radio Telefis Eireann (RTE) and Independent Television Publications Ltd (ITP) v. Commission*, 6 April 1995, [1995] E.C.R. I-743 (ECLI:EU:C:1995:98) (known as the *Magill* case), paras 53–56.

[304] ECJ, Case C-418/01, *IMS Health GmbH & Co. OHG v. NDC Health GmbH & Co. KG*, 29 April 2004, [2004] E.C.R. I-5039 (ECLI:EU:C:2004:257).

[305] General Court, *Microsoft*, *supra* note 302, paras 291–712.

[306] For a more detailed analysis of the "exceptional circumstances" test as it was applied in the *Microsoft* case see *Surblytė, G.*, The Refusal to Disclose Trade Secrets as an Abuse of Market Dominance – *Microsoft* and Beyond, Berne: Stämpfli 2011, pp. XLVII + 263 (Munich Series on European and International Competition Law, Vol. 28), pp. 115–140.

the "Incentives Balance Test", the requirements of the "exceptional circumstances" test remain specific and may be not easy to fulfil in practice.

In contrast to a rather strict compulsory licensing scheme based on EU competition law, pecuniary compensation under the EU Trade Secrets Directive offers a possibility to enable the use of a trade secret in a broader number of cases. Importantly, it does not relate to the requirement of a dominant position in the relevant market, so that cases of smaller market players may also be captured. In contrast to a compulsory licensing scheme under Article 102 TFEU, pecuniary compensation as a remedy in trade secret infringement cases does not depend on dominance.

Yet one particular feature of pecuniary compensation still merits attention. In contrast to a "royalty order injunction", which may not be applied together with damages, the EU Trade Secrets Directive does not exclude such a possibility.

According to Article 14(1) of the EU Trade Secrets Directive, damages for a trade secret infringement shall be "appropriate to the actual prejudice suffered". Such damages may include "lost profits, which the injured party has suffered, any unfair profits made by the infringer and, in appropriate cases, elements other than economic factors, such as the moral prejudice caused to the trade secret holder" (Article 14(2) of the EU Trade Secrets Directive). Furthermore, recital 30 of the EU Trade Secrets Directive explains that "[i]n order [...] to ensure that the injured trade secret holder, to the extent possible, is placed in the position in which he, she or it would have been had that conduct not taken place, it is necessary to provide for adequate compensation for the prejudice suffered as a result of that unlawful conduct". Hence, the purpose of paying damages is not to punish a trade secret infringer, but rather to provide an adequate compensation for a trade secret holder for the prejudice suffered.

In this regard, it could be recalled that the UTSA makes a distinction between a "royalty order injunction" and damages stating that they cannot be claimed simultaneously. This is mainly due to the reason that damages would have to be paid for the past behaviour, whereas a "royalty order injunction" conditions future use of a trade secret. Such a distinction is logical, since, bearing in mind that the person concerned may be not aware of any unlawful conduct involved, no trade secret infringement would have taken place until the moment such a person became aware of such conduct. Awarding damages for the use of a trade secret during the period of time when the person lacked knowledge about unlawful behaviour related to the trade secret, which was acquired in good faith, would actually mean implying liability to a third party without fault.

The fact that the EU Trade Secrets Directive does not make a clear distinction between pecuniary compensation and damages is a major drawback. In fact, the application of both of these remedies simultaneously may result in the cases where a trade secret holder may receive a double compensation. The likelihood of such a risk becomes even higher if we consider that Article 14(2) of the EU Trade Secrets Directive, which speaks about damages, states that the competent judicial authorities may "set the damages as a lump sum on the basis of elements such as, at a minimum, the amount of royalties or fees which would have been due had the infringer requested authorization to use the trade secret in question". Setting damages in such a lump sum may, according to Article 14(2) of the EU Trade Secrets Directive, serve as an alternative for calculating damages. However, the wording of Article 14(2) of the EU Trade Secrets Directive is identical to the wording of Article 13(3), where the latter speaks about the amount of royalty to be calculated in the case of pecuniary compensation.[307] The main difference between these two legal provisions is that, firstly, Article 13(3) sets a time limit when calculating a pecuniary compensation, i.e. "for the period of time for which use of the trade secret could have been prohibited", and, secondly, Article 14(2) speaks about the minimum amount for damages, whereas Article 13(3) sets the limits for the maximum amount of pecuniary compensation. Moreover, recital 30 of the EU Trade Secrets explains that "[a]s an alternative, for example where, considering the intangible nature of trade secrets, it would be difficult to determine the amount of the actual prejudice suffered, the amount of the damages might be derived from elements such as the royalties or fees which would have been due had the infringer requested authorization to use the trade secret in question. The aim of that alternative method is not to introduce an obligation to provide for punitive damages, but to ensure compensation based on an objective criterion while taking account of the expenses incurred by the trade secret holder, such as the costs of identification and research". Accordingly, the alternative provided in Article 14(2) of the EU Trade Secrets Directive is an alternative method of calculating damages, but is not meant to be an alternative to damages as a remedy.

Such deficits of the legal provisions of the EU Trade Secrets Directive, including the risk of a double compensation, may result in pecuniary compensation being a deterrent rather than an incentive for companies to claim for such an alternative remedy. This may be particularly so if we recall that this

---

[307] Article 14(2) 2nd paragraph reads: "Alternatively, the competent judicial authorities may, in appropriate cases, set the damages as a lump sum on the basis of elements such as, at a minimum, *the amount of royalties or fees which would have been due had the infringer requested authorisation to use the trade secret in question*" (emphasis added). Article 13(3) 2nd paragraph reads: "Where pecuniary compensation is ordered instead of the measures referred to in points (a) and (b) of Article 12(1), it shall not exceed *the amount of royalties or fees which would have been due, had that person requested authorisation to use the trade secret in question*, for the period of time for which use of the trade secret could have been prohibited" (emphasis added).

remedy, pursuant to Article 13(3) of the EU Trade Secrets Directive, may be applicable only "at the request of the person liable to be subject to the measures provided for in Article 12". This may be very unfortunate, in particular considering the potential of this remedy if it were applied in the context of the data economy.

3.9 INTERMEDIATE CONCLUSION

Both personal and non-personal data as well as data sets consisting of such data may be eligible for trade secret protection as long as the requirements under a trade secret definition are fulfilled, i.e. relative secrecy, actual or potential commercial value of data (data set) and reasonable steps taken by a trade secret holder to protect information under a trade secret.

The fact that personal data may form part or the whole of a trade secret may raise tensions with personal data protection laws, first and foremost, when it comes to the exercise of the rights of the data subjects provided in the GDPR. In particular, the right to access personal data (Article 15 GDPR) or the right to data portability (Article 20 GDPR) may not only affect the integrity of a data set of a company, but may also risk compromising their trade secrets. Since neither the EU Trade Secrets Directive, nor the GDPR provide clear guidance on how such potential conflicts between trade secret and personal data protection should be solved, solutions will have to be searched for by the courts on the case-by-case basis. Also, the right not to be subject to solely automated decision-making (Article 22 GDPR) may be exercised by a data subject to a limited extent, since an algorithm based on which such a decision is made might be covered by a trade secret.

Although trade secret protection does not grant exclusive rights, this does not mean that trade secrets cannot at all be treated as property or grant ownership. The lack of the notion of a "trade secret owner" in the EU Trade Secrets Directive may thus lead to legal uncertainty, first and foremost, as regards the trade secret owner's rights and obligations related to their trade secrets as well as the enforcement of the protection of trade secrets, including remedies. The question of who the (original) trade secret owner is – as contrasted to further trade secret holders, for example, licensees – may be highly important in the data economy where a number of persons may be involved in different steps and levels of data processing. Also, clarifying the question who a trade secret owner is may solve the question of "data ownership".

One of the fair means of obtaining access to a trade secret by a third party is reverse engineering. In the context of AI technology, the aim that access to technical solutions should remain possible to third parties may lead to trade mark protection for functional signs being refused. Such access may nevertheless be hindered by trade secret law, since, according to the EU Trade

Secrets Directive, contractual restrictions to reverse engineering may be valid. Yet, in light of the importance of such access, not the least for complementary technologies in the data economy, and bearing in mind the cumulative effects of such contractual restrictions, caution may be needed when considering their validity. Furthermore, trade secret law is not meant to reinforce personal data protection, since trade secret law protects information under a trade secret, but does not prohibit access to such information by third parties using fair means, such as reverse engineering. However, should data sets containing (also) personal data be reverse engineered, identifiability of natural persons whose data may form part of such a data set may be enabled. Bearing in mind that such personal data may be further processed, such processing would have to comply with data protection laws in order to be lawful.

Finally, in the case of a trade secret infringement, the EU Trade Secrets Directive provides for an alternative remedy to an injunction or corrective measures, i.e. pecuniary compensation. Such a remedy may be applicable in the case of good faith acquirers of a trade secret. Although pecuniary compensation may serve as compulsory licensing and may thus be an attractive remedy for a trade secret infringement in the data economy, the practical application of this remedy (owing to the deficits of the regulatory norm) will have to be tested in practice. In particular, the fact that pecuniary compensation may be applied together with damages may result in a more cautious application of this remedy in practice.

The analysis above shows that trade secrets may be an important legal tool for the protection of data and (or) data sets as well as algorithms in the data economy. Yet the increasing use of algorithms by business may raise questions that go beyond trade secret law. In fact, the employment of algorithms by business may, first and foremost, raise questions with regard to competition. Thereby, a need may arise to clarify what role competition law plays in the data economy and whether competition law has sufficient tools to tackle the problems that may possibly arise owing to the spread of algorithms used in business.

4. Data- and algorithm-driven economy: issues for competition?

Since the data economy has brought numerous new opportunities for the companies to do business, it may seem at first sight that (drastic) changes may be needed in competition law.[1] The assessment of future risks caused by the developments of the technology may, no doubt, be important. However, the issue often is that an assessment of a problem may remain highly speculative if it is not yet entirely clear what that problem is in the first place. The "phantom" of the so-called "algorithmic collusion"[2] stands here as one of the examples.

Yet the question is how much, if at all, rethinking of competition law, in fact, may be needed. In other words, it might be that the technology is new and innovative, but is this also the case when it comes to the legal questions? It might be that current legal tools that are already available under competition law may be fit for purpose. What may be needed though, is a deeper analysis of their application in the data economy. It might be that such an application may bring to light drawbacks in the existing tool-kit of EU competition law. If this were the case, it may turn out that it is not the data economy that may be challenged by the lack of competition law tools (as the proposals for changing

---

[1]   See, for example, the report for the European Commission by Jacques Crémer, Yves-Alexandre de Montjoye, Heike Schweitzer, Competition Policy for the Digital Era, 2019 (http://ec.europa.eu/competition/publications/reports/kd0419345enn.pdf).
[2]   "Algorithmic collusion" was in particular analysed by Ezrachi and Stucke (see *Ezrachi, A./Stucke, M.E.*, Artificial Intelligence & Collusion: When Computers Inhibit Competition, (2017) University of Illinois Law Review 1775 (Oxford Legal Studies Research Paper No. 18/2015; University of Tennessee Legal Studies Research Paper No. 267, available at SSRN: https://papers.ssrn.com/sol3/papers.cfm?abstract_id=2591874); *Ezrachi, A./Stucke, M.E.*, Two Artificial Neural Networks Meet in an Online Hub and Change the Future (Of Competition, Market Dynamics and Society) (1 July 2017). Oxford Legal Studies Research Paper No. 24/2017; University of Tennessee Legal Studies Research Paper No. 323. Available at SSRN: https://papers.ssrn.com/sol3/papers.cfm?abstract_id=2949434; *Ezrachi, A./Stucke, M.E.*, Sustainable and Unchallenged Algorithmic Tacit Collusion, (2020) 17 Northwestern Journal of Technology and Intellectual Property 217 (University of Tennessee Legal Studies Research Paper No. 366; Oxford Legal Studies Research Paper No. 16/2019. Available at SSRN: https://papers.ssrn.com/sol3/papers.cfm?abstract_id=3282235)). See also *Ezrachi, A./Stucke, M.E.*, Virtual Competition: The Promise and Perils of the Algorithm-Driven Economy, Cambridge, MA: Harvard University Press 2016.

competition law or for filling in its potential gaps in order to tackle "algorithmic collusion" would suggest). In contrast, it might be that the existing competition law tools may be challenged: not because they cannot keep up with the pace of the technological changes, but because their application in light of the data economy and algorithms may help better spotlight the deficits that have existed in some competition law tools for quite some time already.

4.1   ALGORITHMIC PRICE ADJUSTMENTS

In light of an increasing use of algorithms by the business, fears have been raised in terms of a looming danger coming from algorithms. For example, Ezrachi and Stucke, back in 2015, in their seminal article on AI and collusion,[3] identified "four nonexclusive categories of collusion – *Messenger, Hub and Spoke, Predictable Agent*, and *Digital Eye*" (emphasis in original).[4] According to the authors, "[t]he fourth category – *Digital Eye* – is the trickiest. Here, the competitors unilaterally create and use computer algorithms to achieve a given target, such as profit maximization. The machines, through self-learning and experiment, independently determine the means to optimize profit. [...] Noticeably, under this category neither legal concept – intent nor agreement – apply"[5] (footnote omitted).

---

[3]   *Ezrachi, A./Stucke, M.E.*, Artificial Intelligence & Collusion: When Computers Inhibit Competition, (2017) University of Illinois Law Review 1775 (Oxford Legal Studies Research Paper No. 18/2015; University of Tennessee Legal Studies Research Paper No. 267, available at SSRN: https://papers.ssrn.com/sol3/papers.cfm?abstract_id =2591874).

[4]   *Ibid.*, p. 1782. Whether such a *Digital Eye* is meant in terms of an allusion to the HAL 9000 computer in the famous science fiction movie *2001: A Space Odyssey* is an open question. However, the authors seem to have been strongly inspired by the latter in framing their ideas on AI and collusion in the aforementioned article, as the following wording suggests: "The development of self-learning and independent computers has long captured our imagination. The HAL 9000 computer, in the 1968 film, *2001: A Space Odyssey*, for example, assured, 'I am putting myself to the fullest possible use, which is all I think that any conscious entity can ever hope to do.' [...] Today businesses (and governments) are increasingly relying on big data and big analytics. As technology advances and the cost of storing and analyzing data drops, companies are investing in developing 'smart' and 'self-learning' machines to assist in pricing decisions, planning, trade, and logistics" (footnote omitted; *ibid.*, p. 1776).

[5]   *Ibid.*, p. 1783; see also pp. 1795–1796. Further analysis in: *Ezrachi, A./ Stucke, M.E.*, Sustainable and Unchallenged Algorithmic Tacit Collusion, (2020) 17 Northwestern Journal of Technology and Intellectual Property 217, at 250-255 (University of Tennessee Legal Studies Research Paper No. 366; Oxford Legal Studies Research Paper No. 16/2019. Available at SSRN: https://papers.ssrn.com/sol3/papers .cfm?abstract_id=3282235).

The term of "algorithmic collusion" was thus coined, followed by efforts to scrutinize whether such a collusion may raise any new competition law issues that existing competition law tools will not be able to cope with.[6] Few were found though. For example, the UK Competition and Markets Authority, in their study on pricing algorithms,[7] distinguished between two different situations when it comes to assessing the potential risks of algorithms to competition, i.e. firstly, the use of algorithms to monitor and enforce existing coordination, and secondly, the issue of a potential collusion by the use of pricing algorithms by each firm to make their unilateral pricing decisions.[8] The CMA in their study pointed out that out of three risks identified by Ezrachi and Stucke, i.e. the hub-and-spoke cartels, predictive agents and autonomous machines, it was only the hub-and-spoke cartels that could be capable of raising immediate risks to competition.[9] Hence, although the initial debate cautioned against high risks for competition in terms of autonomous collusion by algorithms, it might be that, in reality, these risks remain highly speculative, whereas the more ordinary risks may boil down to traditional competition law problems, such as, for example, the hub-and-spoke cartels.

In fact, the European Commission has already had some practice with cases involving algorithms. In July 2018, the European Commission adopted decisions in four cases,[10] which were among the first examples of real-life cases related to the implementation of algorithms. The European Commission,

---

[6]   See, for example, OECD (2017), Algorithms and Collusion: Competition Policy in the Digital Age (http://www.oecd.org/daf/competition/Algorithms-and-colllusion-competition-policy-in-the-digital-age.pdf); Competition & Markets Authority, Pricing Algorithms. Economic working paper on the use of algorithms to facilitate collusion an personalised pricing, 8 October 2018 (https://www.gov.uk/government/publications/pricing-algorithms-research-collusion-and-personalised-pricing). Bundeskartellamt/ Autorité de la concurrence, Algorithms and Competition, November 2019.

[7]   Competition & Markets Authority, Pricing Algorithms, *supra* note 6, p. 22.

[8]   *Ibid.*, p. 22.

[9]   *Ibid.*, p. 4. According to Ezrachi and Stucke, in the case of a hub-and-spoke cartel, "competitors use the same (or a single) algorithm to determine the market price or react to market changes. In this scenario, the common algorithm, which traders use as a vertical input, leads to horizontal alignment" (*Ezrachi, A./Stucke, M.E.*, Artificial Intelligence & Collusion: When Computers Inhibit Competition, (2017) University of Illinois Law Review 1775, 1787 (Oxford Legal Studies Research Paper No. 18/2015; University of Tennessee Legal Studies Research Paper No. 267, available at SSRN: https://papers.ssrn.com/sol3/papers.cfm?abstract_id=2591874)).

[10]   Commission decision of 24.7.2018 relating to proceedings under Article 101 of the Treaty on the Functioning of the European Union, Case AT.40465 – *ASUS*; Commission decision of 24.7.2018 relating to proceedings under Article 101 of the Treaty on the Functioning of the European Union, Case AT.40469 – *Denon & Marantz*; Commission decision of 24.7.2018 relating to proceedings under Article 101 of the Treaty on the Functioning of the European Union, Case AT.40182 – *Pioneer*;

for the first time, had to deal with the question of price-monitoring software applied by the manufactures of household devices in their online retail distribution network. In these cases, price monitoring software was used to ensure resale prices (hence, the anti-competitive conduct was fixing of a price in the form of a resale price maintenance, RPM). The European Commission imposed fines on the undertakings for restricting such resale prices, thereby infringing Article 101 TFEU. Yet the infringement in this case was rather a traditional one: the fixing of a price in a vertical agreement.

What may pose a potential danger to competition though, might be the horizontal adjustments of a price in cases where pricing algorithms[11] are involved. One of the potential scenarios that may raise concerns for competition may be related to vertical restraints. For example, in the case of a vertical resale price maintenance agreement or the use of the MFN ("most favoured nation") clauses, prices may be fixed between the parties of such agreements. However, the use of algorithmic technology may enable other market participants to follow suit, i.e. to adjust their prices. Although the price would be fixed by the vertical agreement, horizontal price adjustments, with the help of algorithms acting as multipliers of the fixed price, may lead to higher prices in the markets.[12] This shows that vertical agreements, which have normally been considered to pose less danger to competition, may need to be scrutinized more carefully in the light of the business's use of algorithms.[13]

Accordingly, competition concerns in the light of the use of algorithms may relate to "traditional" vertical restrictions, which may also produce horizontal effects (thus, vertical price adjustments with horizontal effects). Also, it might be that such horizontal price adjustments could occur independently of any vertical agreement.

From a competition law perspective, the question is whether such price adjustments in general and algorithmic price adjustments in particular may restrict competition, and if this is answered in an affirmative, whether EU

Commission decision of 24.7.2018 relating to proceedings under Article 101 of the Treaty on the Functioning of the European Union, Case AT.40181 – *Philips*.

[11]   The CMA defines a pricing algorithm as "an algorithm that uses price as an input, and/or uses a computational procedure to determine price as an output" (Competition & Markets Authority, Pricing Algorithms, *supra* note 6, p. 9).

[12]   Owing to the reach of algorithms and their speed, such price adjustments may be instantaneous. It might thus be that the price agreed upon in one anti-competitive agreement (for example, in a form of a resale price maintenance or an MFN (most-favoured nation) clause) may then be spread among the market participants with the help of algorithms.

[13]   Along these lines see also: Bundeskartellamt, "Competition Restraints in Online Sales after Coty and Asics – What's Next?" (Series of papers on "Competition and Consumer Protection in the Digital Economy", October 2018, at p. 1).

competition law, in particular Article 101 TFEU, but possibly also Article 102 TFEU, may capture (sanction) such behaviour.

4.1.1 Article 101 TFEU: A Concerted Practice

Article 101 TFEU prohibits anti-competitive agreements, concerted practices and decisions by associations of undertakings, but does not prohibit parallel behaviour. The concept of an agreement, in the broadest sense, under Article 101 TFEU requires the "concurrence of wills".[14] The question thereby is what implications the application of this legal provision may have for cases where algorithms (algorithmic tools) are employed.

According to the case-law of the ECJ, three elements are necessary for showing an infringement of Article 101 TFEU in the case of a concerted practice, namely a concertation, subsequent behaviour in the market and the causal link between the concertation and the subsequent behaviour in the market.[15] Such a causal link is, however, presumed if the concertation is established and companies remain active in the market.[16]

The ECJ, in the *ICI v. Commission of the European Communities* (known as the "Dyestuffs" case),[17] explained that a concerted practice is "a form of coordination between undertakings which, without having reached the stage where an agreement properly so-called has been concluded, knowingly substitutes practical cooperation between them for the risks of competition".[18] Hence, a concerted practice is, firstly, a reciprocal cooperation, and secondly, it is such cooperation, which *knowingly* substitutes competition. According to the ECJ, a concerted practice, although it does not have all the elements of a contract,

---

[14] See, for example, General Court, Case T-566/08, *Total Raffinage Marketing v. European Commission*, 13 September 2013, ECLI:EU:T:2013:423, para. 32 (with further references).

[15] See, for example, ECJ, Case C-199/92 P, *Hüls AG v. Commission of the European Communities*, 8 July 1999, ECLI:EU:C:1999:358, para. 161.

[16] ECJ, Case C-49/92 P, *Commission of the European Communities v. Anic Partecipazioni SpA*, 8 July 1999, ECLI:EU:C:1999:356, para. 121. See also ECJ, Case C-199/92 P, *Hüls AG v. Commission of the European Communities*, 8 July 1999, ECLI:EU:C:1999:358, para. 162. In the *T-Mobile* case, the ECJ explained that the "causal connection" presumption forms part of EU competition law, so that it has to be applied also by the national courts (ECJ, Case C-8/08, *T-Mobile Netherlands BV, KPN Mobile NV, Orange Nederland NV and Vodafone Libertel NV v. Raad van bestuur van de Nederlandse Mededingingsautoriteit*, 4 June 2009, ECLI:EU:C:2009:343, paras 52–53).

[17] ECJ, Case 48/69, *Imperial Chemical Industries Ltd. v. Commission of the European Communities*, 14 July 1972, ECLI:EU:C:1972:70.

[18] *Ibid.*, para. 64.

"may *inter alia* arise out of coordination which becomes apparent from the behaviour of the participants".[19]

The ECJ distinguished a concerted practice from parallel behaviour by stating that:

> Although *parallel behaviour* may not by itself be identified with a concerted practice, it *may however amount to strong evidence of such a practice* if it leads to *conditions of competition which do not correspond to the normal conditions of the market*, having regard to the nature of the products, the size and number of the undertakings, and the volume of the said market.[20] (Emphasis added)

What "normal conditions of the market" are may be subject to interpretation. Nevertheless, it may be important to bear in mind, following the cited passage above, that parallel behaviour, although it is not as such prohibited by EU competition law, may serve as an evidence that a concerted practice may be taking place.

In this regard, the ECJ further explained that:

> This is especially the case if the parallel conduct is such as to enable those concerned *to attempt to stabilize prices* at a level different from that to which competition would have led, and to consolidate established positions to the detriment of effective freedom of movement of the products in the Common Market and of the freedom of consumers to choose their suppliers.[21] (Emphasis added)

Hence, parallel conduct may, in particular, be an evidence of a concerted practice if indications exist of "an attempt to stabilize prices". In such cases, according to the ECJ, the evidence has to be analysed "not in isolation, but as a whole" and taking account of "the specific features of the market in the products in question".[22]

Such a logic may be highly relevant for a legal assessment of the potential competition law restrictions by using algorithms. In fact, in such cases, it may be even easier to find indications of the "attempts to stabilize prices", since such indications may be integrated in the algorithms themselves.

Furthermore, in the *Sugar Cartel* case, the ECJ held that the criteria of coordination did not require "the working out of an actual plan", but had to be understood "in the light of the concept [...] that each economic operator must

---

19   *Ibid.*, para. 65.
20   *Ibid.*, para. 66.
21   *Ibid.*, para. 67.
22   *Ibid.*, para. 68.

determine independently the policy which he intends to adopt on the common market".[23] In the words of the ECJ:

> Although it is correct to say that this requirement of independence does not deprive economic operators of the right to adapt themselves intelligently to the existing and anticipated conduct of their competitors, it does however strictly preclude any direct or *indirect contact* between such operators, the object or effect whereof is either *to influence the conduct on the market of an actual or potential competitor* or to disclose to such a competitor the course of conduct which they themselves have decided to adopt or contemplate adopting on the market.[24] (Emphasis added)

Hence, a concerted practice may take place not only in terms of a direct contact, but also – and this may be much more complicated – based on indirect contacts. Such a requirement makes sense, since it might be a rare situation in practice that a concerted practice will take place based on direct contacts. Instead, it might be that companies may try to engage with each other indirectly, after all, with the purpose of concealing such a practice.

Yet, a further extension, if not stretching, of a concerted practice was done by the ECJ in the *E-Turas* case,[25] where the ECJ held that a concerted practice may be confirmed also in the cases where "objective and consistent indicia" exist, possibly showing that companies "tacitly assented to an anticompetitive action".[26] Such a statement merits attention, and the case needs to be analysed in more detail.

4.1.1.1 The *E-Turas* case

The *E-Turas* case was not related to any artificial intelligence technology, but was rather about the question of a concerted practice of a number of companies via an online platform.[27] In that case, which started with the investigation by the Competition Council of the Republic of Lithuania,[28] the question was whether a number of travel agencies could be held to have participated in

---

[23] ECJ, Case C-40/73, *Coöperatieve Vereniging "Suiker Unie" UA and others v. Commission of the European Communities*, Joined Cases 40 to 48, 50, 54 to 56, 111, 113 and 114/73, 16 December 1975, ECLI:EU:C:1975:174, para. 173.

[24] *Ibid.*, para. 174.

[25] ECJ, Case C-74/14, *"E-Turas" UAB and Others v. Lietuvos Respublikos konkurencijos taryba*, 21 January 2016, ECLI:EU:C:2016:42.

[26] *Ibid.*, para. 45.

[27] For an analysis of the implications for this case, not the least when it comes to the use of algorithms, see also *Heinemann, A./Gebicka, A.*, Can Computers Form Cartels? About the Need for European Institutions to Revise the Concertation Doctrine in the Information Age, (2016) 7 Journal of European Competition Law & Practice 431.

[28] Decision of the Competition Council of the Republic of Lithuania on the compliance with the actions of the undertakings providing organized trips' sales and other

a concerted practice through the online boking system (E-TURAS), which was administered by the system administrator Eturas. From the competition law point of view, the problematic part of the case was whether it could be said that all travel agencies that used the E-TURAS platform for selling their travel packages could be considered to have participated in a horizontal concerted practice in terms of coordinating their prices via an online booking system of E-TURAS, when the system administrator Eturas introduced a price "cap" on the travel packages sold by those travel agencies on the online booking system E-TURAS.

The Lithuanian Competition Council basically answered this question in the affirmative. According to the Lithuanian Competition Council, 30 travel agencies and Eturas coordinated their behaviour in terms of a concerted practice with regard to the discounts for online travel bookings through the E-TURAS system, and owing to the restriction of competition by object, infringed Article 5[29] of the Law on Competition of the Republic of Lithuania and Article 101 TFEU. Fines were imposed on all undertakings, except for two, i.e. the one that informed the Competition Council about the practice and was thus granted immunity from a fine,[30] and a second that had terminated the agreement with Eturas.[31] As regards Eturas, the company that administered the E-TURAS system, the Competition Council, held that the latter company acted as a facilitator of the concerted practice and, by having restricted competition by object, also infringed Article 5 of the Law on Competition and Article 101 TFEU.[32] Yet, a tricky issue in the case was that the "cap" on the discount rates for the travelling packages offered via the E-TURAS system was technically introduced by the administrator of the E-TURAS system informing the participating travel agencies about such a "cap" by sending an electronic message to their system accounts.[33] However, the arguments of some of the travel agencies that they had not read the aforementioned message, and thus, were not aware of the "cap", was not considered relevant by the Competition Council,[34] as was the fact that some undertakings factually applied higher

---

related services with the requirements of Article 5 of the Law on Competition of the Republic of Lithuania and Article 101 TFEU, 7 June 2012, No. 2S-9.

[29] Law on Competition of the Republic of Lithuania as of 23 March 1999, No. VIII-1099 (with later amendments). Article 5 of the Law on Competition of the Republic of Lithuania is the national equivalent of Article 101 TFEU.

[30] Decision of the Competition Council, *E-Turas*, *supra* note 28, paras 253–258.

[31] *Ibid.*, para. 169.

[32] *Ibid.*, paras 173–177, 179–196.

[33] *Ibid.*, paras 47, 55. Such a "capping" of the discounts was set and technically organized, so that the companies had only limited capabilities to change it (*ibid.*, para. 150).

[34] *Ibid.*, para. 160.

discounts.[35] In the opinion of the Competition Council, the circumstances, such as the features of the E-TURAS system, its functionality principles, systematic notices and visual appearance as well as the information on the websites of the travel agencies themselves that they would apply a discount of 3 per cent, indicated that the travel agencies were aware of the "cap" and could also assume that other undertakings using the E-TURAS system were applying discounts not higher than 3 per cent (the maximum rate set by the E-TURAS system).[36] It was said that, for the assessment whether the behaviour of the travel agencies amounted to a concerted practice, account also had to be taken of circumstances such as the expressed acceptance of such discount caps, a decrease in the applied discounts in reality, as well as the lack of objection to the changes introduced by the administrator of the E-TURAS system.[37]

When the case, by way of the judicial review, reached the Supreme Administrative Court of Lithuania, the latter asked for a preliminary ruling from the ECJ.[38] In particular, the Supreme Administrative Court had doubts "as to the existence of sufficient factors capable of establishing, in the present case, the participation of the travel agencies concerned in a horizontal concerted practice" and thus asked for "clarification as to the correct interpretation of Article 101(1) TFEU and, in particular, as to the allocation of the burden of proof for the purposes of applying that provision".[39] According to the referring court, the main piece of evidence supporting the findings of the infringement, was "a mere presumption that the travel agencies concerned read or should have read the message [...] and should have understood all of the consequences arising from the decision concerning the restriction of the discount rates on bookings".[40] In this regard and bearing in mind that some travel agencies denied that they had had any knowledge of the message, the Supreme Administrative Court expressed concerns with regard to the presumption of innocence applied in competition law.[41] Specifically, the Supreme Administrative Court asked whether "the mere sending of a message concerning a restriction of the discount rate could constitute sufficient evidence to confirm or to raise a presumption that the economic operators participating in the E-TURAS booking system knew or ought to have known about that restriction, even though some of them claim not to have had any knowledge of the restriction, some did not change the actual discount rates applied and

---

[35] *Ibid.*, para. 167.
[36] *Ibid.*, para. 164.
[37] *Ibid.*, para. 165.
[38] ECJ, *E-Turas*, *supra* note 25.
[39] *Ibid.*, para. 21.
[40] *Ibid.*, para. 22.
[41] *Ibid.*, para. 22.

others did not sell any travel packages at all via the E-TURAS system during the relevant period".[42]

The ECJ, first of all, explained that:

> the answer to *the question whether the mere dispatch of a message*, such as that at issue in the main proceedings, *may*, having regard to all of the circumstances before the referring court, *constitute sufficient evidence* to establish that its addressees were aware, or ought to have been aware, of its content, *does not follow from the concept of a "concerted practice"* and is not intrinsically linked to that concept. That question must be regarded as relating to *the assessment of evidence and to the standard of proof*, with the result that it is *governed* – in accordance with the principle of procedural autonomy and subject to the principles of equivalence and effectiveness – *by national law*.[43] (Emphasis added)

Hence, whereas the concept of "awareness" is part of the EU competition law's concept of a concerted practice, the question under what conditions such awareness may be established depends on the assessment of evidence and the standard of proof governed by the national law.

Nevertheless, the ECJ provided further guidance with regard to such an assessment of evidence. It was explained that "in most cases the existence of a concerted practice or an agreement must be inferred from a number of coincidences and indicia which, taken together, may, in the absence of another plausible explanation, constitute evidence of an infringement of the competition rules",[44] so that "an infringement of EU competition law may be proven not only by direct evidence, but also through indicia, provided that they are objective and consistent".[45] Stressing the principle of the presumption of innocence enshrined in Article 48(1) of the EU Charter of Fundamental Rights and applicable to competition law,[46] the ECJ stated that the latter presumption precluded the referring court "from inferring from the mere dispatch of the message at issue in the main proceedings that the travel agencies concerned ought to have been aware of the content of that message".[47] However, the ECJ then held that the presumption of innocence did not preclude the referring court "from considering that the dispatch of the message at issue in the main proceedings may, *in the light of other objective and consistent indicia*, justify the *presumption* that the travel agencies concerned *were aware* of the content of that message as from the date of its dispatch, provided that those agencies

---

[42] *Ibid.*, para. 24.
[43] *Ibid.*, para. 34.
[44] *Ibid.*, para. 36.
[45] *Ibid.*, para. 37.
[46] *Ibid.*, para. 38.
[47] *Ibid.*, para. 39.

still have *the opportunity to rebut it*"[48] (emphasis added). Hence, even in the absence of direct evidence, awareness could be presumed on the basis of other indicia, given that they are objective and consistent, with the result that it would then be for the companies to rebut it.

Yet, almost surprisingly, the ECJ goes on by stating that:

> *if it cannot be established that a travel agency was aware* of that message, *its participation in a concertation cannot be inferred* from the mere existence of a technical restriction implemented in the system at issue in the main proceedings, *unless it is established on the basis of other objective and consistent indicia that it tacitly assented to an anticompetitive action.*[49] (Emphasis added)

The passage is confusing, and several remarks have to be made in this regard.

A direct reading of the passage might raise an impression that the ECJ seems to be saying that a company's participation in the concerted practice could be confirmed even if such company's awareness about the anti-competitive practice cannot be established. Such a finding would be too far-fetched indeed. However, a systemic reading of the ECJ's judgement reveals that this is not necessarily the case. In the final answers to the referring court, the ECJ stresses the importance of awareness, thereby making it clear that the latter is a *conditio sine qua non* for finding a concerted practice.[50] After all, awareness is one of the core requirements for the establishment of a concerted practice. Moreover, such awareness should be actual and cannot be merely potential.[51]

---

[48] *Ibid.*, para. 40. The means of rebutting such a presumption were said to be such as a proof that the travel agencies "did not receive that message or that they did not look at the section in question or did not look at it until some time had passed since that dispatch" (*ibid.*, para. 41), the public distancing from the practice in question or reporting to the administrative authorities (*ibid.*, para. 46) or "by evidence of a systematic application of a discount exceeding the cap in question" (*ibid.*, para. 49).

[49] *Ibid.*, para. 45.

[50] *Ibid.*, para. 50.

[51] See also *Heinemann, A./Gebicka, A.*, Can Computers Form Cartels? About the Need for European Institutions to Revise the Concertation Doctrine in the Information Age, (2016) 7 Journal of European Competition Law & Practice 431, at 436: "It should be noted that concertation requires actual and not only potential awareness of the measures aiming at a restriction of competition." In this regard, the authors take a critical stance as regards the ECJ's statements regarding the question whether companies were aware or ought to have been aware of the system notice. According to Heinemann and Gebicka, in EU competition law the standard for analysing whether there was awareness is and should remain actual awareness, i.e. whether companies knew – instead of "ought to have known" – about the system notice ("it should be clarified that concerted practices only occur where awareness of the restriction can be proved, even if it is by means of (rebuttable) presumptions. For Art. 101 TFEU to be violated, it is not suffi-

However, the ECJ does say in the passage that the finding of the participation in the concerted practice may be based on the finding of a tacit assent (shown by objective and consistent indicia) when "awareness cannot be established".

It is accepted under EU competition law that passive modes of behaviour may be indicative of participation in the concerted practice. In fact, the ECJ, in the *E-Turas* case, refers to its case-law where it was held that "*passive modes* of participation in the infringement, such as *the presence of an undertaking in meetings* at which anticompetitive agreements were concluded, without that undertaking clearly opposing them, are *indicative of collusion* capable of rendering the undertaking liable under Article 101 TFEU, since a party which *tacitly approves* of an unlawful initiative, without publicly distancing itself from its content or reporting it to the administrative authorities, encourages the continuation of the infringement and compromises its discovery".[52] Apart from the fact that establishing awareness when a company was physically present in the meeting may be less problematic, an important point to make is that a tacit approval of an anti-competitive behaviour may be relevant for rebutting the "causal link" presumption.[53] However, this comes after the awareness has already been established.

Bearing in mind that the establishment of a concerted practice should not be possible without establishing awareness, the result of the above-cited passage may be that the assessment of such a tacit assent may have to come into play at an earlier stage, namely, in the first step of considering whether there was a concerted practice, i.e. deciding whether companies were aware of a concerted practice. In such a way, what the ECJ seems to have done in the cited passage is stretched the concept of awareness itself. According to the explanation provided by the ECJ, even if awareness cannot be established either on direct evidence or indicia, then, if not direct evidence, but rather indicia (even

---

cient that ignorance of the system notice is due to negligence. Tacit acquiescence also has to be conscious" (*ibid.*, at 436)).

[52] ECJ, *E-Turas*, *supra* note 25, para. 28 (with further references).

[53] See, for example, ECJ, Case C-194/14 P, *AC-Treuhand AG v. European Commission*, 22 October 2015, ECLI:EU:C:2015:717, para. 31: "In that connection, the Court has held in particular that passive modes of participation in the infringement, such as the presence of an undertaking in meetings at which anticompetitive agreements were concluded, without that undertaking clearly opposing them, are indicative of collusion capable of rendering the undertaking liable under Article 81(1) EC, *since a party which tacitly approves of an unlawful initiative, without publicly distancing itself from its content or reporting it to the administrative authorities, encourages the continuation of the infringement and compromises its discovery* (see, to that effect, judgment in *Dansk Rørindustri and Others v. Commission*, C-189/02 P, C-202/02 P, C-205/02 P to C-208/02 P and C-213/02 P, EU:C:2005:408, paragraphs 142 and 143 and the case-law cited)" (emphasis added).

if consistent and objective) exist that a company – no matter to what extent – tacitly assented to anti-competitive behaviour, it could be still presumed that the company was aware of the anti-competitive conduct, and thus participated in a concerted practice (if other conditions of a concerted practice, namely, the subsequent behaviour in the market and the causal link, are also fulfilled). Although companies would still be given an opportunity to rebut such a presumption, it could be asked whether such a presumption does not go too far, not the least, from the point of view of the presumption of innocence.

It seems to have been the Lithuanian Competition Council that argued in front of the ECJ that travel agencies "tacitly assented" to the concerted practice in question. The ECJ explains in *E-Turas* that:

> The Competition Council contends that the E-TURAS booking system served the applicants in the main proceedings as a tool for coordinating their actions and eliminated the need for meetings. In that respect, it submits that, first, the conditions of use of that system enabled those applicants to reach a "concurrence of wills" on a discounts cap without the need for direct contacts and, secondly, that the failure to oppose the discounts cap *amounted to tacitly assenting* to them. […] According to the Competition Council, the applicants in the main proceedings were obliged to be circumspect and responsible and could not ignore or disregard messages concerning the tools used in their business.[54] (Emphasis added)

However, the main issue in the case might have been that, at least based on the evidence, it was not possible to show that the "concurrence of wills", which is, in fact, the core requirement for establishing a concerted practice, was present with regard to all travel agencies. Such "concurrence of wills" could have hardly been confirmed on the basis of the mere fact that the companies were using the same system. Furthermore, the Competition Council's argument that the companies did not object to anti-competitive behaviour and, therefore, they could be held to have tacitly assented to a concerted practice, seems to leapfrog the very first requirement, i.e. the question whether they could have been held to be aware of the anti-competitive conduct in the first place. A "duty of care" as implied further in the passage is, of course, an important principle for the business. However, it could be questioned to what extent this should play a (decisive) role in the competition law assessment of company's participation in a concerted practice.

In fact, when the case was solved by the Supreme Administrative Court of Lithuania, the Competition Council's decision was partly annulled. Following the guidance of the ECJ, the Supreme Administrative Court issued its

---

[54] ECJ, *E-Turas, supra* note 25, para. 20.

judgement on 2 May 2016.[55] The Supreme Administrative Court noted that, assessing whether there was an infringement of Article 5(1) point 1 of the Law on Competition and Article 101(1) TFEU, three elements with regard to each undertaking had to be analysed: the concertation, the subsequent behaviour in the market and the causal link between the concertation and the subsequent behaviour in the market.[56]

As regards the first element, i.e. the concertation, it was stressed by the Court that it was important to analyse whether there was any direct or indirect contact among the travel agencies bearing in mind that the will of the parties may be expressed directly or indirectly (i.e. tacitly).[57] According to the Court, a situation when the information about the "capping" of the discount is transmitted via an information system and the companies know about it and understand that such a restriction is applied also to other undertakings using the same system, and do not object to such a restriction of the discount, i.e. tacitly accept it, it is to be considered a concerted practice.[58] However, it was crucial, according to the Court, to analyse whether the competition authority had enough evidence to conclude that each of the travel agencies fined by the Competition Council was aware of the discount "cap" and did not object to it.[59]

The Court stressed that finding of a concerted practice was related to the finding of the element of will,[60] so that it was essential to determine whether the evidence in the case confirmed that the travel agencies knew about the "capping" of the discounts as well as to clarify whether the relevant travel agency, by its behaviour, distanced itself from such a concerted practice (thus, rebutting the presumption of the causal link between the concertation and the subsequent behaviour in the market).[61] Based on the national rules of the assessment of evidence, the Court proceeded with the evaluation of evidence related to each of the travel agencies, assessing whether it was aware of the discount "cap" and did not object to it.[62]

The Court agreed with the finding of the Competition Council that, owing to the features of the E-TURAS system, the travel agencies understood that a number of other travel agencies used the same system based on the standard

---

[55] Judgement of the Supreme Administrative Court of Lithuania, 2 May 2016, Case No. A-97-858/2016.
[56] *Ibid.*, para. 353.
[57] *Ibid.*, para. 354.
[58] *Ibid.*, para. 356.
[59] *Ibid.*, para. 356.
[60] *Ibid.*, para. 362.
[61] *Ibid.*, para. 362.
[62] *Ibid.*, paras 363–365 et seq.

conditions.[63] Yet, the circumstance alone that the message about the discount "cap" was sent to the travel agencies to their system accounts was not considered to be sufficient to conclude that the travel agencies read this message and in such a way became aware of its content, i.e. the "capping" of the discount.[64] Referring to the preliminary ruling of the ECJ, the Court stressed that such a finding would run counter to the presumption of innocence.[65] However, in this regard, the Court noted that those undertakings that before the "cap" applied a higher discount could be considered to have been aware of the "cap", first and foremost, owing to the fact that the discount factually applied after the "cap" was smaller and it was impossible for the travel agencies not to have noticed it.[66] In addition, these travel agencies were considered to have understood that the same discount "cap" was also applied to other travel agencies participating in the E-TURAS online platform.[67] Yet the Court noted that sufficient evidence was lacking for finding the awareness of a number of travel agencies.[68] For example, the travel agency that contested the finding that it was aware of the "cap" and which noted that no travel package was sold via the E-TURAS system in the period, which was relevant for the case, was not considered to fulfil the requirement of "awareness" for establishing the participation in the concerted practice.[69] Furthermore, as regards the travel agency that, in fact, had applied a lower discount even before the "cap", the Court held that no sufficient evidence existed to establish that the company was aware of the "cap".[70] The same was held with regard to the travel agency that had been applying the 3 per cent discount (i.e. the amount of the "capped" discount) for a longer time and which provided evidence that it did not even open the message sent by the system administrator of E-TURAS.[71]

As regards two further elements of the concerted practice, i.e. the subsequent behaviour in the market and the causal link between the concertation and the subsequent behaviour in the market,[72] the Court went on with the question whether each travel agency that was considered to have been aware of the "cap" provided sufficient evidence to rebut the "causal link" presumption.[73] Such evidence was said to be, for example, a systemic application of higher

---

63 *Ibid.*, para. 371.
64 *Ibid.*, para. 373.
65 *Ibid.*, para. 373.
66 *Ibid.*, para. 376.
67 *Ibid.*, para. 376.
68 *Ibid.*, paras 392–416.
69 *Ibid.*, para. 393.
70 *Ibid.*, paras 394–395.
71 *Ibid.*, paras 402–404.
72 *Ibid.*, paras 377 et seq.
73 *Ibid.*, paras 378 et seq.

discounts for online travel bookings through the E-TURAS system (thus, not through other channels) after the "capped" discount was introduced.[74] For example, the fact that some of the travel agencies provided an additional possibility to get a loyalty discount was not considered a sufficient evidence to rebut the aforementioned presumption, since, according to the Court, this fact did not amount to a systemic application of such a discount in practice.[75] In fact, the Court said that only if it could be shown that a travel agency systemically applied discounts higher than those "capped" could it be found that such a company did not participate in the concerted practice (thus rebutting the "causal link" presumption).[76] On the basis of such legal analysis and the evaluation of evidence, the Court concluded that only a small number of travel agencies could be found to have participated in the concerted practice.[77] As regards the company Eturas, the Court upheld the findings of the Competition Council.[78]

4.1.1.2 Implications of the *E-Turas* case for algorithm-driven economy

The implications of the *E-Turas* case may be far-reaching in general and with regard to the algorithm-driven economy in particular. The concept of a concerted practice seems to have been broadened by the ECJ in terms of including a tacit assent in the cases where awareness cannot be established based on either direct evidence or indicia. In such a way, the line between a concerted practice and parallel behaviour may be blurred.

Considering a tacit assent at the stage of establishing awareness may be highly problematic. Although it may be considered as indicating a concerted practice in the cases where a company was physically present in the meeting, this may be very different from the cases where such a "contact" is rather remote. Problems with such an interpretation may be not necessarily confined to an online environment. Issues may arise in an offline environment as well. Sending a letter without a clear confirmation that it was received, not to speak of the question whether it was read, may stand as an example. Following the ECJ's explanation in *E-Turas*, participation in a concerted practice could be confirmed if, even upon a failure to establish awareness on the basis of direct evidence or indicia, indications were found of "a tacit assent" by the company to the anti-competitive conduct. Yet it could not be ruled out that such a "tacit assent", in light of the context described above, would, in fact, be parallel behaviour. The criteria of how to draw a line between the latter (which is

---

[74] *Ibid.*, para. 379.
[75] *Ibid.*, para. 379.
[76] *Ibid.*, para. 379.
[77] *Ibid.*, para. 416.
[78] *Ibid.*, paras 417–420.

allowed under EU competition law) and a concerted practice (which is prohibited) may become blurred indeed.

Furthermore, it is not clear to what extent such a tacit assent will always be indicative of reciprocal behaviour. After all, a concerted practice is a form of *coordination* and, as explained before, is a cooperation, which *knowingly* substitutes competition. A tacit assent, almost by definition, indicates a unilateral decision.

As regards markets where algorithms come into play, the concept of a "tacit assent" may be highly problematic. In fact, the application of this concept risks capturing a large number of cases and may have unintended consequences. For example, according to the CMA's study on the pricing algorithms, "the mere fact that firms use the same pricing algorithms is not, by itself, sufficient to establish a tacitly coordinated outcome".[79] Yet the application of a "tacit assent" may result in findings stating exactly the opposite. Hence, when algorithms were used by each firm to make their unilateral pricing decisions, it would be not entirely clear under what circumstances the companies might be considered as participating in a concerted practice (and thus behaving anti-competitively) and when they might be acting in a parallel manner (and thus not engaging in any anti-competitive behaviour). Bearing in mind that algorithms may be protected as a trade secret, cases may possibly come up when pricing algorithms were reverse engineered or similar (or identical) algorithms were independently written and used by different companies. Whether such cases could also fall under the concept of a "tacit assent" remains an open question.

One of the reasons why the "concerted practice" test was broadened in the *E-Turas* case might be the fact that the case did not entirely fit into the framework of a concerted practice with regard to all travel agencies. As illustrated above, at the end of the day, it was only a handful of companies that were found to have participated in the concerted practice. Changing legal concepts on such a basis is a highly risky approach. This is not the first time in EU competition law history, though, that such a situation has arisen. The "exceptional circumstances" test – in its rather flawed form as the EU compulsory licensing scheme – was borne in the *Magill* case as a result of the extensive national legal provisions regarding copyright protection. In the *E-Turas* case, the E-TURAS online platform was the only platform of this kind in Lithuania, so that many travel agencies did not have any alternatives to be visible on the Internet.[80] Furthermore, the capping of the discount was in the interest of the

---

[79] Competition & Markets Authority, Pricing Algorithms, *supra* note 6, p. 25.

[80] The latter fact was noted by the ECJ as well (see ECJ, *E-Turas, supra* note 25, para. 19): "The applicants [...] explain that they continued to use the E-TURAS system

platform, since the commission paid to the platform depended on the price of the travel booking – the higher the price, the higher the commission.[81] This is not surprising, bearing in mind that online platforms function on the basis of generating traffic. So, to some extent, the case was about exercising market power (if not a dominant position) and entering into the agreements with a number of travel agencies (particularly those that were in contact with the platform regarding the prices) and then imposing unfair trading conditions on the others. Some of the undertakings did, in fact, claim that the administrator of the E-TURAS online platform imposed unfair trading conditions on the travel agencies.[82]

The fact that the incentive to cap the discounts was rather (or at least, also) on the side of the online system's operator in order to keep the travel agencies participating in its online E-TURAS system and thereby generating revenues through online travel bookings via the system may be important. In light of the fact that the initiative of "capping" the discount came from a number of undertakings and that the "capping" of the discounts was introduced by the E-TURAS platform on the basis of the direct contact with some of the undertakings,[83] possibly an anti-competitive agreement could have been found as concluded between these companies and the system operator Eturas. As regards the rest of the travel agencies, since there was no other online system similar to E-TURAS in Lithuania, it could be asked whether the behaviour of Eturas could have amounted to an abuse of market dominance (hence, the infringement of Article 7 of the Law on Competition (which is the national equivalent of Article 102 TFEU) and Article 102 TFEU). Bearing in mind that the discount "cap" was imposed by Eturas upon the consultation of some

---

even after the technical implementation of the discounts cap, because there was no other system available and because it would have been too expensive to develop their own system."

[81]   Decision of the Competition Council, *E-Turas, supra* note 28, para. 176; Judgement of the Supreme Administrative Court, *supra* note 55, para. 163. According to the Supreme Administrative Court, however, the initiative of "capping" the discount came from a number of travel agencies (this fact was mentioned in the Competition Council's decision as well (Decision of the Competition Council, *E-Turas, supra* note 28, paras 155, 173)), so even if it were assumed that Eturas could have had an interest in acting unilaterally in order to maintain the loyalty of the travel agencies towards the E-TURAS platform, this circumstance was not considered to be such that could have ruled out the finding on the participation of the travel agencies in the concerted practice, since, it was said, the actions of Eturas would still be based on the interests of such travel agencies (Judgement of the Supreme Administrative Court, *supra* note 55, para. 419).

[82]   Judgement of the Supreme Administrative Court, *supra* note 55, paras 61, 124.

[83]   Decision of the Competition Council, *E-Turas, supra* note 28, paras 155, 173.

(but not all) travel agencies,[84] it could be asked whether other companies that participated in the online system could have been in a position to exert strong buyer power in order to discipline the system administrator. In the *E-Turas* case, some of the travel agencies argued that, although they joined the platform after the "cap" was introduced, they were still held liable for having participated in the concerted practice.[85] For example, one company explained that it became aware of the discount not because of any information exchange with other travel agencies participating in the platform, but through the services agreement with the platform administrator.[86] Owing to the fact that the E-TURAS system was close to a bottleneck platform for those companies, which wanted to have their travel packages booked online, the question could have been whether those companies that applied the capped discount had a choice not to apply the cap on the discount, which was imposed by the system administrator. Hence, it might be that the outcome of the case could have been the finding of a number of anti-competitive agreements between the system operator and some of the travel agencies, whereas the rest of the infringement could have been an abuse of a dominant position by Eturas in terms of imposing unfair business conditions on the travel agencies, which, in fact, could not exert strong buyer power against the online platform.

Be as it is, the *E-Turas* case seems to have brought about some confusion, which will hardly be welcome for several reasons. First of all, it undermines the legal certainty of the companies – a fact that, in the long run, may have negative consequences on the overall competitiveness of the markets. Secondly, it compromises the principle of legality, i.e. the fact that only behaviour that is prohibited by law will be considered anti-competitive. Finally, it raises tensions with the principle of the presumption of innocence in competition law in general and with regard to algorithm-driven markets in particular.

One of the main functions of the legal presumptions in general and in competition law in particular is to facilitate enforcement.[87] Thereby, legal presumptions (including the presumption of innocence) are important for the allocation of the burden of proof. Whereas the assessment of evidence and the standard of proof in national proceedings are governed by national law, the allocation of

---

[84] Judgement of the Supreme Administrative Court, *supra* note 55, paras 30, 317–319; see also Decision of the Competition Council, *E-Turas*, *supra* note 28, para. 155.

[85] See the Judgement of the Supreme Administrative Court, *supra* note 55, paras 16, 157.

[86] *Ibid.*, para. 16.

[87] On a more detailed analysis of the nature and the effect of legal presumptions in EU competition law see, for example, *Bailey, D.*, Presumptions in EU competition law, 31 (2010) E.C.L.R. 20.

the burden of proof is included in EU competition law.[88] According to Article 2 of Regulation 1/2003,[89] "[i]n any national or Community proceedings for the application of Articles 81 and 82 of the Treaty, the burden of proving an infringement of Article 81(1) or of Article 82 of the Treaty shall rest on the party or the authority alleging the infringement. The undertaking or association of undertakings claiming the benefit of Article 81(3) of the Treaty shall bear the burden of proving that the conditions of that paragraph are fulfilled".[90]

Article 48(1) of the EU Charter of Fundamental Rights enshrines the presumption of innocence by stipulating that "[e]veryone who has been charged shall be presumed innocent until proved guilty according to law". Thereby, the scope of the application of the presumption of innocence as stipulated in Article 48(1) of the EU Charter is broader than Article 6(2) of the European Convention on Human Rights, which refers to criminal offences. The fact that the presumption of innocence is also a valid standard in competition law cases has been confirmed by the ECJ. It was said that "[a]ccording to the Court's case-law, the principle of the presumption of innocence applies to the procedures relating to infringements of the competition rules applicable to undertakings that may result in the imposition of fines or periodic penalty payments" (references to case-law omitted).[91]

In the case-law of the ECJ, it has been held that an infringement of competition law may be found if "the established facts cannot be explained other than by the existence of anti-competitive behaviour", unless the undertakings "put forward arguments which cast the facts established by the Commission in a different light and thus allow another plausible explanation of the facts to be substituted for the one adopted by the Commission in concluding that an infringement occurred".[92] In the *Montecatini* case, the ECJ stated that, where the European Commission has established that an undertaking took part in the meeting, it is for an undertaking to provide "another explanation of the tenor of those meetings".[93] In such a case, it was stressed, this does not run counter to the presumption of innocence.

---

[88]　ECJ, *E-Turas*, *supra* note 25, para. 30.

[89]　Council Regulation (EC) No. 1/2003 of 16 December 2002 on the implementation of the rules on competition laid down in Articles 81 and 82 of the Treaty, OJ [2003] L 1/1.

[90]　Articles 81 and 82 of the EC Treaty correlate to Articles 101 and 102 TFEU.

[91]　ECJ, Case C-89/11 P, *E.ON Energie AG v. European Commission*, 22 November 2012, ECLI:EU:C:2012:738, para. 73. See also ECJ, *E-Turas*, *supra* note 25, para. 38.

[92]　ECJ, Case C-89/11 P, *E.ON Energie AG v. European Commission*, 22 November 2012, ECLI:EU:C:2012:738, para. 74.

[93]　ECJ, Case C-235/92 P, *Montecatini SpA v. Commission of the European Communities*, 8 July 1999, ECLI:EU:C:1999:362, para. 181. Cited with approval also

Furthermore, it could be recalled that the ECJ said in *AC-Treuhand* that:

> When, as in the present case, the infringement involves anticompetitive agreements and concerted practices, it is apparent from the Court's case-law that *the Commission must demonstrate*, in order to be able to find that an undertaking participated in an infringement and was liable for all the various elements comprising the infringement, that the undertaking concerned *intended to contribute by its own conduct* to the common objectives pursued by all the participants and *that it was aware* of the actual conduct planned or put into effect by other undertakings in pursuit of the same objectives *or that it could reasonably have foreseen it and that it was prepared to take the risk.*[94] (With further references; emphasis added)

It could be asked whether or how a participation in a concerted practice, shown on the basis of indicia hinting towards a tacit assent, when awareness cannot be established, in fact, complies with this test. According to the holding of the ECJ in *E-Turas*, if awareness cannot be established – either on direct evidence or on the basis of indicia – participation in a concertation can still be established if consistent and objective indicia exist showing tacit assent. In this regard, it would suffice for a competition authority to bring forward indicia hinting towards a tacit assent. However, as also shown by the passage above, much more, in fact, may be needed. Thus, aligning the holding of the ECJ in *E-Turas* with what the ECJ said in *AC-Treuhand*, it could be argued that it would be for a competition authority to bring forward not only convincing indicia that a company joined the anti-competitive conduct, but also to prove that such a company intended to contribute to a concerted practice. Otherwise, the burden of proof may be too quickly shifted to the companies, which, in fact, should be presumed innocent until proven otherwise.

The analysis of the *E-Turas* case shows that, although this case did not involve algorithms, a broader EU competition law concept of the concerted practice that comes out as a result of this case may be highly relevant for analysing future cases when algorithms are involved. After all, should algorithmic price adjustments occur in the market, the argument could go that firms tacitly assented to anti-competitive behaviour. What objective and consistent indicia could be in this regard will depend on the factual context of the case, but the use of the same algorithm could probably stand as one of the examples – the circumstance, which, as explained above, is currently not considered, and probably should not be considered, to amount to anti-competitive behaviour. Thus, from the competition policy perspective, it could be questioned whether

in: ECJ, Case C-89/11 P, *E.ON Energie AG v. European Commission*, 22 November 2012, ECLI:EU:C:2012:738, para. 75.

[94] ECJ, Case C-194/14 P, *AC-Treuhand AG v. European Commission*, 22 October 2015, ECLI:EU:C:2015:717, para. 30.

such a broad coverage of EU competition law is desired. As explained above, this does not seem to have been an intention of the ECJ in *E-Turas* either. A broader concept of a concerted practice was rather borne out of the misconceptions of the *E-Turas* case. However, the result of the case is that more practices may be covered. So, in contrast to the claims that EU competition law may lack tools to capture behaviour related to algorithms, it may be exactly the opposite that may pose higher risks, i.e. a risky potential of the overenforcement of EU competition law.

4.1.2   Algorithmic Price Adjustments and Collective Dominance

Algorithmic price adjustments may occur when companies that are independent from both the economic and the legal points of view, use pricing algorithms in order to observe each other's behaviour and to follow suit. Such parallel behaviour in the markets with a few market players (for example, oligopolistic markets) may amount to collective dominance.

Article 102 TFEU does not condemn a dominant position as such, but rather prohibits an abuse of such a position in the relevant market. Such a dominant position, however, may be single or collective.[95] Whereas single dominance refers to one undertaking, collective dominance covers several undertakings. Hence, as regards parallel behaviour and speaking of unilateral conduct, it might be that cases of algorithmic price adjustments might be caught by Article 102 TFEU in terms of an abuse of collective dominance.

In the case-law of the ECJ,[96] it has been established that collective dominance covers a dominant position held collectively by two or more legally independent undertakings, which, owing to the market structure, align their conduct on the market.

---

[95]   Article 102 TFEU reads: "Any abuse *by one or more undertakings of a dominant position* within the internal market or in a substantial part of it shall be prohibited as incompatible with the internal market in so far as it may affect trade between Member States" (emphasis added) (OJ [2016] C 202/1). For a more detailed analysis of the development of the notion of EU competition law of "collective dominance" see, for example, *Whish, R.*, Competition Law, Sixth edition, Oxford: Oxford University Press 2009, pp. 558–564.

[96]   See, for example, ECJ, Case C-395/96 P, *Compagnie Maritime Belge SA v. Commission of the European Communities*, 16 March 2000, ECLI:EU:C:2000:132; ECJ, Case C-393/92, *Municipality of Almelo and others v. NV Energiebedrijf Ijsselmij*, 27 April 1994, ECLI:EU:C:1994:171.

In *Compagnie Maritime Belge,*[97] the ECJ explained:

> the expression "one or more undertakings" in Article 86 of the Treaty implies that a dominant position may be held by two or more economic entities legally independent of each other, provided that from an economic point of view they present themselves or act together on a particular market as a collective entity.[98]

According to Jones and Suffrin, "independent economic entities may hold a collective dominant position provided that they are united by economic links which enable them to present themselves as a collective entity and to adopt the same conduct on the market. The economic links may be contractual, structural (such as cross shareholdings or common directorships) or provided by the structure of the market which ensures parallelism of behaviour between firms on an oligopolistic market".[99]

Hence, considering that parallel behaviour may amount to a collective dominant position, it might be that companies that are collectively dominant may be held liable under Article 102 TFEU if they abuse such a collective dominant position. Importantly though, such an abuse does not need to be collective, but may rather be an individual one. For example, the General Court in *Irish Sugar v. Commission*[100] held that an individual abuse was possible in the case of a collective dominance. In the words of the General Court:

> Whilst the existence of a joint dominant position may be deduced from the position which the economic entities concerned together hold on the market in question, the abuse does not necessarily have to be the action of all the undertakings in question. It only has to be capable of being identified as one of the manifestations of such a joint dominant position being held. Therefore, undertakings occupying a joint dominant position may engage in joint or individual abusive conduct. It is enough

---

[97] ECJ, Case C-395/96 P, *Compagnie Maritime Belge SA v. Commission of the European Communities*, 16 March 2000, ECLI:EU:C:2000:132.

[98] *Ibid.*, para. 36. See also *ibid.*, para. 45: "The existence of a collective dominant position may therefore flow from the nature and terms of an agreement, from the way in which it is implemented and, consequently, from the links or factors which give rise to a connection between undertakings which result from it. Nevertheless, the existence of an agreement or of other links in law is not indispensable to a finding of a collective dominant position; such a finding may be based on other connecting factors and would depend on an economic assessment and, in particular, on an assessment of the structure of the market in question."

[99] *Jones, A./Suffrin, B.*, EU Competition Law: Texts, Cases, and Materials, Oxford: Oxford University Press 2014, p. 723.

[100] General Court, Case T-228/97, *Irish Sugar plc v. Commission of the European Communities*, 7 October 1999, ECLI:EU:T:1999:246.

for that abusive conduct to relate to the exploitation of the joint dominant position which the undertakings hold in the market.[101]

Accordingly, the company that may be considered to hold a collective dominant position in the market may be held liable under Article 102 TFEU if it engages in conduct that would amount to an abuse. However, it is not required that other companies, forming part of a collective dominant position, also engage in such a conduct.

This may be important for algorithmic price adjustments. Should such adjustments take place in the relevant market with a few market players, it might be that such companies would be considered to hold a collective dominant position in such a market. Yet the mere holding of such a position would not be prohibited under Article 102 TFEU. However, should at least some (or one) of these undertakings engage in behaviour amounting to an abuse of a dominant position in terms of Article 102 TFEU, for example, in terms of excessive pricing (Article 102(a) TFEU), discriminatory behaviour placing other parties at a competitive disadvantage (Article 102(c) TFEU), etc., such conduct could be captured by Article 102 TFEU.

Finally, it can be recalled that the creation or strengthening of a dominant position, including a collective one, is part of the "SIEC" ("significant impediment to effective competition") test that is applied under EU competition law when appraising concentrations.[102] Hence, it might be that such cases may also be captured by the *ex ante* merger control in terms of analysing coordinated effects.

4.2   ALGORITHMIC PRICE ADJUSTMENTS: A RISK OF THE "CELLOPHANE FALLACY" WHEN DEFINING A RELEVANT MARKET?

Algorithmic price adjustments may pose challenges when it comes to delineating markets under EU competition law.

According to the Commission Notice on market definition,[103] "[a] relevant product market comprises all those products and/or services which are regarded as interchangeable or substitutable by the consumer, by reason of the products' characteristics, *their prices* and their intended use" (emphasis

---

[101]   *Ibid.*, para. 66.

[102]   Council Regulation (EC) No. 139/2004 of 20 January 2004 on the control of concentrations between undertakings, [2004] OJ L 24/1, Article 2(3).

[103]   Commission Notice on the definition of relevant market for the purposes of Community competition law, OJ [1997] C 372/5.

added).[104] Accordingly, one of the factors that may be taken into account when checking the interchangeability of the product or service for the purposes of defining the boundaries of the relevant product and geographic market is the price.

In the Notice, the European Commission states that it will be primarily the demand side that will be taken into account when defining relevant markets.[105] One of the tools that can be used for defining a relevant market is the so-called SSNIP test ("small, but significant, non-transitory increase in price"). Based on the latter test, it is analysed whether, in the case of a small but significant (e.g. 5–10 per cent) non-transitory increase in price of a product or service, consumers would tend to switch to another product or service.[106] In case of the affirmative, the relevant market would extend to those products or services to which consumers would be willing to switch.

The potential drawbacks of the application of the SSNIP test in the data economy have already been pointed out. For example, it has been claimed by academia that, since the SSNIP test includes the analysis of the price, such a test may not necessarily be an optimal tool for delineating markets in the data economy where goods or services are often offered for free.[107] As a result, the alternative test – the SSNDQ (small, but significant, non-transitory decrease in quality) – was suggested.[108] The latter test, however, carries great challenges as regards the ability to measure the (reductions in) quality.

Yet the problem with the application of the SSNIP test in the data economy may be a different one. In fact, it may be similar to the well-known "Cellophane Fallacy".[109] The latter cautions against relying on consumers' willingness to switch to another product where the monopolist is already charging a monopoly price. The argument goes that, in such a case, the application of the SSNIP test would show high willingness of consumers to switch (thereby implying a broader definition of the market), although such willingness would not necessarily be related to the elasticity of the price, but rather to the fact that consumers are already paying the higher price and would thus be willing to switch to other products or services in light of any further (even small) price increases. The risk of such a "Cellophane Fallacy" is that the application of the SSNIP test would lead to markets being defined as broader than they are

---

[104] *Ibid.*, para. 7.

[105] *Ibid.*, para. 13.

[106] *Ibid.*, para. 17.

[107] See, for example, *Gebicka, A./Heinemann A.*, Social Media & Competition Law, (2014) 37 World Competition Law and Economics Review 149, at 156–159.

[108] *Ibid.*

[109] On the "Cellophane Fallacy" see, for example, *Whish, R./Bailey, D.*, Competition Law, 7th ed., Oxford: Oxford University Press 2012, pp. 32–33.

in the reality – a fact that may be highly risky, since further competition law assessment may often depend on how relevant markets are defined (this is, in particular, important in cases of an abuse of dominance).

Should algorithms be put into use, it might be that, owing to algorithmic price adjustments, consumers are already paying a higher price.[110] Hence, it might be that, based on the algorithmic price adjustments, companies are already charging a higher price, so that the willingness to switch on the side of consumers may be high (hence, implying a broader market definition than might exist in reality). In other words, it might be that consumers would be willing to switch to other products owing to the fact that they are already paying a higher price. In such a case, similar to the effects of the "Cellophane Fallacy", the use of the SSNIP test would not necessarily provide an accurate picture of the relevant markets.[111]

In this regard, it could be asked whether, in order to achieve more precise delineations of the relevant markets – the circumstance, which may be highly important, including, but not limited to, cases of alleged abuse of market dominance – a need may arise to assess the substitutability of the supply side. In the Commission Notice on market definition it is stated that "from an economic point of view, for the definition of the relevant market, demand substitution constitutes the most immediate and effective disciplinary force on the suppliers of a given product, in particular in relation to their pricing decisions".[112] However, in the Commission's Notice it is also said that "supply-side substitutability may also be taken into account when defining markets in those situations in which its effects are equivalent to those of demand substitution

---

[110] Such a risk was also mentioned by the European Commission when the latter decided four aforementioned cases (*supra* note 10) on the vertical price fixing (see: European Commission, Press release, "Antitrust: Commission fines four consumer electronics manufacturers for fixing online resale prices", Brussels, 24 July 2018, IP/18/4601: "Many, including the biggest online retailers, use pricing algorithms which automatically adapt retail prices to those of competitors. In this way, the pricing restrictions imposed on low pricing online retailers typically had a broader impact on overall online prices for the respective consumer electronics products").

[111] It is noteworthy that the demand side substitutability can be measured by the factors other than the price, thus not applying the SSNIP test. For example, the Federal German Cartel Office, in their decision against Facebook, delineated the relevant market for social media taking into account the factors such as, for example, the intensity of the use of the relevant platform in the time span. It was argued that such factors may also be considered as a characteristic of a product (Decision of the Federal German Cartel Office (Bundeskartellamt), 6 February 2019, No. B6-22/16, para. 248). However, although such characteristics may be suitable for some cases, their application and reliability in all cases may be questioned.

[112] Commission Notice on the definition of relevant market for the purposes of Community competition law, OJ [1997] C 372/5, para. 13.

in terms of effectiveness and immediacy".[113] Thus, given the risks of the application of the SSNIP test for delineating markets where algorithms may be employed, the supply-side substitutability may need to be more often taken into account in order to define relevant markets precisely.

4.3 COMPETITION FOR DATA TRAFFIC

Since data has become a (new) resource in the data economy,[114] it is not surprising that companies that rely on the processing of data in their business compete over it. There are different ways of obtaining data: it can be collected (e.g. personal data or non-personal data such as weather or traffic data), created, compiled (e.g. in a data set), re-engineered (e.g. in a reverse engineering process), extracted from other data (e.g. on the basis of data analytics), etc. A number of – conglomerate – mergers in recent years have been particularly illustrative of business interest in getting access to data (sets). In the EU, the European Commission has time and again been asked to assess such mergers: *Microsoft/LinkedIn*,[115] *Facebook/WhatsApp*,[116] *Google/DoubleClick*[117] are just a few examples. The fact that interest in the "data mergers" has been growing was also stressed by the OECD.[118]

With the rise of digitization, the pattern of doing business has increasingly shifted to the Internet, raising the importance of online platforms. The latter act as intermediaries and are often characterized by (indirect) network effects.[119]

---

[113] *Ibid.*, para. 20.

[114] *Surblytė, G.*, Data as a Digital Resource, Max Planck Institute for Innovation & Competition Research Paper No. 16-12 (6 October 2016), https://papers.ssrn.com/sol3/papers.cfm?abstract_id=2849303. Along these lines see also: *The Economist*, Regulating the Internet Giants. The World's Most Valuable Resource is no Longer Oil, but Data, 6 May 2017 (http://www.economist.com/news/leaders/21721656-data-economy-demands-new-approach-antitrust-rules-worlds-most-valuable-resource); *The Economist*, Fuel of the Future. Data is Giving Rise to a New Economy, 6 May 2017 (http://www.economist.com/news/briefing/21721634-how-it-shaping-up-data-giving-rise-new-economy).

[115] Decision of the European Commission of 6 December 2016, Case M.8124 – *Microsoft/LinkedIn*.

[116] Decision of the European Commission of 3 October 2014, Case No. COMP/M.7217 – *Facebook/WhatsApp*.

[117] Decision of the European Commission of 11 March 2008, Case No. COMP/M.4731 – *Google/DoubleClick*.

[118] OECD (2015), Data-Driven Innovation: Big Data for Growth and Well-Being, Paris: OECD Publishing, p. 23.

[119] See, for example, Bundeskartellamt, Arbeitspapier: Marktmacht von Plattformen und Netzwerken, Juni 2016.

The concept of multi-sided platforms is neither new[120] nor specific to the data economy. Such platforms existed in offline industries as well, for example, in a form of a newspaper. Basically, in multi-sided platforms, one side of the platform is monetized, whereas on the other side services are often provided without any monetary payment. In the context of the data economy, this means that many online services are granted without a payment[121] (although not necessarily "for free"), whereas the data that is collected from the users of such services is monetized on the other sides of the platform, for example, for the purpose of targeted advertising.[122]

The fact that platforms are often monetized on one side shows that the way they generate revenues often depends on the amount of the traffic directed towards the platform. It is, therefore, not surprising that platforms often compete in attracting as much traffic as possible or at least securing the available traffic, because any loss of traffic may lead to loss of revenues. Cases, on both sides of the Atlantic, related to the disputes over the (trade secret) protection for the business's social media accounts stand as one of the examples.[123]

Hence, in the data economy, one important aspect of competition in general, and with regard to online platform competition in particular, is the relevance

---

[120] On the concept of two- or multi-sided platforms see, for example, *Evans, D.S.*, The Antitrust Economics of Multi-Sided Platform Markets, (2003) 20 Yale J. on Reg. 325; *Rochet, J.-C./Tirole, J.*, Platform Competition in Two-Sided Markets, (2003) 1 Journal of the European Economic Association 990; *Evans, D.S./Noel, M.*, Defining Antitrust Markets when Firms Operate Two-Sided Platforms, (2005) Colum. Bus. L. Rev. 667; *Rochet, J.-C./Tirole, J.*, Two-Sided Markets: A Progress Report, (2006) 37 RAND Journal of Economics 645; *Armstrong, M.*, Competition in Two-Sided Markets, (2006) 37 RAND Journal of Economics 668; *Evans, D.S./Schmalensee, R.*, Markets with Two-Sided Platforms (October 1, 2008). Issues in Competition Law and Policy (ABA Section of Antitrust Law), Vol. 1, Chapter 28, 2008. Available at SSRN: http://ssrn.com/abstract=1094820; *Evans, D.S./Schmalensee, R.*, The Antitrust Analysis of Multisided Platform Businesses, in: Roger D. Blair and D. Daniel Sokol (eds), The Oxford Handbook of International Antitrust Economics, Vol. 1, Oxford: Oxford University Press 2015, pp. 404–447.

[121] *Gal, M.S./Rubinfeld, D.L.*, The Hidden Costs of Free Goods: Implications for Antitrust Enforcement (January 2015). UC Berkeley Public Law Research Paper No. 2529425; NYU Law and Economics Research Paper No. 14-44. Available at SSRN: http://ssrn.com/abstract=2529425.

[122] For a more detailed analysis see *Surblytė, G.*, Competition Law at the Crossroads in the Digital Economy: is it all About Google?, (2015) 4 EuCML 170 (Max Planck Institute for Innovation & Competition Research Paper No. 15-13 (7 December 2015), http://papers.ssrn.com/sol3/papers.cfm?abstract_id=2701847), at 173–174.

[123] See *Surblytė, G.*, Data Mobility at the Intersection of Data, Trade Secret Protection and the Mobility of Employees in the Digital Economy, (2016) 65 GRUR Int. 1121 (Max Planck Institute for Innovation & Competition Research Paper No. 16-03 (11 May 2016), http://papers.ssrn.com/sol3/papers.cfm?abstract_id=2752989).

of data traffic. Owing to the fact that a big portion of doing business in the data economy is closely related to (the commercialization of) data, companies compete not only as regards their goods and services, but also over data. After all, data flows to one's own platform may not only reveal information about the preferences, online behaviour, etc., of the platform's users, but may also translate into revenues. The question thereby is whether, or to what extent, the argument of such competition over data traffic may need to be taken into account in a competition law assessment in the data economy.

4.3.1 Selective Distribution: A Restriction Not to Sell in Third-Party Online Marketplaces

Competition for data traffic may be an important factor to consider in assessing restrictions in selective distribution systems, particularly those that might be related to competition in online platforms. Restrictions on selling products in third-party online marketplaces with the aim of preserving the "aura of luxury" of the products, which are subjects of a selective distribution system, stand as an example. The latter restrictions were analysed by the ECJ in the *Coty* case.[124] In that case, the ECJ held that the preservation of the "aura of luxury" of the product in a selective distribution system is a legitimate aim to restrict competition as long as the so-called *Metro* criteria are complied with.

4.3.1.1 "Aura of luxury": part of a legal assessment under EU competition law?

In the *Coty* case, which was based on the request to the ECJ for a preliminary ruling from the Higher Regional Court, Frankfurt am Main, Germany, the ECJ was asked to elaborate on the compatibility of a selective distribution system with Article 101(1) TFEU and, in particular, on the question whether the prohibition imposed on the distributors of the selective distribution system to sell in third-party online marketplaces may infringe Article 101(1) TFEU.[125]

Selective distribution systems often involve products of high quality. Thus, in general terms, the restrictions imposed under a selective distribution system will be not prohibited by Article 101 TFEU if they comply with the so-called

---

[124] ECJ, Case C-230/16, *Coty Germany GmbH v. Parfümerie Akzente GmbH*, 6 December 2017, ECLI:EU:C:2017:941.

[125] *Ibid.*, para. 20. The Higher Regional Court of Frankfurt am Main, which had requested a preliminary ruling from the ECJ in the *Coty* case, followed the explanations provided by the ECJ and on 12 June 2018 delivered the judgement, in which it was stated that the restrictions of the Coty's selective distribution system were compatible with competition law (Oberlandesgericht Frankfurt am Main, Urteil vom 12.07.2018, Az. 11 U 96/14 (Kart)).

Metro criteria,[126] i.e. the nature of the product requires the preservation of its quality, objective criteria are used for the selection of distributors and these criteria are applied in a non-discriminatory manner, and the criteria do not go beyond what is necessary.[127]

In *Coty*, the ECJ held that:

> With particular regard to the question *whether selective distribution may be considered necessary* in respect of *luxury goods*, it must be recalled that the Court has already held that *the quality of such goods* is not just *the result* of their material characteristics, but also *of the allure and prestigious image which bestow on them an aura of luxury*, that that aura is essential in that it enables consumers to distinguish them from similar goods and, therefore, that an impairment to that aura of luxury is likely to affect the actual quality of those goods (see, to that effect, judgement of 23 April 2009, *Copad*, C-59/08, EU:C:2009:260, paragraphs 24 to 26 and the case-law cited).[128] (Emphasis added)

Accordingly, the "aura of luxury" necessitates selective distribution systems, which should serve for safeguarding the quality of goods as well as their "allure and prestigious image". Hence, although the *Metro* criteria are about the nature of the product requiring a selective distribution system to preserve its quality, the ECJ in *Coty* refers to the luxury products and thereby to the "aura of luxury".

As such, preserving the "aura of luxury" through the selection distribution systems is not a bad idea. After all, this is one of the main purposes of such distribution systems. However, making the "aura of luxury" part of a legal assessment may be a different story and begs for further analysis.

In this regard, it should, first of all, be noted that *Coty* was not the first case where the argument of the "aura of luxury" was applied. In fact, in one of the earlier cases, i.e. *Copad v. Dior*,[129] where the ECJ had to assess the provision of a trade mark licence agreement that prohibited the licensee from selling Dior goods to third parties who were not members of the selective distribution system, the ECJ held that:

> Since luxury goods are high-class goods, *the aura of luxury* emanating from them is essential in that it *enables consumers to distinguish them from similar goods.*

---

[126] ECJ, Case C-26/76, *Metro SB-Großmärkte GmbH & Co. KG v. Commission of the European Communities*, 25 October 1977, ECLI:EU:C:1977:167, para. 20. See also: European Commission, Guidelines on Vertical Restraints, 2010/C 130/01, OJ [2010] C 130/1, para. 175.

[127] See also ECJ, *Coty*, *supra* note 124, para. 24.

[128] *Ibid.*, para. 25.

[129] ECJ, Case C-59/08, *Copad SA v. Christian Dior couture SA, Vincent Gladel and Société industrielle lingerie (SIL)*, 23 April 2009, ECLI:EU:C:2009:260.

Therefore, an impairment to that aura of luxury is likely to affect the actual quality of those goods.[130] (Emphasis added)

The ECJ thus confirmed the legitimacy of the restrictions in the trade mark licence related to the sales of Dior goods to discount stores. In the words of the ECJ:

Article 8(2) of the Directive is to be interpreted as meaning that the proprietor of a trade mark can invoke the rights conferred by that trade mark against a licensee who contravenes a provision in a licence agreement prohibiting, on grounds of the trade mark's prestige, sales to discount stores such as the ones at issue in the main proceedings, *provided it has been established that that contravention, by reason of the situation in the main proceedings, damages the allure and prestigious image which bestows on them an aura of luxury.*[131] (Emphasis added)

Hence, in this regard and – importantly – in the context of the EU Trade Mark Directive, the ECJ held that a trade mark owner may prevent the licensee from selling its luxury products beyond the selective distribution system (namely to a discounter) in order to preserve the aura of luxury. The latter, however, as highlighted in the passage above, was specifically meant in terms of a trade mark and thus one of its functions – to enable consumers to distinguish goods. Thus, the *Copad* case was very much related to the question of the scope of the rights of a trade mark licensor, so that the concept of the preservation of the "aura of luxury" in this case was closely related to the factual circumstances, in particular, whether a trade mark licensor can invoke his rights to prevent sales of the licensed product to discount stores.

The question of preserving the "aura of luxury" arose also in another case. In *Pierre Fabre*,[132] the ECJ had to decide whether the restrictions in the latter's selective distribution system were compliant with Article 101 TFEU. The ECJ explained that "[i]t is undisputed that, under Pierre Fabre Dermo-Cosmétique's selective distribution system, resellers are chosen on the basis of objective criteria of a qualitative nature, which are laid down uniformly for all potential resellers. However, it must still be determined whether the restrictions of competition pursue legitimate aims in a proportionate manner in accordance with the considerations set out at paragraph 41 of the present judgment."[133] According to the ECJ in *Pierre Fabre*, "[t]he aim of maintaining a prestigious

---

[130]   *Ibid.*, paras 25–26.
[131]   *Ibid.*, para. 37.
[132]   ECJ, Case C-439/09, *Pierre Fabre Dermo-Cosmétique SAS v. Président de l'Autorité de la concurrence and Ministre de l'Économie, de l'Industrie et de l'Emploi*, 13 October 2011, ECLI:EU:C:2011:649.
[133]   *Ibid.*, para. 43.

image is not a legitimate aim for restricting competition and cannot therefore justify a finding that a contractual clause pursuing such an aim does not fall within Article 101(1) TFEU".[134] Hence, the opposite was said to what the ECJ had held in *Copad v. Dior*.[135]

Yet, in *Coty*, the ECJ takes a stance from *Pierre Fabre* and states that:

> it cannot be inferred from [...] *Pierre Fabre Dermo-Cosmétique* that paragraph 46 thereof sought to establish a statement of principle according to which the preservation of a luxury image can no longer be such as to justify a restriction of competition, such as that which stems from the existence of a selective distribution network, in regard to all goods, including in particular luxury goods, and consequently alter the settled case-law of the Court, as set out in paragraphs 25 to 27 of the present judgment.[136]

The result after *Coty* is thereby the following: whereas in *Pierre Fabre* the ECJ held that the preservation of the prestigious image cannot be a legitimate aim of restricting competition, this, according to the ECJ, is not "a statement of principle", so that the preservation of the aura of luxury can be a legitimate aim of restricting competition. Although this may sound as a plausible solution, the problem comes when it comes to the argumentation. The "aura of luxury" may be a good starting point for a legal assessment under trade mark law, but it is hardly a starting point for such an assessment under competition law. After all, this may have been part of the reasons why the guidance of the ECJ provided in the aforementioned three cases amounted almost to a "ping-pong" effect. This can hardly be welcome in general and when it comes to legal certainty in particular.

The ECJ in the *Coty* case incorporates the concept of the "aura of luxury" into the competition law assessment, by specifying that the preservation of such aura may, in contrast to *Pierre Fabre*, be a legitimate aim of restricting competition. The ECJ explains that "a selective distribution system *designed, primarily, to preserve the luxury image* of those goods is *therefore* compatible with Article 101(1) TFEU on condition that [the Metro criteria are met]"[137] (emphasis added). However, whereas the *Metro* criteria are legal criteria,

---

[134]   *Ibid.*, para. 46.
[135]   The analysis of the *Pierre Fabre* and *Dior* cases provided above is based on the analysis of these cases by Enchelmaier, see: Enchelmaier, S., Selective Distribution and the Internet: Lessons from Case C-439/09 *Pierre Fabre Dermo-Cosmétique* (13 October 2011), in: Surblytė, G. (ed.), Competition on the Internet, Berlin: Springer 2015, pp. 5–23.
[136]   ECJ, *Coty*, *supra* note 124, para. 35.
[137]   *Ibid.*, para 29.

the "aura of luxury" is not. The incorporation of such a criterion into a legal assessment may have risky implications.

First of all, the question may be what a luxury product is in the first place. The fact that this term may be subject to interpretation may be found in the *Coty* case itself. For example, Advocate General, in the opinion,[138] elaborated on the preservation of the "luxury image" in the selective distribution systems not only for luxury and quality products, but also for products of "high technical nature".[139] According to Advocate General, "the properties of the product necessitate a selective distribution system, in the sense that such a system constitutes a legitimate requirement, *having regard to the nature of the products concerned, and in particular their high quality or highly technical nature*, in order to preserve *their quality and to ensure that they are correctly used*"[140] (emphasis added). Furthermore, Advocate General in the opinion held that the purpose of preserving the brand image of the product encompasses the pursuit to preserve "the guarantees of quality, safety and identification of origin".[141] The ECJ, however, speaks about luxury products only,[142] so that it is not clear whether the broader considerations provided in the opinion of Advocate General, such as, for example, the safety of products, may need to be taken into account when considering the "aura of luxury", and more importantly, the compliance of the selective distribution system with Article 101 TFEU.

Moreover, the ECJ in *Coty*, distinguishing the latter case from *Pierre Fabre*, noted that "the goods covered by the selective distribution system at issue in that case were not luxury goods, but cosmetic and body hygiene goods".[143] However, the question is whether such a statement should imply two-tier selective distribution systems, i.e. those that involve "luxury" products, so that the imposed restrictions would not be considered anti-competitive, and such selective distribution systems, the subject-matter of which would be products other than luxury products, in the case of which similar restrictions would be considered anti-competitive. However, it would be hard to believe that the ECJ meant this, since such a two-tier system would hardly be justifiable in general and from a competition law point of view in particular. And yet, this may be exactly the outcome of the *Coty* case. For example, the Federal German Cartel Office has pointed out that, in their view, the ECJ's holding in *Coty* "is limited

---

[138] Opinion of Advocate General Wahl delivered on 26 July 2017, Case C-230/16, *Coty Germany GmbH v. Parfümerie Akzente GmbH*, ECLI:EU:C:2017:603.

[139] *Ibid.*, paras 33, 66, 70.

[140] *Ibid.*, para. 66.

[141] *Ibid.*, para. 102.

[142] ECJ, *Coty*, *supra* note 124, paras 28–29, para. 40.

[143] *Ibid.*, para. 32.

to luxury goods".[144] The implications of such a two-tier system will be seen in practice.

In fact, it may not always be easy to draw a clear-cut line between luxury and non-luxury products, since such lines may be blurred, in particular, in light of the fact that the perception of what a luxury product is may be highly subjective. Furthermore, just as for the concept of luxury, so the concept of the "aura of luxury" may be subjective and undetermined. Thus, in practice, it may be not always clear under what circumstances it may be considered that the "aura of luxury" is sufficiently preserved and when not. For example, if the same luxury product is allowed to be sold at the airport's duty-free shops arguing that the "aura of luxury" is thereby sufficiently preserved, whereas it is not allowed to be sold in a third-party online marketplace arguing that the latter does not preserve such an aura,[145] problems may arise with the assessment when such restrictions may, in fact, be justified and when not. Moreover, issues may arise with regard to the sustainability of the argument on the "aura of luxury". After all, the latter requirement can be easily overcome in practice. It cannot be ruled out that third-party online marketplaces may be optimized in this regard in order to ensure that the "aura of luxury" is preserved. Thereby, a criterion as undetermined as the "aura of luxury" may backfire: whereas it is meant to provide stronger protection for selective distribution systems, it may, at the end of the day, boil down to a rather weak protection, bearing in mind that the restrictions based on the preservation of the "aura of luxury" may appear to be empty, once it turns out that such an "aura" might, in fact, be preserved.

4.3.1.2 Implications of the *Coty* case for platform competition

Owing to the fact that the selective distribution contract in *Pierre Fabre* required the presence of a pharmacist in the case of the sales of its products,[146] the restrictions in the *Pierre Fabre* case amounted to a complete ban of the sales on the Internet. As compared with the *Coty* case, the argument goes that the restriction against selling in third-party online marketplaces does not necessarily amount to a complete ban of the sales on the Internet, since online

---

[144] Bundeskartellamt, "Competition Restraints in Online Sales after Coty and Asics – What's Next?" (Series of papers on "Competition and Consumer Protection in the Digital Economy"), October 2018, at p. 2.

[145] This argument was raised by the defendant in front of the national German courts. However, the Higher Regional Court Frankfurt am Main did not consider that sales in the airports may compromise the luxury image of the product (Oberlandesgericht Frankfurt am Main, Urteil vom 12.07.2018, Az. 11 U 96/14 (Kart), at Section II(1)(b)(bb)(2)).

[146] ECJ, *Pierre Fabre*, *supra* note 132, para. 24.

sales on the distributors' websites are not prohibited.[147] However, it could be asked whether only the restrictions of a selective distribution system, which completely ban sales on the Internet, should be considered anti-competitive. In fact, in light of the data economy, the picture may be more nuanced, so that a deeper analysis of such restrictions may be needed. As argued above, the criterion of the "aura of luxury" can hardly serve the purpose (not only in the cases when there is a complete ban on sales on the Internet, but in other cases as well), since the question may be whether the restrictions on the selective distribution system do not go beyond their purpose and, bearing in mind the principle of proportionality, do not unjustifiably restrict competition.

Third-party online marketplaces are basically online platforms. On the one hand, the restrictions of selective distribution systems could be compared with those applied in the case of the bricks-and-mortar shops (for example, Advocate General in the *Coty* case analysed online selective distribution systems on the basis of complete analogy with the bricks-and-mortar shops[148]). On the other hand, however, bricks-and-mortar shops lack a particular feature that is important in the case of online platform competition, i.e. data traffic. Hence, here the rationale of competing for data traffic (or the incentives to hinder such traffic in the case of (potential) competitors) may come into play. In particular, the long-run rationale behind restricting sales on other (third-party) online marketplaces may, possibly, be related to hindering data traffic of (potential) competitors' websites (and the thereto related potential loss of revenues). As explained, a platform generates revenues through attracting not only sales, but also online (data) traffic to the platform. So, the more traffic the platform attracts, the more likely it is to generate revenues. Thus, the restrictions on sales from third-party online marketplaces may also be targeted towards restricting traffic of such platforms, shielding such a restriction with the argument of a need to preserve an "aura of luxury". After all, the fact in the *Coty* case that sales restrictions related only to the prohibition of such sales in third-party online marketplaces, which were conducted in a discernable manner (thus, when these sales were visible and could have attracted consumers),[149] may be an indicative factor in this regard.

From a comparative point of view, it could be noted that similar issues were decided by some of the national courts. For example, on 12 December 2017 the Federal Supreme Court of Germany delivered its judgement in the *ASICS*

---

[147] ECJ, *Coty, supra* note 124, para. 53. See also, Opinion of AG, *Coty, supra* note 138, para. 109.

[148] Opinion of AG, *Coty, supra* note 138, paras 103, 105.

[149] ECJ, *Coty, supra* note 124, para. 52. Hence, sales in third-party online marketplaces in a non-discernible manner remained allowed.

case,[150] where the selective distribution system of the latter was considered to infringe Article 101 TFEU (and its national equivalent). Thereby, the Court basically upheld the decision of the German Federal Cartel Office,[151] according to which the restrictions in the distribution system used by ASICS Deutschland GmbH vis-à-vis its authorized distributors based in Germany constituted restrictions of competition by object and thereby violated Article 101(1) TFEU and Section 1 of the German Act against Restraints of Competition (GWB). In total, there were three restrictions of the ASICS selective distribution system that were applied, namely: the prohibition to allow a third party to use the ASICS trade mark on third-party Internet websites, in order to direct users' traffic to the Internet websites of selective distributors; the prohibition from supporting the functionality of price comparison websites; and the prohibition from selling the contract goods on third-party Internet websites, unless the name or the logo of third-party's platform was not copied.[152]

According to the Bundeskartellamt, it sufficed for it to analyse some of these restrictions to declare the whole selective distribution system of ASICS as infringing competition law. Thereby, the Bundeskartellamt analysed first two practices. In this regard, it was, for example, held that these practices hindered the improvement of the searchability of the authorized distributors online stores for end customers.[153] The third practice, i.e. the prohibition from selling via online marketplaces, was not analysed by the Bundeskartellamt. Nevertheless, it was noted that the latter practice may, possibly, also be considered a hard-core restriction under Article 4(c) of the BER (block exemption regulation) for vertical agreements, but the question was left open.[154]

The Federal Supreme Court of Germany, in its analysis, drew a line between the *ASICS* and the *Coty* case based on the argument that, firstly, the *ASICS* case was not related to luxury products, and, secondly, in contrast to the *Coty* case, which was related to the restriction to sell in third-party online marketplaces, the combination of the restrictions[155] imposed by the ASICS selective

---

[150] Federal Supreme Court of Germany, 12 December 2017, KVZ 41/17.

[151] Decision of the German Federal Cartel Office (Bundeskartellamt), *ASICS*, 26 August 2015, B2-98/11.

[152] *Ibid.*, paras 4–5, 67–70.

[153] *Ibid.*, paras 253–255.

[154] *Ibid.*, paras 5, 24.

[155] As said, the combination of the restrictions was the following: the prohibition against supporting the functionality of price comparison websites, the prohibition against allowing a third party to use the ASICS trade mark on third-party Internet websites, in order to direct users' traffic to the Internet websites of selective distributors, the prohibition against selling the contract goods on third-party Internet websites, unless the name or the logo of third-party's platform was not copied (Federal Supreme Court of Germany, 12 December 2017, KVZ 41/17, para. 30).

distribution system was said to have been such that it did not allow users who were interested in a particular product to a considerable extent to get access to the Internet offers of selective distributors.[156] The Court also explained that, in contrast to the *Pierre Fabre* case, which was related to a complete ban on sales on the Internet, the restrictions in the *ASICS* case limited the possibilities generally offered by the Internet channel.[157] The Court analysed in more detail the restrictions related to price comparison. In the legal analysis, the Court did not rely on the argument of the "aura of luxury", but referred rather to the role of price comparison websites in terms of increasing the visibility of online offers in light of their amount on the Internet.[158] Furthermore, the selective distribution restrictions on price comparison websites were not considered to be exempted by the Block Exemption Regulation of vertical agreements,[159] since such restrictions were said to amount to a hardcore restriction in terms of Article 4(c).[160]

The German *ASICS* case shows that the restrictions in the selective distribution systems may (need to) be assessed on the basis of criteria other than the preservation of the "aura of luxury". In fact, this case also shows that making the latter argument part of the legal test may, at the end of the day, result in the "Coty test" being relevant for a rather limited number of cases. Although the Federal Supreme Court of Germany analysed in more detail and gave a definite answer as regards the anti-competitiveness of one of the restrictions, i.e. the restrictions related to price comparison websites, thereby giving no direct answer whether other restrictions could similarly be considered anti-competitive, it should not be ruled out that this might be the case. After all, as mentioned above, this was also indicated (although, again, not directly stated) by the Bundeskartellamt. The answer to the question on the restrictions from selling in third-party online marketplaces is, in fact, nuanced, but also for this reason it could hardly be assessed based on the criteria as undefined as the preservation of the "aura of luxury" is. Furthermore, since it was stated in the *ASICS* case that some of the restrictions were related to the users' traffic, this case serves as a good illustration of the fact that the rationale behind such restrictions may, indeed, be related to the issue of online traffic. Moreover, the Federal Supreme Court of Germany did not consider that at least the restrictions related to price comparison could be exempted under the EU BER.

---

[156] Federal Supreme Court of Germany, 12 December 2017, KVZ 41/17, para. 30.

[157] *Ibid.*, para. 22.

[158] *Ibid.*, paras 24–25.

[159] Commission Regulation (EU) No. 330/2010 of 20 April 2010 on the application of Article 101(3) of the Treaty on the Functioning of the European Union to categories of vertical agreements and concerted practices, OJ [2010] L 102/1.

[160] Federal Supreme Court of Germany, 12 December 2017, KVZ 41/17, para. 23.

Finally, the Court did not focus on the question whether it was a complete ban on Internet sales that resulted from the restriction, but rather on the extent to which competition could have been distorted, thereby harming consumers. In this regard, this case also indicates that the analysis of online platforms has to take account of the particular features of the Internet that distinguish it from the bricks-and-mortar shops. One of such features is the importance of visibility of the goods placed on the Internet.

Indeed, one broader question may merit attention when it comes to online platforms, i.e. their role in increasing the visibility of the products given the reach of the Internet.[161] In fact, the role of platforms in terms of facilitating finding the products and the thereto related risks arising from the restriction to sell in third-party online marketplaces was addressed by the ECJ in the *Coty* case: the ECJ, which did not consider the aforementioned restrictions as anti-competitive, referred to the possibility of using online search engines and thus the ability of customers to find the relevant online offers of authorized distributors.[162] Yet, in light of the specifics as regards the listing of search results in online searches in general[163] and with regard to the European Commission's decision on the abuse of a dominant position by Google[164] in particular, the argument relating to the effectiveness of the use of online search engines as regards the visibility of the goods placed on the Internet remains open. From a comparative point of view, it could be noted that, for example, the Federal German Cartel Office in the ASICS decision explained that a possibility of online search often does not suffice for the products to be easily found on the Internet; stressing an increasingly wide spectrum of the Internet, it was pointed out that companies often use paid advertisements in order to facilitate/optimise the finding of their products online.[165] It was thus said that presence

---

[161] On the role of the "visibility" on the Internet, also for competition law assessment, see, for example, *Surblytė, G.*, Competition Law at the Crossroads in the Digital Economy: is it all About Google?, (2015) 4 EuCML 170 (Max Planck Institute for Innovation & Competition Research Paper No. 15-13 (7 December 2015), http://papers.ssrn.com/sol3/papers.cfm?abstract_id=2701847).

[162] ECJ, *Coty*, *supra* note 124, para. 67. See also Opinion of AG, *supra* note 138, para. 147.

[163] To this end see also: the Decision of the German Federal Cartel Office (Bundeskartellamt), *ASICS*, 26 August 2015, B2-98/11, para. 41.

[164] Commission Decision of 27 June 2017, Case AT.39740 – *Google Search (Shopping)*. Accordingly, the abuse of a dominant position by Google was found owing to the fact that the latter, in general search results page, positioned and displayed more favourably its own comparison shopping service compared with its rivals. The case is pending before the General Court (Case T-612/17, *Google and Alphabet v. Commission*, action brought on 11 September 2017).

[165] Decision of the German Federal Cartel Office (Bundeskartellamt), *ASICS*, 26 August 2015, B2-98/11, para. 15. See also *ibid.*, paras 86–95.

in third-party online marketplaces could contribute to the products being more easily found.[166] Finally, although the safety measures as regards Internet platforms were not addressed by the ECJ in *Coty*, the question of what kind of platforms could be in a position to offer safe online sales may need to be taken into account when it comes to examining the competitive landscape of online platform competition.[167] After all, the safety of the website may be determined on more objective criteria than the "aura of luxury".

It is also noteworthy that the legal assessment provided in the *Coty* case seems to reflect a "screen-shot" picture of today without considering the increasing (potential) role of online platforms. For example, Advocate General in the opinion stated that:

> In fact, unlike the absolute ban imposed on authorised distributors making use of the internet in order to distribute the contract products, a prohibition on the use of third-party platforms does not – *at least at this stage of the development of e-commerce, which may undergo changes in the shorter or longer term* – have such a degree of harm to competition.[168] (Emphasis added)

Yet, relying on the argument that third-party online marketplaces are not – as of today – important distribution channels is not necessarily convincing. First of all, according to the European Commission's sector inquiry,[169] this circumstance differs in the Member states.[170] The latter fact may also be important when assessing the effects of the restrictions on the online visibility of the distributors. This may be important with regard to the online platforms, which are most important online sales channel. Thereby, the potential effects that the restrictions to sell in third-party online marketplaces may have on the visibility of the distributors on the Internet may possibly lead to such restrictions being considered anti-competitive under Article 4(c) of the BER of vertical agreements.[171] In *Coty*, the ECJ did not consider the restriction to sell in third-party

---

[166] *Ibid.*, paras 15, 40.

[167] *Ibid.*, para. 42.

[168] Opinion of AG, *Coty*, *supra* note 138, para. 118. See also *ibid.*, paras 111, 149.

[169] European Commission, Report from the Commission to the Council and the European Parliament: Final Report on the E-commerce Sector Inquiry, Brussels, 10.5.2017, COM(2017) 229 final.

[170] *Ibid.*, para. 39. Along these lines see also: Bundeskartellamt, "Competition Restraints in Online Sales after Coty and Asics – What's Next?" (Series of papers on "Competition and Consumer Protection in the Digital Economy"), October 2018, p. 3.

[171] See also: Bundeskartellamt, "Competition Restraints in Online Sales after Coty and Asics – What's Next?" (Series of papers on "Competition and Consumer Protection in the Digital Economy"), October 2018, p. 3: "it remains unclear at which point general platform restrictions and other restrictions of online sales activities reduce a dealer's visibility to an extent that fulfils the criterion of the restriction of passive sales

online marketplaces as a hardcore restriction under Article 4(b) and Article 4(c) of the BER of vertical agreements.[172] However, it may be asked whether the restrictions to sell in third-party online marketplaces could, under the circumstances, fall under such hardcore restrictions, but not only in terms of restricting passive, but also active sales. Further, the circumstance that online sales are closely related to online advertising raises the question of what implications the *Coty* case may have for, for example, advertisement aggregators. The advertising of the product and offering it online may be closely related, so that the restriction on the latter may also restrict the former. The question is also whether competition authorities should wait for "changes in the shorter or longer term" (in the words of AG) in order to step in. Bearing in mind that these restrictions may carry a risk of distorting competition among online platforms, it could be asked whether restrictions that would be considered legitimate for the purpose of preserving the "aura of luxury" from the perspective of today, will remain so tomorrow.

Finally, another hypothetical scenario that might be related to the restrictions against selling in third-party online marketplaces may be the use of pricing algorithms. The ECJ in *Coty* held that restrictions in a selective distribution system not to sell in third-party online marketplaces may be compatible with Article 101 TFEU. Yet, should such third-party online marketplace use its own pricing algorithms, it may be difficult for the selective distribution system owner to monitor the prices of the retailers. In such a case, a rationale behind the restriction to sell in third-party online marketplaces may, in fact, be better monitoring of the retailer's price and, shielding it with the preservation of the "aura of luxury", an avoidance of the risk that the price of the relevant (luxury?) product may, in fact, go down. In other words, it could be speculated that, in the case where a manufacture of a product recommends retail prices, it may be easier to monitor such prices by cutting the possibilities of retailers selling in third-party online marketplaces shielding such a restriction with a need to preserve the "aura of luxury". Thereby, the argument of the "aura of luxury", which looks perplexing if it is considered that, in *Coty*, sales in airport duty-free shops were allowed and were not considered impairing such an aura, may find its "logic" from the point of view of the owner of the selective distribution system. After all, offline shops do not use pricing algorithms. The outcome of such a speculation would be that, while assessing the restrictions in an online environment, a need may arise to take account of factors other than those present in an offline environment, namely, the use of pricing algorithms

---

pursuant to Article 4(c) VBER. Furthermore, it remains unclear whether an overall assessment of different restrictions is required."

[172]   ECJ, *Coty, supra* note 124, para. 68.

and the question of the extent to which such algorithms may incentivize the owner of a selective distribution network to shield their products from algorithmic price adjustments that may "risk" lowering the price of the product that is part of a selective distribution system. In such a case, as long as resale prices were recommended, there would be no anti-competitive behaviour; however, negative effects may arise not only (or merely) from limiting the sales channels, but, in fact, from limiting the possibilities of intensifying price competition in terms of algorithmic price adjustments.

4.3.2   "Rights Relating to a Data Set" and Contractual Restrictions on "Screen Scraping"

Competition for data traffic may also need to be taken into account in cases assessing so-called "screen scraping". In the case of a data set, which does not qualify for database protection, the question may arise to what extent contractual restrictions hindering access to data may be legitimate. A tricky issue in this regard is not only a competition law perspective. When it comes to a data set, which does not qualify for database protection, the limitations on the contractual restrictions enshrined in Article 15 of the EU Database Directive[173] would not apply. Based on the freedom of contract, companies may thereby be able to restrict extraction or reutilization of a data set by means of their terms and conditions.

The legitimacy of the contractual restrictions on "screen scraping" was analysed by the ECJ in the *Ryanair v. Aviation* case.[174] In that case, Ryanair claimed that PR Aviation "infringed its rights to its data set"[175] by having obtained the necessary information for its website from a dataset that was linked to the Ryanair website.[176] The latter, however, was accessible by consumers.[177]

4.3.2.1 The ECJ's preliminary ruling in *Ryanair v. PR Aviation*
The dispute in the *Ryanair* case was related to the use by PR Aviation of the data from Ryanair's data set for the sake of the operation of PR Aviation's website, on which consumers could not only compare prices of low-cost air

---

[173] Directive 96/9/EC of the European Parliament and of the Council of 11 March 1996 on the legal protection of databases, [1996] OJ L 77/20 (hereinafter: Database Directive).

[174] ECJ, Case C-30/14, *Ryanair Ltd v. PR Aviation BV*, 15 January 2015, ECLI:EU: C:2015:10.

[175] *Ibid.*, para. 17.

[176] *Ibid.*, para. 15.

[177] *Ibid.*, para. 15.

companies, but could also book flights on payment of commission.[178] Visitors to the Ryanair website had to accept its general terms and conditions (by ticking a box), which included a clause on the exclusive distribution of Ryanair services only by the Ryanair website and the Ryanair call center, so that any other website could not be authorized to sell Ryanair's flights. The use of the website was allowed solely for private, non-commercial purposes, whereas the extraction of data by third parties (using any automated systems or software) from the Ryanair website for commercial purposes (so-called "screen scraping"[179]) was prohibited, unless they had concluded a written licence agreement granting "access to Ryanair's price, flight and timetable information for the sole purpose of price comparison".[180] Ryanair claimed that PR Aviation breached such terms and conditions, which it had accepted, and infringed Ryanair's "rights relating to its data set".[181]

The question in this case was thereby the legitimacy of the contractual clauses restricting the commercial use of data from the Ryanair's data set by third parties. In the request, which was related to the interpretation of the EU Database Directive, the Netherlands Supreme Court referred the following question to the ECJ:

> Does the operation of [Directive 96/9] also extend to online databases which are not protected by copyright on the basis of Chapter II of [that directive], and also not by a sui generis right on the basis of Chapter III, in the sense that the freedom to use such databases through the (whether or not analogous) application of Article[s] 6(1) and 8 in conjunction with Article 15 [of Directive 96/9], may not be limited contractually?[182]

In other words, the question in the case was whether third parties – by means of a contract (or, to be more precise, by means of terms and conditions) – may be prohibited from accessing an online data set that does not qualify for database protection.

In the preliminary ruling, the ECJ held that the Database Directive does not cover databases that are not protected by copyright or a *sui generis* right, so

---

[178] *Ibid.*, para. 15.

[179] "Screen scraping" has to be distinguished from "data portability". The right to data portability, which is anchored in Article 20 of the EU General Data Protection Regulation, enables the data subject (thus, a natural person) to transfer personal data from one electronic system to the other. Yet data portability relates, firstly, to personal data only, and secondly, to the transfers of such personal data upon the request of the data subject (not third parties).

[180] ECJ, Case C-30/14 *Ryanair Ltd v. PR Aviation BV*, 15 January 2015, ECLI:EU:C:2015:10, para. 16.

[181] *Ibid.*, para. 17.

[182] *Ibid.*, para. 28.

that also the nullity and voidness of contractual clauses which limit access and further use of such databases, as stipulated in Article 15 of the EU Database Directive, does not apply. Consequently, the holders of an online data set, which does not qualify for database protection, can – by way of a contract (in their terms and conditions) – impose on third parties limitations as regards access to and commercial use of such an online data set if the applicable national law does not provide for the opposite.[183]

4.3.2.2 Scope of EU database protection

Database protection was introduced in the EU in 1996 with the EU Database Directive. According to the Directive, a database is defined as "a collection of independent works, data or other materials arranged in a systematic or methodical way and individually accessible by electronic or other means" (Article 1(2)).

In the EU, a database can either be protected by copyright, if the selection or the arrangement of the contents of the database constitute the author's own intellectual creation (Article 3(1) of the Database Directive), or it can fall under the *sui generis* protection upon the condition of "a substantial investment" in obtaining, verifying or presenting the contents of the database (Article 7(1)).[184] By including the protection of databases by the *sui generis* right, the Database Directive sought "to safeguard the position of makers of databases against misappropriation of the results of the financial and professional investment made in obtaining and collection the contents by protecting the whole or substantial parts of a database against certain acts by a user or competitor".[185] Thus, whereas "original" databases may be protected by copyright (given that the structure of the database amounts to the "author's own intellectual creation"[186]), "non-original" databases may fall under database protection when there has been a substantial investment in obtaining, verifying or presenting the content of the database. Such an investment, as explained in recital 40 of the Database Directive, "may consist in the deployment of financial resources and/or the expending of time, effort and energy".

---

[183] *Ibid.*, para. 45.

[184] On the appropriateness of database protection see, for example, Commission of the European Communities, DG Internal Market and Services Working Paper: First evaluation of Directive 96/9/EC on the legal protection of databases, Brussels, 12 December 2005. For a detailed analysis of the requirements for database protection, also with a focus on the intersection with competition law, see, for example, *Leistner, M.*, The Protection of Databases, in: Derclaye, E. (ed.), Research Handbook on the Future of EU Copyright, Cheltenham: Edward Elgar, 2009, pp. 427–456.

[185] Recital 39 of the EU Database Directive.

[186] See also recital 15 of the EU Database Directive.

As regards the latter, it could be recalled that the ECJ, in the *British Horseracing Board*, explained that "the expression 'investment in ... the obtaining, verification or presentation of the contents' of a database must be understood, generally, to refer to investment in the creation of that database as such".[187] In the words of the ECJ:

> the expression "investment in ... the obtaining ... of the contents" of a database must [...] be understood to refer to the resources used to seek out existing independent materials and collect them in the database, and not to the resources used for the creation as such of independent materials. The purpose of the protection by the *sui generis* right provided for by the directive is to promote the establishment of storage and processing systems for existing information and not the creation of materials capable of being collected subsequently in a database.[188]

Accordingly, the investment in the obtaining of the contents of a database "excludes the creation of the materials contained in a database from the definition of obtaining".[189]

The users of so protected databases may be restricted in the acts that they can perform as regards such databases (Article 5 as regards copyright and Article 8 as regards the *sui generis* right); yet the Database Directive also provides for exceptions to such restricted acts. For example, according to Article 6(1) of the Database Directive, which speaks of the exceptions to restricted acts in the case of a database protected by copyright, a lawful user of a database may – without the authorization of the author of the database – perform acts of the reproduction of a database, its translation, adaptation, arrangement or any alteration or any other acts listed in Article 5 if such acts are necessary to access the contents of a database for a normal use of such a content. However, what a normal use is is an open concept and thereby subject to interpretation.

Furthermore, Article 8 of the Database Directive, which elaborates on the rights and obligations of the lawful users of the databases protected by the *sui generis* right, says in Article 8(1) that:

> The maker of a database which is made available to the public in whatever manner may not prevent a lawful user of the database from extracting and/or re-utilizing *insubstantial parts* of its contents, evaluated qualitatively and/or quantitatively, *for any purposes whatsoever*. (Emphasis added)

---

[187] ECJ, Case C-203/02, *The British Horseracing Board Ltd and Others*, 9 November 2004, ECLI:EU:C:2004:695, para. 30.

[188] *Ibid.*, para. 31.

[189] *Ibid.*, para. 32.

Thereby, the extraction and (or) the re-utilization of the database is allowed – for any purpose (thus, including the commercial one), yet only to the extent that it relates to insubstantial parts of such a database.

The ECJ, in the *British Horseracing Board* case, explained that a "substantial part, evaluated quantitatively" refers to "the volume extracted from the database",[190] whereas "substantial part, evaluated qualitatively" refers to "the scale of investment in the obtaining, verification or presentation of the contents of the subject of the act of extraction and/or re-utilisation".[191]

Importantly though, according to Article 15 of the Database Directive, "any contractual provisions contrary to Articles 6(1) and 8 shall be null and void". Hence, in the case of a database protection by the *sui generis* right, the extraction (i.e. "the transfer of the contents of the database to another medium"[192]) or the re-utilization (i.e. "the making available to the public of the contents of a database"[193]) of insubstantial parts of a database cannot be prohibited contractually.

4.3.2.3 Legal challenges of the "rights relating to a data set"

The ECJ's *Ryanair* case described above raises several legal questions. First of all, the case is an illustration of the situation where the ECJ had to provide guidance on the question, which falls into a legal gap. In fact, the case, back in 2015, sent a clear signal of the (emerging) problem in the data economy, i.e. firstly, how to treat data that is not covered by the existing legal tools, such as, for example, database protection, and secondly, how to assess what impact the (contractual) restrictions on access to such data may have in general and on (platform) competition in particular. In fact, the term, which is used in the case, i.e. the "rights relating to a data set", is rather unusual. Such a legal creature is not known under the EU Database Directive. Indeed, the rights relating to a data set did not stem from database protection. Instead, such rights were rather of a contractual nature, or, to be more precise, they stemmed from the terms and conditions.

It is, of course, true that, owing to the freedom of contract, companies should be free to agree on such rights on the basis of their terms and conditions. However, the question is how to treat such rights in the light of the existing regulation, i.e. the Database Directive, which, in fact, prohibits the contractual restrictions of a nature similar to the rights relating to the data set which were under dispute in *Ryanair*. So, on the one hand, it could be argued that, based

---

[190] *Ibid.*, para. 70.
[191] *Ibid.*, para. 71.
[192] *Ibid.*, para. 61.
[193] *Ibid.*, para. 61.

on the freedom of contract, a company may restrict access to data and may choose any tools (such as, for example, terms and conditions) for doing so. On the other hand, however, the question is whether a different treatment of the freedom of contract as regards data (sets) protected under the legal framework of the database protection and those that do not fall under such protection may be justified.

The question in the *Ryanair* case was about the "rights related to a data set", which does not qualify for database protection. Based on Article 15 of the Database Directive, the holders of the databases are restricted to imposing contractual provisions that limit the exceptions to restricted acts (including the extraction and re-utilization of insubstantial parts of the database). Such contractual restrictions are considered to be null and void. However, in the case of sets of data that do not qualify for database protection (i.e. are "too simple" to qualify for such a protection or do not live up to the standard of a "substantial investment"), such contractual provisions, according to the ECJ's judgement, should be valid. Yet the question is whether there is, in fact, any legal basis for such a different treatment, particularly bearing in mind that contractual protection would, accordingly, be allowed for data sets that do not fulfil the requirement of creativity or substantial investment in terms of the EU Database Directive. In other words, should such contractual restrictions be considered legitimate, the protection as regards "simple" data sets (for example, consisting of information such as prices, which – owing to their simplicity – do not enjoy any legal protection) may become much stronger than the protection of databases that qualify for database protection. Thus, in light of the fact that the Database Directive stipulates that contractual provisions that limit the exceptions to restricted acts (including the extraction and the re-utilization of insubstantial parts of the database) should be null and void, it could be questioned whether similar contractual provisions as regards data sets that do not qualify for database protection, could be considered a proportionate tool to restrict the extraction of data that forms part of a data set that is basically "too simple" to qualify for database protection. In such a way, the contractual restrictions (or to be more precise, the restrictions involved in the terms and conditions) could extend the scope of protection of such data, which by its nature does not qualify for any intellectual property or intellectual property-like protection.

The ECJ basically affirmed the right of the holder of an online data set that is not entitled to the protection provided for in the framework of the Database Directive to contractually forbid access to it and the commercial use of it by third parties. The outcome of the *Ryanair* judgement is therefore the following: the owner of a database that, based on the criterion of creativity or a substantial investment, enjoys the copyright or the *sui generis* protection of a database, respectively, may not restrict access to or the use of the content of a database by third parties on the basis of a contract, as this is expressly forbidden in

Article 15 of the Database Directive. However, the holders of a data set that does not qualify for protection (thus, basically, it is "too simple" to qualify), may, in the end, enjoy a much stronger protection as regards its access and the use of its contents, since the latter may be forbidden by a contract, based solely on the discretion of the holder of online data. Such an outcome is confusing – yet not only from the point of view of the Database Directive.

While assessing the "rights related to a data set" it could be asked whether the Database Directive should play a crucial role here. In the *Ryanair* case, the ECJ had to elaborate on it, because this was the question asked by the national court. However, it could be argued that the "rights related to a data set", in fact, aim at hindering access to data as such (thus, not to a database). Database protection does not amount to the protection of its content, but rather, as explained above, it protects the creation of a database as such. For example, the fact that the EU Database Directive does not grant protection to data as such was part of the scepticism expressed by the European Commission as regards the appropriateness of such protection for data sets in the data economy.[194]

Although providing a careful and systematic view of the Database Directive, the ECJ's judgement in no way elaborates on the impact that such clauses may have for competition, in particular as regards a potentially negative impact which the contractual restrictions in question may have on platform competition.

The restrictions on "screen scraping" may be directly related to restricting data traffic. In fact, using contractual restrictions to "screen scrape" information from one's own website, access seems to be hindered to non-personal data such as, for example, information on the prices available on the website, etc. Yet, on a closer look, through hindering access to non-personal data (such as information on prices, etc.), access may, at the end of the day, be hindered to personal data in terms of restricting traffic from potential visitors. The rationale behind the restrictions on "screen scraping" may be related to attracting as many users as possible to *one's own* platform. This rationale as such is not necessarily harmful. However, recalling that competition in the case of online platforms translates into competition for data traffic, the effects of "screen scraping" may boil down to hindering the traffic of data of (potentially) competing platforms. The effects of such contractual restrictions may be that they restrict access to personal data through hindering access to non-personal data, in order to increase data traffic from visitors to the company's own website and

---

[194] See, for example, European Commission, Commission Staff Working Document on the free flow of data and emerging issues of the European data economy. Accompanying the document: Communication, "Building a European Data Economy", Brussels, 10.1.2017, SWD(2017) 2 final, p. 20.

in such a way to generate more revenue. Bearing in mind that data traffic may be closely related to the economic viability of some online platforms (not only in terms of revenues, but also in terms of users' data as well), such restrictions may turn out to be a powerful tool to restrict the economic performance of (potential) competitors.

A legal assessment of such restrictions seems to go to the heart of balancing the interests of the companies, so that the argument could follow that this should be left for the companies to solve. This is rightly so, since the economic rationale of increasing data traffic and generating revenues will also be present on the side of companies willing to perform "screen scraping". However, such restrictions may also negatively affect consumers. Having more choice for consumers when it comes to online platforms may, first and foremost, be beneficial if we consider the rise of personalized pricing and the potential risks of online behavioural discrimination. Furthermore, it cannot be ruled out that platforms might exist offering better services than the platform owner (e.g. in terms of service packages, the quality of services, the processing of personal data, etc.), so that having a choice in this regard may also be highly relevant. Finally, considering the benefits of price comparison websites, it could also be argued that the restrictions on "screen scraping" may deprive consumers of such benefits. Bearing in mind that the visibility of the information provided on the Internet is becoming increasingly important for consumers (particularly, in making their choices), such restrictions may thus negatively affect consumers' interests, including, but not limited to cases when such restrictions were applied to price comparison websites.

Yet the question is whether any legal basis exists that could serve to limit the contractual restrictions on "screen scraping". After all, as explained above, the limits set by the EU Database Directive would not be applicable, since particular data sets may fall outside database protection. EU competition law, specifically, Article 102 TFEU, could be applied only in a limited number of cases, mostly owing to the fact that a dominant position would need to be established. Thus, it might be that the legal provisions against unfair competition may come into play in this regard, as illustrated by the German case described below.

4.3.2.4 "Screen scraping": judgement of the Federal Supreme Court of Germany

An approach to the legal assessment of "screen scraping" different from that of the ECJ can be found in the national law. The Federal Supreme Court of Germany, for example, rejected the allegations of unfair competition against an online flight-booking platform, which was using "screen scraping" for its online flight-booking, although it had previously accepted the flight company's terms and conditions forbidding such automated scraping of the flight data.[195] In other words, a breach of the accepted terms and conditions was not considered an act of unfair competition. It was stressed by the Court that the fact alone that the defendant – a competitor of the plaintiff – contrary to the will of the plaintiff, offered the flights on its own website could not be considered unfair competition even if the purpose of the defendant were to make the website visitors aware of the advertisements and the deals offered for a payment on its own website.[196] Furthermore, the Court explained that, in the light of the general interest of the functionality of the Internet, companies that provide offers on the Internet, should bear in mind that the information publicly provided by them may be found by the users on the basis of the commonly used search mechanisms, so that companies should accept the circumstance that revenues may be lost owing to the fact that users, while using the search mechanisms, will not necessarily visit directly the websites of the companies.[197] The Court also noted that the terms and conditions were related to information that had, in fact, been made publicly available, so the Court made a distinction between the latter case and the cases where technical protective measures are employed in advance[198] stressing that, as regards the assessment of the acts of unfair competition, acceptance of the terms and conditions cannot stand on an equal footing to cases where the restrictions are provided by the protection of the technical protective measures.[199]

In light of the features of online platform competition and the role of data traffic, it could be argued that the German judgement takes a more balanced approach when it comes to the assessment of the legality of "screen scraping". As said above, on the one hand, companies do enjoy a freedom of contract and can freely decide not only with whom they contract, but also on what terms. On the other hand, however, it should be recalled that such terms and conditions may amount to restrictions that may negatively affect competition and thereby also the interests of consumers. Bearing in mind that the aggregation of data is part of the life-blood of the data economy, it may be of crucial importance to achieve legal clarity as regards the assessment of "screen scraping", in particular when restrictions are imposed unilaterally by such contract-like clauses as terms and conditions.

---

[195] Federal Supreme Court of Germany, 30 April 2014 (I ZR 224/12).

[196] *Ibid.*, para. 34.

[197] *Ibid.*, para. 37. In this regard, the Court referred to the following two cases: Federal Supreme Court of Germany, 17 July 2003 (I ZR 259/00) and Federal Supreme Court of Germany, 22 June 2011 (I ZR 159/10).

[198] *Ibid.*, para. 37. In this regard, the Court referred to the following two cases: Federal Supreme Court of Germany, 17 July 2003 (I ZR 259/00) and Federal Supreme Court of Germany, 22 June 2011 (I ZR 159/10).

[199] *Ibid.*, para. 38.

4.4   ARTICLE 102 TFEU: A LEGAL BASIS TO ACCESS DATA?

Article 102 TFEU is the EU competition law provision that prohibits the abuse of a dominant position, although it does not prohibit the dominant position as such. In the case-law of the ECJ, this legal norm has been the basis for the licensing of intellectual property rights or granting access to information protected as a trade secret in the framework of the "exceptional circumstances" test. Whereas, in the *Magill* case, the "exceptional circumstances" test related to copyright[200] and, in the *IMS Health* case, to database rights,[201] in the *Microsoft* case, access was requested to information protected as a trade secret.[202]

Bearing in mind that data may be eligible for trade secret protection and that data sets may, under the circumstances, enjoy database protection, it could be tempting to argue that the application of Article 102 TFEU may be called into question in disputes over access to data.

Yet one of these cases – the *IMS Health* case – was not necessarily related to Article 102 TFEU. In fact, although the ECJ in this case provided guidance on the EU compulsory licensing scheme (in casu: a database) in terms of an abuse of a dominant position under Article 102 TFEU, the case involved one particular issue, which allows this case to be explained from a different perspective, namely the fact that the *IMS Health* case was about the "departing employee" and the question of the right of the latter to use information from the company which the person had left, in the framework of the law against unfair competition.

It might be that, owing to the factual circumstances of the *IMS Health* case, it in fact does not (and did not) entirely fit into the "exceptional circumstances" test. So, the question is, therefore, firstly, whether the issues similar to those that arose in the *IMS Health* case should indeed be solved on the basis of Article 102 TFEU, and secondly, whether the analysis of the *IMS Health* case – different from the "exceptional circumstances" test – may help to better spotlight issues that may be problematic in the data economy, and, thirdly, whether access to data in cases of Article 102 TFEU, in particular in the case

---

[200]   ECJ, Joined cases C-241/91 P and C-242/91 P, *Radio Telefis Eireann (RTE) and Independent Television Publications Ltd (ITP) v. Commission*, 6 April 1995, [1995] E.C.R. I-743 (ECLI:EU:C:1995:98) (known as the *Magill* case).

[201]   ECJ, Case C-418/01, *IMS Health GmbH & Co. OHG v. NDC Health GmbH & Co. KG*, 29 April 2004, [2004] E.C.R. I-5039 (ECLI:EU:C:2004:257).

[202]   General Court, Case T-201/04, *Microsoft v. Commission*, 17 September 2007, [2007] E.C.R. II-3601 (ECLI:EU:T:2007:289).

of a single-source database, should rather be based on the so-called "Bronner test", instead of applying the EU compulsory licensing scheme.

4.4.1 *IMS Health*: Beyond the "Exceptional Circumstances" Test

The *IMS Health* case was the second case in a row (following *Magill* and followed by *Microsoft*) out of three compulsory licensing cases addressed by the EU courts (the ECJ and the General Court). In this case, it was the application of the so-called "exceptional circumstances test" – the scheme of the EU compulsory licensing – that was called into question.

In the *IMS Health* case, the ECJ provided guidance for the application of the "exceptional circumstances" test,[203] as created by the ECJ in the *Magill* case.[204] Accordingly, the "exceptional circumstances" test is a compulsory licensing scheme applicable in cases where a dominant company, by refusing to grant a licence to other companies, may be found to have abused its dominant position in the relevant market in terms of Article 102 TFEU. The "exceptional circumstances" test, as analysed by the ECJ in *Magill* and *IMS Health*, consisted of four cumulative conditions: (i) the indispensability of an input; (ii) elimination of competition in a secondary market in the case of a refusal to license; (iii) hindering an appearance of a "new" product, for which there is a consumer demand; and (iv) the lack of objective justification for a refusal to grant a licence.[205] In *Microsoft*, this test was reinterpreted and consists of the four-step test, namely: firstly, access to a particular input is indispensable; secondly, there is a risk of the elimination of effective competition in the related markets; thirdly, technical development is hindered to the prejudice of consumers; and fourthly, there is no objective justification, in terms of the "Incentives Balance Test", as regards the refusal to grant access to the input requested.[206]

The *IMS Health* case has been widely debated by academia – but with regard to the "exceptional circumstances" test.[207] However, it should be recalled that

---

[203] ECJ, *IMS Health, supra* note 201, para. 52.

[204] ECJ, *Magill, supra* note 200, paras 53–56.

[205] ECJ, *Magill, supra* note 200, paras 53–56; ECJ, *IMS Health, supra* note 201, para. 52.

[206] General Court, *Microsoft, supra* note 202, paras 291–712. See also: *Surblytė, G.,* The Refusal to Disclose Trade Secrets as an Abuse of Market Dominance – *Microsoft* and Beyond, Berne: Stämpfli 2011, pp. XLVII + 263 (Munich Series on European and International Competition Law, Volume 28), pp. 115–140.

[207] See, for example, *Conde Gallego, B.,* Die Anwendung des kartellrechtlichen Missbrauchsverbots auf "unerlässliche" Immaterialgüterrechte im Lichte der *IMS Health-* und *Standard-Spundfass*-Urteile, (2006) GRUR Int. 16; *Drexl, J.,* Intellectual Property and Antitrust Law – IMS Health and Trinko – Antitrust Placebo for Consumers

the ECJ, in the *IMS Health* case, provided a preliminary ruling, so that the case was subsequently solved by the national court. It is also this latter part that may be highly interesting, since the national court solved the case on a completely different legal basis.

The legal dispute in this case started in front of the German courts. The issue in the *IMS Health* case evolved around the use by the NDC of the "brick structure" – a database developed by the IMS Health for the provision of the regional sales data on pharmaceuticals. Since such a "brick structure" was considered to be a database protected by copyright under the German law, the German courts prohibited the use of the "1860 brick structure" by the NDC.[208]

In 2000, the NDC referred to the European Commission with the claim that the IMS Health was abusing its dominant position (Article 102 TFEU) by refusing to grant a licence on the use of the aforementioned database.[209] Although the European Commission, by its interim measure decision,[210] ordered the IMS Health to grant a licence,[211] the interim measures decision was suspended by the order of the Court of First Instance (CFI) [now the General Court (GC)],[212] which, in turn, was upheld by the ECJ.[213] The decision was finally withdrawn by the European Commission.[214] The CFI [now GC] stated in its judgement that "the contested decision disappeared from the Community legal system with effect from 13 August 2003" and that the "German courts

---

Instead of Sound Economics in Refusal-to-Deal Cases, (2004) 35 IIC 788; *Leistner, M.*, Intellectual Property and Competition Law: The European Development from Magill to IMS Health compared to recent German and US Case Law, (2005) ZWeR 138.

[208]   ECJ, *IMS Health, supra* note 201, paras 9–10.

[209]   ECJ, *IMS Health, supra* note 201, para. 11.

[210]   Commission Decision of 3 July 2001 relating to a proceeding pursuant to Article 82 of the EC Treaty (Case COMP D3/38.044 – NDC Health/IMS HEALTH: Interim measures), OJ [2002] L 59/18.

[211]   *Ibid.*, Article 1.

[212]   Order of the President of the Court of First Instance, Case T-184/01 R, 10 August 2001, ECLI:EU:T:2001:200.

[213]   Order of the President of the Court, Case C-481/01 P(R), 11 April 2002, ECLI: EU:C:2002:223.

[214]   Commission Decision of 13 August 2003 relating to a proceeding under Article 82 of the EC Treaty (Case COMP D3/38.044 – NDC Health/IMS Health: Interim measures), OJ [2003] L 268/69. "The threat of extinction of NDC, posed to NDC and to the public interest in competition, no longer has the urgency to require the grant of a licence to NDC which was identified by the Commission at the time of adoption of its Decision and which is necessary to justify the maintenance of interim measures" (*ibid.*, para. 16).

therefore have complete freedom as to how to decide the cases before them, as the contested decision in any event only adopted interim measures".[215]

Yet, at the time when the European Commission's interim measure decision was withdrawn, the case, based on the request for a preliminary ruling from the Landgericht Frankfurt am Main on the same issue, was pending at the ECJ. In 2004, the ECJ delivered a preliminary ruling in the *IMS Health* case.[216] In the preliminary ruling, the ECJ provided guidance on the application of the "exceptional circumstances test" with regard to the IMS Health's refusal to license its copyright for the database at dispute. The *IMS Health* case was thereby treated as a case related to a compulsory licence of a database, which was addressed by the ECJ from the perspective of EU competition law (Article 102 TFEU).

However, the defendant in the *IMS Health* case was a former employee – actually a former director – of IMS Health, which is mentioned in the decision of the European Commission,[217] the opinion of Advocate General[218] as well as in the preliminary ruling of the ECJ. The ECJ, for example, pointed out that:

> After leaving his post in 1998, a former manager of IMS created Pharma Intranet Information AG ("PII"), whose activity also consisted in marketing regional data on pharmaceutical products in Germany formatted on the basis of brick structures. At first, PII tried to market structures consisting of 2 201 bricks. On account of reticence manifested by potential clients, who were accustomed to structures consisting of 1 860 or 2 847 bricks, it decided to use structures of 1 860 or 3 000 bricks, very similar to those used by IMS. PII was acquired by NDC.[219]

Hence, a crucial point in the *IMS Health* case was that the former manager of the company wanted to use the "brick structure" that was developed by the IMS Health, first and foremost, owing to the fact that such a "brick structure" was an industry standard, as explained in the passage above. Since such a "brick structure", as a database, was protected under copyright under the German law,

---

[215] Order of the Court of First Instance, Case T-184/01, 10 March 2005, ECLI:EU: T:2005:95, para. 46.

[216] ECJ, *IMS Health*, *supra* note 201.

[217] NDC (the US company, which entered the EU market in 1998 via two acquisitions in the UK) was established by a former employee of IMS Health, and in 2000 NDC concluded the purchase agreement of PI Pharmaintranet (PI), which provided it an operational platform in the German market (Commission Decision of 3 July 2001 relating to a proceeding pursuant to Article 82 of the EC Treaty (Case COMP D3/38.044 – NDC Health/IMS HEALTH: Interim measures), OJ [2002] L 59/18, para. 4).

[218] Opinion of Advocate General Tizzano delivered on 2 October 2003 in Case C-418/01, *IMS Health GmbH & Co. OHG v. NDC Health GmbH & Co. KG*, ECLI:EU: C:2003:537, para. 8: "PII, founded by a former director of IMS".

[219] ECJ, *IMS Health*, *supra* note 201, paras 7–8.

the IMS Health refused to grant a licence for NDC to use it. Hence, the issue in the case was not so much related to an abuse of a dominant position under Article 102 TFEU, but was rather about possibly unfair competition between the two companies.

The fact that a former director of the IMS Health became a director of PII played an important role in the decision of the Federal Supreme Court of Germany.[220] In fact, in front of the German courts, the plaintiff argued that the defendant was using an exact copy of the brick structure, which was based on a "pirate copy" (*Raubkopie*) that was claimed to have been illegally acquired by the defendant.[221] The dispute was, *inter alia*, about Section 4(3) of the German Law against Unfair Competition (UWG), which enshrines different types of conduct and prohibits the offering of the goods/services which are the copies of the goods/services of the competitors. The Federal Supreme Court of Germany stressed that, for the conduct to be considered unfair competition, it was not only that copied goods had to be offered, but also that other additional conditions relating to the aforementioned different types of behaviour had to be fulfilled.[222] In this regard, the Court referred to the judgement of the appellate court, which, in its judgement, had held that the defendant, by having taken over the brick structure directly and without their own efforts in terms of the time, costs and tools which would have been needed for conquering the market, was competing unfairly.[223] The Federal Supreme Court of Germany did not agree with the latter finding. The Federal Supreme Court of Germany pointed out that the findings of the appellate court as regards copying in terms of the mere traceability of the plaintiff's segment structure in the defendant's segment structure could not be upheld.[224] It was stressed that it was not the direct copy of the product that was used, but rather the scheme of the product that enabled the original data structure to be traced back (e.g. based on a "conversion table" (*Konvertierungstabelle*)).[225] So, the use of a similar brick structure was not considered to amount to unfair behaviour.

The analysis above shows that the role of the *IMS Health* case in terms of the application of Article 102 TFEU and thus granting access to data on this legal basis should not be overestimated. The case was not so much about Article 102 TFEU, but rather about the issue of whether the employee who left the company was possibly competing unfairly. Thus, the case came from a completely different angle and went beyond the EU compulsory licensing scheme

---

[220] Federal Supreme Court of Germany, 4 May 2016, I ZR 58/14, para. 5.
[221] *Ibid.*, para. 6.
[222] *Ibid.*, para. 40.
[223] *Ibid.*, para. 41.
[224] *Ibid.*, para. 68.
[225] *Ibid.*, paras 69–75.

in terms of the "exceptional circumstances" test. Accordingly, the question was not so much about access to data, but rather whether a particular data structure could be used by a former director of the company, so that the case was finally solved by the national courts on the basis of unfair competition law. In its nature, the issue in this case comes very close to the issues that come under trade secret law, i.e. the question whether or to what extent a departing employee may use their knowledge and the information acquired with the former employer without compromising the employer's trade secrets. Such cases will not necessarily be solved on the basis of Article 102 TFEU, but may rather involve considerations relating to unfair behaviour (unfair competition).

The explanations provided by the Federal Supreme Court of Germany in the *IMS Health* case may be highly relevant for the data economy. After all, in the latter, it is increasingly intelligent machines and algorithms that are used. The question therefore is how cases should be solved when a departing employee takes with them knowledge, for example, about the algorithms used by their previous employers. Although the use of identical algorithms could probably be prohibited on the basis of trade secret protection, the question may be more complicated if algorithms were used that would be not identical, but merely similar. In such cases, issues may arise that come under the so-called "Inevitable Disclosure Doctrine", which has been developed under US trade secret law.

The Inevitable Disclosure Doctrine was born in the US in the *PepsiCo* case.[226] In that case, the plaintiff (PepsiCo Inc.) asked for an injunction to be applied to the former General Manager of one of the units of the company, who moved to work for a competitor in soft drinks. The request was based on the reason that it was inevitable that such a senior manager who moved to a close competitor would disclose strategic knowledge to the competitor. Thus, the problem in the case was related to the strategic information (e.g. sensitive information about the "pricing architecture") that the former general manager was aware of.[227] It was claimed that "knowing PCNA's pricing architecture would allow a competitor to anticipate PCNA's pricing moves and underbid PCNA strategically whenever and wherever the competitor so desired".[228] Given the information that the former general manager possessed, the US Court of Appeals upheld the judgement of the US District Court for the Northern District of Illinois, which granted a temporary injunction against a former employee as regards "assuming his responsibilities" at the new

---

[226] *PepsiCo, Inc. v. Redmond*, 54 F.3d 1262 (7th Cir. 1995).
[227] *Ibid.*, at 1265.
[228] *Ibid.*, at 1265.

employer and prevented the former employee forever from disclosing former employer's trade secrets and confidential information.[229]

The Inevitable Disclosure Doctrine in the US is based on the concept of the "threatened misappropriation" of a trade secret. In fact, the Uniform Trade Secrets Act in the US, which is a model act followed by most of the States in issuing their Trade Secrets Act, stipulates that the misappropriation of a trade secret may be actual or threatened.[230] Since the same wording was also enshrined in the Illinois Trade Secrets Act, the Court held in *PepsiCo* that "[t]he question of threatened or inevitable misappropriation in this case lies at the heart of a basic tension in trade secret law. Trade secret law serves to protect 'standards of commercial morality' and 'encourage[ ] invention and innovation' while maintaining 'the public interest in having free and open competition in the manufacture and sale of unpatented goods'. Yet that same law should not prevent workers from pursuing their livelihoods when they leave their current positions" (reference to the citation omitted).[231]

As regards "threatened misappropriation", the Court analysed it in terms of high likelihood that trade secrets will inevitably and immediately be used.[232] It was stated by the Court that:

> Admittedly, PepsiCo has not brought a traditional trade secret case, in which a former employee has knowledge of a special manufacturing process or customer list and can give a competitor an unfair advantage by transferring the technology or customers to that competitor. [...] Rather PepsiCo has asserted that Redmond cannot help but rely on PCNA trade secrets as he helps plot Gatorade and Snapple's new course, and that these trade secrets will enable Quaker to achieve a substantial advantage by knowing exactly how PCNA will price, distribute, and market its sports drinks and new age drinks and being able to respond strategically. [...] This type of trade secret problem may arise less often, but it nevertheless falls within the realm of trade secret protection under the present circumstances.[233] (Footnote and references to the case-law omitted)

It is noteworthy that the Court referred to the finding of the district court in that case that unless the former employee "possessed an uncanny ability to compartmentalize information, he would necessarily be making decisions about Gatorade and Snapple by relying on his knowledge of PCNA trade secrets".[234] Also, an important factual feature of the *PepsiCo* case was that a confidenti-

---

[229] *Ibid.*, at 1272.
[230] National Conference of Commissioners on Uniform State Laws, Uniform Trade Secrets Act, 1979, as amended in 1985, Section 2, p. 7.
[231] *PepsiCo, Inc. v. Redmond*, 54 F.3d 1262 (7th Cir. 1995), at 1268.
[232] *Ibid.*, at 1268.
[233] *Ibid.*, at 1270.
[234] *Ibid.*, at 1269.

ality agreement signed by the former employee was not considered a factor countervailing the inevitable disclosure of a trade secret.[235] In the words of the Court:

> the danger of misappropriation in the present case is not that Quaker threatens to use PCNA's trade secrets to create distribution systems or co-opt PCNA's advertising and marketing ideas. Rather, PepsiCo believes that Quaker, *unfairly armed with knowledge of PCNA's plans, will be able to anticipate its distribution, packaging, pricing, and marketing moves.* [...] In other words, PepsiCo finds itself in the position of a coach, one of whose players has left, playbook in hand, to join the opposing team before the big game.[236] (Emphasis added)

Controversial as it is, the Inevitable Disclosure Doctrine allows the prevention of a former employee, who may possess knowledge about the strategic information related to the business of the former employer, from working – at least, temporarily – at a competitive business. The doctrine rests on the basis that it may be inevitable that such a former employee will use or disclose trade secrets of a former employer in their new business. When it comes to algorithms, the issue may sound very similar: should a departing employee possess knowledge about or related to the algorithms used by the company, it may be inevitable that such employees will use or disclose such algorithms (or the information related to them) when working for their new employers in a competing business. However, the risk of following the Inevitable Disclosure Doctrine would be that a good number of departing employees might be enjoined from working at all, particularly bearing in mind the widespread use of algorithms in business.[237] Hence, it might be that, in this regard, non-compete agreements may become even more widely used. The latter, however, restrict ability to work for a limited period of time on the basis of granting compensation.

On the basis of what was said above, it could be argued that, based on the approach of the Federal Supreme Court of Germany, cases like *IMS Health*

---

[235] *Ibid.*, at 1264, 1270, 1271.

[236] *Ibid.*, at 1270.

[237] The question whether the "Inevitable Disclosure Doctrine" may need to be applied to intelligent machines themselves is, for the time being, rather speculative and can be left open. On the one hand, intelligent machines, in contrast to people, may be better capable of "compartmentalising" information, so that the risk of the disclosure of a trade secret would not arise in the first place. On the other hand, however, should not only people, but also machines be "moving" among different employers, account may need to be taken of the fact that it might be inevitable that such machines will use or disclose the knowledge they possess from the previous employment. A kind of a "cool-off" period might thereby be needed (if we consider the fact that also in *PepsiCo* a temporary injunction was applied, thus implying that the information protected by a trade secret may "get old").

may have to be solved on the basis of the legal framework against unfair competition where it may need to be analysed whether any additional acts of unfair behaviour might have been involved. It is namely in this regard, thus, not in terms of a compulsory licensing under Article 102 TFEU, that the *IMS Health* case may turn out to be most important in general and for the data economy in particular.

4.4.2   Access to "Single-Source" Data Sets: The "*Bronner*-Case" Standard

"Single-source" databases are described by the European Commission as "databases where the database maker and the proprietor of the underlying information are the same person or entity".[238] Hence, in the case of a single-source database, both the database and its contents (e.g. individual data) are in the hands of one person or entity. Bearing in mind the role of data in the data economy, competition law concerns, in the cases of single-source data sets, may be at their peak, since, as long as it is not possible for competitors to independently collect data, access to such a database may be indispensable.

Recital 47 of the EU Database Directive stipulates that:

> in the interests of competition between suppliers of information products and services, protection by the *sui generis* right must not be afforded in such a way as to facilitate abuses of a dominant position, in particular as regards the creation and distribution of new products and services which have an intellectual, documentary, technical, economic or commercial added value; [...] therefore, the provisions of this Directive are without prejudice to the application of Community or national competition rules.

Thereby, the EU Database Directive does not entail the compulsory licensing clause in the case when a database is protected by the *sui generis* right, but leaves the door open, as stipulated in recital 47, to apply competition law. Hence, compulsory licensing of a database may be granted on the basis of Article 102 TFEU, i.e. an abuse of a dominant position.

In this regard, it is noteworthy that the proposal for the EU Database Directive[239] included legal provisions on the compulsory licensing of the

---

[238] Commission of the European Communities, DG Internal Market and Services Working Paper: First evaluation of Directive 96/9/EC on the legal protection of databases, Brussels, 12 December 2005, p. 15.

[239] Commission of the European Communities, Proposal for a Council Directive on the legal protection of databases (92/C 156/03), COM(92) 24 final – SYN 393 (submitted by the Commission on 15 April 1992), OJ [1992] C 156/4 (hereinafter: Proposal for the Database Directive).

single-source databases. Article Article 8(1) of the Proposal for the Database Directive read:

> Notwithstanding the right provided for in Article 2(5) to prevent the unauthorized extraction and re-utilization of the contents of a database, *if the works or materials contained in a database which is made publicly available cannot be independently created, collected or obtained from any other source*, the right to extract and re-utilize, in whole or substantial part, works or materials from that database for commercial purposes, *shall be licensed on fair and non-discriminatory terms.* (Emphasis added)[240]

Thereby, the Proposal for the EU Database Directive included a compulsory licensing provision in the case where, firstly, a database was made publicly available, and, secondly, it was impossible for other companies to independently create, collect or obtain the works or materials, i.e. the contents of the database, from any other sources. Hence, a compulsory licensing provision in the proposed Database Directive was related to access to the contents of a database. This fact was also reflected in the title of Article 8, namely, in the acts performed in relation to the contents of a database – unfair extraction of the contents.[241]

Recital 31 of the Proposal for the Database Directive further explained that:

> in the interests of competition between suppliers of information products and services, the maker of a database which is commercially distributed, whose database is the sole possible source of a given work or material, *should make that work or material available under licence for use by others*, providing that the works or materials so licensed are used in the independent creation of new works, and providing that no prior rights in or obligations incurred in respect of those works or materials are infringed. (Emphasis added)

Thereby, the licence in the proposed Database Directive was meant in terms of the works or materials that formed part of a database. Such licences, according to recital 33 of the proposed Database Directive, "should not be requested for reasons of commercial expediency such as economy of time, effort or financial investment". Article 8(3) of the proposed Database Directive stipulated that

---

[240] Article 2(5) of the proposed Database Directive reads: "Member States shall provide for a right for the maker of a database to prevent the unauthorized extraction or re-utilization, from that database, of its contents, in whole or in substantial part, for commercial purposes. This right to prevent unfair extraction of the contents of a database shall apply irrespective of the eligibility of that database for protection under copyright. It shall not apply to the contents of a database where these are works already protected by copyright or neighbouring rights."

[241] It is noteworthy that the "right of unfair extraction" later on became the *sui generis* right that was enshrined in the EU Database Directive.

"Member States shall provide appropriate measures for arbitration between the parties in respect of such licences".[242]

The legal provision on such compulsory licensing was preserved in the European Commission's amended proposal for the EU Database Directive.[243] Article 11(1) of the amended proposal stipulated that:

> Notwithstanding the right provided for in Article 10(2) to prevent the unauthorised extraction and re-utilisation of the contents of a database, if the works or materials contained in a database which is made publicly available cannot be independently created, collected or obtained from any other source, the right to extract and re-utilise, in whole or substantial part, works or materials from that database for commercial purposes that are not for reasons such as economy of time, effort or financial investment, shall be licensed on fair and non-discriminatory terms. A declaration shall be submitted clearly setting out the justification of the commercial purposes pursued and requiring the issue of a licence.

However, the legal provision on a compulsory licensing was not included in the final text of the EU Database Directive. The analysis of the preparatory materials of the directive nevertheless shows that the initial idea was to include a legal provision on a compulsory licensing of the databases protected under the *sui generis* right. After all, the standard of protection of the latter right is lower than in the case of copyright, which protects originality. Instead, in the case of the *sui generis* right it is rather the investment (in the broadest sense) that is protected. For such cases, it is more the "sweat of the brow" standard that applies. So, it could be asked whether, in the case when such a database constitutes a single-source database, a standard for a compulsory access should apply that would be lower than the standard for a compulsory licensing of copyright. The latter would fall under the EU compulsory licensing scheme in terms of the "exceptional circumstances" test.

Hence, bearing in mind that the *sui generis* database protection right highly reflects the "sweat of the brow" standard, which grants protection on the basis of skills and labour involved, it could, in fact, be more justified to apply a standard lower than that of the "exceptional circumstances" test when it comes to the request to grant access to a database protected by the *sui generis* right. After all, the granting of such a right, in contrast to copyright, is not based on any "intellectual" creation, but rather seeks to protect investment.

---

[242] Recital 34 of the proposed Directive explained that "in the event that licences are refused or the parties cannot reach agreement on terms to be concluded, a system of arbitration should be provided for by the Member States".

[243] Commission of the European Communities, Amended proposal for a Council Directive on the legal protection of databases, COM(93) 464 final – SYN 393, Brussels, 4 October 1993.

The ECJ in the *British Horseracing Board* case noted that, according to the 48th recital of the preamble to the EU Database Directive, "the *sui generis* right has an economic justification, which is to afford protection to the maker of the database and guarantee a return on his investment in the creation and maintenance of the database".[244]

Bearing in mind that access to single-source databases may be highly important for companies operating in the data economy, it could be asked whether it is the "exceptional circumstances" test that should be the governing standard for solving such cases. After all, it is not only access to a database, but also access to data that forms the whole or a substantial part of such a database that may be needed. It could be argued that such cases, i.e. cases of access to single-source databases, should be solved on the basis of the "pure" indispensability standard, bearing in mind that crystalizing the legal criteria for defining indispensability may be crucial for legal certainty. In other words, it could be asked whether such cases should be solved as refusal to deal cases, instead of being considered refusal to license cases.

The "indispensability" requirement in the refusal to deal context (thus, not a refusal to license), was analysed by the ECJ in the *Bronner* case.[245] Thereby, the question is the following: if access to a single-source data set should be granted on the basis of the standard of indispensability provided for in the *Bronner* case, what should the relevant legal requirements be and how may they be applied in the data economy?

In the *Bronner* case, the ECJ was asked to provide a preliminary ruling on the question whether access requested by Oscar Bronner in terms of including their published newspaper in the nationwide home-delivery scheme established by Mediaprint could be granted on the basis of the legal provisions of an abuse of a dominant position.[246] In answering that question, the ECJ, first of all, noted that the national court should analyse whether home-delivery schemes constitute a separate market,[247] and, in the words of the ECJ:

> If that examination leads the national court to conclude that a separate market in home-delivery schemes does exist, and that there is an insufficient degree of interchangeability between Mediaprint's nationwide scheme and other, regional, schemes, it must hold that Mediaprint, which according to the information in the

---

[244] ECJ, Case C-203/02, *The British Horseracing Board Ltd and Others*, 9 November 2004, ECLI:EU:C:2004:695, para. 46.

[245] ECJ, Case C-7/97, *Oscar Bronner GmbH & Co. KG v. Mediaprint Zeitungs- und Zeitschriftenverlag GmbH & Co. KG, Mediaprint Zeitungsvertriebsgesellschaft mbH & Co. KG and Mediaprint Anzeigengesellschaft mbH & Co. KG*, 26 November 1998, ECLI:EU:C:1998:569.

[246] *Ibid.*, paras 7–8.

[247] *Ibid.*, para. 34.

order for reference operates the only nationwide home-delivery service in Austria, is *de facto* in a monopoly situation in the market thus defined, and thus holds a dominant position in it.[248]

Furthermore, the ECJ said that the national court had to analyse whether a refusal to include the newspaper in the home-delivery system could amount to an abuse of a dominant position "on the ground that such refusal deprives that competitor of a means of distribution judged essential for the sale of its newspaper".[249] Explaining the criterion of indispensability, the ECJ noted that account should be taken of whether other methods of distribution exist, "even though they may be less advantageous".[250] Moreover, it was noted that, in that case, there did not seem to be "any technical, legal or even economic obstacles capable of making it impossible, or even unreasonably difficult, for any other publisher of daily newspapers to establish, alone or in cooperation with other publishers, its own nationwide home-delivery scheme and use it to distribute its own daily newspapers".[251] Importantly though, the ECJ said that, for establishing indispensability, it was not sufficient to claim that it was "not economically viable by reason of the small circulation of the daily newspaper or newspapers to be distributed",[252] but that it "would be necessary at the very least to establish" that it was "not economically viable to create a second home-delivery scheme for the distribution of daily newspapers with a circulation comparable to that of the daily newspapers distributed by the existing scheme".[253]

Hence, based on the Bronner standard, a refusal to deal may amount to an abuse of a dominant position under Article 102 TFEU when an input is indispensable in terms of technical, legal or economic obstacles existing owing to which it may be impossible or unreasonably difficult for competitors to create their own infrastructure in order to provide their services. Transferred to the data economy, indispensability would mean that the aforementioned obstacles should exist in terms of making it impossible or unreasonably difficult for competitors to collect or create data on their own. Such an argument seems to strike a balance between a too broad right of access to data and thereby related risks of "free-riding", on the one hand, and the need to promote competition in the markets driven by data on the other. After all, companies in general and in data markets in particular should compete on the basis of their own capacities

---

248   *Ibid.*, para. 35.
249   *Ibid.*, para. 37.
250   *Ibid.*, para. 43.
251   *Ibid.*, para. 44.
252   *Ibid.*, para. 45.
253   *Ibid.*, para. 46.

and on their own performance. Such a performance is driven by the economic incentives of such companies to do business and to further innovate. The indispensability requirement under the Bronner standard takes this into account: only in cases where technical, legal or economic obstacles exist that deprive companies of the possibility to compete should access be granted. It should also be borne in mind that a refusal to grant access by a dominant company may be considered not to amount to an abuse of a dominant position if it can be objectively justified.[254]

Bearing in mind that a refusal to grant access to a single-source data set may amount to an abuse of a dominant position if the creation of an alternative data set may be impossible, or unreasonably difficult, from an economic, technological, or a legal point of view, the question may arise in the data economy whether the rules on personal data protection may amount to indispensability in terms of the legal obstacles that may make it impossible or unreasonably difficult for companies to create their own infrastructures, or alternative data sets.

In fact, the circumstance that it may be impossible to create an alternative infrastructure from a legal point of view owing to personal data protection laws was argued in the *IMS Health* case. In that case, it was pointed out that the IMS Health's database was created in collaboration with the pharmaceutical industry, so that the "brick structure" created by IMS Health was established in the market as a *de facto* standard.[255] Yet, in the *IMS Health* case, the argument was raised by the party seeking access to and the right to use the database that the creation of a similar database was not possible owing to data protection laws, thereby substantiating the claim why the use of the original "brick structure" was needed.[256] The fact that data and privacy protection laws could act

---

[254] See, for example, ECJ, Joined Cases 6/73 and 7/73, *Istituto Chemioterapico Italiano S.p.A. and Commercial Solvents Corporation v. Commission of the European Communities*, 6 March 1974, ECLI:EU:C:1974:18, para. 25; ECJ, Case C-7/97, *Oscar Bronner GmbH & Co. KG v. Mediaprint Zeitungs- und Zeitschriftenverlag GmbH & Co. KG, Mediaprint Zeitungsvertriebsgesellschaft mbH & Co. KG and Mediaprint Anzeigengesellschaft mbH & Co. KG*, 26 November 1998, ECLI:EU:C:1998:569, para. 25.

[255] ECJ, *IMS Health, supra* note 201, paras 4–6. NDC, in fact, did try to develop a different "brick structure", but the latter was rejected by the industry: the company "initially drew up its reports on the basis of a segmentation of German territory into 2201 areas. It emerged from contacts with potential customers that data processed in that form would be difficult to market because it did not follow the structures with which the pharmaceutical undertakings had brought themselves into line. Accordingly, PII went over to working with 1860 and 3000 brick structures which were very close to those used by IMS" (footnote omitted). (Opinion of Advocate General Tizzano, *IMS Health, supra* note 218, para. 8.)

[256] Commission Decision of 3 July 2001 relating to a proceeding pursuant to Article 82 of the EC Treaty (Case COMP D3/38.044 – NDC Health/IMS HEALTH: Interim measures), OJ [2002] L 59/18, paras 17, 138–142, 153.

as a barrier for creating a second "brick structure" in Germany was discussed in the *IMS Health* European Commission's decision.[257] It was argued by NDC – the company that requested the use of the "1860 brick structure" – that the creation of another data structure would violate data protection laws, since the comparison of data in the different structures would allow the identification of the sales data of individual pharmacies.[258] In this regard, it could be recalled that the "brick structure" developed by IMS Health involved a particular segmentation – it consisted of 1860 bricks, which were constructed on the basis and the segmentation of the map of Germany. It was noted in the European Commission's decision that the primary purpose of creating such a structure was to enable the reporting of the regional sales data, while at the same time avoiding the identification of sales to individual pharmacies.[259] It was stated that a number of companies, also in other markets, provide their services using "brick structures", including "1860 brick structures",[260] in order to, *inter alia*, comply with data protection laws,[261] whereas in countries with no data protection laws no "brick structure" was used.[262] It was explained that, in particular in the European countries, owing to the protection of personal data, brick structures were used in terms of creating the "bricks", which were "formed by aggregating several postcodes".[263]

Accordingly, it might be that a particular structure of the database may serve the purpose of complying with data protection laws. The circumstance that data protection laws might have been relevant in terms of the potential obstacles to the creation of an alternative database is an important part of the *IMS Health* case. It may indeed be highly relevant in the context of the data economy, particularly bearing in mind the use of the (identifiable) data sets and a broad definition of personal data in the GDPR. Following *IMS Health*, it might be that the use of a different structure of a database may compromise the data included in the database in terms of enabling the identification of individuals. Therefore, the request to use the database with a particular structure may be based on the claim for a licence in order not to infringe data protection laws. In other words, a choice in creating one's own infrastructure may be limited by personal data protection. In the data economy, this may often be the case.

---

[257] *Ibid.*, paras 138–142.
[258] *Ibid.*, para. 138. Interestingly though, IMS argued that this was "only a theoretical possibility, because no party would have a commercial reason to carry out this comparison work, and it would involve disproportionate effort" (*ibid.*).
[259] *Ibid.*, para. 14.
[260] *Ibid.*, paras 24–25.
[261] *Ibid.*, para. 17.
[262] *Ibid.*, para. 153.
[263] *Ibid.*, para. 153.

In terms of the *Bronner* case, this may, under circumstances, amount to legal indispensability, i.e. the impossibility of creating an alternative system on the basis of legal requirements.

Coming back to the Proposal for the EU Database Directive, it could indeed be asked whether an obligation to provide access to single-source databases on fair, reasonable and non-discriminatory terms should be included in the law. After all, such an obligation is known, for example, in the telecommunications industries. In this regard, the legal provision in the Proposal for the EU Database Directive saying that fair and non-discriminatory terms may need to be decided by an arbitrator may also sound reasonable. After all, determining the amount of royalties under the so-called FRAND licensing is known in the context of licensing standard-essential patents. In this regard, the ECJ in the *Huawei* case stated that:

> where no agreement is reached on the details of the FRAND terms following the counter-offer by the alleged infringer, the parties may, by common agreement, request that the amount of the royalty be determined by an independent third party, by decision without delay.[264]

It could also be recalled that the EU Database Directive in recital 42 states that "the special right to prevent unauthorized extraction and/or re-utilization relates to acts by the user which go beyond his legitimate rights and thereby harm the investment; [...] the right to prohibit extraction and/or re-utilization of all or a substantial part of the contents relates not only to the manufacture of a parasitical competing product but also to any user who, through his acts, causes significant detriment, evaluated qualitatively or quantitatively, to the investment". Hence, in line with the EU Database Directive, a refusal to grant access to a single-source database may be considered justified, for example, in cases where acts of unfair competition are involved or detriment to the investment of a database holder may be caused in any other way.

In the absence of such a compulsory access clause in the law, it could be advocated for the application of the *Bronner* – instead of the *IMS Health* – test for granting access to single-source databases protected by the *sui generis* right.

---

[264] ECJ, Case C-170/13, *Huawei Technologies Co. Ltd v. ZTE Corp., ZTE Deutschland GmbH*, 16 July 2015, ECLI:EU:C:2015:477, para. 68.

4.5   UNILATERAL CONDUCT: IS THE TIME RIPE FOR A "MONOPOLIZATION" TYPE OF ABUSE?

In the EU, a dominant position is not prohibited. Article 102 TFEU prohibits an abuse of a dominant position, but not a dominant position as such. In contrast to Section 2 of the Sherman Act in the US,[265] there is no "attempt to monopolise" claim in the EU.

Data economy has already raised the need to adapt some of the competition law concepts. For example, the German Act against Restraints of Competition (GWB) was supplemented with new criterion for a legal assessment of a dominant position. On 9 June 2017 the so-called "9. GWB-Novelle" (the 9th amendment of the aforementioned law) entered into force.[266] According to Section 18(3a) GWB, when assessing a dominant position, in particular, in multi-sided markets, criteria have to be taken into account such as direct and indirect network effects, multi-homing and switching possibilities of the users, economies of scale related to network effects, access to data relevant for competition and competitive pressure driven by innovation. Hence, the abilities of the companies to access data have become part of a legal assessment of a dominant position.

In fact, the EU Commissioner for Competition, *Margrethe Vestager*, has referred to the unique sets, which, on the one hand, may be a valuable asset in the data economy, yet, on the other hand, may pose a danger to competition.[267] The argument could go that, once a large database has been created, it can be increasingly difficult for the competitors to catch up.

Yet it could be questioned whether it is, in fact, data, and the question of access to data, that may be most problematic from the EU competition law point of view. As argued before, EU competition law seems to have enough legal tools to tackle most of the problems arising in the data economy. However, one particular issue may still merit attention, namely, the circumstance where the use of algorithms may lead to a dominant position, yet not in terms of the competition on the merits, but rather in the case of the manipu-

---

[265] The US Section 2 of the Sherman Act reads: "Every person who shall monopolize, or attempt to monopolize, or combine or conspire with any other person or persons, to monopolize any part of the trade or commerce among the several States, or with foreign nations."

[266] Neuntes Gesetz zur Änderung des Gesetzes gegen Wettbewerbsbeschränkungen vom 1. Juni 2017, Bundesgesetzblatt, Jahrgang 2017, Teil I Nr. 33, ausgegeben zu Bonn am 8. Juni 2017.

[267] *Vestager, M.*, "Making Data Work for Us", Speech, 9 September 2016 (https://ec .europa.eu/competition/speeches/index_2016.html).

lation of algorithms. After all, not only data, but also algorithms may play an important role in establishing a dominant position in the data economy.

The definition of a dominant position was provided by the ECJ in *United Brands*: accordingly, a dominant position "relates to a position of economic strength enjoyed by an undertaking which enables it to prevent effective competition being maintained on the relevant market by giving it the power to behave to an appreciable extent independently of its competitors, customers and ultimately of its consumers".[268] Thereby, a dominant position is a position of such economic strength that it, firstly, enables the undertaking to prevent effective competition being maintained, and secondly, gives it the power to behave independently of its competitors, customers and consumers. Although a dominant position has been explained in terms of the ability of a company to behave independently,[269] the definition consists of two parts. After all, a dominant position, although not prohibited as such under Article 102 TFEU, is one that enables a company "to prevent effective competition being maintained on the relevant market". A precise reading thereof reveals that a dominant position enables the prevention of effective competition, and yet such a position is not prohibited under Article 102 TFEU. In this regard, it is not entirely clear how the part of the definition of a dominant position in terms of it enabling the company to prevent effective competition being maintained relates to the concept of an abuse of a dominant position, which includes similar wording.[270] The two definitions are contradictory, in particular if we bear in mind that a dominant position (although it says that it enables the prevention of effective competition) is allowed, whereas an abuse (stipulating the same) is prohibited.[271]

---

[268] ECJ, Case 27/76, *United Brands v. Commission*, 14 February 1978, [1978] E.C.R. 207 (ECLI:EU:C:1978:22), para. 65.

[269] See, for example, *Whish, R./Bailey, D.*, Competition Law, 7th ed., Oxford: Oxford University Press 2012, p. 180.

[270] According to the ECJ in *Hoffmann-La Roche*: "The concept of an abuse is an objective concept relating to the behaviour of an undertaking in a dominant position which is such as to influence the structure of the market where, as a result of the very presence of the undertaking in question, the degree of competition is weakened and which, through recourse to methods different from those which condition normal competition in products or services on the basis of the transactions of commercial operators, has the effect of hindering the maintenance of the degree of competition still existing in the market or the growth of that competition" (ECJ, Case 85/76, *Hoffmann-La Roche & Co. AG v. Commission of the European Communities*, 13 February 1979, ECLI:EU:C: 1979:36, para. 91).

[271] For a more detailed analysis on this issue see *Surblytė, G.*, The Refusal to Disclose Trade Secrets as an Abuse of Market Dominance – *Microsoft* and Beyond, Berne: Stämpfli 2011, pp. XLVII + 263 (Munich Series on European and International Competition Law, Vol. 28), pp. 124–128.

Although the wording of Article 82 EC, which was a direct predecessor of Article 102 TFEU, is identical, digging deeper into the historical development of this European legal provision on the abuse of a dominant position[272] reveals that the original text of this provision was slightly different. In the European Coal and Steel Community Treaty (which pre-dated the EC Treaty), Article 66(7) stipulated:

> If the High Authority finds that public or private undertakings which, in law or in fact, hold or *acquire* in the market for one of the products within its jurisdiction a dominant position shielding them against effective competition in a substantial part of the common market are using that position for purposes contrary to the objectives of this Treaty, it shall make to them such recommendations as may be appropriate to prevent the position from being so used.[273] (Emphasis added)

Although the latter legal provision speaks about the acquisition of a dominant position shielding a company from effective competition, it still condemns the behaviour, namely, the use of such a position, not the acquisition of such a position as such. Thus, looking at the origins of Article 102 TFEU reveals that this legal provision, in contrast to the US Sherman Act, was not meant to condemn the acquisition of a dominant position as such, even if the drafting of the competition law provisions of the ECSC Treaty seems to have involved US scholars.[274]

A legal gap, in terms of EU competition law may exist when a dominant position was acquired on the basis of the manipulation of algorithms. In fact, in the data economy, algorithmic manipulation may need a closer look from the regulators, not the least for the sake of consumer protection.[275] As regards competition, an acquisition of a dominant position on the basis of algorithmic manipulation would not be based on competition on the merits. Since EU competition law prohibits an abuse of an existing dominant position, but does not elaborate the acquisition of such a position, EU competition rules would be not applicable, for example, in cases where a dominant undertaking, which acquired a dominant position on the basis of algorithmic manipulation, does

---

[272] For more see *O'Donoghue, R./Padilla, A.J.*, The Law and Economics of Article 82 EC, Oxford and Portland, OR: Hart Publishing 2006, pp. 8 et seq.

[273] Treaty establishing the European Coal and Steel Community, 1951. The English translation of this legal provision from: *O'Donoghue, R./Padilla, A.J.*, The Law and Economics of Article 82 EC, Oxford and Portland, Oregon: Hart Publishing 2006, p. 10 footnote 29.

[274] See *O'Donoghue, R./Padilla, A.J.*, The Law and Economics of Article 82 EC, Oxford and Portland, Oregon: Hart Publishing 2006, p. 11 footnote 31 (with further references).

[275] On the need for regulatory rules as regards algorithmic manipulation see *infra* Chapter 5, Section 5.1.

not further engage in abusive conduct. However, even in the absence of such an abuse, competition in the market may be weakened – in fact, on the way to a dominant position, competitors may be forced out from the market or weakened, yet, not because they would be not in a position to compete, but rather owing to the behaviour of a company in terms of the manipulation of algorithms. In light of this, the acquisition of power in the data-driven markets could simply be based on the manipulation of algorithms (rather than on the competition on the merits).

In this regard, it could be asked whether a monopolization-type claim, similar to that in the US under Section 2 of the Sherman Act, may need to be introduced into EU competition law. Section 2 of the Sherman Act condemns the acts of "[e]very person who shall monopolize, or attempt to monopolize, or combine or conspire with any other person or persons, to monopolize any part of the trade or commerce among the several States, or with foreign nations". Bearing in mind that the manipulation of algorithms may, in fact, lead to such a monopolization, or an attempt to monopolize, changes in EU competition law in this regard may need to be considered.

4.6   SCHUMPETERIAN COMPETITION FOR AI MARKETS: ANY ROOM FOR REGULATION?

Since competition law reacts to potential competition law infringements, i.e. it steps in *ex post*, the question is whether the increasing use of algorithms by the business raises the need for any earlier intervention in terms of a more general regulatory approach. Yet, in light of intensive competition that might amount to the so-called Schumpeterian competition, any regulatory intervention may do more harm than good. Thus, the question is the following: should it be Schumpeterian competition that drives the data economy, is there a need – or, in fact, any room – for any regulatory intervention in the first place.

4.6.1   Schumpeterian Competition for Emerging (AI) Markets

Back in 1942, in the book "Capitalism, Socialism and Democracy",[276] Joseph Schumpeter, elaborating on the capitalist markets that function under the "perennial gale of creative destruction",[277] criticized the traditional concept of

---

[276] *Schumpeter, J.A.*, Capitalism, Socialism and Democracy, 1942, reprint, London and New York: Routledge 1992.

[277] *Ibid.*, pp. 83–84.

the "*modus operandi* of competition", which mostly focused on price,[278] and argued that:

> it is not that kind of competition which counts but the competition from the new commodity, the new technology, the new source of supply, the new type of organization [...] – competition which commands a decisive cost or quality advantage and which strikes not at the margins of the profits and the outputs of the existing firms but at their foundations and their very lives. This kind of competition is as much more effective than the other as a bombardment is in comparison with forcing a door.[279]

Thereby, Schumpeterian competition is an aggressive type of competition, characterized by leapfrogging existing products, technologies, etc. According to Schumpeter, even monopolistic markets may be competitive – in fact, highly competitive – as long as monopolies remain subject to strong competitive pressure. In his words:

> competition of the kind we now have in mind acts not only when in being but also when it is merely an ever-present threat. It disciplines before it attacks. The businessman feels himself to be in a competitive situation even if he is alone in his field.[280]

Hence, temporary monopolies[281] would "rise and fall" owing to drastic developments of competing products/services, and thus, innovation.[282] Such competition is mostly intensive in terms of innovation and is of a temporary nature. It may be mostly important in some periods, in particular when it comes to introducing new products. Schumpeterian competition is competition *for* the (new) markets as contrasted with another type of competition, i.e. competition *within* the market.[283] Schumpeterian competition is very intensive, if not

---

[278]   *Ibid.*, p. 84.

[279]   *Ibid.*, p. 84.

[280]   *Ibid.*, p. 85.

[281]   *Ibid.*, p. 99: "pure cases of long-run monopoly must be of the rarest occurence and that even tolerable approximations to the requirements of the concept must be still rarer than are cases of perfect competition".

[282]   *Ibid.*, p. 102: "For, especially in manufacturing industry, a monopoly position is in general no cushion to sleep on. As it can be gained, so it can be retained only by alertness and energy."

[283]   For a more detailed analysis of the distinction between competition *for* the market and competition *within* the market see, for example, *Surblytė, G.*, The Refusal to Disclose Trade Secrets as an Abuse of Market Dominance – *Microsoft* and Beyond, Berne: Stämpfli 2011, pp. XLVII + 263 (Munich Series on European and International Competition Law, Volume 28), pp. 162–163.

aggressive. In fact, it describes the competitive process where those which are first and the strongest win.

Bearing in mind the topicality of the issue of data access and observing current competition for data in the form of the "data wars" that have been going on for developing new data-based technologies, it is not difficult to spot that Schumpeterian competition has been taking place in the data economy.[284] In fact, the competitive landscape as it is today is not necessarily meant for today – but rather, for tomorrow. In this regard, it could be recalled that it was noted by Arrow that:

> The crucial empirical point is that markets for most future commodities do not exist. It is an interesting and illuminating question why they do not exist, but this is not the place to examine that. But in their absence *behavior on current markets largely reflects anticipations of the future if the present is unimportant.*[285] (Emphasis added)

According to the passage, competition, although it takes place on current markets, may be competition, which is much more important for the future markets, i.e. such markets that are about to emerge. This is exactly what could be said to be happening with the data markets: it could be argued that a big portion of current competitive processes does not necessarily target the existing markets, but instead those of the future. Hence, current competition as regards the developments of intelligent machines, and in particular (general) AI, may be described as Schumpeterian competition for future (emerging) AI markets.

This insight – in light of the fact that data is crucial for learning algorithms and, thus, for the developments of AI technology – explains why the question of access to data might be so important for the industry. After all, data is an essential tool in the race towards AI technology, which may have potential for granting a "first mover advantage". Yet this also shows how careful an assessment should be to create a regulatory framework for granting access to data: instead of stimulating a competitive process, a regulatory rule that would enable such access without taking into account the fact that it might be Schumpeterian competition that has been taking place, could at the end of the day, distort the conditions of competition, where companies should compete on the basis of their own capacities and capabilities driven by strong economic incentives to be the first at the end of the racing track.

---

[284] For a more detailed analysis see *Surblytė, G.*, Data-Driven Economy and Artificial Intelligence: Emerging Competition Law Issues, (2017) 67 WuW 120.

[285] *Arrow, K.J.*, The Future and the Present in Economic Life, (1978) 16 Economic Inquiry 157, 159–160.

Yet this is not to say that Schumpeterian competition can not at all be subject to regulation. In fact, whereas Schumpeter's "perennial gale of creative destruction" – by definition – does not sound very much like something that is prone to regulation, Schumpeter himself was not entirely against state regulation, but rather pleaded for a rational, instead of vindictive, regulation:

> This is why our argument does not amount to a case against state regulation. It does show that there is no general case for indiscriminate "trust-busting" or for the prosecution of everything that qualifies as a restraint of trade. Rational as distinguished from vindictive regulation by public authority turns out to be an extremely delicate problem which not every government agency, particularly when in full cry against big business, can be trusted to solve.[286] (Footnote omitted)

Hence, even in light of Schumpeterian competition, state regulation is possible. However, such regulation should delicately find a "gold standard" in order not to destroy economic incentives, while promoting competition.

Bearing this in mind, it is also noteworthy that Schumpeterian competition is but one type of competition. Schumpeter himself considered this type of competition being of highest importance for a new entry:

> Perfect competition implies free entry into every industry. [...] But perfectly free entry into a *new* field may make it impossible to enter at all. The introduction of new methods of production and new commodities is hardly conceivable with perfect – and perfectly prompt – competition from the start. [...] As a matter of fact, perfect competition is and always has been temporarily suspended whenever anything new is being introduced [...] even in otherwise perfectly competitive conditions.[287] (Emphasis in original)

In this regard, he stressed the role of trade secrets as a "protecting device" necessary under the circumstances of "creative destruction". According to him:

> Long-range investing under rapidly changing conditions, especially under conditions that change or may change at any moment under the impact of new commodities and technologies, is like shooting at a target that is not only indistinct but moving – and moving jerkily at that. Hence it becomes necessary to resort to such protecting devices as patents or *temporary secrecy of processes or, some cases, long-period contracts secured in advance*.[288] (Emphasis added)

Hence, as a "new entry" competition, Schumpeterian competition rests on the need for strong incentive mechanisms, which can be safeguarded by some of

---

[286] *Schumpeter, J.A.*, Capitalism, Socialism and Democracy, 1942, reprint, London and New York: Routledge 1992, p. 91.

[287] *Ibid.*, pp. 104–105.

[288] *Ibid.*, p. 88.

the types of legal protection, such as, for example, trade secret protection. The latter fact is one of the reasons (but not the only one) why a deeper analysis of the eligibility of trade secret protection for data and data sets may be crucial.[289] However, a more fundamental question is how to find that "gold standard" when it comes to Schumpeterian competition and regulation.

4.6.2 "Creative Destruction" and "Self-Interest"

In the "History of Economic Analysis", Joseph Schumpeter took a critical stance on Adam Smith's *The Wealth of Nations*.[290] According to him, *The Wealth of Nations* did not "contain a single *analytic* idea, or method that was entirely new in 1776" (emphasis in original).[291] He furthermore noted that "A.Smith's political principles and recipes – his guarded advocacy of free trade and the rest – are but the cloak of a great analytic achievement".[292]

One of the harshest points of criticism related to the concept of monopolies. The attitude of Adam Smith towards monopolies was rather critical, first and foremost, owing to their ability to raise prices. In his words:

> The price of monopoly is upon every occasion the highest which can be got. The natural price, or the price of free competition, on the contrary, is the lowest which can be taken, not upon every occasion indeed, but for any considerable time altogether.[293]

---

[289] See *supra* Chapter 3, Section 3.2.

[290] *Schumpeter, J.A.*, History of Economic Analysis (edited from manuscript by Elizabeth Boody Schumpeter), 1954, reprint, New York: Routledge 1994, pp. 181–194.

[291] *Ibid.*, p. 184. The division of labour, as developed by Adam Smith, was one of a few concepts acknowledged by Schumpeter in his otherwise rather critical analysis of Smith's economic theory: "Though, as we know, there is nothing original about it, one feature must be mentioned that has not received the attention it deserves: nobody, either before or after A.Smith, ever thought of putting such a burden upon division of labor. With A.Smith it is practically the only factor in economic progress" (*ibid.*, p. 187).

[292] *Ibid.*, p. 38. See also *ibid.*, p. 185: "His mental stature was up to mastering the unwieldy material that flowed from many sources and to subjecting it, with a strong hand, to the rule of a small number of coherent principles: the builder who built solidly, regardless of cost, was also a great architect. His very limitations made for success. Had he been more brilliant, he would not have been taken so seriously. Had he dug more deeply, had he unearthed more recondite truth, had he used difficult and ingenious methods, he would not have been understood. But he had no such ambitions; in fact he disliked whatever went beyond plain common sense. He never moved above the heads of even the dullest readers."

[293] *Smith, A.*, An Inquiry into the Nature and Causes of the Wealth of Nations, Chicago: The University of Chicago Press 1976, p. 69.

Picking up on this sentence, written by Adam Smith, Schumpeter argued that:

> There is no theory of monopoly price beyond the meaningless (or even false) sentence that the "price of monopoly is upon every occasion the highest which can be got," whereas "the price of free competition ... is the lowest which can be taken" in the long run – an important theorem though Smith does not seem to have had any notion of the difficulties of a satisfactory proof.[294]

Schumpeter furthermore explained that:

> There was more excuse for that uncritical attitude in the case of Adam Smith and the classics in general than there is in the case of their successors because big business in our sense had not then emerged. But even so they went too far. In part this was due to the fact that they had no satisfactory theory of monopoly which induced them not only to apply the term rather promiscuously (Adam Smith and even Senior interpreted for instance the rent of land as a monopoly gain) but also to look upon the monopolists' power of exploitation as practically unlimited which is of course wrong even for the most extreme cases.[295]

Hence, for Schumpeter, the perspective of becoming a monopolist and getting the monopoly gain was the whole driving force behind the "perennial gale of creative destruction". In this regard, it could be argued that such a perspective comes close to Adam Smith's concept of self-interest as the main human factor driving economic behaviour. In this aspect, Schumpeter's and Smith's theories did not diverge that much. However, an important difference between the two theories was when it comes to a monopoly itself: whereas Smith had concerns about the monopolies when they are constant, monopolies in Schumpeter's theory are in motion, in process, i.e. they were meant to be fragile and operating under the "perennial gale of creative destruction", i.e. constant (potential) competitive pressure.

In fact, Adam Smith compared the effects of the monopoly with those of a trade secret. He distinguished between trade secrets in trade and trade secrets in manufacture, considering the former as a concealment of an increased price.[296] According to him, such trade secrets cannot be kept for long. In con-

---

[294] *Schumpeter, J.A.*, History of Economic Analysis (edited from manuscript by Elizabeth Boody Schumpeter), 1954, reprint, New York: Routledge 1994, p. 189.

[295] *Schumpeter, J.A.*, Capitalism, Socialism and Democracy, 1942, reprint, London and New York: Routledge 1992, p. 100 footnote 17.

[296] *Smith, A.*, An Inquiry into the Nature and Causes of the Wealth of Nations, Chicago: The University of Chicago Press 1976, pp. 67–68: "When by an increase in the effectual demand, the market price of some particular commodity happens to rise a good level above the natural price, those who employ their stocks in supplying that market are generally careful to conceal this change. If it was commonly known, their great profit would tempt so many new rivals to employ their stocks in the same way,

trast, trade secrets in manufacture were considered more durable, since they were said to be "capable of being longer kept than secrets in trade".[297] In the words of Adam Smith:

> A monopoly granted either to an individual or to a trading company has the same effect as a secret in trade or manufactures. The monopolists, by keeping the market constantly under-stocked, by never fully supplying the effectual demand, sell their commodities much above the natural price, and raise their emoluments, whether they consist in wages or profit, greatly above their natural rate.[298]

Accordingly, when speaking about trade secrets in trade, Adam Smith does not refer to trade secrets in a classic sense. The latter are described by him as trade secrets in manufacture. In fact, what he referred to was the effect of a monopoly in terms of their ability to raise prices and, at least for some time, to conceal this. Thus, Adam Smith did not oppose to legal tools such as trade secrets themselves, but was, instead, concerned about the monopolist's ability to raise prices in the absence of competition. In other words, Adam Smith was concerned about the risk of the monopolistic markets being constantly under-supplied, so that a higher market price may be maintained.

The analysis above shows that Adam Smith's economic theory remains valid for the data economy. Despite the criticism from Joseph Schumpeter, who pleaded for a "new entry" competition, the economic theory of Adam Smith could be said to supplement, rather than to contradict, the theory of Schumpeter. It could be argued that, although Adam Smith was so harshly criticized by Schumpeter, he provides a broader economic theory and thereby lays the foundations for any type of competition, including the Schumpeterian one. The latter may be relevant for particular periods of time, such as when conquering completely new markets. This insight may be highly important when searching for the "gold – regulatory – standard", particularly in the cases of Schumpeterian competition.

4.6.3   The (Meaning of the) "Invisible Hand"

The concept of the "invisible hand" of Adam Smith seems to be doomed to misinterpretation. Whereas in earlier times it was often misinterpreted in

---

that, the effectual demand being fully supplied, the market price would soon be reduced to the natural price, and perhaps for some time even below it. If the market is at a great distance from the residence of those who supply it, they may sometimes be able to keep the secret for several years altogether, and may so long enjoy their extraordinary profits without any new rivals."

[297]   *Ibid.*, p. 68.
[298]   *Ibid.*, p. 69.

terms of an unlimited "laissez-faire" principle,[299] in the data economy, the "invisible hand" has been turned into a "digitized hand". In their book *Virtual Competition: The Promise and Perils of the Algorithm-Driven Economy* Ezrachi and Stucke write:

> The displacement of the invisible hand by the "digitized hand" heralds a change in dynamics which requires us to carefully recalibrate our approach to markets and intervention.[300]

And yet, the meaning that Adam Smith himself attributed to this concept[301] was neither unlimited liberalism, nor, even more so, a "digitized hand".

In the works of Adam Smith, there are only a number of passages devoted to the "invisible hand". In *The Wealth of Nations* Smith wrote:

> every individual necessarily labours to render the annual revenue of the society as great as he can. He generally, indeed, neither intends to promote the public interest, nor knows how much he is promoting it. By preferring the support of domestic to that of foreign industry, he intends only his own security; and by directing that industry in such a manner as its produce may be of the greatest values, *he intends only his own gain, and he is in this, as in many other cases, led by an invisible hand to promote an end which was no part of his intention.* Nor is it always the worse for the society that it was no part of it. By pursuing his own interest he frequently promotes that of the society more effectually than when he really intends to promote it.[302] (Emphasis added)

The term of the "invisible hand" can also be found in his earlier work. In *The Theory of Moral Sentiments*[303] – a less known book by Adam Smith devoted to

---

[299] For a more detailed analysis of the reasons of such a misinterpretation see, for example, *Recktenwald, H.C.*, Adam Smiths Paradigmen: Bewahrtes und Unvollendetes, Stuttgart: Steiner 1986, p. 25.

[300] *Ezrachi, A./Stucke, M.E.*, Virtual Competition: The Promise and Perils of the Algorithm-Driven Economy, Cambridge, MA: Harvard University Press 2016, p. 203. See also *ibid.*, pp. 209–210.

[301] For a more detailed analysis, see also, for example, *Sedláček, T.*, Die Ökonomie von Gut und Böse, München: Wilhelm Goldmann Verlag 2013, pp. 247–249; *Grampp, W.D.*, What Did Smith Mean by the Invisible Hand?, (2000) 108 Journal of Political Economy 441.

[302] *Smith, A.*, An Inquiry into the Nature and Causes of the Wealth of Nations, Chicago: The University of Chicago Press 1976, pp. 477–478.

[303] *Smith, A.*, The Theory of Moral Sentiments, London: Henry G. Bohn, York Street, Covent Garden 1853.

his moral theory – the following passage may be found, which is worthwhile quoting in full:

> The produce of the soil maintains at all times nearly that number of inhabitants which it is capable of maintaining. The rich only select from the heap what is most precious and agreeable. They consume little more than the poor; and in spite of their natural selfishness and rapacity, though they mean only their own conveniency, though the sole end which they propose from the labours of all the thousands whom they employ be the gratification of their own vain and insatiable desires, they divide with the poor the produce of all their improvements. *They are led by an invisible hand to make nearly the same distribution of the necessaries of life* which would have been made had the earth been divided into equal portions among all its inhabitants; and thus, without intending it, without knowing it, advance the interest of the society, and afford means to the multiplication of the species. When providence divided the earth among a few lordly masters, it neither forgot nor abandoned those who seemed to have been left out in the partition. These last, too, enjoy their share of all that it produces. In what constitutes the real happiness of human life, they are in no respect inferior to those who would seem so much above them. In ease of body and peace of mind, all the different ranks of life are nearly upon a level, and the beggar, who suns himself by the side of the highway, possesses that security which kings are fighting for.[304] (Emphasis added)

Accordingly, the meaning that Adam Smith attributed to the "invisible hand" was not related to any regulatory context. In fact, in *The Wealth of Nations*, Adam Smith, as regards the "invisible hand", repeats what he said in his previous work, i.e. in *The Theory of Moral Sentiments*.[305] The "invisible hand", as is clear from the passages above, is neither the state nor the regulator. Moreover, it is no force related to the market. Instead, the "invisible hand" in terms of Adam Smith has almost a metaphysical meaning. Indeed, Smith is said to have had confidence in the theism of his times, so that his meaning of the "invisible hand" could, in fact, have been thereby affected.[306] The "invisible hand" in the meaning of Smith thus comes close to the divine Providence (as mentioned in the cited passage) instead of being the (invisible) hand of the state or the

---

[304] *Ibid.*, pp. 264–265.

[305] See also *Viner, J.*, Adam Smith und Laissez-faire, in: H.C. Recktenwald (ed.), Ethik, Wirtschaft und Staat: Adam Smiths politische Ökonomie heute, Darmstadt: Wissenschaftliche Buchgesellschaft 1985, p. 82.

[306] *Ibid.*, pp. 76–77. The author explains that Smith's moral theory was highly based on the principles of (the natural flow of) nature and that much of his theory rests on the idea of the harmonic order of nature, which in turn leaves him striving for harmony also in the relationship of human beings. As further explained by Viner, such a harmonic order of nature exists under a divine guidance, which increases the wealth of people through the outcome of their individual inclinations (*ibid.*, p. 80).

market. Thereby, the "invisible hand" for Smith was something metaphysical rather than (purely) economical.

The clarification of the meaning of the "invisible hand" attributed to it by Smith himself is important not only in terms of avoiding any further possible misinterpretations of this concept. In fact, it shows that Smith was not necessarily so much against regulation as the (misleading) use of his concept of the "invisible hand" would advocate for. Indeed, in contrast to what is often attributed to him, Smith never pleaded for a "night watchman state", but rather postulated that the state had to fulfil its duty in such an efficient and fair way that the market economy could function and the commonwealth would be viable.[307] Nor did he plead for an unlimited "laissez-faire" principle.[308]

4.7 INTERMEDIATE CONCLUSION

EU competition law has sufficient tools to tackle problems that may arise in the data economy. In fact, as a result of the ECJ's guidance in *E-Turas* related to the notion of concerted practice, the application of competition law to algorithms-based behaviour may lead to an overenforcement of competition law, for example, in terms of capturing parallel behaviour. This insight stands in stark contrast to the fears that have time and again been raised by academia, namely, that competition law may be not capable of capturing competition law issues related to algorithms.

In the data economy, the competitive process may be closely related to competition for data traffic. This fact may have to be taken into account in competition law assessment related to online platforms. In particular, it may have to be scrutinized whether the actions of companies competing for data traffic may, in fact, hinder (potential) competitors from competing or result in unfair competition.

---

[307] *Recktenwald, H.C.*, Adam Smiths Paradigmen: Bewahrtes und Unvollendetes, Stuttgart: Steiner 1986, pp. 22–23. See also: *Köhler, B.*, Adam Smith: Der Vater der Nationalökonomie, in: Lüchinger, R. (ed), Die zwölf wichtigsten Ökonomen der Welt: Von Smith bis Stiglitz, Zürich: Orell Füssli Verlag 2009, pp. 23–39, at p. 34; *Viner, J.*, Adam Smith und Laissez-faire, in: H.C. Recktenwald (ed.), Ethik, Wirtschaft und Staat: Adam Smiths politische Ökonomie heute, Darmstadt: Wissenschaftliche Buchgesellschaft 1985, pp. 107–108.

[308] On the contrary, as *Viner* explains, according to Adam Smith, a natural order, if completely unlimited, may, in fact, work against, rather than for, an overall welfare (*Viner, J.*, Adam Smith und Laissez-faire, in: H.C. Recktenwald (ed.), Ethik, Wirtschaft und Staat: Adam Smiths politische Ökonomie heute, Darmstadt: Wissenschaftliche Buchgesellschaft 1985, p. 93). For a more detailed analysis of the role of the state in the Adam Smith's theory see *ibid.*, pp. 92–109.

Access to data may have to be granted on the basis of Article 102 TFEU – not on the basis of the compulsory licensing scheme (i.e. the "exceptional circumstances" test), but rather on the basis of the Bronner test, i.e. the "pure" indispensability requirement. This may be particularly so in cases of requests to access single-source databases protected by the *sui generis* right. For access to such single-source data sets, a legal provision stipulating compulsory access on fair, reasonable and non-discriminatory terms of a database protected by the *sui generis* right may be needed.

Although Schumpeterian competition may be said to take place for (emerging) AI markets, such intensive competition is but one type of competition. Schumpeterian competition describes aggressive and intense competition, yet, it is mostly important as "new entry" competition. Hence, it cannot be ruled out that, even in light of Schumpeterian competition, regulation in the data economy may be needed. Yet the question as regards the need for regulation should not be confined to the issue that has often been debated by academia, i.e. how to ensure data access. A more fundamental, yet more nuanced, question is how to find a balanced solution between preserving economic incentives, which stimulate competition (including, but not limited to, Schumpeterian competition), and protecting different interests that might be at stake, first and foremost, the interests of individuals.

5. Regulation beyond competition?

Analysing the question whether any regulation in the data economy may be needed beyond competition, it could, first of all, be recalled that competition law, on the remedies side, provides a possibility for the European Commission[1] and the national competition authorities[2] to adopt a commitment decision. Such a commitment decision, which was included as the new instrument in EU Regulation 1/2003 with a purpose of making the process of solving competition law cases more effectively,[3] may be adopted without a final finding that there was a competition law infringement if companies, during the process, offer commitments which may solve a potential competition law problem and the competition authority accepts and makes such commitments binding on them. The question thereby is whether, in the light of the lack of regulation, commitment decisions could serve the purpose, i.e. fill in the gaps, which may be left by regulation (in other words, fill in the regulatory gaps).

National competition authorities have already used this tool for filling in the regulatory gaps. For example, the Competition Council of the Republic of Lithuania terminated the investigation, by accepting commitments, against AB "Swedbank" on the alleged abuse of its dominant position by preventing other companies, such as Paysera LT, to provide payment initiation services.[4] In that case, the competition authority accepted commitments from AB "Swedbank", which was suspected to have abused its dominant position in terms of an infringement of Article 7 of the Lithuanian Law on Competition (the national equivalent of Article 102 TFEU). One of the arguments of the Competition

---

[1]   Council Regulation (EC) No. 1/2003 of 16 December 2002 on the implementation of the rules on competition laid down in Articles 81 and 82 of the Treaty, OJ [2003] L 1/1, Article 9.

[2]   Directive (EU) 2019/1 of the European Parliament and of the Council of 11 December 2018 to empower the competition authorities of the Member States to be more effective enforcers and to ensure the proper functioning of the internal market, OJ [2019] L 11/3, Article 12.

[3]   ECJ, Case C-441/07 P, *European Commission v. Alrosa Company Ltd*, 29 June 2010, ECLI:EU:C:2010:377, para. 35.

[4]   Decision of the Competition Council of the Republic of Lithuania on the termination of the investigation on the compliance of actions of AB "Swedbank" with the requirements of Article 7 of the Law on Competition of the Republic of Lithuania, 12 June 2018, No. 1S-79 (2018).

Council was that commitments may provide clarity for the whole industry while the regulation (in casu: on payment initiation services) was, at that time, still lacking.[5]

However, from a broader perspective, it could be questioned whether commitment decisions should serve as a regulatory measure substituting any need for legislative regulation in general and in the data economy in particular. Apart from a number of downsides of a commitment decision,[6] a commitment decision solves the case between particular parties, whereas a legislative norm has a broader application. Thus, commitments are addressed to particular undertakings, so that their effect should not be overestimated when it comes to the whole industry. Furthermore, if it were commitment decisions that would serve as filling in the gaps for regulation, a risk may arise of divergences in the EU Member States. Finally, a commitment decision may also risk undermining legal certainty, which is highly important in general and for doing business in particular. It should also be stressed that competition authorities are the enforcers of competition law. They are not and should not become regulators. Thereby, a cautious approach may be needed when it comes to the commitment decisions, in particular, as regards their role in the data economy.

Hence, it may be asked whether any (new) regulation may, in fact, be needed in the data economy. In considering this, account should be taken of the increase in private power and the widening of the gap between private parties and consumers, in particular, with regard to information asymmetry. It could be recalled that, even in light of Schumpeterian competition taking place, regulation, as explained, should not necessarily be ruled out. After all, neither Schumpeter, nor Adam Smith, as shown,[7] were against regulation. However, the question is what type of regulation may be needed and what issues should be regulated.

Although EU competition law may solve a big portion of issues in the data economy, one particular area of the data economy may, in fact, need the closer attention of regulators, i.e. the area of algorithmic manipulation. Although algorithmic manipulation as such is not a new concept (since regulation

---

[5]   *Ibid.*, para. 65.

[6]   See, for example, *Wils, W.P.J.*, Ten Years of Commitment Decisions Under Article 9 of Regulation 1/2003: Too Much of a Good Thing? (12 June 2015). Concurrences Journal 6th International Conference "New Frontiers of Antitrust" (Paris, 15 June 2015). Available at SSRN: https://papers.ssrn.com/sol3/papers.cfm?abstract_id=2617580; *Geradin, D./Mattioli, E.*, The Transactionalization of EU Competition Law: A Positive Development? (20 September 2017). TILEC Discussion Paper No. DP 2017-035. Available at SSRN: https://papers.ssrn.com/sol3/papers.cfm?abstract_id=3040306.

[7]   See *supra* Chapter 4, Section 4.6.

related to algorithmic manipulation has been known in the financial sector), the increasing use of algorithms in the data economy may increase the risk of algorithmic manipulation beyond the financial markets. Hence, bearing in mind that, in the data economy, algorithmic manipulation may occur in any market, the effects of such manipulation may be broader and may severely affect final consumers. Since competition law might not be able to adequately capture the cases of algorithmic manipulation that, for example, go beyond an abuse of a dominant position, the question is whether it is this area where the widest regulatory gap may exist in the data economy and where thus the regulatory intervention may be most needed.

Thus, bearing in mind an increasing use of algorithms, it should, first of all, be analysed whether any rules may be needed in the data economy that should tackle the risks that may arise from algorithmic manipulation. Furthermore, in light of a growing private power, the question is whether more robust state control of the terms and conditions may be needed in the data economy, first and foremost, for the sake of consumer protection. Finally, it should be analysed how much room may be left for co- and self-regulation.

5.1   ALGORITHMIC MANIPULATION

In 2017, in her speech, the EU Commissioner for Competition *Margrethe Vestager* said:

> But more and more, we're being asked to put our trust not just in other people, but in computers and algorithms. Algorithms most of us don't fully understand. Whose workings might be a mystery even to those who use them to run their businesses. So today, the biggest challenge to the future of innovation isn't whether we have enough ideas. It's whether that new technology can succeed in winning the public's trust.[8]

Back in 2016 she raised the question whether "as competition enforcers, we need to ask ourselves whether we can help solve the problem of trust, by making markets more competitive".[9] Yet, apart from the fact that competition law, as explained before,[10] may capture a good number of cases in the data economy, including those related to the use of algorithms, the question of "trust" as regards AI may often be related to the issues of safety rather than competitive markets. The need for "trustworthy AI" has been stressed by the

---

[8]   *Vestager, M.,* "Clearing the Path for Innovation", Speech, 7 November 2017 (https://ec.europa.eu/competition/speeches/index_2017.html).
[9]   *Vestager, M.,* "Making Data Work for Us", Speech, 9 September 2016 (https://ec.europa.eu/competition/speeches/index_2016.html).
[10]   See *supra* Chapter 4.

European Commission in the Communication on "Shaping Europe's digital future"[11] as well as in the White Paper on Artificial Intelligence.[12] According to the European Commission, "lack of trust is a main factor holding back a broader uptake of AI".[13] Thus, although the notion of trust has been used by the European Commission in various contexts as regards AI, the red thread seems to be the concern of the "black-box" effect of algorithms. In fact, one particular issue that may have broader implications and thus may need to be addressed beyond the competition law enforcement may be the manipulation of algorithms.

Attention has already been drawn to the fact that algorithms may increase market transparency. It has been noted that such market transparency may pose a danger to competition. For example, when discussing "algorithmic collusion", Ezrachi and Stucke, while elaborating on the benefits of market transparency for competitive markets,[14] also pointed out the risks related to "'excessive' market transparency" when algorithms were employed and to the limits of the competition law enforcement in this regard.[15]

---

[11]   European Commission, Communication: Shaping Europe's digital future, 19 February 2020.

[12]   European Commission, White Paper on Artificial Intelligence – A European Approach to Excellence and Trust, Brussels, 19.2.2020, COM(2020) 65 final. In the White Paper, the European Commission states that "[b]uilding an ecosystem of trust is a policy objective in itself, and should give citizens the confidence to take up AI applications and give companies and public organisations the legal certainty to innovate using AI" (*ibid.*, p. 3).

[13]   *Ibid.*, p. 9. See also *ibid.*, p. 1: "As digital technology becomes an ever more central part of every aspect of people's lives, people should be able to trust it. Trustworthiness is also a prerequisite for its uptake." Interestingly though, the European Commission considers a "trustworthy AI" in terms of "AI based on European values and rules" (*ibid.*, p. 3). It could be argued, however, that, in essence, one of the main issues when it comes to a "trustworthy AI" is probably the safety and security of such a technology.

[14]   *Ezrachi, A./Stucke, M.E.*, Artificial Intelligence & Collusion: When Computers Inhibit Competition, (2017) University of Illinois Law Review 1775, at 1797 (Oxford Legal Studies Research Paper No. 18/2015; University of Tennessee Legal Studies Research Paper No. 267, available at SSRN: https://papers.ssrn.com/sol3/papers.cfm?abstract_id=2591874).

[15]   *Ibid.*, at 1798. See also: *Ezrachi, A./Stucke, M.E.*, Sustainable and Unchallenged Algorithmic Tacit Collusion, (2020) 17 Northwestern Journal of Technology and Intellectual Property 217 (University of Tennessee Legal Studies Research Paper No. 366; Oxford Legal Studies Research Paper No. 16/2019. Available at SSRN: https://papers.ssrn.com/sol3/papers.cfm?abstract_id=3282235).

Similarly, in the OECD's paper as of 2017 on algorithms and collusion[16] concerns have been raised that:

> Economic theory suggests that there is a considerable risk that algorithms, by improving market transparency and enabling high-frequency trading, increase the likelihood of collusion in market structures that would traditionally be characterized by fierce competition.[17]

Although market transparency can indeed increase the likelihood of parallel behaviour, EU competition law, as explained in the previous chapter,[18] seems to have enough tools to solve the cases where algorithms would be involved. In fact, as explained, the issue may even be one of overenforcement. However, the problem with competition law enforcement may be that it would capture cases sporadically, whereas algorithmic manipulation may need to be disciplined more widely, thus going beyond a number of cases that may be solved on the basis of competition law. Yet, before delving into the analysis of such a regulatory rule, the question that has to be answered is whether there is a need for such a rule in the first place. After all, market transparency may also bring many beneficial gains. Yet while this will often be true for the business, the question is whether the same holds true when it comes to consumers.

5.1.1 Predictive Efficiency and Personal Welfare

The concept of efficiencies is known under EU competition law. Efficiencies may be argued in the framework of Article 101 TFEU[19] and Article 102 TFEU,[20] and they can also serve as a defence in the framework of the appraisal of concentrations.[21] The concept of "predictive efficiency" is rather new.

---

[16] See, for example, OECD (2017), Algorithms and Collusion: Competition Policy in the Digital Age (http://www.oecd.org/daf/competition/Algorithms-and-colllusion-competition-policy-in-the-digital-age.pdf).

[17] *Ibid.*, p. 7.

[18] See *supra* Chapter 4, Section 4.1.

[19] Communication from the Commission, Notice, Guidelines on the application of Article 81(3) of the Treaty, 2004/C 101/08, OJ [2004] C 101/97.

[20] On the "efficiency defence" see, for example, the European Commission's Discussion Paper on Article 82 EC (European Commission, DG Competition discussion paper on the application of Article 82 of the Treaty to exclusionary abuses, Brussels, December 2005, paras 84–92).

[21] See: Council Regulation (EC) No. 139/2004 of 20 January 2004 on the control of concentrations between undertakings, [2004] OJ L 24/1, recital 29. See also: Guidelines on the assessment of horizontal mergers under the Council Regulation on the control of concentrations between undertakings, [2004] OJ C 31/5, paras 76–88; Guidelines on

However, it may be highly relevant in the context of the data economy, thus going beyond the role of the efficiencies under EU competition law.

The concept of "predictive efficiency" was analysed in more detail by Kenneth Arrow.[22] He stressed that, in contrast to a pure neoclassical model, where the market participants know their "own production possibilities [...] together with market information on the rest of the economy",[23] in the information economy, "any variables which improve his ability to predict the future have a very meaningful economic value to him".[24] The latter fact, according to Arrow, induces companies to seek more information of predictive value and on this basis "information-acquisition activities and information markets [...] appear on the economic landscape".[25] Accordingly:

> Efficiency in the operation of firms ceases to be purely productive efficiency; *it involves efficiency in prediction as well.*[26] (Emphasis added)

Hence, in the data economy, any tools that may help to enhance the possibilities of the companies "to predict the future" may be highly valuable in economic terms. After all, information about consumers in the hands of the companies may often turn into a "crystal ball". Thereby, predictive efficiency is a very important concept in the data economy.

It is needless to say that algorithms may be one of the core tools in the data economy that may serve this purpose. Although the use of algorithms will not necessarily pull the demand,[27] they do enable companies to better predict such a demand – importantly though, not the absolute, but rather the effectual demand.

The concept of the "effectual demand" was described by Adam Smith. According to him, the effectual demand is the demand of those people, "who are willing to pay the natural price of the commodity, or the whole value of the rent, labour, and profit" (footnote omitted).[28] Such effectual demand, in the words of Adam Smith, has to be distinguished from the absolute demand: "[a]

---

the assessment of non-horizontal mergers under the Council Regulation on the control of concentrations between undertakings, OJ [2008] C 265/6.

[22] *Arrow, K.J.*, Limited Knowledge and Economic Analysis, reprinted in: Collected Papers of Kenneth J. Arrow, The Economics of Information, Vol. 4, Cambridge, MA: The Belknap Press of Harvard University Press 1984, pp. 153–166.

[23] *Ibid.*, p. 161.

[24] *Ibid.*, pp. 161–162.

[25] *Ibid.*, p. 162.

[26] *Ibid.*, p. 162.

[27] See *supra* Chapter 2, Section 2.3.1.

[28] *Smith, A.*, An Inquiry into the Nature and Causes of the Wealth of Nations, Chicago: The University of Chicago Press 1976, p. 63.

very poor man may be said in some sense to have a demand for a coach and six; he might like to have it; but his demand is not an effectual demand, as the commodity can never be brought to market in order to satisfy it".[29]

Companies that operate in the data economy often target an effectual demand. An increasing use of personalized services stands as an example. In fact, in the data economy, companies tend to increasingly personalize the services they provide and, in such a way, to gather even more personal data. As a result, companies may better predict (yet not necessarily pull) the effectual demand.

Yet effectual demand, as described by Adam Smith, is also about a personal ability to pay. Technological developments enable the collection and the analysis of consumers' data. Such data carries information and thereby enables companies to get knowledge not only about the preferences and habits of the users, but also about their ability to pay. Should a company possess both information about the needs and the preferences of a consumer as well as information about their ability to pay, a risk may arise with regard to the misuse of such information to the detriment of a consumer. Such a risk has already been identified and is not entirely new. Attention has been drawn to the risks associated with the behavioural price discrimination[30] or personalized pricing.[31] According to the OECD, personalized pricing is "any practice of price discriminating final consumers based on their personal characteristics and conduct, resulting in prices being set as an increasing function of consumers' willingness to pay".[32] Thus, personalized pricing is about effectual demand.

---

[29] *Ibid.*, p. 63.

[30] See, for example, *Ezrachi, A./Stucke, M.E.*, Virtual Competition: The Promise and Perils of the Algorithm-Driven Economy, Cambridge: Harvard University Press 2016, p. 101.

[31] See, for example, Office of Fair Trading, Personalised Pricing: Increasing Transparency to Improve Trust, May 2013 (https://webarchive.nationalarchives.gov .uk/20140402165101/http:/oft.gov.uk/shared_oft/markets-work/personalised-pricing/ oft1489.pdf); OECD, Personalised Pricing in the Digital Era – Background Note by the Secretariat, 20 November 2018, DAF/COMP(2018)13; European Commission, Consumer market study on online market segmentation through personalised pricing/ offers in the European Union, June 2018 (https://ec.europa.eu/info/sites/info/files/ aid_development_cooperation_fundamental_rights/aid_and_development_by_topic/ documents/synthesis_report_online_personalisation_study_final_0.pdf).

[32] OECD, Personalised Pricing in the Digital Era – Background Note by the Secretariat, 28 November 2018, DAF/COMP(2018)13, p. 9. See also: Office of Fair Trading, Personalised Pricing: Increasing Transparency to Improve Trust, May 2013 (https://webarchive.nationalarchives.gov.uk/20140402165101/http:/oft.gov.uk/shared _oft/markets-work/personalised-pricing/oft1489.pdf), p. 2: personalised pricing refers "to the practice where businesses may use information that is observed, volunteered, inferred, or collected about individuals' conduct or characteristics, to set different

Such a pricing is seen as a form of price discrimination,[33] the risks of which are mostly associated with market power.[34]

However, should companies increasingly use algorithms and continue to provide personalized services, it should not be ruled out that algorithmic manipulation may become a broader issue, going beyond personalized pricing. In fact, when such an effectual demand becomes predictable, risks may arise as regards manipulation, not only as regards the effectual demand, but also with regard to the absolute demand. For example, although practices of direct personal pricing are said to be still rather rare,[35] it has been claimed that such pricing may be exercised indirectly, for example, in a form of personal discounts, i.e. cases when uniform prices are offered, but discounts to such prices are personalized.[36] However, the question might be whether, having extensive information about effectual demand, a company, lacking sufficient competitive pressure, may, at some point in time, start manipulating the absolute demand as well, for example, in terms of undersupply, if not higher prices. Thus, in addition to the fears expressed with regard to personalized pricing that the price may be artificially raised for those whose personal information in the hands of a company reveals their ability (including that based on a particular wish or a dire need) to pay (even) a higher price, the effect of algorithmic manipulation may be broader, thus, affecting also the absolute demand.

It is worthwhile recalling that Kenneth Arrow cautioned that "uncertainty can tend to destroy markets".[37] Yet, in light of the data economy, it could be

---

prices to different consumers (whether on an individual or group basis), based on what the business thinks they are willing to pay".

[33] Office of Fair Trading, Personalised Pricing: Increasing Transparency to Improve Trust, May 2013 (https://webarchive.nationalarchives.gov.uk/20140402165101/http://oft.gov.uk/shared_oft/markets-work/personalised-pricing/oft1489.pdf), p. 2.

[34] See, for example, OECD, Personalised Pricing in the Digital Era – Note by the European Union, 28 November 2018, DAF/COMP/WD(2018)128, p. 4 ("To achieve such personalized pricing, three conditions must be present: (a) the ability to accurately sort consumers into such ever smaller groups based on their maximum willingness to pay; (b) market power; and (c) consumers must not be reselling items on a significant scale"). See also OECD, Personalised Pricing in the Digital Era – Note by BIAC, 28 November 2018, DAF/COMP/WD(2018)123, p. 6.

[35] OECD, Personalised Pricing in the Digital Era – Background Note by the Secretariat, 28 November 2018, DAF/COMP(2018)13, pp. 5, 14; OECD, Personalised Pricing in the Digital Era – Note by BIAC, 28 November 2018, DAF/COMP/WD(2018)123, pp. 3–4.

[36] OECD, The regulation of personalised pricing in the digital era – Note by Marc Bourreau and Alexandre de Streel, 21 November 2018, DAF/COMP/WD(2018)150, p. 3.

[37] *Arrow, K.J.*, Limited Knowledge and Economic Analysis, reprinted in: Collected Papers of Kenneth J. Arrow, The Economics of Information, Vol. 4, Cambridge, MA: The Belknap Press of Harvard University Press 1984, pp. 153–166, at p. 164.

asked whether the opposite may nowadays be equally, if not more risky, i.e. whether it might be a certainty that can tend to destroy markets. Interestingly, Kenneth Arrow, although he did not write during the era of AI, wrote the following passage, which neatly suits this context:

> I do not wish to face here the question of whether or not there is any "objective" uncertainty in the economic universe, *in the sense that a supremely intelligent mind knowing completely all the available data could know the future with certainty.*[38] (Emphasis added)

Such a "supremely intelligent mind" should probably not be claimed to exist in terms of AI. What may be important though, is the fact that the more relevant information a firm has, the better it can predict – thus, the higher the certainty. According to Arrow, "[w]hen there is uncertainty, there is usually the possibility of reducing it by the acquisition of *information*. Indeed, information is merely the negative measure of uncertainty, so to speak" (emphasis in original).[39] Information thus reduces uncertainty. For the data economy, it could be added that such uncertainty would be reduced by the acquisition of not any, but rather relevant information, for example, that related to the effectual demand.

Hence, on the one hand, technological tools that have improved the predictive abilities of companies may have enhanced their predictive efficiency.[40] Algorithms play an important role in this regard. On the other hand, however, such predictive efficiency, even if it does not lead to absolute certainty, may

---

[38]   *Arrow, K.J.*, Alternative Approaches to the Theory of Choice in Risk-Taking Situations, reprinted in: Collected Papers of Kenneth J. Arrow, Individual Choice under Certainty and Uncertainty, Vol. 3, Cambridge, MA: The Belknap Press of Harvard University Press 1984, pp. 5–41, at p. 7.

[39]   *Arrow, K.J.*, Information and Economic Behavior, reprinted in: Collected Papers of Kenneth J. Arrow, The Economics of Information, Vol. 4, Cambridge, MA: The Belknap Press of Harvard University Press 1984, pp. 136–152, at p. 138.

[40]   It is noteworthy that "predictive efficiency" does not mean that the notion of competition being the "discovery procedure" – in terms of *von Hayek* – is eliminated (*von Hayek, F.A.*, Der Wettbewerb als Entdeckungsverfahren, in: Erich Schneider, Kieler Vorträge, Kiel: Institut für Weltwirtschaft an der Universität Kiel 1968). In fact, as explained, predictive efficiency may facilitate the prediction of the effectual demand, but it does not eliminate the unpredictability of the overall process of competition. Although datification facilitates the predictability of demand, it does not predict the result of competition. Hence, competition remains "a discovery procedure". The fact that data may increase the predictability does not yet mean that the "journey of competition" has ended. In fact, it has merely begun. Another opinion by Ezrachi and Stucke who ask how much is left for competition as "the discovery procedure" in light of Big Data being in the hands of companies (*Ezrachi, A./Stucke, M.E.*, Virtual Competition: The Promise and Perils of the Algorithm-Driven Economy, Cambridge, MA: Harvard University Press 2016, pp. 208–217).

increase existing private power.[41] Thereby, the risk arises that the benefits of predictive efficiency, as regards consumers, may be outweighed by the commercial benefits to companies. It may be difficult for consumers to counterbalance such a behaviour, first and foremost, owing to the information asymmetry between both sides.

In fact, it could be asked whether consumers may exert countervailing buyer power. For example, with regard to personalized pricing, it has been argued that the latter may be less harmful when "consumers know it is happening, understand how it works and can exercise effective choice, for example, where consumers receive personalized discounts as a result of the membership of a loyalty scheme".[42] However, should algorithms be manipulated, it may be that consumers will not even know about it, not to mention their ability to understand how it works. After all, algorithms will often be kept as trade secrets, so that the way such algorithms work will hardly be disclosed to the public.

Hence, when it comes to the risk of algorithmic manipulation in the data economy, there seems to be a regulatory gap and, thus, a need for intervention. In this regard, it should be noted that account may need to be taken of another economic category, i.e. personal welfare. The latter is not meant in terms of consumer welfare known under EU competition law.

"Personal welfare" – as an economic, yet not a moral category – was analysed by Kenneth Arrow.[43] When talking about personal welfare, Arrow elaborated on "the preference systems of individuals" as a "basic raw material for the formulation of social choice".[44] Hence, personal welfare takes into account individual preferences for the sake of making a collective decision.[45] Arrow notes:

> In general, this agreement will not be the best possible decision for any single individual, according to his own personal preference scale. Each one carries out his part of the agreement, not because he wants to undertake this obligation for its own sake, but because it is part of an agreement, *the net result of which is beneficial to him as*

---

[41] For more detail about private power see *Möslein, F.* (ed.), Private Macht, Tübingen: Mohr Siebeck 2016.

[42] Office of Fair Trading, Personalised Pricing: Increasing Transparency to Improve Trust, May 2013 (https://webarchive.nationalarchives.gov.uk/20140402165101/http:/oft.gov.uk/shared_oft/markets-work/personalised-pricing/oft1489.pdf), p. 5.

[43] *Arrow, K.J.*, The Place of Moral Obligation in Preference Systems, reprinted in: Collected Papers of Kenneth J. Arrow, Social Choice and Justice, Vol. 1, Cambridge, MA: The Belknap Press of Harvard University Press 1983, pp. 78–80.

[44] *Ibid.*, p. 78.

[45] *Ibid.*, p. 78: "We rather think of a set of individuals, each with his own personal preference scales, who have to make a collective decision of some kind."

compared with the alternative of no agreement – though not as compared with the best state he could achieve if he were a perfect dictator.[46] (Emphasis added)

Accordingly, "personal welfare" should not be understood as "individual welfare". Personal welfare is such a welfare, where an individual benefit features in and arises from a collective decision. Although this does not yet necessarily imply making binding collective decisions – the circumstance, which has, for example, been considered by Luhmann as the highest evolutionary achievement[47] – "personal welfare" is a powerful reflection of a collective decision made on the basis of the preferences (as a system) of individuals. Thereby, personal welfare is considered a set of personal preferences that can be limited by the (expected) benefits of the collective decisions.

Transferred to the data economy, the concept of "personal welfare" should be considered in the context of the whole ecosystem of the data economy. The acceptance of data-based goods and services as part of a collective agreement on the data economy as a whole may not always provide the best possible solution in terms of individual welfare, but the overall gains may often be greater than without it. In other words, in the data economy, the preference systems of individuals, although not always satisfactory as regards each of them, pave the way for a social choice of the data economy as a whole. Yet such a hypothesis may be valid only upon the condition that the choice is voluntary and could hold only as long as the benefits of the "net result" of participating in such a collective agreement, compared with the alternative of no agreement, are not outweighed by the substantial losses that could, for example, arise when the balance of powers in terms of the private power on the side of the companies and the power of the users gets distorted.

In fact, although not expressly, this has already been hinted at regarding achieving personal welfare. For example, as regards the personalization in the data economy, it has been stated that "[i]n order for personalization to work, we believe the outcome should not just be reasonable from the perspective of an individual consumer, but also for society as a whole".[48]

---

[46] *Ibid.*, at p. 78.

[47] *Luhmann, N.*, Systemtheorie der Gesellschaft, Berlin: Suhrkamp Verlag 2017 (edited by Johannes F.K. Schmidt and André Kieserling, under cooperation of Christoph Gesigora), p. 398.

[48] OECD, Personalised Pricing in the Digital Era – Note by the Netherlands, 28 November 2018, DAF/COMP/WD(2018)124, p. 7.

5.1.2   Regulating Algorithmic Manipulations

As such, algorithmic manipulation is not a new phenomenon. For example, in the financial sector, a number of EU legal acts exist with the rules prohibiting market manipulation in order to preserve confidence in the markets for financial instruments.[49] So, in the light of the use of algorithms by the business when providing more "traditional" services, the question is whether similar rules may be needed with regard to potential algorithmic manipulations in the data economy,[50] including algorithmic manipulations in the business-to-consumer relationship.

To some extent, the question of manipulating algorithms in the case of ranking by online platforms is addressed in the Regulation on promoting fairness and transparency for business users of online intermediation services[51] (hereinafter Regulation 2019/1150). This Regulation covers the business-to-business relationship, i.e. the providers of online intermediation services and online search engines, on the one hand, and business users and corporate website users, on the other (Article 1(2)). Article 5(1) stipulates that "[p]roviders of online intermediation services shall set out in their terms and conditions the main parameters determining ranking and the reasons for the relative importance of those main parameters as opposed to other parameters". A similar obligation is foreseen for the providers of online search engines (Article 5(2)). Thereby, Regulation 2019/1150 sets the transparency require-

---

[49]   See, for example, Directive 2014/65/EU of the European Parliament and of the Council of 15 May 2014 on markets in financial instruments and amending Directive 2002/92/EC and Directive 2011/61/EU (recast), OJ [2014] L 173/349; Regulation (EU) No. 596/2014 of the European Parliament and of the Council of 16 April 2014 on market abuse (market abuse regulation) and repealing Directive 2003/6/EC of the European Parliament and of the Council and Commission Directives 2003/124/EC, 2003/125/EC and 2004/72/EC, OJ [2014] L 173/1; Directive 2014/57/EU of the European Parliament and of the Council of 16 April 2014 on criminal sanctions for market abuse, OJ [2014] L 173/179.

[50]   To some extent, this question is addressed by *Picht, P.G./Loderer, G.*, Framing Algorithms – Competition Law and (Other) Regulatory Tools (30 October 2018). Max Planck Institute for Innovation & Competition Research Paper No. 18-24. Available at SSRN: https://papers.ssrn.com/sol3/papers.cfm?abstract_id=3275198. However, the authors rather focus on the question of how competition law could learn from the legal acts regulating algorithmic trading.

[51]   Regulation (EU) 2019/1150 of the European Parliament and of the Council of 20 June 2019 on promoting fairness and transparency for business users of online intermediation services, OJ [2019] L 186/57. See also: European Commission, Proposal for a Regulation of the European Parliament and of the Council on promoting fairness and transparency for business users of online intermediation services, Brussels, 26.4.2018, COM(2018) 238 final, 2018/0112 (COD).

ment[52] for the providers of online intermediation services and the providers of online search engines. According to Article 5(6) of Regulation 2019/1150, while complying with the aforementioned obligation, providers of online intermediation services and of online search engines will not be required to disclose their algorithms, or – as specified by recital 27 – "to disclose the detailed functioning of their ranking mechanisms, including algorithms". Importantly, Article 5(6) stipulates that it will be without prejudice to the EU Trade Secrets Directive[53] – the circumstance that may be relevant bearing in mind that ranking algorithms may indeed fall under trade secret protection. It is, nevertheless, noteworthy that recital 27 explains that, even in light of trade secret protection, "the description given should at least be based on actual data on the relevance of the ranking parameters used".

Since a detailed analysis of the aforementioned Regulation goes beyond the scope of this book, it suffices to mention that, although it includes a rule on transparency that could tackle the issue of algorithmic manipulation, the Regulation, as explained, firstly, touches upon behaviour related to online platforms (only) and, secondly, addresses the business-to-business relationship, so that the relationship with consumers falls outside the scope of the Regulation.

Hence, with regard to potential algorithmic price manipulations, which may affect final consumers, there seems to be a gap in regulation. However, as argued above, there may be a need for such a regulatory rule. The question thereby is whether rules similar to those existing in the financial markets should be adopted for algorithmic manipulations in the markets where goods and services are provided to final consumers.

EU Directive 2014/65/EU on markets in financial instruments[54] defines algorithmic trading as "trading in financial instruments where a computer

---

[52]   See also recitals 7–8 of Regulation 2019/1150.

[53]   In this regard, it could be noted that the wording in the final text of the Regulation is slightly different from the proposal of the Regulation, where Article 5(4) stipulated that providers of online intermediation services and providers of online search engines were not required to disclose their trade secrets (Proposal for a Regulation of the European Parliament and of the Council on promoting fairness and transparency for business users of online intermediation services, Brussels, 26.4.2018, COM(2018) 238 final, 2018/0012(COD)). Furthermore, recital 18 said that "[w]hilst the providers are under no circumstances required to disclose any trade secrets as defined in Directive (EU) 2016/943 of the European Parliament and of the Council [...] when complying with this requirement to disclose the main ranking parameters, *the description given should at least be based on actual data on the relevance of the ranking parameters used*" (footnote omitted; emphasis added).

[54]   Directive 2014/65/EU of the European Parliament and of the Council of 15 May 2014 on markets in financial instruments and amending Directive 2002/92/EC and Directive 2011/61/EU (recast), OJ [2014] L 173/349.

algorithm automatically determines individual parameters of orders such as whether *to initiate the order, the timing, price or quantity of the order* or *how to manage the order after its submission,* with limited or no human intervention, and does not include any system that is only used for the purpose of routing orders to one or more trading venues or for the processing of orders involving no determination of any trading parameters or for the confirmation of orders or the post-trade processing of executed transactions" (Article 4(1) point 39) (emphasis added).[55] Based on this definition and owing to the fact that algorithms are used by the business to provide goods or services to final consumers, it could be argued that a similar definition may be applicable in these cases as well. After all, in such cases it might be that it will be algorithms that initiate the order or decide on the parameters of the order such as the timing, price, quantity, etc.

Recital 62 of Directive 2014/65/EU explains that "algorithmic trading or high-frequency algorithmic trading techniques can, like any other form of trading, lend themselves to certain forms of behaviour which is prohibited under Regulation (EU) No 596/2014".

EU Regulation No. 596/2014 – the market abuse Regulation[56] – stipulates in Article 15 that "[a] person shall not engage in or attempt to engage in market manipulation". Article 1 of Regulation 596/2014 says that "[t]his Regulation establishes a common regulatory framework on [...] market manipulation (market abuse) as well as measures to prevent market abuse to ensure the integrity of financial markets in the Union and to enhance investor protection and confidence in those markets".

It can be recalled that the role of trusting the markets where algorithms are employed has been stressed, including the EU Commissioner for Competition *Margrethe Vestager.*[57] In fact, the role of (building) trust as regards the data economy was also pointed out in the Communication on Building a European Data Economy, where the European Commission noted that "an increased level of consumer trust will benefit both EU and external commercial operators".[58] It was explained that "strong data protection rules create the trust that

---

[55]   Directive 2014/65/EU, Article 4(1) point 40, also provides a definition of a high-frequency algorithmic trading technique.

[56]   Regulation (EU) No. 596/2014 of the European Parliament and of the Council of 16 April 2014 on market abuse (market abuse regulation) and repealing Directive 2003/6/EC of the European Parliament and of the Council and Commission Directives 2003/124/EC, 2003/125/EC and 2004/72/EC, OJ [2014] L 173/1.

[57]   See *supra* in this chapter, Section 5.1, note 8.

[58]   European Commission, Communication from the Commission to the European Parliament, the Council, the European Economic and Social Committee and the Committee of the Regions, "Building a European Data Economy", Brussels, 10.1.2017, COM(2017) 9 final, at p. 2.

will allow the digital economy to develop across the internal market".[59] In a similar way, recital 7 GDPR states that technological developments "require a strong and more coherent data protection framework in the Union, backed by strong enforcement, given the importance of creating the trust that will allow the digital economy to develop across the internal market".

Data protection rules and their robust enforcement are, no doubt, important for raising trust in the data economy. However, the functioning of the data economy is based not only on data, but also on algorithms. So the question is rather about the data ecosystem as a whole, so that the issue may be whether, or what type of, control may be needed in the light of a potential risk of algorithmic manipulation.

Regulation 596/2014 provides a list with a number of actions that may be considered market manipulation. Notably, pursuant to Article 12(1)(a) of Regulation 596/2014, market manipulation shall comprise

> entering into a transaction, placing an order to trade or any other behaviour which:
> (i)   gives, or is likely to give, false or misleading signals as to the supply of, demand for, or price of, a financial instrument, a related spot commodity contract or an auctioned product based on emission allowances; or
> (ii)   secures, or is likely to secure, the price of one or several financial instruments, a related spot commodity contract or an auctioned product based on emission allowances at an abnormal or artificial level;
> unless the person entering into a transaction, placing an order to trade or engaging in any other behaviour establishes that such transaction, order or behaviour have been carried out for legitimate reasons, and conform with an accepted market practice as established in accordance with Article 13.

A careful reading of this legal provision reveals that the actions mentioned may also be highly relevant for the cases when the goods or services were provided by companies to final consumers on the basis of ordinary business-to-consumer transactions. As it was argued before, on the basis of the information about the effectual demand, misleading information could be provided to those who would form part of the absolute demand. Hence, a prohibition along similar lines might be needed not only for the financial sector.

As it can be seen from the legal provision cited above, it includes an important exception when the aforementioned conduct would not be considered market manipulation. Such an exception refers to the legitimate reasons and the conformity with "an accepted practice" pursuant to Article 13 of Regulation 596/2014.

Article 13, which elaborates on accepted market practices, in paragraph 2, lists the criteria that would have to be taken into account by a competent

---

[59]   *Ibid.*, at p. 3.

authority establishing an accepted market practice. One of such criteria is "whether the market practice provides for a substantial level of transparency to the market" (Article 13(2)(a) of Regulation 596/2014). Hence, in contrast to what has been claimed regarding market transparency posing a danger when it comes to the use of algorithms,[60] a deeper analysis of the relevant legal provisions that deal with similar issues reveals that this may be exactly the opposite. In light of the specific features of algorithmic trading, market transparency may, in fact, be one of the important factors when considering whether such trading may amount to market manipulation. In other words, such transparency, in the case of the use of algorithms, may be desirable in order to prevent market manipulation. The latter insight may also be important bearing in mind that algorithms may be protected as trade secrets. After all, competent authorities (supervisory authorities), possibly sector-based, would have to be designated for dealing with questions of market manipulation.[61] Importantly though, creating a network of such institutions similar to the European Competition Network may be important bearing in mind that algorithmic trading may be cross-border.

The analysis above shows that the issues raised by business use of algorithms may be similar to the issues known in the context of algorithmic trading of financial instruments. In particular, the risk of market manipulation may arise and thereby the need for regulatory rules in this regard. Importantly though, such rules should not merely deal with the business-to-business relationship, but should rather strike a balance in the relationship of business-to-consumer.

5.2 CONSUMER PROTECTION: THE CONTROL OF TERMS AND CONDITIONS BY PUBLIC BODIES

According to Article 38 of the EU Charter of Fundamental Rights, "Union policies shall ensure a high level of consumer protection". In light of the rise of private power[62] and a growing gap between business and consumers, particularly, in terms of the information asymmetry and differences in their negotiating power, it may be asked whether such consumer protection can still effectively be ensured. On the one hand, the EU rules on personal data protection have been strengthened, for example, by issuing the EU General Data Protection Regulation, which has been applicable in the EU Member States since May 2018. On the other hand, however, it could be asked whether

---

[60] See *supra* in this chapter, Section 5.1, note 15.

[61] Possibly, based on the example of Regulation 596/2014, Articles 22–23 (elaborating on the competent authorities and their powers) as well as Articles 27–29 (elaborating on professional secrecy and data protection).

[62] See *Möslein, F.* (ed.), Private Macht, Tübingen: Mohr Siebeck 2016.

consumers are in a position to counterbalance – by themselves – the potential pressure that may be exerted upon them by the business. This may be particularly the case when it comes to the numerous terms and conditions that consumers are often requested to accept if they want to acquire goods or services in the data economy.

In this regard, state intervention may be needed. Bearing in mind that the freedom of contract covers not only the freedom to enter into a contract, but also on what terms, it might be asked whether limitations to the exercise of this freedom might be needed and whether it should be the task of a public authority to control the terms and conditions for the sake of consumer protection. Hence, one of the options of state intervention might be the control – by state bodies – of the terms and conditions that consumers are often requested to accept in order to be able to acquire goods or services in the data economy.

5.2.1   *Kontrahierungszwang* and *diktierter Vertrag*: The Concepts Developed by Nipperdey

Back in 1920, the question of the restriction of the private rights of individuals, in particular their right to the freedom of contract, was analysed by the German scholar Hans Carl Nipperdey.[63] In his book "Kontrahierungszwang und diktierter Vertrag", he elaborated not only on the duty to enter into a contract (*Kontrahierungszwang*), but also on the duty to enter into a contract on prescribed terms (*diktierter Vertrag*).

In the opinion of Nipperdey, a society may require not to be disadvantaged by the behaviour of its individual members even if such behaviour falls into the framework of the acknowledged private rights and freedoms. According to him, in such a case this framework is just too wide. He stressed that a society may require that the exercise of private freedoms does not lead to a suppression of those members of society who are economically weaker. Should this be the case, Nipperdey said, intervention of the state may be needed.[64]

Nipperdey defined a duty to enter into contract as a duty, based on a legal norm, ordering a legal subject, without their will, to enter into a contract with a predefined terms or terms defined by an independent third party.[65] Accordingly, the restriction of the freedom of contract is meant not only in terms of a duty to enter into a contract, but also in terms of a duty to enter into a contract with predefined terms. In the opinion of Nipperdey, a duty to enter

---

[63]   *Nipperdey, H.C.*, Kontrahierungszwang und diktierter Vertrag, Jena: Verlag von Gustav Fischer 1920.

[64]   *Ibid.*, p. 2.

[65]   *Ibid.*, p. 7.

into a contract translates into an acceptance of a constraint based on the will of others (*ein willensfremder Zwang*[66]). Importantly though, such a duty is not confined to a vertical (public) relationship, but may also cover the horizontal (thus, private) relationship (for example, rental contracts). In this regard, a freedom of contract can thus be limited also in cases of horizontal relationships, i.e. between private legal subjects.

Nipperdey distinguished between an inner legal ground for a duty to enter into a contract (*der innere Rechtsgrund des Kontrahierungszwangs*) and an explicit, or a formal, legal ground. As to the former, he noted that an inner legal ground for a duty to enter into a contract is the social interest.[67] Such an inner legal ground, according to Nipperdey, has to be expressed formally (thus, an explicit, or a formal, legal ground), namely, it must be enshrined in a legal norm.[68] However, although the law, in his opinion, is the most important legal basis where such a duty can be anchored, Nipperdey also speaks about the delegated powers of legislature, so that a duty to enter into a contract may also be anchored in the lower-ranking legal norms, such as regulations or even administrative acts.[69] According to him, a legal source for a duty to enter into a contract may also be the autonomous statutes of the self-regulatory bodies (even those that are private).[70]

The analysis above shows that a state intervention, when it comes to a duty to enter into a contract in broader terms, may be needed when part of society may be suppressed by others. In such a case, as it is shown by the analysis of the concept developed by Nipperdey, a framework of particular private freedoms may be considered to be too wide and could be restricted in the light of the social interest (an inner legal ground) and on the basis of a legal norm (a formal legal ground). The question thereby is whether this may be the case in the data economy.

5.2.2 Data Economy: Is There a Need for the State Control of Terms and Conditions?

In order to answer the question whether there might be a need for state intervention, it has to be analysed whether the existing legal framework, in particular the legal framework on personal data protection, provides insufficient control for individuals when it comes to the processing of their personal data.

---

[66] *Ibid.*, p. 15.
[67] *Ibid.*, pp. 5, 8.
[68] *Ibid.*, p. 8.
[69] *Ibid.*, pp. 9–10.
[70] *Ibid.*, p. 11.

After all, one of the goals of the GDPR was to strengthen the control of data subjects over their data.[71]

5.2.2.1   A lack of a "freely given" and "informed" consent?

According to Article 6(1)(a) GDPR, consent of the data subject is one of the legal bases for a lawful processing of personal data. Also, Article 8(2) of the EU Charter of Fundamental Rights stipulates that personal data "must be processed fairly for specified purposes and on the basis of the consent of the person concerned or some other legitimate basis laid down by law".

Article 4(11) GDPR defines a consent as "any freely given, specific, informed and unambiguous indication of the data subject's wishes by which he or she, by a statement or by a clear affirmative action, signifies agreement to the processing of personal data relating to him or her".[72] Thus, four cumulative requirements apply in order to determine whether a consent is valid, i.e. such a consent should be freely given, specific, informed and unambiguous. In addition, a consent has to be expressed "by a statement or by a clear affirmative action", so that any passive behaviour will not be considered a valid consent. Preselected ticks in a checkbox[73] or a requirement for a customer to express, in handwriting, a refusal to consent to particular clauses of the standardized contract[74] may stand as examples of such passive behaviour.

Recital 42 GDPR explains that "[c]onsent should not be regarded as freely given if the data subject has no genuine or free choice or is unable to refuse or withdraw consent without detriment". The GDPR does not explain what such "detriment" should mean. It could be asked whether, for example, cases where, on the basis of a loyalty card, which includes personal data, a purchaser gets a discount, could be considered as providing "detriment" for those who refuse to provide their personal data and thus are not granted such a loyalty card with a result that they have to pay the ordinary price (i.e. without a discount). On

---

[71]   See, for example, recitals 6–7 GDPR.

[72]   See also recital 32 GDPR.

[73]   See, for example, ECJ, Case C-673/17, *Bundesverband der Verbraucherzentralen und Verbraucherverbände — Verbraucherzentrale Bundesverband eV v. Planet49 GmbH*, 1 October 2019, ECLI:EU:C:2019:801, para. 52.

[74]   See, for example, Opinion of Advocate General Szpunar delivered on 4 March 2020, Case C-61/19, *Orange România SA v. Autoritatea Națională de Supraveghere a Prelucrării Datelor cu Caracter Personal (ANSPDCP)*, ECLI:EU:C:2020:158 ("A data subject intending to enter into a contractual relationship for the provision of telecommunication services with an undertaking does not give his or her 'consent', that is, does not indicate his or her 'specific and informed' and 'freely given' wishes [...] to that undertaking when he or she is required to state, in handwriting, on an otherwise standardised contract, that he or she refuses to consent to the photocopying and storage of his or her ID documents" (*ibid.*, para. 63)).

the one hand, it could be argued that such cases mean that a data subject is not able to refuse the processing of their personal data without detriment. On the other hand, however, it should probably be said that such processing rather provides a possibility of getting an advantage (in terms of a discount), but does not directly cause any detriment. As a result, such situations would probably not amount to the cases where it could be claimed that a data subject could not refuse the processing of their personal data without suffering any detriment.

Furthermore, according to recital 43 GDPR:

> In order to ensure that consent is freely given, consent should not provide a valid legal ground for the processing of personal data in a specific case where there is a clear imbalance between the data subject and the controller, in particular where the controller is a public authority and it is therefore unlikely that consent was freely given in all the circumstances of that specific situation.

Hence, in the case of a "clear imbalance", a consent will not necessarily be considered valid. However, apart from the example that such a clear imbalance may exist in the cases when a public authority would be involved, the GDPR does not further explain what such a clear imbalance should mean. Other examples of such cases are said to involve, for example, cases of the employer–employee relationship.[75]

Article 7 GDPR lists further, rather strict, requirements for a valid consent.[76] Importantly, Article 7(4) GDPR stipulates that "[w]hen assessing whether consent is freely given, utmost account shall be taken of whether, *inter alia*, the performance of a contract, including the provision of a service, is conditional on consent to the processing of personal data that is not necessary for the performance of that contract".[77] First of all, it should be noted that consent is not needed when the processing of personal data is necessary for the performance of a contract – in such a case, a legal basis for lawful processing will be Article 6(1)(b) GDPR. However, when the processing of such data is not necessary for the performance of the contract, a consent may be needed if personal data will be processed in the context of the contract.[78] Importantly though, Article 7(4) GDPR speaks about cases where there may be a strong position of the party requesting the consent, for example, cases when a data subject would not have

---

[75]   *Ernst, S.* in: Paal, B.P./Pauly, D.A., Datenschutz-Grundverordnung, München: C.H. Beck 2017, Art. 4, p. 46, para. 71.

[76]   It is noteworthy that sanctions are foreseen in Article 83(5)(a) GDPR for the infringements of the legal provisions related to the consent, including Article 7 GDPR.

[77]   See also recital 43 GDPR.

[78]   See also: *Frenzel, E.M.* in: Paal, B.P./Pauly, D.A., Datenschutz-Grundverordnung, München: C.H. Beck 2017, Art. 7, p. 114, para. 20.

the possibility to obtain the desired services from elsewhere.[79] Article 7(4) GDPR condemns such cases and stipulates that consent will not be considered freely given. However, it has been claimed that, in cases when the exchange of data itself is an essential part of a contract (i.e. in the cases when consumers "pay" with their data in order to be provided a service), the overall freedom of the data subject to enter into a contract will depend on what (market) power the other party has, so that "freely given" will be not so much related to the concept of a consent (and thus Article 7(4) GDPR), but may rather need to be interpreted in the framework of the whole contract itself on the basis of, for example, Article 102 TFEU (or equivalent national provisions), instead of being explained with the help of Article 7(4) GDPR.[80] It could be argued, however, that in such a case, consent should not be considered freely given if a data subject lacks the freedom to enter into a contract in the first place.[81]

The requirements for a consent, pursuant to Article 4(11) GDPR, include that such a consent has to be not only specific and unambiguous, but also "informed". Recital 42 GDPR explains that "[f]or consent to be informed, the data subject should be aware at least of the identity of the controller and the purposes of the processing for which the personal data are intended". In general terms, the "informed" consent means that a data subject should be able to understand the contents of such a consent, in order to be fully aware of it.[82] Thereby, a consent should be comprehensible to the data subject (not only in terms of the language, but also when it comes to any technical or other specific terms used).[83] Yet a tricky question is whether an "informed" consent should mean the consent granted after the relevant text has been read.

In fact, one of the issues in the data economy is that terms and conditions often seem to be accepted by consumers without having actually read them.[84] Naturally, the question may arise whether, in such cases, it might be possible to speak about an "informed" consent in the first place. On the one hand, the argument could go that, as long as terms and conditions were accepted without having actually read them, the consent would be "not informed". On the other

---

[79] *Frenzel, E.M.* in: Paal, B.P./Pauly, D.A., Datenschutz-Grundverordnung, München: C.H. Beck 2017, Art. 7, pp. 114–115, para. 20.

[80] *Ibid.*, p. 115, para. 21.

[81] Along these lines see also: *Ernst, S.* in: Paal, B.P./Pauly, D.A., Datenschutz-Grundverordnung, München: C.H. Beck 2017, Art. 4, p. 47, paras 73, 76.

[82] *Ernst, S.* in: Paal, B.P./Pauly, D.A., Datenschutz-Grundverordnung, München: C.H. Beck 2017, Art. 4, p. 48, para. 79.

[83] *Ibid.*, pp. 48–49, paras 81, 84.

[84] For more see, for example, *Acquisti, A./Brandimarte, L./Loewenstein, G.*, Privacy and human behavior in the age of information, (2015) 347 Science 509; *Acquisti, A./John, L.K./Loewenstein, G.*, What is Privacy Worth, (2013) 42 The Journal of Legal Studies 249.

hand, however, it should probably be asked whether the terms and conditions were "readable", even if, in a particular factual situation, they were not necessarily read by the data subject. In such a way, in cases of disproportionately extensive terms and conditions, it would be possible to argue that consent could not be considered to be "informed".[85] Yet this would not necessarily be in all cases and would depend on the factual circumstances. After all, this will be closely related to the accountability principle enshrined in the GDPR (Article 5(2)), according to which a data controller has to prove compliance with the principles related to the processing of personal data.

Based on what was said above, it could be argued that, on the one hand, the consent given by a data subject may, based on the rules of personal data protection, often be considered to be valid. On the other hand, however, the problem in the data economy may be that consumers accept the terms and conditions without a clear understanding of their content. Therefore, a more robust state control of the terms and conditions may be needed.

5.2.2.2 Enforcement of the control of terms and conditions

In the EU, steps have already been taken to strengthen the enforcement of EU consumer law.[86] In November 2019, the Directive 2019/2161 as regards the better enforcement and modernisation of EU consumer protection rules was adopted.[87] However, as explained above, for the sake of consumer protection, *ex ante* control of such terms and conditions by public bodies may be needed in the data economy. After all, the question would often be not only whether to enter into the contract, but also on what terms. The beauty of such *ex ante* control would not only be the prevention of the potential conflicts that may arise after particular terms and conditions are accepted by consumers, but it would also create a more uniform approach when it comes to the control of the terms and conditions.

---

[85] Along these lines see also: *Ernst, S.* in: Paal, B.P./Pauly, D.A., Datenschutz-Grundverordnung, München: C.H. Beck 2017, Art. 4, p. 49, para. 86.

[86] See the "New Deal for Consumers" initiative of the European Commission: https://ec.europa.eu/info/law/law-topic/consumers/review-eu-consumer-law-new-deal -consumers_en. See also: European Commission, Press Release, A New Deal for Consumers: Commission strengthens EU consumer rights and enforcement, Brussels, 11 April 2018, IP/18/3041 (http://europa.eu/rapid/press-release_IP-18-3041_en.htm); see also: https://ec.europa.eu/newsroom/just/item-detail.cfm?item_id=620435.

[87] Directive (EU) 2019/2161 of the European Parliament and of the Council of 27 November 2019 amending Council Directive 93/13/EEC and Directives 98/6/EC, 2005/29/EC and 2011/83/EU of the European Parliament and of the Council as regards the better enforcement and modernisation of Union consumer protection rules, OJ [2019] L 328/7.

The fact that there may be a need for the state control of the terms and conditions in the data economy is clearly illustrated by the case of the Federal German Cartel Office (Bundeskartellamt) against Facebook.[88] In that case, the German competition authority held that Facebook abused its dominant position in the social media market by imposing such terms and conditions on the users of its social media platform that were considered by the competition authority as exploitative (*Konditionenmissbrauch*) and thus infringing Section 19(1) of the German Act against Restraints of Competition (GWB).[89] The Bundeskartellamt did not examine the use of data, which was generated by the use of Facebook's social network itself, but rather looked at the terms and conditions that Facebook enforced with regard to data obtained from third-party sources ("off Facebook").[90] As regards the abuse through exploitative conditions (*Konditionenmissbrauch*), the Bundeskartellamt, relying on the case-law of the Federal Supreme Court of Germany, explained that "to protect constitutional rights, § 19 GWB must be applied in cases where one contractual party is so powerful that it is practically able to dictate the terms of the contract and the contractual autonomy of the other party is abolished".[91] According to the competition authority, conditions that contradict data protection laws may, when a relation to a dominant position is established, infringe Section 19(1) GWB.[92]

In the *Facebook* case, the German competition authority scrutinized the compliance of the terms and conditions with personal data protection, i.e. the GDPR, in much detail.[93] In fact, its analysis comes close to the supervision of such terms and conditions – a circumstance that raises the question whether

---

[88]   Decision of the Federal German Cartel Office (Bundeskartellamt), 6 February 2019, No. B6-22/16.

[89]   *Ibid.*, paras 163, 522 et seq.

[90]   *Ibid.*, para. 522. The German competition authority looked at whether the conditions imposed by Facebook on its users amounted to an exploitative abuse of a dominant position in terms of making them choose "between accepting 'the whole Facebook package', including an extensive disclosure of personal data, or not using Facebook at all" (Bundeskartellamt, Background information on the Facebook proceeding, 19 December 2017 (http://www.bundeskartellamt.de/SharedDocs/Publikation/EN/Diskussions_Hintergrundpapiere/2017/Hintergrundpapier_Facebook.html?nn=3591286), p. 2). Therefore, the Bundeskartellamt delved into a deeper analysis whether such terms complied with the EU data protection laws, i.e. the GDPR.

[91]   Bundeskartellamt, Background information on the Facebook proceeding, 19 December 2017 (http://www.bundeskartellamt.de/SharedDocs/Publikation/EN/Diskussions_Hintergrundpapiere/2017/Hintergrundpapier_Facebook.html?nn=3591286), p. 5. Decision of the Bundeskartellamt, *Facebook, supra* note 88, paras 525 et seq.

[92]   Decision of the Bundeskartellamt, *Facebook, supra* note 88, para. 532.

[93]   *Ibid.*, paras 535–870.

such broad competences are meant to be vested in competition authorities. This question is also reflected in the remedy,[94] where a fine was not imposed, but Facebook was obliged to adjust its terms and conditions under the supervision of the Bundeskartellamt. Thus, on the one hand, the terms and conditions may, no doubt, be a problematic issue in the data economy, as the *Facebook* case illustrates. On the other hand, however, it could be argued that the control of the terms and conditions should form part of a broader policy, rather than be based on sporadic cases against some companies.

A more important issue though arises when it comes to the legal basis on which the German competition authority found Facebook's infringement of competition law. As said above, the competition authority claimed that Facebook infringed Section 19(1) of the German Act against Restraints of Competition (GWB). The competition authority did not apply Article 102 TFEU.[95] The problematic part of the legal analysis in the *Facebook* case is the causal link between Facebook's dominant position and the abuse. Namely, as explained below, under German competition law, the establishment of such a causal link is required for proving an infringement under Section 19 GWB, whereas the causal link does not necessarily form part of the requirements under EU competition law, namely Article 102 TFEU. Several remarks have to be made in this regard.

First of all, although, according to the Bundeskartellamt, Facebook's abuse was causally linked to its dominant position,[96] the link to the causality in this case is rather weak, if existing at all. In this aspect, the *Facebook* case is problematic, and the part related to the causality is probably one of the most problematic parts of the decision. In the opinion of the Bundeskartellamt:

> According to the case-law it is not necessary to determine that the conduct, i.e. the violation, was only possible in the first place because of market dominance and that other market participants did not have a chance to behave in a similar way. Instead, it is sufficient to determine that the two aspects are linked by a causality which is either based on normative aspects or the outcome. Both aspects can be assumed to be fulfilled in this case.[97]

---

[94] *Ibid.*, paras 946 et seq.
[95] See *ibid.*, para. 914.
[96] *Ibid.*, paras 871 et seq. See also: Bundeskartellamt, Case Summary, Facebook, Exploitative business terms pursuant to Section 19(1) GWB for inadequate data processing, 15 February 2019, Case reference: B6-22/16 (https://www.bundeskartellamt .de/SharedDocs/Entscheidung/EN/Fallberichte/Missbrauchsaufsicht/2019/B6-22-16 .pdf?__blob=publicationFile&v=3), p. 7: "being a manifestation of market power, the terms violate the stipulations of the GDPR and are abusive within the meaning of Section 19(1) GWB".
[97] Bundeskartellamt, Case Summary, Facebook, Exploitative business terms pursuant to Section 19(1) GWB for inadequate data processing, 15 February 2019, Case

The fact that a company would be able to behave in a particular way solely because of its dominant position (and that other companies, thus, would not be able to behave in a similar way)[98] would, according to the competition authority, require a strict causal link to be established, which is not required under the German competition law.[99] The competition authority stresses that "the violation of data protection requirements found is a manifestation of Facebook's market power".[100] It points out the imbalances of negotiating power.[101] Yet the tricky aspect in the *Facebook* case is that it might be that the infringement on exploitative terms (*Konditionenmissbrauch*) did not necessarily stem from or was related to a dominant position of Facebook, but was rather caused by the fact that consumers simply did not read the terms and conditions of Facebook before accepting them. In other words, it might be that the users of Facebook's social media platform accepted their terms and conditions not because the latter platform was dominant (thus, the users were not forced by the platform to accept these terms[102]), but because the users simply did not read them.[103] Following such a logic, the causal link between Facebook's dominant

---

reference: B6-22/16 (https://www.bundeskartellamt.de/SharedDocs/Entscheidung/EN/Fallberichte/Missbrauchsaufsicht/2019/B6-22-16.pdf?__blob=publicationFile&v=3), p. 11. See also: Decision of the Bundeskartellamt, *Facebook, supra* note 88, para. 873.

[98]   This was the argument of Facebook, which argued that the causality between Facebook's dominant position and their abuse was missing, since a number of other companies behaved similarly as regards personal data (Decision of the Bundeskartellamt, *Facebook, supra* note 88, para. 156). Facebook claimed that the Bundeskartellamt did not sufficiently prove the causal link (*ibid.*, para. 158).

[99]   Decision of the Bundeskartellamt, *Facebook, supra* note 88, para. 873.

[100]   Bundeskartellamt, Case Summary, Facebook, Exploitative business terms pursuant to Section 19(1) GWB for inadequate data processing, 15 February 2019, Case reference: B6-22/16 (https://www.bundeskartellamt.de/SharedDocs/Entscheidung/EN/Fallberichte/Missbrauchsaufsicht/2019/B6-22-16.pdf?__blob=publicationFile&v=3), pp. 7, 11.

[101]   Decision of the Bundeskartellamt, *Facebook, supra* note 88, paras 383, 527–528, 530.

[102]   The Bundeskartellamt, by contrast, seems to indicate that users were forced to accept the terms and conditions by Facebook. See Bundeskartellamt, Background information on the Facebook proceeding, 19 December 2017 (http://www.bundeskartellamt.de/SharedDocs/Publikation/EN/Diskussions_Hintergrundpapiere/2017/Hintergrundpapier_Facebook.html?nn=3591286), p. 4: "the Bundeskartellamt also applies data protection principles in its assessment of Facebook's terms and conditions. In this regard, data protection law has the same objective as competition law, which is to protect individuals from having their personal data exploited by the opposite market side. Data protection legislation seeks to ensure that users can decide *freely and without coercion* on how their personal data are used" (emphasis added).

[103]   Interestingly, this fact is mentioned in the Bundeskartellamt's decision, but it is stated that, since the user, owing to the platform's dominant position, would have to accept the terms and conditions anyway, they skip their reading (Decision of the

position and its alleged abuse when it comes to "exploitative" terms would be interrupted. This may be so even if we recall that, under German competition law, strict causality (i.e. market dominance would enable another company to act in the same or similar way) is not required, but rather an "effects based causality" or a "normative causality" suffices, i.e. "it is sufficient that the conduct has anti-competitive effects specifically because the abuser holds a dominant position on the market".[104] Thus, if it were so that the terms and conditions were accepted by the users of the platform just because they did not read them, negative effects on consumers that may follow would not be related to a dominant position of the company, but, instead triggered by the negligent behaviour of the users themselves. In other words, even if Facebook were not dominant, similar negative effects on consumers could also arise from its broad terms and conditions. Furthermore, the insight that the terms and conditions may be accepted by consumers because they do not read them brings in even more confusion as regards the position of the Bundeskartellamt: recalling that the mere fact that a data subject did not read the terms and conditions before accepting them does not necessarily render the consent invalid,[105] processing of personal data on this legal basis may be lawful. Bearing in mind that the breaches of data protection laws were the basis for the Bundeskartellamt's holding that there was an abuse of a dominant position, it could be asked whether such a finding can still hold.

Secondly, the *Facebook* case shows that there may be problems when it comes to the terms and conditions accepted by consumers in the data economy, first and foremost, owing to the imbalance of power between companies and consumers – this is the strong side of this case. However, it also shows – and this is the weakness of the case – that legal tools such as competition law may not be the most appropriate ones to deal with these kinds of cases. In fact, their application may rather have unintended consequences and may bring negative results. For example, the fact that the Federal German Cartel Office analysed the terms and conditions of Facebook while leaving out those of WhatsApp

---

Bundeskartellamt, *Facebook, supra* note 88, para. 385). However, it could be asked, firstly, whether there was indeed no other alternative for the user, and, secondly, even if it were so, whether such a straightforward conclusion can be made that the users do not read the terms and conditions because of the company's dominant position. It could be argued that consumers often do not read the terms and conditions, irrespective of the market power of the companies.

[104] *Körber, T.*, Is Knowledge (Market) Power? – On the Relationship Between Data Protection, "Data Power" and Competition Law (29 January 2018). NZKart 2016, 303 et seq. and 348 et seq. (German version). Available at SSRN: https://papers.ssrn.com/sol3/papers.cfm?abstract_id=3112232, p. 22 with further references to the relevant German case-law.

[105] See *supra* in this chapter, Section 5.2.2.1.

raises questions, first and foremost, as regards the equal treatment of companies, not the least bearing in mind the merger of these two companies that took place some years before.[106] Furthermore, stretching, if not misinterpreting, existing competition law concepts – when trying to squeeze in cases that may not necessarily fall under the existing legal framework – may be a highly risky approach. Finally, although the legal effect of such a case may be national, it may have broader consequences if we recall the global presence of the companies such as Facebook. In fact, it could be asked whether the terms and conditions written under the supervision of the German competition authority would have to be amended, at least when it comes to Facebook's presence in other EU Member States. Since this is not given, it might be that different terms and conditions may exist as regards consumers in different countries.

Thirdly, should cases like *Facebook* be further solved on the basis of competition law, proving causality in competition law may be essential. Although such a causality, as explained above, forms part of the German law, it is not entirely clear whether it also forms part of EU competition law. The ECJ, for example, in the *Continental Can* case[107] held that "[s]uch being the meaning and the scope of Article 86 of the EEC Treaty, the question of the link of causality raised by the applicants [...] between the dominant position and its abuse, is of no consequence".[108] However, the ECJ, in *Tetra Pak II*,[109] noted that "application of Article 86 presupposes a link between the dominant position and the alleged abusive conduct, which is normally not present where conduct on a market distinct from the dominated market produces effects on that distinct market".[110] And yet, it could be debated whether the introduction of a requirement for causality may be needed also under EU competition law. This may be particularly so if the control of terms and conditions were done by competition authorities. Should the terms and conditions be analysed under the EU competition law standard, the introduction of the causality requirement in the cases of Article 102 TFEU may need to be considered. It could be argued that, if not strict causality, at least an effects-based causality may have to be considered.[111]

---

[106] Decision of the European Commission of 3 October 2014, Case No. COMP/M.7217 – *Facebook/WhatsApp*.

[107] ECJ, Case 6/72, *Europemballage Corporation and Continental Can Company Inc. v. Commission of the European Communities*, 21 February 1973, ECLI:EU:C:1973:22.

[108] *Ibid.*, para. 27.

[109] ECJ, Case C-333/94 P, *Tetra Pak International SA v. Commission of the European Communities*, 14 November 1996, ECLI:EU:C:1996:436.

[110] *Ibid.*, para. 27.

[111] Along these lines, advocating for an "effects-based causality" rather than strict causality, see *Körber, T.*, Is Knowledge (Market) Power? – On the Relationship

Fourthly, from a broader policy perspective, it could be advocated that it should not be competition authorities that would be vested with such powers. Instead, it could be argued that a public authority (for example, such as data protection authorities and authorities for consumer protection) should be vested with powers to control such terms and conditions.[112] In such a case, this would be done on a regular basis and in a more consistent manner. This would help to avoid situations where the terms and conditions are controlled when an abuse of a dominant position is established. Instead, more companies would be addressed, independently of their market power. Thus, bearing in mind the role of the terms and conditions in the data economy, a more consistent policy of the control of terms and conditions may be needed.

Finally, criticism by academia has been expressed as regards a too extensive integration of the analysis of data protection laws by the Bundeskartellamt in *Facebook*.[113] Indeed, the extensive application of data protection laws by the Bundeskartellamt in *Facebook* may be critical. However, such a criticism, which may be correct with regard to that particular case, should not amount to broader conclusions saying that data protection laws should in no way be integrated in the analysis of competition law. On the one hand, it is true that privacy issues have, time and again, been rejected by the ECJ or the European Commission from being considered in the framework of competition law. For example, in the *Asnef Equifax* case,[114] the ECJ held that:

> any possible issues relating to the sensitivity of personal data are not, as such, a matter for competition law, they may be resolved on the basis of the relevant provisions governing data protection.[115]

Between Data Protection, "Data Power" and Competition Law (29 January 2018). NZKart 2016, 303 et seq. and 348 et seq. (German version). Available at SSRN: https://papers.ssrn.com/sol3/papers.cfm?abstract_id=3112232, p. 23.

[112] Along these lines, see *ibid.*, p. 23.

[113] See, for example, *Picht, P.G./Loderer, G.*, Framing Algorithms – Competition Law and (Other) Regulatory Tools (30 October 2018). Max Planck Institute for Innovation & Competition Research Paper No. 18-24. Available at SSRN: https://papers.ssrn.com/sol3/papers.cfm?abstract_id=3275198, pp. 24-26; *Davilla, M.*, Is Big Data a Different Kind of Animal? The Treatment of Big Data Under the EU Competition Rules, (2017) 8 Journal of European Competition Law & Practice 370; *Körber, T.*, Is Knowledge (Market) Power? – On the Relationship Between Data Protection, "Data Power" and Competition Law (29 January 2018). NZKart 2016, 303 et seq. and 348 et seq. (German version). Available at SSRN: https://papers.ssrn.com/sol3/papers.cfm?abstract_id=3112232.

[114] ECJ, Case C-238/05, *Asnef-Equifax, Servicios de Información sobre Solvencia y Crédito, SL, Administración del Estado v. Asociación de Usuarios de Servicios Bancarios (Ausbanc)*, 23 November 2006, ECLI:EU:C:2006:734.

[115] *Ibid.*, para. 63.

Similarly, the European Commission, in the *Facebook/WhatsApp* merger,[116] stated that "[a]ny privacy-related concerns flowing from the increased concentration of data within the control of Facebook as a result of the Transaction do not fall within the scope of the EU competition law rules but within the scope of the EU data protection rules".[117] On the other hand, however, data protection and privacy questions have been taken into account in other cases in the assessment of competition law.[118]

Thus, it should probably not be ruled out at the outset that data protection issues may have to be analysed in the framework of the competition law assessment. After all, the intersection of competition law with other areas of law is not new. A prominent example is the intersection of competition law and intellectual property law. In fact, it has been claimed by Ohlhausen and Okuliar that privacy could be considered "a non-price dimension of competition",[119] yet, it should be the type of harm that should govern the choice of law.[120] Thus, it could be argued that data protection and privacy laws may have to be taken into account under competition law assessment if – and only if – the theory of harm of a particular behaviour would predominantly be related to competition.

Based on what was said above, it could be argued that competition authorities are not necessarily best placed to supervise the terms and conditions imposed by companies on consumers in the data economy. If at all, such authorities can sporadically capture cases on an abuse of dominance, but proving such cases may turn out to be challenging. Hence, it could be argued that data protection authorities or consumer protection authorities could be vested with the power to control such terms and conditions.

5.3   CO- AND SELF-REGULATION: AN OPTIMAL SOLUTION FOR THE DATA ECONOMY?

In the data economy, it has been suggested that the codes of conduct should, for example, be developed as regards AI technology, namely, for "the ethical implementation of intelligent technologies" as part of the Global Initiative for

---

[116] Decision of the European Commission of 3 October 2014, Case No. COMP/M.7217 – *Facebook/WhatsApp*.

[117] *Ibid.*, para. 164.

[118] See, for example, Decision of the European Commission of 6 December 2016, Case No. M.8124 – *Microsoft/LinkedIn* (see, for example, para. 255; also, para. 350 speaks about privacy as "an important parameter of competition").

[119] *Ohlhausen, M.K./Okuliar, A.*, Competition, Consumer Protection, and the Right (Approach) to Privacy (6 February 2015). Antitrust Law Journal, Forthcoming. Available at SSRN: https://papers.ssrn.com/sol3/papers.cfm?abstract_id=2561563, p. 36 ("Privacy therefore increasingly represents a non-price dimension of competition").

[120] *Ibid.*, p. 39.

Ethical Considerations in the Design of Autonomous Systems introduced by the IEEE Standards Association in 2016.[121]

Codes of conduct, as a form of self-regulation, may be beneficial in many aspects. For example, it was pointed out by Kenneth Arrow that:

> I expect that ethical codes and informal nonprice organizations will continue to evolve where needed, for example in the control of product quality, to permit transactions which would be impossible because of differential information in markets where all individuals behaved in a purely selfish manner.[122]

Thereby, one of the circumstances when the codes of conduct could be needed is "differential information in markets".

However, the role of self- or co-regulation should not be overestimated when it comes to the data economy. On the one hand, solutions based on co-regulation may be beneficial in terms of the latter being able to provide sector-specific solutions. For example, a co-regulatory approach has been discussed with regard to Internet regulation and net neutrality.[123] In the data economy, the fact that co-regulation may be adapted to sector-specific solutions may be relevant in light of the variety of industries where data-driven companies have been branching out. When it comes to self-regulation, an agreement of ethical standards (with regard to the AI technology, for example) may be included in the ethical code.

On the other hand, however, when it comes to personal data and the fundamental rights involved, alternative regulatory mechanisms should be applied with caution. After all, the enforcement of voluntary codes may be problematic.[124]

Alternative regulatory mechanisms, such as co- and self-regulation, were listed in the "Interinstitutional Agreement on better law-making" of the European Parliament, the Council of the European Union and the European

---

[121] http://standards.ieee.org/news/2016/ieee_autonomous_systems.html. The programme launched aims at identifying the needs and building the "consensus for standards, certifications and codes of conduct regarding the ethical implementation of intelligent technologies" (*ibid.*).

[122] *Arrow, K.J.*, Information and Economic Behavior, in: Collected Papers of Kenneth J. Arrow, The Economics of Information, Vol. 4, Cambridge, MA: The Belknap Press of Harvard University Press 1984, pp. 136–184, at p. 150.

[123] *Marsden, C.T.*, Internet Co-Regulation: European Law, Regulatory Governance and Legitimacy in Cyberspace, Cambridge: Cambridge University Press 2011; *Marsden, C.T.*, Net Neutrality: Towards a Co-Regulatory Solution, New York: Bloomsbury Academic 2010.

[124] See, for example, *Tapscott, D.*, The Digital Economy: Promise and Peril in the Age of Networked Intelligence, New York: McGraw-Hill 1996, p. 279.

Commission of the year 2003.[125] Co-regulation, as defined in the aforementioned Agreement, means "the mechanism whereby a Community legislative act entrusts the attainment of the objectives defined by the legislative authority to parties which are recognized in the field (such as economic operators, the social partners, non-governmental organisations, or associations). This mechanism may be used on the basis of criteria defined in the legislative act so as to enable the legislation to be adapted to the problems and sectors concerned, to reduce the legislative burden by concentrating on essential aspects and to draw on the experience of the parties concerned".[126] Accordingly, in the case of co-regulation, the objectives and the criteria would be defined by the legislative act, whereas the means to achieve them can be chosen by the economic operators themselves. When it comes to the question of access to data, co-regulation would mean that the legislative act would have to state the objective and the criteria based on which access should be granted, whereas economic operators would further define them based on the terms on which such access is granted.

The aforementioned Agreement also defined self-regulation, namely as "the possibility for economic operators, the social partners, non-governmental organisations or associations to adopt amongst themselves and for themselves common guidelines at European level (particularly codes of practice or sectoral agreements)".[127] It was further clarified that "[a]s a general rule, this type of voluntary initiative does not imply that the Institutions have adopted any particular stance".[128] Hence, in the case of self-regulation, the EU institutions do not take any stance with regard to a specific question, since the regulation of the issue is left completely to the economic operators. In the context of the data economy, self-regulation would mean that the EU legislator does not take any steps as regards the question of data access, since the solutions to this question would be left to the industry.

Although the aforementioned two alternative regulation mechanisms were not included in the Interinstitutional Agreement on Better Law-Making of 13 April 2016,[129] which replaced the Interinstitutional Agreement as of 2003,

---

[125]   The European Parliament, the Council of the European Union, the Commission of the European Communities, "Interinstitutional Agreement on Better Law-Making", OJ [2003] C 321/1, paras 16–23.

[126]   *Ibid.*, para. 18.

[127]   *Ibid.*, para. 22.

[128]   *Ibid.*, para. 22.

[129]   Interinstitutional Agreement between the European Parliament, the Council of the European Union and the European Commission on better law-making (13 April 2016), OJ [2016] L 123/1.

the aforementioned alternative regulation mechanisms have not lost their importance.[130]

In fact, one form of an alternative regulation mechanism, i.e. the codes of conduct, is enshrined in the GDPR. In contrast to the EU Data Protection Directive,[131] according to which codes of conduct could be used for providing guidance on the anonymization of data,[132] the GDPR provides broader possibilities for issuing such codes. According to Article 40(1) GDPR, "[t]he Member States, the supervisory authorities, the Board and the Commission shall encourage the drawing up of codes of conduct intended to contribute to the proper application of this Regulation, taking account of the specific features of the various processing sectors and the specific needs of micro, small and medium-sized enterprises". Thereby, codes of conduct could be issued for the purpose of specifying a proper application of the GDPR.[133] In fact, while the Interinstitutional Agreement as of 2003 stipulated that co-regulation and self-regulation "will not be applicable where fundamental rights […] are at stake",[134] the latter provision is not found in the Interinstitutional Agreement as of 2016, which does not elaborate on either co- or self-regulation. Bearing in mind the fundamental right to personal data protection and the eligibility of the codes of conduct pursuant to the GDPR, the codes of conduct would be valid if issued under the conditions set in Article 40 GDPR. In fact, such codes of conduct may be adhered to by controllers or processors that are not subject to GDPR (Article 40(3) GDPR) and, according to Article 40(9) GDPR, may, upon the decision of the European Commission, have general validity within the Union.

Codes of conduct are also included in Regulation 2018/1807[135] on the free flow of non-personal data. For example, the Proposal for the regulation of non-personal data[136] stipulated in recital 7 that "a clear, comprehensive and

---

[130] See: https://ec.europa.eu/digital-single-market/en/community-practice-better-self-and-co-regulation-cop.

[131] Directive 95/46/EC of the European Parliament and of the Council of 24 October 1995 on the protection of individuals with regard to the processing of personal data and on the free movement of such data, OJ [1995] L 281/31.

[132] *Ibid.*, recital 26.

[133] See also Article 40(2) GDPR.

[134] The European Parliament, the Council of the European Union, the Commission of the European Communities, "Interinstitutional Agreement on Better Law-Making", OJ [2003] C 321/1, at para. 17.

[135] Regulation (EU) 2018/1807 of the European Parliament and of the Council of 14 November 2018 on a framework for the free flow of non-personal data in the European Union, OJ [2018] L 303/59.

[136] European Commission, Proposal for a Regulation of the European Parliament and of the Council on a framework for the free flow of non-personal data in the European Union, Brussels, 13.9.2017, COM(2017) 495 final.

predictable legal framework" for the processing of non-personal data was crucial for laying the foundations of the data economy, while also saying that "self-regulation should ensure that the framework is flexible". Yet, Regulation 2018/1807 foresees the development of such codes of conduct for the portability of non-personal data. Article 6, which elaborates on the "porting of data", paragraph 1, of Regulation 2018/1807 stipulates that "[t]he Commission shall encourage and facilitate the development of self-regulatory codes of conduct at Union level ('codes of conduct'), in order to contribute to a competitive data economy, based on the principles of transparency and interoperability and taking due account of open standards". It is further stated that such codes of conduct should, *inter alia*, cover aspects such as "best practices for facilitating the switching of service providers and the porting of data in a structured, commonly used and machine-readable format including open standard formats", information requirements, approaches to certification schemes, "communication roadmaps [...] to raise awareness of the codes of conduct among relevant stakeholders" (Article 6(1) letters a–d). Whereas recital 30 stipulates that "the detailed information and operational requirements for data porting should be defined by market players through self-regulation, encouraged, facilitated and monitored by the Commission, in the form of Union codes of conduct which might include model contractual terms and conditions", recital 31 explains what aspects should be covered by such codes of conduct, including that such codes of conduct "should also make clear that vendor lock-in is not an acceptable business practice". Finally, according to Article 7, each Member State shall designate a single point of contact, which "shall provide users with general information on this Regulation, including on the codes of conduct" (Article 7(6)).

Regulation 2018/1807, at least to some extent, fulfills the agenda of the European Commission on the "free flow of data". As explained,[137] the latter initiative focused on non-personal data. The possibility for the members of the industry – in the codes of conduct – agreeing on the model terms and conditions of the portability of non-personal data allows them to engage in self-regulation. However, the choice of such an alternative regulation mechanism for the portability of non-personal data may raise serious concerns, in particular, with regard to the fundamental rights that might be involved. As argued before,[138] cases of pure non-personal data may be rare, since, in the data economy, data will often be mixed and may be interlinked with other data, with a result that identifiable data sets may be produced that would, in fact, contain personal data.

---

[137] See *supra* Chapter 2, Section 2.4.1.
[138] See *supra* Chapter 2, Section 2.4.2.

5.4 EUROPEAN COMMISSION'S WHITE PAPER ON AI: WHAT IS "HIGH RISK"?

In February 2020, the European Commission issued the White Paper on Artificial Intelligence.[139] In the White Paper, the European Commission analyses the regulatory framework of AI in terms of possible adjustments that may have to be made to the existing legal framework, such as the legal norms on the safety of products and the liability regimes, as well as the scope of a potential future regulatory framework of AI.[140] As regards the latter, the European Commission, stressing the importance of a proportionate regulatory intervention, suggests following a "risk-based approach".[141] In other words, the European Commission considers a mandatory regulation as regards AI applications identified as "high-risk", whereas voluntary labelling schemes would be possible for no-high risk AI applications.[142] Specifically, the European Commission envisages a list of mandatory requirements that would be applicable to the AI applications identified as "high-risk".[143] Among such mandatory requirements the European Commission mentions requirements such as transparency, robustness and accuracy, but also measures that are rather intrusive, such as keeping of records and data used for AI training and making them available upon request in case of inspection by the competent authorities or human oversight of AI systems identified as "high risk".[144]

The principle of proportionality would imply that the means of the regulatory intervention are proportionate to the goal that such a regulation strives to achieve. However, as regards the notion of "high-risk", the European Commission, in the White Paper, says that "[t]he Commission is of the opinion that a given AI application should generally be considered high-risk in light of what is at stake, considering whether both the sector <u>and</u> the intended use involve significant risks, in particular from the viewpoint of protection of safety, consumer rights and fundamental rights"[145] (emphasis in original). Such a definition of "high-risk" is broad in general and in light of the above-mentioned mandatory requirements in particular. In fact, following the definition of "high-risk" as suggested by the European Commission, the regulatory framework could cover a large number of cases, so that the question may

---

[139] European Commission, White Paper on Artificial Intelligence – A European approach to excellence and trust, Brussels, 19.2.2020, COM(2020) 65 final.

[140] *Ibid.*, pp. 9 et seq.

[141] *Ibid.*, p. 17.

[142] See *ibid.*, p. 24.

[143] *Ibid.*, pp. 17 et seq.

[144] *Ibid.*, pp. 18–22.

[145] *Ibid.*, p. 17.

arise whether the regulatory intervention would still comply with the principle of proportionality.

Yet, precisely because the principle of proportionality may be highly important when considering the potential regulatory framework of AI, not the least in light of the fact that trade secrets might also be involved,[146] it may be crucial to specify and possibly narrow down the notion of "high-risk" in order to avoid a broad interpretation of this notion while applying future regulatory norms for AI. Whereas sector-specific solutions may indeed be a welcome approach when considering a potential regulatory framework of AI, the notion of "high-risk" should be defined in a more precise way, for example, covering cases when the life or health of individuals might be at stake or when AI applications would be used for strategic decision-making.

While considering any potential regulatory framework of AI, sector-specific solutions and a possibly narrow, but in any case more specified, "high-risk" approach may be helpful in avoiding risks of overregulation related to AI. Avoiding such overregulation would be important not only for the sake of economic incentives related to innovations in the field of AI, but also for not depriving consumers of the benefits that they could enjoy from the developments of AI.

5.5   INTERMEDIATE CONCLUSION

A regulatory intervention may be needed for tackling algorithmic manipulation in the business-to-consumer relationship. The framing of the regulatory rules in this regard could be based on the example of the regulatory prohibition of market manipulation in the financial sector. The transparency requirement would be essential in enforcing the prohibition of algorithmic manipulation. Furthermore, for the sake of consumer protection, public bodies, such as data protection authorities or authorities for consumer protection, should exercise *ex ante* control of terms and conditions before they are provided for acceptance to consumers, particularly in the context of the provision of services in exchange of their data. Finally, although alternative regulatory mechanisms, such as co- or self-regulation, may be important in areas such as setting ethical standards for AI technology, such alternative regulatory mechanisms may have to be used cautiously when fundamental rights such as the right to protect personal data and privacy might be at stake. In any case, while framing the

---

[146] As regards the mandatory requirement of keeping records and data that might be requested to be made available in the case of inspections, the White Paper merely states that "[w]here necessary, arrangements should be made to ensure that confidential information, such as trade secrets, is protected" (*ibid.*, p. 20).

(future) regulatory norms for AI, it is of utmost importance that the principle of proportionality is respected.

6.   Conclusions

Despite the fact that there has been much academic debate over the allegedly revolutionary issues raised by the development of the AI technology, a closer look at the fundamental principles of the data economy shows that economic and technological changes have not necessarily raised revolutionary legal questions. Instead, the issue that has become most pressing in light of AI developments is how to strike a balance between the economic incentives of AI developers and the protection of consumers who might also be data subjects.

In light of the fact that personal data might be a critical input for a major portion of AI technology, personal data protection has become increasingly important. Although, in the academic debate, the role of personal data has often been overshadowed by the focus on non-personal data as an allegedly new type of data, the fact remains that in many cases it will be personal data that will be processed in the context of AI. This is particularly so if we consider "identifiable" data sets that might be processed in the data economy. Thus, a large portion of data that might be considered to be non-personal at first sight may turn out to be personal data and will have to be processed in compliance with the data protection laws.

The fact that it will often be not only non-personal, but also personal data that might be processed in the context of AI is highly important for trade secret protection that could apply to data sets. Bearing in mind that personal data could form part or the whole of a trade secret, tensions may arise between the protection of data sets as trade secrets by AI developers and the data subjects' rights provided in the GDPR. In particular, while exercising the right to access personal data (Article 15 GDPR) and the right to data portability (Article 20 GDPR), problems may arise not only with regard to the integrity of a data set, but also, and arguably more importantly, as regards the risks of compromising the whole trade secret protecting a data set, part of which may cover personal data requested by the data subject. Since neither the EU Trade Secrets Directive nor the GDPR provide clear guidance on how to solve such issues, the solutions may have to be sought by the courts on a case-by-case basis. Also, the eligibility of algorithms for trade secret protection may result in the right not to be subject to solely automated decision-making (Article 22 GDPR) being exercised by a data subject to a limited extent owing to the trade secret protection of the algorithm that the decision is based on.

Trade secret protection does not grant exclusive rights. However, this does not mean that trade secrets cannot be treated as property or grant ownership. The fact that the notion of "a trade secret owner" is completely missing in the EU Trade Secrets Directive may result in a major drawback, not to mention legal uncertainty, in the data economy where a number of persons may be involved in different steps and levels of data processing. Thus, it may be crucial to clarify who the (original) trade secret owner is – not only as regards any further legal relationships (e.g. licensing), but also when it comes to the rights and obligations of a trade secret owner.

Trade secrets may be reverse engineered. The possibility for third parties to gain access to the information under a trade secret by fair means, such as reverse engineering, may be important in the context of AI technology, not least when it comes to complementary technologies. Based on the aim that technical solutions should remain accessible to third parties, trade mark protection may be refused for functional signs. However, such access could still be hindered on the basis of trade secret law, since the EU Trade Secrets Directive provides that contractual restrictions on reverse engineering may be valid. Yet, bearing in mind the cumulative effects of such contractual restrictions and in light of the importance of maintaining access to technical solutions, such contractual restrictions on reverse engineering may need to be considered with caution. Furthermore, reverse engineering a trade secret, which covers a data set, may have implications for personal data. Trade secret law is not meant to reinforce personal data protection. It protects information under a trade secret, but does not prohibit access to such information by third parties using fair means such as reverse engineering. Should a data set, which includes personal data, be reverse engineered, the identifiability of natural persons may be enabled. Owing to the fact that the GDPR lists several legal bases for a lawful processing of data, personal data gained by way of reverse engineering might further be processed, even in the absence of the consent of a data subject.

In light of AI technology, including connected technology such as the IoT, it may be crucial to use a trade secret, in particular in cases where it was initially acquired in good faith. The remedy provided by the EU Trade Secrets Directive – pecuniary compensation – may be an attractive remedy in the data economy, first and foremost, owing to the fact that it offers an alternative to an injunction and corrective measures in the case of a trade secret infringement. Such a remedy could amount to a compulsory licensing. However, the flaws of this remedy as enshrined in the EU Trade Secrets Directive, in particular, the fact that it may be applied together with damages, may result in a rather cautious application of pecuniary compensation in practice.

The increasing use of algorithms by business may raise questions related to competition. Although, in academia, the weakness of competition law in capturing "algorithmic collusion" has been highlighted, EU competition law has sufficient tools to deal with algorithmic price adjustments. Owing to a broad interpretation of the notion of "a concerted practice" by the ECJ in *E-Turas*, the tackling of algorithmic price adjustments may, in fact, lead to merely parallel behaviour being condemned, and thus conduct that has normally been allowed under EU competition law. Thus, in contrast to the expressed fears of an underenforcement of EU competition law, the risk when applying EU competition law to algorithm-based behaviour may rather be an overenforcement of EU competition law.

In the data economy, account may need to be taken of the fact that the competitive process may often be related to competition for data traffic. This may be particularly so in the case of online platform competition. Thus, the question whether the actions of companies that compete for data traffic may, in fact, result in (potential) competitors being hindered from competing or amount to acts of unfair competition may have to be analysed in the cases of online platforms.

As regards access to data, such access may have to be granted on the basis of Article 102 TFEU, i.e. the legal norm of EU competition law that prohibits an abuse of a dominant position. However, access to data, in particular, in the cases of the single-source databases protected by the *sui generis* right, should be provided on the basis of the *Bronner*-case standard, i.e. the standard that includes the "pure" indispensability requirement, instead of applying the "exceptional circumstances" test, i.e. the scheme for a compulsory licensing of intellectual property rights. In cases of access requests to a single-source database, it should be adequate to require fulfilment of the indispensability requirement for granting a compulsory access without requiring the fulfilment of the "exceptional circumstances" test. Also, a legal norm elaborating on such access to the single-source databases protected by the *sui generis* right on fair, reasonable and non-discriminatory terms may have to be considered.

Despite Schumpeterian competition in the data economy, regulatory intervention may be needed. After all, Schumpeterian competition is but one type of competition and is mostly important for a new entry. In light of an increasing use of algorithms in the data economy, regulatory intervention may be needed in broader terms in order to find a balance between the economic incentives of the companies (including those that are part of Schumpeterian competition) and the protection of consumers' interests.

In this regard, in the area of algorithmic manipulation in the data economy, in particular when it comes to the business-to-consumer relationship, there seems to be a significant legal gap. Although rules tackling the risk of ranking manipulation are present as regards online intermediaries, they apply to the business-to-business relationship. Thus, the introduction of rules regulating algorithmic manipulation in the business-to-consumer relationship may have to be considered. Such rules could be framed on the example of the rules prohibiting market manipulation on the basis of algorithms in the financial sector.

For the sake of consumer protection and in light of the fact that data protection laws may not grant sufficient tools for consumers to exercise countervailing power against private companies, public authorities should be vested with powers to exercise a robust control of the terms and conditions in the business-to-consumer relationship.

Although co- and self-regulation may have many advantages in the data economy, first and foremost, for providing companies with the flexibility to agree on issues such as, for example, ethical standards for AI, the use of such alternative regulatory mechanisms should not be overestimated, particularly in cases when fundamentals rights such as the right to personal data protection and the right to privacy are be involved.

Finally, should any (new) regulatory framework for AI be considered, it is of utmost importance that the principle of proportionality be respected in order to avoid risks of overregulation related to AI.

The overall analysis in this book shows that the data economy has not triggered a need for drastic legal changes. However, some fine-tuning of the legal framework may be needed. It is important to do this in a timely manner in order to extract the maximum benefit from the data economy for both business and consumers.

Index